Strategies of
Information Processing

Edited by
GEOFFREY UNDERWOOD
Department of Psychology,
University of Nottingham

1978

ACADEMIC PRESS
London   New York   San Francisco
A Subsidiary of Harcourt Brace Jovanovich, Publishers

ACADEMIC PRESS INC. (LONDON) LTD.
24/28 Oval Road
London NW1

United States Edition published by
ACADEMIC PRESS INC.
111 Fifth Avenue
New York, New York 10003

Library of Congress Catalog Card Number: 77 93215
ISBN: 0 12 708950 0

Printed in Great Britain by
The Garden City Press Limited
Letchworth, Hertfordshire

List of Contributors

JONATHON BARON, Department of Psychology, University of Pennsylvania, Philadelphia, Pennsylvania 19174, U.S.A.

M. P. BRYDEN, Department of Psychology, University of Waterloo, Waterloo, Ontario N2L 3G1, Canada.

RONALD A. COLE, Department of Psychology, Carnegie-Mellon University, Pittsburg, Pennsylvania 15213, U.S.A.

MAX COLTHEART, Department of Psychology, Birkbeck College, University of London, London WC1E 7HX, England.

JOHN FOX, MRC Social and Applied Psychology Unit, Department of Psychology, University of Sheffield, Sheffield S10 2TN, England.

C. I. HOWARTH, Department of Psychology, University of Nottingham, Nottingham NG7 2RD, England.

JOLA JAKIMIK, Department of Psychology, Carnegie-Mellon University, Pittsburg, Pennsylvania 15213, U.S.A.

ALAN KENNEDY, Department of Psychology, University of Dundee, Dundee DD1 4HN, Scotland.

NEVILLE MORAY, Department of Psychology, University of Stirling, Stirling FK9 4LA, Scotland.

GEOFFREY UNDERWOOD, Department of Psychology, University of Nottingham, Nottingham NG7 2RD, England.

DAVID J. WOOD, Department of Psychology, University of Nottingham, Nottingham NG7 2RD, England.

RICHARD M. YOUNG, Department of Artificial Intelligence, University of Edinburgh, Forrest Hill, Edinburgh EH1 2QL, Scotland.

Preface

In one sense this book is a statement of faith. The information processing model of human cognition has experienced a considerable amount
of attack recently from critics of "mechanism" in psychology, and these
essays represent a strong argument in support of the image of man as a
processor of information. Central to this argument is the notion that
man is free to select his own information and responses as well as
selecting the strategies with which the information will be processed.
Critics of the information processing model have argued from ground
in the domain of social psychology and interpersonal behaviour, and
from within cognitive psychology, but both groups have repeatedly
used one argument in particular. This criticism is that the model fails
to take account of the subjective, experiential aspect of mental life,
and a variation of this argument says that we have no means of
describing the goals and intentions of the individual as he moves
around in a complex social environment. The description of subjective
experience is out of reach, as yet, of any model in psychology, but this
book indicates how the information processing model will develop
to use the concept of intention as it accounts for increasingly wider
aspects of mental life. Without entering into the dialogue directly we
have described a stage in the evolution of the model in which the
variability of behaviour, and the choices made by the individual, can
be understood together with his goals and intentions. These concepts
are vital to a description of the strategies which the individual selects
in his interactions with the world. This position is specified more
thoroughly in the introductory chapter, but is apparent in each of the
major content chapters which deal with the application of the analysis
of strategical information processing in a variety of cognitive domains.
It remains to be seen whether the model can evolve further to take full
account of the description of subjective experience and consciousness.
If it does, then the strategies of processing will surely be an integral
part of that description.

I would have liked to thank an enormous number of people for their
discussions during the formulation and preparation of this book—far
more names than I have space for here. Discussions with people

committed to the empirical investigation of cognitive behaviour have been essential in the derivation of arguments involving the theory of strategies of processing, but just as vital have been discussions with the non-committed and with the outright heretics. The authors of the contributions here not only responded eagerly to the development of the theory, but also produced enthusiastic and provocative arguments to demonstrate the power of the theory within their areas of interest. As well as expressing gratitude to the contributors for their enthusiasm, I must also thank Jean Underwood for her editorial assistance and support (at times when the heretics appeared to be at their strongest), and Alan Beggs, Mark Haggard and Roger Henry for their guidance on editorial matters concerning the contributed chapters.

Nottingham,   GEOFFREY UNDERWOOD
June 1978

Contents

One

Concepts in Information Processing Theory

Geoffrey Underwood
University of Nottingham

1. THE STRUCTURE OF COGNITIVE PROCESS

At one level of explanation it is surely undeniable that the brain can be considered to be a machine. To the physiologist concerned with patterns of electrochemical activity in the striate cortex associated with retinal stimulation, a particular input will provide a particular change. There is little room for uncertainty at this level of explanation, just as I am reasonably confident that depression of the accelerator pedal of my car will result in an increase in the engine speed. Both systems have the characteristic features of a machine: they have well specified S–R relationships. Problems arise, however, when we attempt to extend the machine analogy to the psychological level of explanation. When one experimental subject attempts to encode a passage of text, his success will depend upon limits imposed by physiological structure, and by the psychological structure which reflects its underlying physiology, but a major source of variation which gives rise to our uncertainty about his performance will be the *strategies* of encoding and retrieval which the learner *chooses* to employ in the experiment.

It is the purpose of this book to illustrate this analysis of structural

1

and strategical limitation on behaviour, by reviewing evidence relating to cognitive structure and indicating some of the influences upon behaviour when this structure is strategically manipulated. Implicit in this view is the consideration that the flow-chart of cognitive activity is incomplete and without use unless it takes into account the variability of processing sequences. When information is presented to an individual the sequence of processing is not pre-determined, but the individual is able to select certain processes and reject others. The traditional flow-chart of information processing suggests that once sensory data are entered into the system, then the response is structurally determined. The view here is that the response may be structurally limited, but that the strategies used by the processor—the individual—play a vital role. The subject may decide to remember the sentences of the passage as a list of items, or he may construct a series of visual images of the events described or he may attempt to remember the pattern of words on the page. Whichever strategy he chooses in this simple task will be a manipulation of the information by the experimenter, using available cognitive structures which will themselves transform and encode the information in a variety of ways. The cognitive structures here are the systems which analyse the information passed to them by earlier systems and which perform such functions as perception, encoding, language comprehension, problem solving and the control of overt action. Each of these functions, and the stages of processing which they envelop, has its own structural limitations and capacity restrictions, and the limits of one stage will necessarily have implications for the processing by all other stages. Thus, our limitations in solving problems, given any one strategy, will be a composite of the speed of comprehension and assimilation of the information comprising the problem, of the storage limits of working memory, of the forgetting characteristics of the memory systems used, of the efficiency of the access code for retrieving information stored in permanent memory and which may be relevant to the problem, and of the speed and efficiency of any other system used in the total activity. It has been the task of the cognitive psychologist to describe which processes are necessary for the performance of the cognitive activities in which man engages, and to describe the limits and characteristics of these processes. Their success in investigation and interpretation may be judged by the plethora of criticism of their methods and assumptions produced during recent years. These criticisms are based around the "artificial" laboratory setting as the location for investigations of "real world" behaviour (e.g. Neisser, 1976; Newell, 1973a). These are interpretive errors, however, for the cognitive structure available to an individual is the same whether he is sat in his garden or sat by the laboratory bench. But whereas the invariant structures may be accessed quite easily in the laboratory we have more difficulty in accessing the variable strategies which are more than likely to change when the naïve subject enters the novel environment of the laboratory. Similar misconceptions form the basis of Shotter's (1975) complaints against experimentation made on the grounds that subjects behave as experimenters expect them to behave. Shotter suggests that our conclusions about the flow of information are a result of men acting *as if* they were an information channel, without saying anything about the fundamental nature of man. The two errors here are to say that we can go beyond our structural limitations in the performance of any cognitive task, and secondly, that experimenters are naïve enough to seek only confirmation of their pet theory. Structural limitations can only be overcome by the strategical manipulation of information *within* those limitations. When the subject enters the laboratory he takes with him his structural limitations and a repertoire of strategies. The problem is to separate out structure from strategy, and indeed this is the basis of Newell's (1973b) own solution to paradigm-bound investigation.

The capriciousness of behaviour in slightly different experimental situations, a problem giving rise to the unclear evidence reviewed pessimistically by Newell (1973a), is not a condemnation of the experimental method used in cognitive psychology, rather, it is an indication of how the demands of an experiment can induce a subject to employ different strategies of handling the presented stimuli. The profusion of paradigm-bound investigations is an indication of a narrow concern for the structure of cognitive process—decay rates, capacity limits, feature detectors, search and recognition rates, the hierarchical organization of semantic memory, effects of repetition and of rehearsal, and physical and name codes. Most of Newell's "phenomena of contemporary psychology" are concerned with the detail of structure. Not that the notion of strategies is anything new to psychology, for Bartlett's schemata, the plans of Miller, Galanter and Pribram, Minsky's frames, and the production systems of Newell and Simon, are all bound up with the adaptability, expectation and creativity of the active subject, as well as the more direct discussions of strategies by Bruner, Simon and Restle, among others. Within the framework of information processing theory we have been rather more concerned with cognitive structure than with behavioural strategy, and it may be this bias which is producing our frustration with the phenomena. The physicist finds it inappropriate to ask "What is force?" or "What is matter?", and prefers to investigate events rather than elementary particles. The psychologist might profitably take this lead. In preference to asking questions about storage systems and capacity limits we may be better equipped to investigate the manipulation of information—the events of cognition.

The two fundamental questions for the cognitive psychologist concerned with the dynamics of processing are (1) how can we isolate the effects of strategies from those of structure, and (2) what should be the defining characteristics of any strategy? The first of these questions is by far the more tricky, and will be answered by the ingenuity of experiments which use a combination of tasks to induce one strategy rather than another. This is followed by an analysis where operations are converged with behaviour and introspective data relating to performance. The following chapters in this volume will give a preliminary indication of the success with which we can separate the effects of structural limitations from those of strategical variation. The strategies which we can isolate will be defined in terms of the information used by the subject, of the stages of processing which are applied, and of the effects of strategy upon behaviour. Our description of a strategy will look something like a physicist's description of a force, and will take the form of a description of an effect upon certain elements. In our case these will be elements of behaviour and elements of the environment. The elements of a particular strategy can only be defined in terms of its effects. By way an introduction to the descriptions of strategies of information processing contained here and for purposes of context, we need first to review briefly the basic concepts of contemporary information processing theory, following some of the more structural notions of Broadbent (1958), Haber (1974), Neisser (1967) and Sperling (1967).

1.1 The processing of information

The current environmental evidence which we select and use, in conjunction with previously encoded evidence and inference, is best described as information. Any piece of datum which is selected can be quantified in terms of the amount of uncertainty which is reduced, and therefore it might appear that the amount of information required to perform a task can be defined by the number of binary decisions necessary to remove all doubt as to what the transmission to the subject contained. Such is the assumption of Information Theory applied to the communication of messages, but whereas the assumption may hold, before we can identify the information which is received by the individual we need to know more about the strategy of reception. For a simple message with the objective information value of the message defined and known to the receiver, then Information Theory holds, but for the complex visual and auditory arrays in the environment the receiver can attend to whatever aspect he chooses, and process it in any number of ways. The subjective information content of such an environment may be impossible to assess, for the receiver interacts with the environment according to his own needs. The goals of the receiver will determine what information is received, and the same visual scene will offer very different information to two very different individuals. The expectations of the receiver, defined generally as the products of a lifetime of experience in the selection of environmental information, will also affect the quantified information content of a message. For an individual with a vocabulary of 50,000 or 60,000 words, each of these words contains between fifteen and sixteen bits of information, where one bit is sufficient to distinguish between two equiprobable alternatives. The word "equiprobable" is the key here, for not only are words used in language with greatly differing frequencies, but a word in isolation conveys more information to the individual than the same word in legal linguistic context. Consider the sentence "The cat sat on the map". The final word here contains more information than the word "mat" in the same sentential position but less information than the word "map" presented in isolation. The experience and culture of the perceiver will necessarily enable more or less information to be extracted from this word, and here we come to two fallacious criticisms of information processing theory suggested by Neisser (1976). The theory, he argues (his p. 7), is "indifferent to culture", whereas it can certainly account for cultural differences in behaviour by assuming that cultural expectations will suggest their own unique strategies for perceiving the world as well as unique strategies for responding to it. Neisser also suggests that an information processing system pays "little heed to the kind of information the environment actually offers" and that such systems would ". . . leave the perceiver lost in his own processing system . . ." (his p. 53). Such a system as this would without doubt be incapable of responding to anything but an impoverished environment, but we are not suggesting a model in which information is selected for the processor, for selection itself is a process fundamental to the system. The individual actively seeks the information most relevant to his goals, in the ways suggested by Neisser, but we need to specify what it is about selected (and non-selected) information that is useful, and how it is used both to reach his goals and seek more information used in that activity. Thus the individual is in constant interaction with the world, but it is as much an oversimplification to refer to "the individual" without specifying the systems and processes which go to make an individual, as it is to refer exclusively to the environment with which those systems and processes interact.

Miller (1956) recognized this interaction on a local level when he changed the measure of information from "bits" to "chunks". Whereas "bits" are objective, and transferable between individuals, "chunks" are subjective and restricted to the individual in that the information content of a message accepted can only be specified in the terms of the decoding strategy employed by that individual. The information which is processed is not objectively quantifiable, and cannot be specified in advance of its processing unless we can specify the acquisition strategy which will be used. The strategy will of course depend upon the history of the processor. I can remember Chinese logographs best by the visual relationships of the component marks, just as the Chinese person unfamiliar with English script would possibly decode our written words, but the fluent Chinese reader may pay little heed of pattern other than to extract the distinctive features, and will remember the meaning of the character easier than the visual structure. Similarly, the chess-master will see a smaller variety of patterns on the board being used by another two masters than I would. Such a board could be said to contain less information than the board being used by two novices, but only to the eye of the chess-master. Experience facilitates perception of the regular by reducing the number of possible displays which the environment can offer, but a regular world cannot be appreciated by an inexperienced perceiver, and an irregular world cannot be anticipated by the skilled perceiver. In all of these instances we can refer to the information available in the environment, to the selection of information and to the influence of experience in that selection process. The consequent processes which follow selection may also be specified, but they all act upon information received using information previously stored as "experiences".

1.2. Stages of processing

Information in the environment is received by our sensory systems not in a passive fashion but by an active process of selection based upon previous experience and the current goals of the organism. The process does not stop there, however, for the model argues that the information in the display must be *processed* before it can be related to those goals, and it is said to be processed through a series of stages of transformation. Thus my comprehension of a Chinese logograph and of an English word differs by the stages of transformation which can be applied. My processing of a printed English word may progress through the discrimination of the features which distinguish it from other English words, to the comprehension of its structural or lexical meaning, and finally to its integration with the other words in the sentence. These transformations, from an appreciation of (1) the visual features, to (2) the lexical features, to (3) the associative contextual features, may be represented as being effected by stages of processing. For the logographs I have developed a stage of processing which allows me only to discriminate the visual features of the pattern, without the transformation from word to meaning being possible. Given that I had the meaning of each logograph available presumably I would be able to make an approximation towards the comprehension of each individual series of logographs because my knowledge of "language" (which is necessary for the transformation (3) above) could then be applied to the symbols, and their visual form would be inconsequential. The total task of reading, and indeed the processing of any information extracted from the environment, can be analysed into a series of transformations applied to the input, and which are identified as occurring at stages of processing.

These stages are not directly observable, of course, and we must infer their existence by performance on a number of tasks and by using the procedure of converging operations (Garner et al., 1956). Only by observing the effects of a theoretical stage of processing under a set of circumstances which allow these effects to be isolated from those of other stages, can we establish the characteristics of each stage. The loss of information which has been presented can only be stage-localized by a series of operations to examine the possibilities of imperfect reception, storage or retrieval. Although we cannot observe "reception" directly, we can observe the effects of good reception, and those of impoverished perception, and so we can consider the possibilities of the stage of reception as being the locus of the failure of subsequent recall. In a similar way Corcoran (1966) established the strategy of using an acoustic stage of transformation in the reading of prose. Subjects were asked to cross out every instance of the letter *e* in a passage while reading silently, but they tended to miss more instances from words in which the *e* would have been pronounced as an *e* had the passage been read aloud. So, the *e* in "beard" would be less likely to be missed than the *e* in "bared". From this experiment and others we can infer the existence of a strategy of articulatory mediation whilst reading. This is only an optional strategy, of course, for a number of experiments have demonstrated that words may be read without articulatory or phonemic mediation, and indeed even whilst the attention of the reader is diverted elsewhere (e.g. Bradshaw, 1977; Gray, 1975; Kleiman, 1975; Underwood, 1976a); this point is taken up in the discussions by Coltheart, Kennedy and Underwood in this volume. Articulatory recoding of print may be seen as a stage of processing in which the visual information is transformed into an acoustic representation before the response is organized.

Use of the stage of processing of articulatory recoding may be optional whilst reading, and may thus be a learnt strategy of reading, but not all stages are optional in the information processing sequence. For certain tasks successful performance depends upon the passage of information through invariant stages. When reading, for instance, each word must at some point contact its representation in lexical memory. The transformation achieved here is that from a set of distinctive visual features into a symbolic representative of some event or object met in the individual's psychological past. If we are to understand sentences and books of sentences then we must have some understanding of the component words. Once the visual features are transformed into individual meaningful units the next process might involve the integration of these words into the general schema of the sentence in a stage which might be labelled working memory. The perception of spoken language involves a parallel set of structural stages of processing. The distinctive features of speech, once detected, are incorporated into meaningful segments and their lexical representations contacted before the lexical units themselves are integrated into the context of the whole speech. Perhaps one of the best-known accounts of the derivation by inference of the stages of information processing necessary for the performance of a specific task, is that of Sperling's (1967) discussion of the partial report procedure in the description of iconic memory. The basic evidence upon which Sperling built his model was the limit of four or five items recalled following brief tachistoscopic exposure, given his previous inference of the existence of a visual information store, or iconic memory. The first model which he considered proposed that between storage of the complete visual display in the invariant stage of iconic memory and the output of the information by the observer, the information must be transformed into a state appropriate to the response. If this stage of motor translation reads information out of iconic memory at a fixed rate then the icon may have decayed by the time four or five items have been transferred, thereby preventing more than four or five items being read out. However, this model is inadequate because decay of information in iconic memory precedes any response. It is necessary to interpose at least one other stage of processing between the visual information store and response preparation, and in Sperling's second model the contents of iconic memory are said to be read into an acoustic store prior to output. A problem here is that the rate of output from iconic memory is faster than the rate of subvocal rehearsal. The processing of information into an auditory code could not keep up with the rate of extraction of information from the iconic store, and so Sperling suggested a third model which maintains the stages of iconic storage and auditory storage. The rehearsal process from the second model is now given a series of functions rather than simply transforming the visual input into an auditory form. The images selected by a scanning mechanism (taking instructions according to the partial report cue) are transformed into a set of motor instructions for use by the rehearsal procedure. These motor instructions are said to be set up at a rate which coincides with the rate of extraction of information from iconic memory, but the execution of these instructions (finishing with an acoustic trace) occurs at the rate at which we can subvocally rehearse information which is available. The limit in report in "span of apprehension" experiments might then be a function of the disparity between the speed of readout from the icon and the speed of setting up an acoustic representation of the information displayed. In this model storage in, and readout from, iconic memory, and the rate of transformation into acoustic memory, are processes subject to structural limitations. They are stages of processing which, when selected by the observer, impose a series of accumulating limits upon performance. The transformation of the input into an acoustic form may itself be a strategy of processing which is optional, but once employed the performance of the whole task will be subject to the efficiency of performance of acoustic encoding, storage and retrieval. The demands of the task will dictate the strategy used, and in Sperling's partial report experiment all subjects may have selected an acoustic recoding strategy. In a slightly different experimental situation this strategy might be inappropriate and very different performance characteristics would then change. This feature of the great variability of strategies in the employment of a number of invariable stages of processing seems to be responsible for the despondent review of the recent progress of experimental psychology provided by Newell (1973a).

One further point to make about this analysis of performance into constituent processes of information transformation, is that it assumes that the perception of events, being a function of finite processes, is non-immediate (Haber, 1974). The world which we experience is the world as it *was* rather than the world as it *is*. The reality which we experience is quite artificial, despite our "immersion in the world" (Shotter, 1975), for the world of which we are conscious is the product of a series of processes applied to sensory data over a period of time. Our "immediate" contact with the world is illusory, if consistent, and is relative to the contact available in the previous psychological moment. It can say nothing of those aspects of the world for which we have no sensory detectors, and which presumably are of no adaptive concern to us. We can be aware of only those aspects of "reality" for which we have sensory detectors, and in consequence we must realize that the world *as we know it* is incomplete. Given that our experiences are representations based upon the processing of our private sensory evidence, and that this processing is not instantaneous, then it follows that our perceptual constructions are outdated in the same sense that our knowledge of events in outer space is outdated by the time required for the transmission of that information. Our experiences are as wide, rich and appropriate as our sense receptors and cognitive processes allow them to be.

1.3. The limited capacity of structural processes

Information processing models assume that the processor and its components have a limited amount of processing capacity available at any one time. The rejection of this assumption rests upon the argument that all information is processed and made available to the response systems instantaneously, and that we can perform any number of tasks simultaneously. Instances of apparent multiple-task performance, or even of the simultaneous operation of two stages of processing are common (e.g. Allport et al., 1972; Shaffer, 1971; Underwood, 1974) and tend to result from overpractice. Such instances of the auto-matization of skill do not negate the concept of limited capacity. Rather, they demonstrate the strategical operation of expectancy and the appreciation of redundancy both in the environment and in the capacities of our response systems. Men do not resemble finite-state automata whose individual responses are governed by individual stimuli, but our choice of response is suggested by any number of relationships between the most recently presented stimulus, stimuli remembered from previous occasions, and inferred relationships bet-ween these sets of stimuli. The continuity of sequential responses can be taken into account by the inclusion of a buffer memory prior to each stage of processing. If one stage is occupied on presentation of informa-tion by the previous stage, then no information will be lost and perfor-mance will both be continuous and have the characteristics of simul-taneity of activity of more than one stage.

The limited capacity of any stage of processing may be described in a number of alternate forms. To state that primary memory has a storage capacity of approximately three words is equivalent to the statement that the interaction between the decay rate of an item in primary memory and the time required for regeneration of an item is such that only three items may be maintained in an accessible form. If storage of four items is attempted then an item is lost ("forgotten") because regeneration of the fourth item allows one of the other items to decay beyond reconstruction. To argue that the capacity can be described as being three words is the structural equivalent to this dynamic process description. Cavanagh's (1972) curious conclusion that it takes us approximately a quarter of a second to scan the contents of consciousness, regardless of the type of material being considered, can be interpreted by this dynamic process model. The scanning rate (and presumably the renewal rate for retention) seems to be a constant number of features per unit time, and so an item containing fewer features can be scanned and renewed at a faster rate per item than a span of items containing more features per item. The model does not assume a limited capacity of storage, or number of "slots" available, but views the limit as being one of the rate of review and renewal. The two events of review and renewal do not necessarily occur independently of course, and reviewing an item can be considered to result in re-entry of that item into the system. Tulving's (1972) episodic-semantic memory distinction is similar in this point, with the retrieval of a piece of information into awareness being considered as a new entry into our time-dependent autobiographical episodic memory each time a retrieval is made. An impression of limited capacity is given by this process by the limited number of retrievals and entries which can be made per unit time.

Structural limitations to the processing of information such as readout rates from iconic memory and scanning rates in primary memory are confounded by limitations posed by the strategical manipulation of attention. The limited capacity of a processing system is exemplified by the limited amount of information to which we can attend at any one time. Indeed, the structural limit of storage in "primary memory" has on different occasions been described as the "span of apprehension", "the span of attention" and the "contents of consciousness", suggesting that this apparent capacity limit is determined by the power of the attention process. That which is attended to, and which gains entry to consciousness may be said to be stored in primary memory, and the capacity of primary memory is likewise a function of the amount of information which can be attended to without loss. With simultaneous presentations this ambiguous picture is not clarified, even though the limits become even more obvious. The dichotic listening experiments which led Broadbent (1958) to conclude that the (initial) limit in processing was at the stage of word recognition can still be interpreted alternatively as resulting from limits in the perceptual system (Treisman, 1960), the response system (Deutsch and Deutsch, 1963), an intermediate system or systems (Erdelyi, 1974; Underwood, 1976b), or indeed from a strategy of switching between messages during presentation (Moray, 1969). Reporting both halves of a short dichotic message is a complex task involving the processes of speech perception, lexical access, message separation (labelling), buffer storage, retrieval, subvocal rehearsal and response organization. Each of these processes have their own structural limitations, and so we should expect a variety of strategies to appear from unpractised subjects who are perhaps uncertain as to how to best direct their attention in this novel situation. The highly-practised dichotic listener has little trouble in dividing his attention optimally to pick up the most relevant information from two competing messages (Underwood, 1974), and demonstrations of skills such as this may be an indication of strategies of processing being used to overcome the processing limits of the structural features in the system. The appreciation of redundancy in the display, and the automatization of regularly used skills are features of an adaptive individual manipulating the attention which he has available so as to extract as much as he needs from a complex environment, or so that attention and volitional processing can be directed elsewhere in a simple environment.

1.4. The continuity of processing

Implicit in the preceding discussions is the assumption that cognitive processes do not operate independently, but that the activity of one process will affect the activity of all other processes involved in the performance of the task in hand. We are unable, for instance, to investigate a problem-solving subsystem without knowing how the problem was presented and perceived, which features of the problem attracted the attention of the subject, which features were remembered and, in general, which structural stages of processing were involved in the solution of the problem. The processing of information must be considered in the context of all of the processing stages concerned, for the strategy involving one stage will depend upon the information presented to it by the previous stages. The use of acoustic memory by subjects in the visual memory partial report studies of Sperling (1967), is an indication of the interaction of processes employed to solve demanding experimental tasks. The study of language comprehension also provides examples of the interactions, in both directions, between stages of processing. The comprehension of self-embedded sentences, such as "The man the waiter the chef the owner hired today gave the meal to served died", is governed by the limits of a variety of processes. Aside from such factors as the appreciation of the roles of agents in the world and the generation associations between agents and actions in our representation of knowledge, comprehension will be determined by the requirement to remember each agent until late in the sentence when its action is clarified. To learn what the waiter did we must postpone processing until we have learnt what the chef and the owner did, and each postponement increases the amount of information which must be held in buffer storage. The perception of complex sentences involves more than lexical decoding, buffer storage, the representation of inferential knowledge and syntactic knowledge, however, and constructive processes employing visual imagery have been implicated. The interactions between each of these processes with all others demands an interpretation of the whole task as presented to the subject. Attempting to describe the qualities of "buffer storage" by using tasks such as this can only lead to a restricted understanding of how that stage can be operated under certain processing demands. The intensive investigation of one component process produces Newell's (1973a) phenomenon-driven science which lacks cohesion and fails to accumulate. Stages *can* be investigated in series of experiments employing converging operations, but a separate issue is whether this approach is one which *should be* used to describe the complete characteristics of an isolated stage. Newell's argument against this approach, in favour of the investigation of problems in terms of the necessary processes and systems, is an argument which implicitly recognizes the continuity of information processing and the reciprocal effects which associated processes have upon each other.

2. STRATEGIES AND THE VARIABILITY OF BEHAVIOUR

By emphasizing the importance of the concept of *strategy* we are acknowledging the variability of human behaviour. Two individuals will behave differently in the same environmental situation, and the same individual will behave differently in the same situation at different times. These variations may be attributed to strategy changes when-ever they are not the direct result of a physical change to the individual (e.g. illness, injury), or of learning, or of a failure to remember. The cases of learning and forgetting (*superior* and *inferior* information) may impose a strategy change upon the behaviour of the individual, but even when identical information is available about the environmental situation, behaviour may vary. In most cases, however, there will be a difference in the experiences of the individuals which can be used to account for the variability. Previous success with one strategy will lead to its recurrent use, as will a lack of awareness of alternative strate-gies. The process of learning may lead to a strategy change with or without the individual being aware of the change. Awareness of the alternatives is not a necessary condition for the emergence of what we shall describe as a strategy, although in some circumstances the perfor-mance will be facilitated by the information. Thus the skilled reader who is a poor speller may be using the strategy of spelling words as they sound (*fite*, *clime*, for *fight* and *climb*), whereas this strategy is clearly inappropriate (Frith, 1976). The poor speller may be unaware of the alternatives to his well learned strategy of articulating his print.

If we are to accept the point that strategies may be selected without any volitional choice, in that behaviour which is strategy-governed may not be considered against its alternative by the individual, then we must also accept the definition of the concept implied by the ethologists Maynard Smith and Price (1973) and Dawkins (1976), in their discussions of Evolutionary Stable Strategies. A population of potentially aggressive organisms will maximize their own success by employing individual strategies which will depend upon the strategies of the other members of the population. If most members of the population select that particular strategy then each individual will fare better than if a different strategy had been adopted. Dawkins defines a strategy as a "programmed behavioural policy" (his p. 74), where the programming is contained in the gene. The complex behavioural strategy described by Maynard Smith and Price as "retaliator" is an Evolutionary Stable Strategy in that its adoption by most members of the population will lead to a stable population of "retaliators" in the face of intrusions into the group by deviants who use other strategies. A "dove" strategy of non-aggression is stable until an aggressive "hawk" appears, at which point the "hawks" take over. A population of "hawks" will accordingly kill themselves off. "Retaliators" behave conditionally, and act as "doves" initially, but fight if provoked. A population of "retaliators" will be non-aggressive until a deviant "hawk" is presented to them, and then they fight back. Their behaviour depends entirely upon the behaviour of other individuals. These behavioural styles may be described as strategies in the present context because choice is available, not to the individual, but to the genes of the population. At an individual level there may be no choice in the strategy employed, for it is already programmed, but there is choice for the population. Choice does not need to be reflective, but alternatives need to be available for the population as a whole.

The discussions contained in this book assume a number of definitions of the concept of a strategy, but all have the notion of choice as a central feature. The choice is not always apparent to the individual, but it is present in the population. A poor speller may not "choose" to articulate the words which he is writing, but he *could* behave differently in different circumstances, and thereby give the appearance of choosing.

Strategies can be chosen by the individual, and this is perhaps most apparent with social behaviour. The roles which we play in our contact with other individuals are in themselves strategies. They are programmes to guide our behaviour in new or difficult environmental conditions, and are often selected intentionally with a view to obtaining a favourable outcome to an interaction. The application of the concept of strategy to social behaviour is outside of the scope of this book, but can be found in descriptions of role theory (Secord and Backman, 1961).

Between these two views of strategies—as genetically programmed and as a method of social interaction—is the theme of the present collection of discussions. We shall consider the structural concepts in information processing theory in relation to the strategical manipulation of information through cognitive structure, and the contributors apply this structure–strategy analysis to a number of areas in the investigation of cognition. The particular information processing models assumed in each discussion vary around the outline presented above, but a common assumption is that we must take into account the variability of processing applied by the individual. This is not a condemnation of the machine analogy, so much as an extension of it to give the machine flexibility.

The first three chapters, those by Fox, by Cole and Jakimik, and by Bryden, are concerned with processes and phenomena which might be considered by some theoretical models to be dictated more by structure than by strategy. The chapter by Fox, entitled *Continuity, Concealment and Visual Attention*, concerns the ecology of visual perception and develops both the Gibsonian view of visual events and the analysis of those events by feature detectors in the visual system. The reliance by cognitive psychology upon developments in computer science is very apparent in this discussion, in which Fox goes beyond the simple activation of individual feature detectors to show how an interactive and predictive system which is in contact with the world can detect concealed objects by strategical operations rather than by structural detectors. The interaction between feature detectors and the manipulation of their outputs is also a theme of the following chapter. In their report of a detailed set of experiments involving the comprehension of natural speech, Cole and Jakimik describe the features used in the recognition of spoken words (*Understanding Speech: How Words are Heard*). Words are recognized using a variety of sources of information —acoustic, syntactic, semantic etc.—and this chapter provides evidence of the interaction of information during listening. The empirical problems under review include the detection of mispronunciations (the detection of a misplaced phoneme depends upon its similarities with the correct phoneme) and the segmentation of continuous speech into the perceptual units of the sentence. An assumption underlying this work is that word recognition is an active and interactive process, yet the chapters by Coltheart, Kennedy and Underwood question this assumption with data from natural listening and reading situations. This is one of Newell's (1973a) binary oppositions: active *vs.* passive processing. We stand accused by Newell not only of investigating *phenomena* intensively, but also of posing opposites (e.g. peripheral *vs.* central, and stages *vs.* continuous development), and certainly these opposites can be found thriving in most investigations. They are not always at the centre of the investigation, however, but if they emerge regularly as alternative interpretations this cannot be the symptom of the inappropriate research procedure that Newell is worried about. So far as the current active–passive disagreement is concerned, we can gain by its appearance by using apparently contradictory evidence to support a more detailed theory. For instance, words may be recognized passively when clearly segmented, but actively whenever ambiguity is to be resolved or whenever the relationships between words must be established by the perceiver and a deep level of coding achieved.

Bryden's chapter on *Strategy Effects in the Assessment of Hemispheric Asymmetry* is a theoretical discussion of the effects of strategical information handling in relation to hemispheric superiority for the processing of certain stimuli over others. The processing of handwriting might be found to be more fully lateralized in the left cerebral hemisphere in one individual in comparison with another individual. This might mean that handwriting analysis is processed more in the left hemisphere for one individual over the other, or that one individual prefers to use a linguistic strategy in the analysis of handwriting (and hence a left hemisphere superiority), and the other individual a non-linguistic strategy. Asymmetries may appear following structural or strategical preferences, but as Bryden points out, one will affect the other in profound interactions.

The chapters by Coltheart, by Kennedy and by Underwood discuss the investigation of specific problems in the processing of verbal information. Coltheart's discussion of *Lexical Access in Simple Reading Tasks* considers the question of how the skilled reader is able to derive the meanings of words from their written form. Given the word "cat", for example, how are we able to go beyond the visual pattern on the page (in the process of "lexical access") to comprehend the object denoted? The process by which the meaningful associates (the object "cat") are evoked by a written symbol (the word "cat") is considered to proceed through one of two possible routes. Meaning may be accessed via a phonological representation of the word, or access may depend upon a decoding of the orthography of the print. Coltheart suggests a number of strategies within each of these two theories, and resolves some apparent contradictions from previous research by appealing to the possibility of different strategies being appropriate under different experimental conditions.

In contrast to Coltheart's approach to the investigation of reading skill, the chapter by Kennedy looks at ongoing reading processes, as indicated by his title *Reading Sentences: some observations on the control of eye movements*. Kennedy reviews the major theories of the relationship between eye movements and reading, which range from those advocating no relationship to those which advocate that eye movements are under the control of the text not yet fixated. This description of the influence of peripheral information during reading is concluded with a new experiment in which Kennedy demonstrates that words in advance of fixation do affect the pattern of eye movements. Readers also spent more time looking at the second member of the semantically associated word pair than at control words, as well as being influenced by the presence or absence of this associate when it was ahead of the eyes. It is not possible to investigate the reading process unless we are aware of the purposes of the text being read. Reading strategies can be affected very shortly after the skill has been acquired, as second-grade schoolchildren readers perform differently (as measured by the eye–voice span) with instructions to "read carefully in preparation for questioning" or to "read for the general idea" (Levin and Cohn, 1968).

The chapter by Underwood on *Attentional Selectivity and Behavioural Control* pursues some of the theoretical points raised by Coltheart and Kennedy in the access of meaning by words which are not fixated (and not attended?) or not listened to, in relation to attention strategies and in relation to the functions of attention. The selective admittance of information to consciousness is seen as a preparation for response, but information which is not admitted can be processed pre-attentively at the level of lexical access, and can influence ongoing performance.

The chapters by Howarth and by Moray discuss the strategies used by the skilled individual—respectively, the skilled integration of sensory information in the control of bodily movement, and the skills apparent in man–machine control systems. Howarth's discussion of *Strategies in the Control of Movement* reviews evidence relating to movement within a theoretical framework which assumes that strategies are used by the individual to resolve problems caused by the need to combine different sources of sensory information for the control of a wide range of possible movements. The three general strategies discussed are continuous recalibration of the senses, changed weighting of information according to its reliability, and the continuous correction of movement. Howarth argues that these strategies lead to the appearance of various phenomena which have been described elsewhere as resulting from structural mechanisms, and discusses autokinesis, the displacing prism adaptation, ventriloquism, the intermittent control of movement, speed–error trade-off, and the relationship between eye movements and visual search within this strategical framework. Moray's chapter on *The Strategic Control of Information Processing* is very much more involved with behaviour than with cognitive structure in its analysis of the ongoing control of machine systems by the human operator. In any system which provides information of its own changing status the skilled operator develops optimal monitoring strategies, and Moray's discussion of the behaviour of air-traffic controllers, of the steering control of ships and automobiles, and of the monitoring of informative instruments, is largely a discussion of the *use* of cognitive structure rather than one of its formulation. Sutherland's (1977) review of Colin Blakemore's Reith Lecture series holds the same warning for physiology when he concludes that

> the knowledge that a particular function is localized in one part of the brain is of itself no help in understanding the mechanisms involved: at best, it can only be a useful first step to more detailed behavioural, neurophysiological and neuroanatomical work that may help unravel the underlying processes.

Evidence of the localization of a cognitive process tells us little of the functioning of that process in behaviour, and Moray's chapter presents similar arguments against a psychologist's structural view of behaviour.

The final section, comprising three chapters by Wood, Young and Baron, centres on more general domains of behaviour than do the earlier sections. These chapters discuss the application of the information processing system to the problems faced by the adaptive individual. Wood's discussion of *Problem Solving—The Nature and Development of Strategies* contains most of the points necessary in the definition of the concept of strategy. Within the domain of problem-solving behaviour, Wood explains the need to account for the variability of behaviour by different individuals, and by the same individual on different occasions, and demonstrates how short-term (practice) and long-term (developmental) improvements in problem-solving capabilities may by attributed to strategy changes. This chapter also provides an indication of how information processing theory can come to grips with cultural differences. Members of very different cultures not only solve their problems in very different ways, but they also perceive the problems very differently. Strategical differences will be effective throughout the sequence of processing information, and culture will necessarily produce vast disparities in the strategies which are selected. In contrast to Wood's analysis of strategies in problem solving, Young's chapter on *Strategies and the Structure of a Cognitive Skill* prefers to emphasize the use of the concept of production systems, leaning heavily upon computer science, rather than that of strategy. There is a consideration here of the variability of behaviour, as with strategies, but production systems give detailed protocols of the individual's behaviour on his way to the current goal. Young's comparative discussion of production systems and strategies uses cognitive development as its arena, and argues forcibly that we must distinguish carefully between overt behaviour and the cognitive processes used to generate that behaviour. Behaviour is generated by, but does not correspond to, process; just as strategies are indicated by differences in behaviour without implying differences in the underlying cognitive structure. The reliance upon production systems in Young's chapter does give access to the problem of how different strategies can arise—they are generated by different production systems—but the same production system can give rise to different strategies under different circumstances of course.

The final chapter in this section is Baron's discussion of *Intelligence and General Strategies*, which outlines a number of strategies and their necessary application in the generation of what we describe as intelligent behaviour. This *tour de force* necessarily touches upon a large number of areas of investigation in its organization of purposeful behaviour. Integrated into Baron's discussion are considerations of the specific use of the knowledge systems in the retrieval of information from memory, the relationships between individual differences in memory tasks and the use of adaptive strategies, and between the stages of cognitive development and the acquisition of such strategies. Population differences between retarded and normal children, and between cultures, are also introduced as being associated with strategy differences. Together with Wood's review of problem solving behaviour, Baron also considers the relationship between instruction and cognitive flexibility, exploring some of the conditions necessary for the assisted development of adaptive strategies.

As a book concerned with the application of the concept of strategy to the investigation of cognitive processing, there has been no attempt to apply the concept exhaustively to every area of investigation which is available. These chapters are representative of a wide range of investigations, from phoneme perception and object recognition to problem solving and intelligence. The common thread, and indeed the purpose of the book, is the demonstration of the power of an analysis of behaviour in terms of the strategies of information processing. The underlying cognitive structure may or may not be vital—we have no unified theory of these relationships here—but strategy cannot be overlooked at the expense of structure. This selective review of problem areas in the context of the variability of behaviour, which is endorsed by the analysis of strategies, looks more at the description of behaviour than at the areas themselves. Thus, although memory and language appear frequently in discussions, as they should do once we have admitted the principle of continuity of information processing, there are no intensive reviews of these domains. Indeed, the continuity principle can be seen to be operating at its best in current studies of memory *for* language: it would be pointless to attempt to describe the use of knowledge in a communicating system as an isolated problem in the investigation of semantic memory or sentence comprehension. It is a problem in its own right, with its own relationships to these other two abstract areas.

Perhaps one of the more important and most attractive features of this development in information processing theory is that implicit in the description of any strategy is the acknowledgement of the goals and intentions of the individual. For the individual to choose one strategy rather than another he must have his goals in mind, as well as what he thinks is the best route to those goals. Problems arise in the laboratory, of course, because the goals of the experimental subject do not always coincide with the goals of the experimenter. A description of the strategical use of cognitive processes has the power to resolve the conflict suggested by the phrase "the social psychology of the psychology experiment".

Developments of the use of strategical analyses will be intensive within the current bounds of "cognitive psychology", and extensive to bring currently esoteric problems under greater consideration. To account for the variability of behaviour between individuals we need to look specifically at strategies and their manifestation as personality differences, cultural differences and intelligence differences. As a catalogue of general strategies appears we shall be producing a theory of personality, and the roots of this development are quite apparent in Baron's chapter here. Individuals with particular personality traits, and cognitive styles, may use particular strategies consistently, and these strategies for processing information may vary widely over a population of personalities. If one of our main aims is to account for variations in behaviour, then strategies must take a central role in our explanations.

REFERENCES

Allport, D. A., Antonis, G. and Reynolds, P. (1972). On the division of attention: A disproof of the single channel hypothesis. *Quarterly Journal of Experimental Psychology* **24**, 225–235.

Bradshaw, J. L. (1974). Peripherally presented and unreported words may bias the perceived meaning of a centrally fixated homograph. *Journal of Experimental Psychology* **103**, 1200–1202.

Broadbent, D. E. (1958). "Perception and Communication". Pergamon Press, Oxford.

Cavanagh, J. P. (1972). Relation between the immediate memory span and the memory search rate. *Psychological Review* **79**, 525–530.

Corcoran, D. W. J. (1966). An acoustic factor in letter cancellation. *Nature* **210**, 658.

Dawkins, R. (1976). "The Selfish Gene". Oxford University Press, Oxford.

Deutsch, J. A. and Deutsch, D. (1963). Attention: Some theoretical considerations. *Psychological Review* **70**, 80–90

Erdelyi, M. H. (1974). A new look at the new look: Perceptual defense and vigilance. *Psychological Review* **81**, 1–25.

Frith, U. (1976). How to read without knowing how to spell. Paper read at the Lancaster meeting of the British Association for the Advancement of Science.

Garner, W. R., Hake, H. W. and Eriksen, C. W. (1956). Operationism and the concept of perception. *Psychological Review* **63**, 317–329.

Gray, M. J. (1975). Effects of shadowing on reading. *Journal of Experimental Psychology: Human Learning and Memory* **104**, 423–428.

Haber, R. N. (1974). Information processing. *In* "Handbook of Perception: Historical and Philosophical Roots of Perception" (E. C. Carterette and M. P. Friedman, eds), Vol. 1. Academic Press, New York and London.

Kleiman, G. M. (1975). Speech recoding in reading. *Journal of Verbal Learning and Verbal Behaviour* **14**, 323–339.

Levin, H. and Cohn, J. A. (1968). Studies of oral reading: XII. Effects of instructions on the eye–voice span. *In* "The Analysis of Reading Skill" (H. Levin, E. J. Gibson, and L. J. Gibson, eds), Final report, Project No. 5-1213, Contract No. OE6-10-156. Cornell University and US Office of Education.

Maynard Smith, J. and Price, G. A. (1973). The logic of animal conflicts. *Nature* **246**, 15–18.

Miller, G. A. (1956). The magical number seven, plus or minus two: Some limits on our capacity for processing information. *Psychological Review* **63**,81–97.

Moray, N. (1969). "Attention: Selective Processes in Vision and Hearing". Hutchinson, London.

Neisser, U. (1967). "Cognitive Psychology". Appleton-Century-Crofts, New York.

Neisser, U. (1976). "Cognition and Reality". Freeman, San Francisco.

Newell, A. (1973a). You can't play 20 questions with nature and win: Projective comments on the papers of this symposium. *In* "Visual Information Processing" (W. G. Chase, ed). Academic Press, New York and London.

Newell, A. (1973b). Production systems: Models of control structures. *In* "Visual Information Processing" (W. G. Chase, ed.). Academic Press, New York and London.

Secord, P. F. and Backman, C. W. (1961). Personality theory and the problem of stability and change in individual behaviour: An inter-personal approach. *Psychological Review* **68**, 21–32.

Shaffer, L. H. (1971). Attention in transcription skill. *Quarterly Journal of Experimental Psychology* **23**, 107–112.

Shotter, J. (1975). "Images of Man in Psychological Research". Methuen, London.

Sperling, G. (1967). Successive approximations to a model for short-term memory. *Acta Psychologica* **27**, 285–292.

Sutherland, N. S. (1977). Review of *Mechanics of the Mind*, by C. Blakemore. *The Times Higher Education Supplement*, 29.7.77.

Treisman, A. M. (1960). Contextual cues in selective listening. *Quarterly Journal of Experimental Psychology* **12**, 242–248.

Tulving, E. (1972). Episodic and semantic memory. *In* "Organization of Memory". (E. Tulving and W. Donaldson, eds). Academic Press, New York and London.

Underwood, G. (1974). Moray *vs.* the rest: The effects of extended shadowing practice. *Quarterly Journal of Experimental Psychology* **26**, 368–372.

Underwood, G. (1976a). Semantic interference from unattended print. *British Journal of Psychology* **67**, 372–338.

Underwood, G. (1976b). "Attention and Memory". Pergamon Press, Oxford.

Two

Continuity, Concealment and Visual Attention

John Fox

University of Sheffield

INTRODUCTION

Some things are immediately evident in the visual world that confronts us, requiring little in the way of effort to find them, while some things are concealed. Those things which are evident to an organism, and those which aren't, tell us a great deal about the kinds of process that its perceptual system is capable of carrying out. A moving fly, we are told, is evident to a frog while a stationary fly is not. The differences between certain sorts of pattern and others are evident to a human observer while other kinds of difference cannot be seen without considerable effort, as we shall see later. These observations have greatly helped us to understand perceptual systems in themselves and potentially they will help us understand more about the ecological aspects of perception. After all, the richness of the optical distinctions that an organism can make is critically important to it; the range of distinctions that it can make, by whatever means, is one of the factors that confine the range of ecologies in which it could manage. A frog cannot survive in an environment in which its food doesn't move.

One must say that it is to the credit of the higher organisms that they overcome many of the "concealment" problems that are posed by their environments though admittedly often by rather roundabout means. The range of methods for achieving this is, at least for man, rather large and probably includes many techniques of which we are largely unaware. We can expose a concealed predator by gross movements to look behind an obscuring obstacle, by probing for details with careful, searching eye-movements and fixations, and we can pay special attention to certain places and patterns by subtle changes in the "tuning" of the perceptual system. Most concealed things, whether they are concealed physically, intellectually or only optically, can usually be revealed in a variety of ways, so it seems appropriate that in a volume concerned with strategies we should consider some of the information processing techniques that are available when we are faced with one or another kind of concealment difficulty.

But if we are to discuss this with anything approaching clarity it seems prerequisite that we should have a clear idea of some of the conditions that can mediate visual concealment. Trivially, of course, the opacity of an object is sufficient to prevent something being seen; in itself we normally regard this as the province of physics rather than psychology. However, the characteristics of visual systems themselves also afford certain kinds of concealment, as the example of the frog illustrates, which go beyond the obvious cases of objects being obscured by others or the equally clear cases where we simply fail to pay enough attention or fail to "notice" aspects of detail. We must, therefore, spend some time discussing the ways in which we typically process information during perception before tackling these issues directly.

My plan in this chapter, therefore, is to outline some of the many kinds of visual concealment and then to present a partial theory of visual information processing in the hope that this will shed some light on why these difficulties occur. Only on this basis will the "strategic" processes proposed in Section 3 make any sense. This is probably a chapter that one should start at the beginning and read through to the end; an unfashionable admission but the reader should blame the perversity of the material, rather than that of the author, for such an odd organization. The nature of the argument, though not its present form, owes much to the criticisms and writings of others, particularly David Marr on early visual processing, J. J. Gibson and Ulric Neisser on the relationships between perception and attention, and Allen Newell and Richard Young who have good ways of talking about perception without making it seem trivial. These debts should be acknowledged at the outset.

1. CONTINUITY AND CONCEALMENT

1.1. The concealment problem

It is, as I think J. J. Gibson would put it, a matter of ecological optics that things that are the same or have the same significance for an organism often *look* the same (but of course not always), while the things that look the same often *are* the same. Within limits the various regions of a lawn are similarly coloured, similarly textured and so forth. Perceptually grouping such regions together as a single surface, under one heading as it were, seems to have the straightforward value of summarizing the scene. This helps perception to take place more quickly and reduces mental effort. If mental processes determine that one part of the lawn is flat, and will provide a satisfactory surface of support, then it would seem strangely wasteful of mental resources* if this had to be done for every region of the lawn; that is, if all the regions *look* the same then one could do worse than to assume that they were part of the same, flat, supporting surface. Better that the system first uses some reasonably reliable criterion to rough out those parts of the optic array that probably correspond to significant perceptual entities, and then one can assign functional properties to them just once, as it becomes possible, and as it becomes necessary. What more relevant criterion can one think of for "roughing out" than an optical criterion? To a first approximation, regions of the optic array that have similar

---

* I am, of course, begging an important question here. One can only be "wasteful" of anything if one is, in practice, short of that thing. The pre-attentive visual system appears to have an enormous capacity for handling information and it is generally assumed that such operations as finding groups of identically coloured fragments corresponding to "lawns" are carried out pre-attentively; it is the more central "attentive" processes whose information processing capacity is considered to be significantly limited. However, I take the view that whether attentive processes are necessarily involved in the *assembly* of such descriptions as "satisfactory surface of support", or whether they merely accept them as the results of more primitive mechanisms, it makes sense that there should be as few descriptions as possible.

optical properties will not share those properties by chance but are likely to have the same or similar functional significance for the perceiver. Conversely, those regions which do not have similar optical properties (having different colours or brightnesses or grossly different textures) *should* be treated as functionally distinct until enough evidence is accumulated to establish their equivalence. Whether or not the similarities or dissimilarities of objects noticeably affect the final course of behaviour will depend upon some degree of processing of such similarities being carried out; optical continuity detection involves a minimum commitment of resources while at the same time providing a rich basis for further processing if that proves necessary. An abrupt brightness discontinuity, caused by a shadow for example, is significant whether it is later taken to indicate coolness, the presence of another organism, a place to hide, or whatever. The elementary optical discontinuities, as a matter of fact, map quite nicely on to the objects, structures and events that are likely to turn out to be of significance for us. So long as an organism is capable of recovering from the occasional, inevitable error little harm should result from the application of this "principle of continuity". (This name for the principle is borrowed from Musatti (1931) who first pointed out the feature common to much of the Gestalt thinking on principles of perceptual organization.)

The reader will have guessed that the reason for this emphasis on continuity and discontinuity has to do with the problem of concealment. On occasion things that are grouped together on the basis of optical continuity will prove *not* to have the same significance; the whole purpose of camouflage is to create the maximum likelihood that unwelcome observers will make continuity errors. And of course the converse error must also occur; one occasionally mistakes a shadow seen out of the corner of one's eye as something one is about to trip over, though fortunately such errors appear to be the exception rather than the rule. Such errors of assignment, and how we manage to recover from them, are the subject of this discussion; my first task, therefore, is to attempt to identify some of the more obvious sources of such errors.

1.2. Examples of concealment

1.2.1. Continuity of elementary sensory properties

Two of the most dominant optical properties appear to be brightness and colour. However similar in form two objects or patterns may be, if their colours are different (even if only "slightly" different) they will tend to be distinguished in our minds. Two rows of letters, one in red and one in black, clearly break up into two groups even if the letters within a row are quite different from each other but identical to the letters in the other row. Brightness differences can produce comparable grouping effects.

The ability of colour and brightness to influence the perceived organization of complex displays is attested to by our experience and a host of experimental demonstrations. We need mention only a handful of examples; it appears to be straightforward to use colour as a basis for search, more effective than shape (e.g. Williams, 1966), and similarly it is an effective basis for distinguishing patterns in visual sensory (iconic) memory (e.g. Clark, 1969). Brightness and colour are considerably more effective retrieval cues than shape, category or other "complex" properties (Von Wright, 1968, 1970). The simple point to be established is that colour and brightness are compelling attributes of visual stimuli; they dominate perceived continuity and the assignment of "groups" by the visual system.

(One must be wary of oversimple interpretations of the macrobiological significance of these observations. There are cases in the animal world where sensory *distinctiveness* is used as part of a complex system of *concealment*. The Californian skink, for example, is a lizard that is quite well camouflaged for its habitat with the exception of a long, bright blue tail. This tail, however, breaks off easily and may serve to distract the attention of a predator as the lizard escapes.)

Fig. 1. Grouping by continuity of orientation of lines.

It is also quite clear that the orientation of edges and lines has a comparable effect. Olson and Attneave (1970) have shown that line orientation has considerable influence on perceived continuity and Beck (1966) has shown that orientation factors are more influential than factors of arrangement in the perceptual grouping of lines. There is also some evidence that the visual system treats continuity of pattern elements as especially significant by providing a mechanism for mutual facilitation of encoding (Treisman *et al.*, 1975). An example of grouping by continuity of orientation is shown in Fig. 1.

1.2.2. *Continuity over proximity and location*

The visual system treats things which are next to each other, and things which are relatively close together, with a special sort of respect. Of course this is only as it should be—there *is* something special about adjacency. The parts of any object or continuous surface are bound together at infinitesimal sites; they are adjacent. A simple matter of physics it might seem but one which has substantial consequences for the design of an effective visual mechanism. It is true that objects, surfaces and contours are often broken through the interposition of other surfaces, but as a first approximation adjacency is a very useful basis for identifying underlying physical continuity. Figure 2 illustrates the importance of adjacency. Figure 2 is much the same as Fig. 1 except that the needles have been mixed up; elements with the same orientation properties are no longer guaranteed to be directly adjacent to each other. Only if there is continuity with a majority of adjacent elements is there a chance of them aggregating to form a distinct region—otherwise we see a composite surface composed of two kinds of element.

FIG. 2. Mixing up lines of distinct orientations makes it difficult to perceive two distinct groups of elements, unlike Fig. 1. Adjacency of identical elements appears to be important in grouping and perceived continuity, in this case only a single pattern is seen.

This important component of adjacency is of course implicit in our discussion of continuity of sensory properties above. But while adjacency often goes together with identity of sensory (and other) properties, it can contribute something in isolation; it is possible to construct contours, i.e. perceived contours, composed of objects which only appear to be consistently related by being immediate neighbours, as illustrated in Fig. 3.

Proximity also contributes to perceived continuity (a fact which the Gestalt psychologist canonized) quite separately from adjacency. O'Callaghan (1974) investigates this phenomenon in detail and gives examples of random dot patterns in which some regions are immediately evident; the dots in the two regions have stochastically similar adjacency relations but are distinguished by the average proximity of the dots in the two regions. This example, however, begins to blur into differences of the "structure" of the spatial layout so let us turn directly to this topic.

Fig. 3. A "contour" composed of highly distinct elements is formed under the influence of adjacency relations.

1.2.3. Continuity by structural similarity

We discussed above how the perception of continuity in a structure that is as complex as that of a lawn can be influenced by continuity of colour and brightness. Similarly with orientation—those blades of grass that have been mowed in the same direction generally lean at the same orientation to produce the characteristic stripes. Adjacency is also important but this is by no means the whole story; other more subtle relationships between the fragments of an object also have a profound effect on perceived continuity. To take a familiar case which the Gestalt psychologists referred to as *good continuation*, it is obvious that the dots in Fig. 4 cohere to form two major elements, even though the dots themselves are locally indistinguishable. Of course the dots are configured in highly systematic ways; adjacent pairs of dots in a row

Fig. 4. Continuity of spacing and axial relations cause the dots to split up into two groups, while a variety of other, repetitive structures such as quadrilaterals are not seen without deliberate attention.

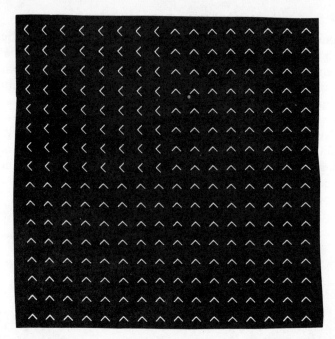

FIG. 5. Although the populations of lines are confined to + 45° and − 45° throughout the texture, other structural properties give rise to the perception of two distinct regions.

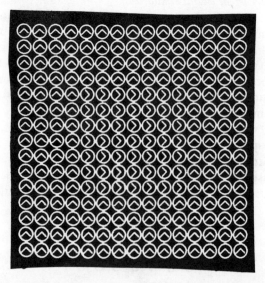

FIG. 6. A texture similar to that in Fig. 5 contains an odd region which is concealed from the cursory glance by the addition of a surround to each of the texture elements.

have the same proximity to each other as all other adjacent pairs in a row, but do not have the same relationships with dots in the other row. Similarly the orientation of the arcs between dots within the same row are consistent, and all the dots are coaxial. Many such observations are characterized by being continuities of the relationships between elements rather than continuities across local properties.

With respect to my theme of concealment one might also note the multiplicity of structures hidden within Fig. 4. There are pairs and triples of dots, triangles and quadrilaterals galore; without deliberate attention all fall victim to the principle of continuity.

Structural properties can give rise to some striking and unexpected changes in perceived continuity and discontinuity. Figure 5, for example, contains a 16×16 array of right-angle elements all of which are composed of identical diagonal elements. Yet it is quite evident that two distinct regions are present. The sensory properties of the texture elements are identical; it is only the way that they are arranged that makes the regions so easy to discriminate.

There are yet more oddities in the way that our visual mechanisms are engineered, oddities that are shown up by some strikingly simple changes that can be made to this "texture"; as Fig. 6 illustrates, placing a circular surround around each of the texture elements results in the odd patch being concealed from the cursory glance. A number of examples of related phenomena will be illustrated later. They demonstrate the subtlety of the concealment problem; continuity and discontinuity are not merely matters of optical properties as they are registered by peripheral sensory mechanisms, nor a matter of "similarity" in any obvious intuitive sense. In order to understand this we need to develop some rather clear concept of the nature of optical relationships and structure. This observation is underlined by the strange case of visual symmetry.

1.2.4. *Continuity by symmetry*

The Gestalt psychologists set one particular grouping mechanism apart from all others—grouping by symmetry. They noticed that symmetrical patterns, particularly bilaterally symmetrical patterns, tend to cohere to form a strongly unitary whole. In present terms such patterns have a very salient internal continuity. The insight of these investigators was that the mechanisms required to register this kind of continuity would have to be rather different from the simple kind of "continuity detector" that might suffice for the examples discussed above—an insight that has often been forgotten to judge from some of the proposals for mechanisms of early visual processing. The difficulty associated with the perception of symmetry is illustrated in Fig. 7.

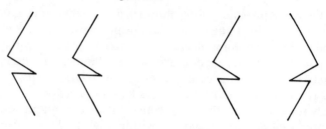

Fig. 7. *Left.* A pattern made up of two components one of which is an exact translation of the other. *Right.* A pattern made up of components in a reflection relationship. Many experiments have shown that patterns like the one on the right have a greater perceptual unity than patterns like the one on the left.

On the left of Fig. 7 is a pair of patterns, one of which is an exact copy and translation of the other—the pattern has been constructed with the intention that the two parts should be identical in every sense. The pattern on the right is similar, except that one component is a "reflection" rather than a translation of the other. In most obvious senses the two halves of the symmetrical pattern are less similar to each other than are the two halves of the repeated pattern; reflection changes the orientation of lines, repetition does not; reflection switches all left–right relations and so on.

The great puzzle is that reflected patterns often tend to produce *more* perceived continuity than repeated patterns. Julesz (1975), for example, has observed that certain textures which are globally symmetrical about a midline are quickly perceived as such, while textural *repetition* is often missed and generally harder to see. Corballis and Roldan (1974) have shown that symmetry is perceived more quickly than repetition, and Bruce and Morgan (1975) have found that small violations to bilateral symmetry are more immediately evident than violations of a perfect repetition. More directly on the matter of continuity, Fox (1975a) has found that the *identity* of pattern pairs is picked up more quickly if the pairs are in a reflection relationship than if they are only in a translation relationship. Bryant (1974) and Huttenlocher (1967) have found that young children find difficulty in discriminating pairs of simple patterns which combine to form a bilaterally symmetrical display (e.g. ⊏ ⊐) than patterns arranged in different ways* (e.g. ⊓ ⊔). On a general level all these phenomena suggest that

* Bryant also points out that in the stimuli used differences of discrimination can also be explained by the observation that some of the pattern elements were "in line", i.e. had the same orientation and were coaxial. This seems to be a special case of the continuity of orientation discussed above; the data are consistent with the idea that symmetry and continuity of orientation are *both* contributing to the overall unitariness of the patterns.

symmetry *conceals* the very changes that are introduced by the reflection transformation. In my view this is a paradox that has not received a satisfactory explanation in any of the contemporary accounts of visual processing; I shall attempt such an account later in the discussion.

1.2.5. Continuity and temporal invariance

Of course perception doesn't take place in a world having only dimensions of space; the temporal dimension is just as fundamental though temporal perception is harder to study. Continuity and discontinuity are concomitantly temporal as well as spatial concepts—objects sometimes change over time and sometimes remain invariant. The argument that it is important for the perceptual system to be able to summarize the spatial continuities that it encounters applies no less here—it is important that the objects that are changing in time and those that are invariant over time should be economically represented.

The concealment problem also remains fundamental. It is possible for an object to be hidden, and an organism to conceal itself, by altering its temporal behaviour, and a sophisticated observer acquires significant advantages if he is able to overcome this concealment. A familiar "strategy" of any predatory animal is to freeze should his intended prey glance around, but slight changes in head posture or grosser movements will often suffice to reveal the embarrassed impostor by the exploitation of parallax. The risk of detection from an incautious movement is very real; the human visual system has prodigious abilities to detect continuities and discontinuities in temporal relationships. Johannson (1971), for example, has carried out his famous series of experiments in which lights are placed on a person's shoulders, ankles, elbows etc. and filmed in an otherwise totally dark setting. While stationary the image appears as a random cluster of lights, but let the model walk, dance or turn for a moment then the observer, after only the briefest of pauses, recognizes what he is seeing. It is not only the frog who is doomed to being unable to perceive contours if the right sort of information is not available to distinguish them.

Invariance of spatial relations is also of significance on a much more detailed scale in identifying object boundaries. As an object moves against a background, it sets up a number of microstructures that are optically quite characteristic to a suitably talented observer. I am thinking here of the dynamic edges produced by objects in motion—leading edges, trailing edges and "shearing" edges. Leading and trailing edges appear to be characterized by shared motion and invariance of spatial relations, between the fragments of the moving object; in the case of an opaque object this is coupled with systematic patterns of occlusion and reappearance of fragments of the background. The shearing edge produced by an opaque object, such as an edge parallel to the direction of motion, results from temporal consistency of the spatial relations of the fragments of the edge (assuming of course that the body is rigid!) together with discontinuity of spatial relations with background elements. As with Johannson's dancer, the absence of motion results in the collapse of all these edges and, if the object is distinguished from its background by no other discontinuity, perfect camouflage results.

All perceivers have a great deal of knowledge about how to conceal themselves and how to reveal others, though that knowledge may be tacit. These examples capture many of the concealment problems that we know about and set the stage for the remainder of the discussion. The next section attempts to explain how and why the problems arise from the way our nervous systems are designed; the final section tries to describe the way our tacit knowledge can be expressed as methods for revealing objects that have become concealed by misleading continuities.

2. FOUNDATIONS OF A THEORY OF VISUAL INFORMATION PROCESSING

2.1. Evaluation criteria

Any theory of information processing must satisfy one main criterion before one should, or indeed can, attempt to put it to an empirical test. The criterion is that the theory should be *manageably complete*. Completeness requires that one should be satisfied that the theory, if it were embodied in some sort of mechanism, would actually *do* the task for which the theory was intended. In order to achieve this it is necessary to deal with issues of control, stability and adequacy, whether at a concrete or an abstract level. When circumstances are particularly propitious this can result in a theoretical module, a self-contained process or mechanism which will do the job asked of it and can form part of a more comprehensive theory without modification.

This volume recognizes explicitly that mental processes recruit and continually activate "pieces" of knowledge embodied in skills and their component habitual acts. But whether habitual or creative, behaviour is concerned with *doing* things and psychological theories must reflect this. Mental processes must make use of mental resources, like coding mechanisms and memory buffers, to be sure, but the ways in which they must be used have a great deal to do with what they are being used *for* and psychological theories make little sense if they confine themselves to the resource aspects alone. It seems clear that we learn, and accumulate, a great deal less from theories of "pattern recognition", for example, than from theories of "how to find things"; theories that deal with the latter kind of activity lend themselves much more readily to explicating complex streams of behaviour.

(One caveat is necessary; completeness does not imply unwieldy masses of detail, which is why I have included the informal qualification of *manageableness*. Completeness can be achieved at any level that is appropriate—appropriateness of course being judged differently according to whether one is interested in visual perception, problem solving or management techniques.)

In a word, it is *procedural* aspects of behaviour which are missing from many contemporary psychological theories, and in their absence it is hard to see whether a theoretical proposal is realistic. This point is emphasized for two reasons. Firstly, in order to add a voice to those others calling for more productive evaluation criteria in psychology (e.g. Newell, 1973). Secondly, it is necessary to explain an assumption running throughout this discussion which is controversial in some quarters. I have assumed that the representation of the world embodied in man's visual system is, from first to last, discrete, for we know and understand little of mechanisms that lend themselves to procedural representation that do not require the discreteness property.

There are a number of alternative directions that I have chosen not to take; for example it has often been suggested that the visual system implements processes that transform the retinal image in a way that resembles two-dimensional Fourier analysis or two-dimensional autocorrelation. Both classes of theory assume to all intents and purposes that the visual input should be regarded as a complex and continuous waveform, rather than a collection of discrete fragments. For some purposes there is little doubt that these approaches lead to valuable insights into the kinds of things that the visual system is capable of, but neither is either manageable or complete in that they have not proved to assist the description of the ongoing moment-to-moment aspects of perception. Since the seminal work of Campbell and his colleagues (e.g. Campbell *et al.*, 1968; Blakemore and Campbell, 1969) there have been no proposals made as to how, for example, spatial–frequency descriptions of the invariants of objects may be set down. It is true that some of the classical problems of stimulus equivalance such as equivalence over size and location are dealt with by the spatial–frequency approach, but the problem of *description* of objects has not been. We may be able to describe certain gratings and bull's-eyes in spatial–frequency terms, but we have had little success in capturing the families of edges (sharp or fuzzy, intact or interrupted) or the families of surfaces (flat or curved, shaded or textured) which are the stuff of the perceptual stream. Before we can have theories of how edges and surfaces are dealt with in perception and action, we must have theoretical languages which naturally express these concepts.

As will become clear in what follows, discrete representations do exist in which it is possible to make sense of such concepts. They are conceptually manageable and make it possible to contemplate the development of complete theories of visual information processing.

2.2. Marr's theory of peripheral visual mechanisms

At the time of writing, the most comprehensive theory of early visual processing is that developed by Marr (1976), and this section essentially presents Marr's ideas on the peripheral visual mechanisms with few additions. This theory is used as the groundwork on which more cognitive processes can be discussed; this is possible because of the completeness of Marr's account, completeness and modularity being central, also, to his views on theoretical development. Of course this is something of a commitment because Marr's theory may be incorrect but it seems to me that since the theory is consistent with known physiology and effective (it has been implemented as a computer program), it will probably prove to be theoretically productive for some time to come.

Be that as it may I doubt anyway whether the psychological ideas that I shall explore really stand or fall on the correctness of Marr's theory—because of its modularity a quite different theory doing the same job could be "plugged in" in its place if that were necessary. The purpose of describing it in some detail is to satisfy the completeness criterion—it would be most unsatisfactory if the comments made on perception and attention relied on assumptions whose consistency and adequacy were uncertain.

The account of Marr's theory is necessarily sketchy; the interested reader is strongly urged to consult his original paper. The part of the theory that we shall focus on particularly is the account of peripheral mechanisms which recover something akin to an artist's sketch from a natural (i.e. photographic) image. To do this, familiar concepts from neurophysiology are used—the excitatory/inhibitory receptive fields associated with cortical units such as those discovered in the celebrated work of Hübel and Wiesel and others. But Marr emphasizes the view that these units are not merely "triggers" that respond to the presence of certain sorts of feature with either a present/absent or even graded response, rather they have a sophisticated function of *measuring* the stimulus; the results of the measurements are a huge collection of localized but rich *descriptions* of the parts of the stimulus. Several steps are involved in the process:

1. For each locale of the image the brightness distribution over the locale is convolved with the excitatory/inhibitory profile of a set of "masks" (corresponding to simplified receptive fields). Each mask is made up of two or three parallel and alternating strips of excitatory or inhibitory elements which model the physiological units rather coarsely but nevertheless satisfactorily. Such strips must, of course, have both a size and an orientation and in fact Marr makes use of a large range of sizes and orientations when convolving with each locale. (Convolution is rather like correlating a matrix representing the brightness distribution in the image with a matrix representing the excitation/inhibition strips of the mask.*) The result of the convolution can be thought of as a value which specifies how well each mask, with such and such a size and such and such an orientation, describes the brightness pattern at the locale. The masks respond to brightness *changes* (discontinuities) in the image such as edges and lines, and each mask records how each discontinuity matches up to its preferred orientation and preferred size.

2. But obtaining a set of possible descriptions is not enough, the system must also pick out which *one* description gives the best account of the luminance pattern in its locale. Marr achieves this in two ways: first, by taking the straightforward step of identifying the orientation of the masks that best describe the local stimulus, and secondly by identifying the best size of mask for describing it. This is rather tricky because at this point the system cannot know what kind of discontinuity is confronting it; it might be a sharp or fuzzy edge or a bar or a very gradual ramp, and the shape and size descriptions of the discontinuity are closely interrelated. This can be sorted out satisfactorily, however, because different kinds of intensity change, like smooth gradients and abrupt edges, produce different responses through the range of mask sizes. Specifically the size of mask is determined by the point at which increasing the size of the mask doesn't much change the response obtained to the input brightness distribution.

3. The next step is to sort out exactly what kind of intensity change is present in the locale. Marr has found that the set of neighbouring receptive fields (masks) selected in Step 2 which are looking at the locale, has a profile of convolution values that is quite characteristic

---

* Those readers familiar with spatial–frequency filtering theory will recognize that these operations are formally equivalent to filters of different kinds. The emphasis in Marr's theory is, however, placed upon the discrete, symbolic representation of the visual image which is the final outcome of the measurement process rather than the formal fact that the mechanisms are tuned to a particular band in the spectrum.

for different kinds of intensity change. On the basis of these profiles, therefore, the system identifies all the intensity changes in the image.

4. Finally the information from the various processes is assembled into what Marr calls a *symbolic assertion* describing the local brightness change in detail. An example of such an assertion is:

$$
\begin{aligned}
&\text{(Shading-edge (Position (34 48) (73 48))}\\
&\qquad\qquad\text{(Contrast 18)}\\
&\qquad\qquad\text{(Fuzziness 17)}\\
&\qquad\qquad\text{(Orientation 0))}
\end{aligned}
$$

Which is simply to say that the system has recorded the presence of an edge running between positions (34 48) and (73 48), and that its contrast is 18 units and orientation 0 degrees. The edge is not sharp, however, but is characterized as a *Shading-edge* with a "fuzziness" value of 17 units. The result of all these processes is a vast collection of symbolic assertions which Marr refers to collectively as the "primal sketch" because they record the contours and slight changes of intensity much as an artist might sketch them.

As was observed in Section 1 the places where there are significant optical changes in the stimulus capture a good deal of the important structure of the visual environment; the location of objects, their boundaries and so forth. It is for this reason that Marr chooses to distinguish the derivative of the optical luminance waveform in the primal sketch—the *changes* in luminance rather than those adjacent locales with identical luminances. It seems clear that Marr is right to make this emphasis but for our purposes it is necessary to reinstate the properties of these uniform regions. The reason for this is that the primal sketch does not carry all the information that must be assumed for later discussion; and it also accords with conscious experience that we perceive the uniformity of brightness or colour of a region and not just its edges. But in the spirit of Marr's approach I shall not attempt to modify the notion of the primal sketch, rather to introduce an additional representation which for convenience will be referred to as the "property map" of the retinal image. The property map preserves a point-for-point map of the brightness and colour properties of the input stimulus.

I have also to add an assumption about the temporal aspects of early visual processing, though I do so with considerable trepidation because much less is known about temporal than spatial visual mechanisms. As such the conjectures have a purely functional status (though one can envisage temporal mechanisms analogous to Marr's spatial masks) in that the information that the putative processes provide has to be provided somehow. Specifically I shall assume in what follows that two sets of processes contribute to the production of temporal representations analogous to the property map and primal sketch of the spatial system. The temporal property map records all events and is almost like a series of spatial property maps "back-to-back" in time; the temporal sketch specifies *onsets* and *offsets* of visual events (appearances and disappearances), their *abruptness* and so forth. The *duration* of events is assumed to be recoverable from one or the other of these records.

We return now to the main theme of this discussion, continuity and the summary of the visual lay-out.

2.3. Perception of continuity and the assignment of object-tokens

Marr introduces the important concept of the *place-token* in his paper on early visual processing. The place-token is a purely information processing concept; it may be thought of as a symbol that is internal to the perceptual system by which it keeps a note of the structure of the stimulus in an economical way. As we observed earlier, it would seem of value if a perceptual system could internally represent the significant sectors of its input, such as that corresponding to a "lawn", by some relatively simple data structure which compactly captured the continuities and other important properties of the sector. Such a data structure can be referenced by other processes such as those concerned with the control of walking without creating problems of selecting relevant information unnecessarily—if more detail is needed it can generally be remembered or picked up by an additional glance. Marr's concept of the place-token is very much like this in that place-tokens identify regions of interest in the primal sketch, and he discusses certain processes of statistical aggregation and similarity grouping which can lead to the assignment of place-tokens to portions of the sketch.

The view put here, while in very much the same spirit as Marr's, differs from it in a number of ways (e.g. Fox and Mayhew, 1977). In particular I shall assume a greater degree of uniformity in the processes of token assignment. In order to keep Marr's views distinct from my own, therefore, and to avoid putting words into that author's mouth I shall modify the terminology very slightly—the vocation of early visual processing is seen as the *assignment of object-tokens to regions and structures showing significant degrees of continuity*. Object-tokens are the precursors of object-descriptions, becoming more and more elaborate as information becomes available. Our main concern here is with the early part of this process, the assignment of the object-token on the basis of optical continuity, but I do not want to restrict the idea of an object-token to the simple case alone. An example of a hypothetical elaborated object-token follows; neither its form nor content should be taken too seriously but it captures something of the flavour of the idea:

```
(Region (Geography (Flat)
                   (Location nasal)
                   (Slant horizontal) . . .)
        (Continuities (Colour green)
                      (Texture (description))
                      (Brightness bright) . . .)
        (Components . . .))
```

This summarizes the sort of information one might need during the control of an overt activity directed at the object (Geography), the evidence on which the region was identified (Continuities), and a "message" saying where additional information might be accessed from or otherwise obtained (Components). Once again the example should not be regarded as a definite proposal, its concreteness goes far beyond what either evidence or even the most persuasive argument could justify. At a somewhat more abstract level, however, the concept of the object-token can be clarified in several respects:

(a) An object-token is a convenient name for portions of the visual stimulus which are treated as a single aggregate by subsequent perceptual processes. It is composed of a shorthand description of the optical continuities of that portion of the stimulus, a description of any structural continuities that have been identified, and might specify complex attributes, such as Geography, when these have been identified.

(b) Object-tokens are assigned as the result of symbolic correlational processes carried out on the property map, primal sketch and "proximity graph" (*see below*); the proposed continuity mechanisms are described later.

(c) Object-tokens can be assigned by combining subordinate object-tokens *if the relation between the subordinates can be derived from the continuity mechanism.**

(d) Object-tokens may refer to structures that are coincident in the

---

* This is an important point because if the idea that object-tokens are elaborated over time is to be plausible, then it must be possible to reduce all elaborations to a definite set of more primitive mechanisms. The wisdom of arbitrarily defining a large set of formal descriptive terms without any attempt to consider the genesis of those terms is debatable. The discussion of Miller and Johnson-Laird (1976) is somewhat exposed in this respect. Perhaps surprisingly a wide range of relations that would be of value in building complex descriptions can be derived entirely from the repeated application of continuity operations (Fox, 1975b).

outside world. For example one object-token may refer to a region on the basis of textural continuity while part of the region is referred to by another object-token on the basis of brightness continuity.

(e) Object-tokens are prenominal, they do not have "names" in the linguistic sense though they may refer to stimulus entities which are, in fact, nameable.

(f) Object-tokens must be referred to by cognitive processes in transactions with the outside world. They are the only means of obtaining access to information about the visual layout (cf. Marr's view that we have access to the outputs of simple cells). The processes of attention, naming and thought all act on the object-token assembly.

(g) Assignment of ego-coordinates (left–right, up–down) to the object-token occurs relatively late in processing and may be dependent on, or synonymous with, attention to the object-token (e.g. see Fig. 8).

(h) Some limited global processes can influence the assignment of object-tokens, other than changes of fixation, posture etc., but they can operate only on a representation subsequent to the primal sketch (the proximity graph) as described later.

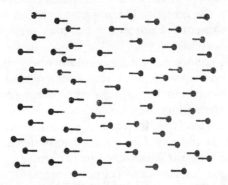

Fig. 8. The elements of this figure are organized into two distinct regions on the basis of whether the dot is on the *left* or *right* end of the line. The regions are not, however, immediately apparent suggesting that continuity analysis is not sensitive to this kind of polarity.

I have chosen to make these firm commitments at the outset for polemical reasons, however it will be clear that several of the above assertions differ very radically in their status. The basic assertion (a) may have a purely epistemological status, and not be amenable to an empirical test. One may simply have to tolerate this and look elsewhere for grounds for falsification. Assertions (f) and (g) on the other hand may well turn out to be testable at some point, and I think that there is little doubt that (b) and (h) are immediately subject to empirical

evaluation—the elementary continuity mechanisms and the mechanisms
to be proposed for global control may turn out to be neither necessary
nor sufficient to deal with the phenomena of perceived continuity
and concealment.

2.3.1. Assignment of object-tokens on the basis of sensory properties

Given the premise that the contents of the primal sketch and the
property map are available in the form of discrete assertions we may
propose a mechanism embodying a matching operator applied to
adjacent* assertions: if an assertion a_i shares a property (in the body of
the assertion) with an *adjacent* assertion a_j then the properties p_i, p_j may
be linked to the *token* property p_{ij}. The character of p_{ij} is identical to
that of each progenitor and thus regions and contours of identical
neighbours can be "grown" recursively, growth being simultaneously
initiated at many sites. The properties on which such growth can be
based include colour, brightness, and the orientation of line- and edge-
segments.

The region may, in information processing parlance, be "accessed"
or referenced by other processes by referencing the object-token p_{ijk} . . .
that results from the growth. The object-token can be dealt with as a
single entity in subsequent processing but may preserve connections to
its progenitor assertions.

On this basis, connected, uniform colour and brightness regions of
the property map acquire shared object-tokens, and adjacent *collinear*
and *parallel* elements can be aggregated to form complete or broken
contours. This elementary mechanism copes nicely with the simpler
cases of concealment. It is, for example, hard to see green things on
green backgrounds and one does not tend to notice any particular part
of a straight line unless it is smudged or broken.

It has also been asserted that cognitive access to the optic array is
only through the object-tokens; that is if a portion of the stimulus has
been distinguished by the assignment of an object-token then it will be
possible to respond selectively to that portion, if not then selection will
not be possible. Some evidence for the correctness of this assertion
comes from the research into retrieval from sensory memory referred
to in Section 1.2.1. A variety of studies have shown that it is straightforward to selectively retrieve information from iconic memory on the

---

* The sense of *adjacent* cannot be specified with certainty as yet, but in the spirit of
completeness one computable definition might run as follows: two assertions of
the property map are adjacent if they can be regarded as the end points of a diameter
of a circle and the circle contains no other assertions. Two assertions of the primal
sketch are adjacent if their circle circumscribes a set of assertions in the property
map which are all referenced by the same (property generated) object-token.

basis of elementary sensory "features" such as colour and brightness (Von Wright, 1968; Dick, 1969; Clark, 1969). The instruction "Report all the red letters but ignore all the black" poses no difficulty because all the red letters are referenced by a common object-token. But the instruction "Report all the letters but ignore the mirror-image letters" cannot be complied with in the space of a tachistoscopic exposure (Von Wright, 1970) because the left-handed and right-handed versions of the letters are not distinguished by the assignment of separate object-tokens. Of course, given sufficient time to scrutinize a display normal and reversed letters can be distinguished, but this brings us into the realm of "strategic" processes which are the topic of Section 3.

Little in the way of understanding has been gained of how iconic selection takes place, though Broadbent (1971) has applied his well known "filter" formula to the problem with some success. Broadbent's view is that information from the icon is selectively attenuated prior to the central decision-making processes. According to the Filter Theory, selection is carried out on the basis of the "physical features" of the input, which in vision include colour and brightness. I take no issue with the Filter Theory since its validity is well attested, but the present approach does provide it with some nourishment. On the one hand the term "physical features" which is never explicated by Broadbent could now be taken to mean *continuities in the property map and primal sketch,* and the mechanism of selection could be equated with *referencing of a particular object-token.*

2.3.2. *Object-token assignment and the proximity graph*

There are certain aggregation phenomena, however, which seem to indicate that the account of object-token assignment offered so far isn't comprehensive, and incidentally raises the possibility that Broadbent's view of the filter acting only on "physical" features is incomplete. Figure 5, for example, contains two clearly distinguishable regions as we have discussed; we almost see "edges" at the region boundaries. And yet neither the property maps of the two regions, nor the primal sketches, differ in their complements of assertions. If we are to account for this discrimination phenomenon in terms of "physical features" then the operation of the filter must be spelled out in considerably more detail than it has been; on the other hand, a more straightforward solution might be to drop the term "physical" and replace it with a more comprehensive representational scheme.

J. E. W. Mayhew and I took the latter approach (Fox and Mayhew, 1977). We noticed that although the local properties of the texture regions and their elements (brightness, line-orientation) would give rise to uniform complements of assertions in the property map and

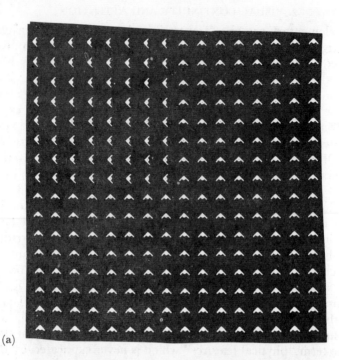

(a)

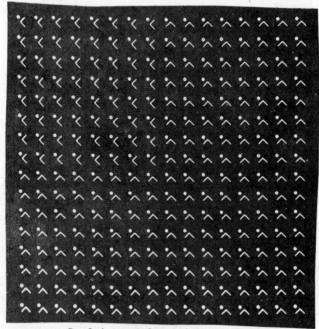

(b)

See facing page for caption.

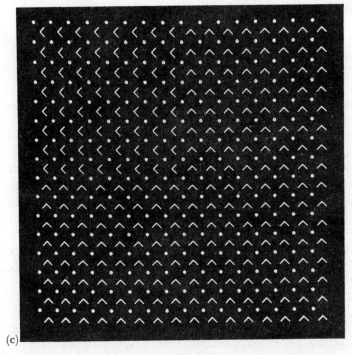

(c)

FIG. 9. An example of concealment by manipulation of proximity relations (*see text*).

primal sketch, the regions had quite different properties in what one might call the proximity domain. We suggested that subsequent to the assembly of the primal sketch was an additional stage of processing in which spatial relations, specifically proximity relations, between the assertions in the primal sketch were analysed. We found that while proximity relations well inside the regions tended to be very homogeneous, there were marked inhomogeneities at the region boundary. We concluded that the perception of the region in Fig. 5 resulted from the detection of the discontinuity of proximity relations at the boundary—and thus the assignment of distinct object-tokens to the two regions.

Some support for this suggestion was obtained from a careful analysis of the rather striking phenomenon illustrated in Fig. 9. Figure 9a shows a texture that is identical to that in Fig. 5 except that a small dot has been added to the centre of each texture element—the region is immediately evident as before. Figure 9b shows the same texture again but with a very slight change—the dots have been moved diagonally a little way. What is immediately apparent in Fig. 9a is that the region has been concealed; we have confirmed experimentally that, as one would expect, observers take considerably longer to identify it. But even more puzzling is the fact that moving the dot a little further way again, so that it is midway between texture elements, *reveals* the odd region again (Fig. 9c)!

Mayhew and I considered the proximity relations of these textures in detail and found that the concealing effects of the dot were directly tied to the degree to which the continuity of proximity relations within the regions was disrupted at the boundary. In order to account for these results it is necessary to suppose that each assertion in the primal sketch becomes the vertex of a "graph" specifying local proximity relations. It is as though one stood on the top of a hill and estimated how far away all the hills around one were, wrote this down, then went to another hill and so on. The list of distances for each hill is analogous to the proximity graph of the assertions in the primal sketch. If all the local proximity graphs (p-graphs) for each assertion are like many of those in their locality then the stimulus will appear very "regular", but any disruption of this regularity will be perceived as a discontinuity, as in the examples.

2.3.3. Proximity and continuity by symmetry

A quite separate source of evidence that continuity of proximity relations, as represented in the proximity graph, is fundamental to perceived continuity is provided by the phenomena of bilateral symmetry that have been discussed above. As has been shown, the ease with which one picks up reflection relationships poses a problem for simple hierarchical feature theories of continuity perception and simple correlational mechanisms such as autocorrelation. Symmetrical patterns are *optically* less regular than repeated patterns though their regularity is more easily seen. However, in terms of their *structural* descriptions symmetrical patterns turn out to be more regular.

I suggested in the last section that after the assembly of the primal sketch the visual system turns to the analysis of proximity relations, the result of which is the proximity graph. The proximity graph is composed of a set of p-graphs, each one associated with an assertion in the primal sketch and corresponding to an unordered list of proximity relations. These p-graphs have some important properties for understanding the nature of bilateral symmetry and repetition. If we consider a symmetrical pattern, such as the letter pair T T, then you will see that no matter what point of the pattern you consider, it is identical in its complement of spatial relationships to a least one other point of the pattern (the mirror-image point). If one imagines drawing lines from the chosen point to every other point and measuring the length of each—the list of measurements being the p-graph—then the set of measurements for the mirror-image point is identical. On the other hand, suppose one carried out the identical procedure for a repeated pattern such as L L. Now one can see that the proximity of the corner point of the left L and the rightmost point of the right L is *not* the same as the proximity of the corner point of the right L and rightmost point of the left L. In short, the proximity relations of the two points do not match up; in general the regularity of proximity relations of symmetrical patterns is not matched by the regularity of proximity relations of repeated patterns. In order to understand why mirror-image patterns tend to cohere together as a unitary whole, concealing the differences between the components, as found by Bryant (1974) and Huttenlocher (1967), one needs to look carefully into the continuity of proximity relations as well as the continuity of sensory elements like orientation.

As in the case of the examples of texture discrimination given in the last section, the visual system finds the continuity of proximity relations in symmetrical patterns so persuasive that it is prepared to assign an object-token to the whole array under a wide range of conditions.

2.3.4. Continuity and temporal invariance

Continuity of spatial proximity may also underlie the perception of invariance in patterns which are changing in time, particularly the invariance of rigid or firm objects moving against patterned backgrounds. While the identification of a moving object benefits greatly from any physical discontinuities with the background, such as colour or brightness discontinuities, they are not necessary for the detection of motion. Retinal motion is itself not satisfactory since it is very hard to recover such motion if the observer is himself in motion; the important thing is the *relative* motion of patterns in the world. It is a matter of ecological optics that things which move together or in the same way, generally tend to be associated together; a fact that has been enshrined in an additional continuity principle, the principle of common fate, by the Gestalt psychologists.

Again I take no issue with this well established insight but only suggest that in information processing terms we might think of those elements of the optic array in common motion as being referenced by a single object-token. However, the question of how the continuity is detected is not solved by this addition since we still need to say something about the conditions underlying perceived common motion. Proximity again offers a basis for understanding this. After all, the distances between parts of a rigid object do not change as it moves. Even when the rigid objects are in more complex motion than simple translation there are very often portions whose parts preserve their proximity structure invariant over time. In contrast, proximity relations with background elements are not invariant—in front of the leading edge, proximities between background fragments and object fragments are continually decreasing while behind the trailing edge they are increasing, together with appearance and disappearance of fragments at the boundaries. At the prototypical shearing edge there are no disappearing or appearing elements, but the graph of proximity relations contains two subgraphs which are invariant from moment to moment.

Continuity of proximity relations over time is *sufficient* for the assignment of an object-token as an experiment by Gibson *et al.* showed (1959). They sprinkled two glass plates with talcum powder and cast the shadows of the plates on to the back of a ground-glass screen. When both plates were stationary, or moving at the same speed, the observer saw a single flat pattern. However, if the plates were moved at different speeds they immediately split up and appeared to be separated in depth. In present terms one can say that two distinct object-tokens have been assigned to those dot subsets whose internal proximities remain invariant.

At this point let me be absolutely clear about the value of the object-token concept. The idea that an object-token is assigned in visual processing offers *no insights* into the detection of proximity invariance, or the other continuities, as such; that is not its purpose. Its purpose is to help clarify our mental picture of the abstract mechanisms of information flow and control, and to provide a bridge between our conceptions of peripheral and cognitive perceptual processes.

It can also be argued that invariance of proximity relations underlies much of our ability to interpret compound motions. Johansson's demonstrations can be interpreted in this way (Johansson, 1971). It will be remembered that Johansson placed lights on the joints of a helper and then photographed him moving around in the dark. While the figure was stationary an observer saw a random meaningless pattern of lights, but as soon as the figure moved, the pattern of motion plotted by the lights was immediately recognizable. For our purposes the important observation is that the lights were placed at the ends of rigid bones with the result that lights at the ends of a single long-bone would preserve their proximity as the actor walked. I would suggest that these local invariances are detected, and assigned object-tokens. Subsequently, invoking the rule that object-tokens can be combined together if the relationship between them can be recognized, the repetitive pendular activities of the limbs would be recorded, with the final outcome that a single object-token for the whole group of lights is assigned.

A prediction from this approach is that placing lights at the centres of the limbs, rather than at the ends, will result in a failure to perceive the repetitive motion of the figure because the proximities of adjacent lights now vary as the joints bend. Under such conditions the prediction is confirmed, and the figure is not recognized.

Johansson also observed that when the figure walks towards the point of observation, rather than across the line of sight, it is still recognizable even though all retinal proximities now vary due to the looming of the figure. A variety of solutions to this problem may be considered, including short-term approximation to invariance of proximity, or the detection of continuities in *relative* proximity; but this point must be resolved before the approach can be regarded as wholly satisfactory for Johansson's demonstrations.

2.4. A continuity mechanism

In this section a first approximation to a theory of the continuity mechanism is formally presented. The formal presentation is necessary because it prevents any concealment of unwarranted assumptions. The notation used in this section and the remainder of the article is summarized in the Appendix.

I have chosen to represent the mechanism as having four subordinate mechanisms, each of which is a procedure for specifying a certain kind of continuity such as sensory continuity, structural continuity and so forth. However, one can also take the view that a single continuity mechanism is involved throughout processing; what distinguishes the kinds of continuity detected is the kind of information *available* as processing progresses—the mechanism is "data-limited" during early processing (Norman and Bobrow, 1975). First, there is sensory information available, then the sketch, and then information about the spatial lay-out is captured in the proximity graph. There is much to recommend this view. However, for clarity of exposition I shall stick with formally dividing up the parts to reflect the different kinds of continuity discussed.

The mechanisms are presented as "production rules" (Newell and Simon, 1972) in which the left-hand side of a symbolic expression specifies a continuity condition, and the right-hand side summarizes the result of obtaining a continuity. All such results are written in the form $E(N, N')$, simply specifying that two networks of properties and relations have been found to be *equal*, i.e. a continuity has been detected and an object-token can be assigned. In the final section of the chapter production rules are encountered again and discussed in more detail; the continuity $E(N, N')$ will be found to be central to that discussion.

The first mechanism represents continuity of sensory properties of adjacent fragments of the stimulus:

$(\forall a_i)$ where $a_i \in L$,
    $(\exists a_j \in L')$ such that $adjacent(a_i, a_j)$ and $p_i = p_j$ $\Rightarrow$ $E(L, L')$

which is to say that all assertions that are *adjacent* and have a shared property give rise to the joining of the localities of which they are members; that is the localities L and L' are joined under the same object-token.

In order to satisfy feature (c) in the characterization of object-tokens in Section 2.3, a generalized continuity operator has to be defined in which continuity over higher-order relations (denoted $\langle\ \rangle$) can be detected. This makes it possible, for example, to define a property such as *parallel* and then to apply the continuity mechanism as usual to assign an object-token to a network, N, of *parallel* elements:

$(\tilde{\forall} \langle\ \rangle \in N)$ such that $a_i \langle\ \rangle a_j$
    $(\exists (a_i', a_j') \in N')$ such that $a_i' \langle\ \rangle a_j'$ $\Rightarrow$ $E(N, N')$.

Continuity of proximity relations has been specially distinguished; the detection of continuity of proximity relations (denoted $\langle p \rangle$) is roughly similar to the generalized case mentioned last except that a boundary condition *pmax* is included. The term *pmax* specifies the maximum distance over which proximity relations are analysed and is a variable.

$(\tilde{\forall} \langle p \rangle \in N)$ such that $a_i \langle p \rangle a_j$
              and $|p| \leqslant pmax$,
   $(\exists (a_i', a_j') \in N')$ such that $a_i' \langle p \rangle a_j'$ $\Rightarrow$ $E(N_{pmax}, N'_{pmax})$

In order to be consistent with the observation that continuity of temporal events is also easily perceived a comparable mechanism for detection of duration–delay continuity is defined with boundary condition *dmax*:

$(\tilde{\forall} \langle d \rangle \in N)$ such that $a_i \langle d \rangle a_j$,
              and $|d| \leqslant dmax$,
   $(\exists (a_i', a_j') \in N')$ such that $a_i' \langle d \rangle a_j'$ $\Rightarrow$ $E(N_{dmax}, N'_{dmax})$

Where *networks* (N, N') are being matched it is intended that the *adjacent* requirements may be relaxed, depending on empirical findings.

Let us now turn to how such mechanisms might be put to use in the ongoing stream of perceptual behaviour.

3. ATTENTION, REINTERPRETATION AND RECOVERY FROM ERROR

3.1. Continuity errors

While the world often changes quite sharply or abruptly, significant structures or events are often only distinguished from their context by smooth, gradual transitions. The general rule that I have adopted is that the processes embodying the *principle of continuity* will reflect the abrupt changes, whether the changes are spatial or temporal, in the complement of object-tokens that are assembled. Sharp discontinuities in colour, brightness, spatial regularity or temporal regularity result in segmentation of the input and assignment of distinct object-tokens to the segments. Smooth transitions, however, will often be missed. Continuity errors of this kind must occur with almost any conceivable mechanism and indeed it is a matter of common experience that we make them. If circumstances permit, however, recovery from such errors is often swift and fluent. In the texture in Fig. 6, for example, the odd region is not immediately evident at first glance, and for a moment we see the whole region as uniform; but it is not long before differences in detail are noticed. The slow creep of the predator may be invisible but any abrupt movement will attract the vigilant and sustained stare of its intended victim. The result of such concentrated attention may well be the discovery of the concealed enemy. Such experiences are, in a sense, ambiguous—the first interpretation gives way to a second, quite different one. Laboratory demonstrations of the phenomena abound but relatively little effort has been put into providing a detailed account of the information processing that underlies our flexibility.

One would like to ask then, what is the mechanism of recovery? But some care must be taken because this way of putting it may be misleading. Everyday language offers important hints about why this is; we have many ways of expressing the fact that we can "see things in different ways". We speak for example of "paying attention to detail" or "seeing things as a whole"; we talk of "scrutinizing" new objects and "peering" at things; we "notice" and we "ignore". One thing seems clear—there is not just one process or mechanism for the reinterpretation of events, there are many. A range of miniature skills and mental habits are coordinated to form a fluent stream of overt and covert activity, one of whose purposes is to make continual alterations and adjustments to the posture and state of apprehension of the perceiver. The stream can include head movements and eye movements in addition to various covert forms of attention change. But I

suggest that all these diverse acts serve the function of changing the
way in which the principle of continuity is applied and object-tokens
assembled; the principle is, by its very simplicity, a source of irreme-
diable error if rigidly exploited.

3.2. Production system models of information processing

The following section gives quasi-computational descriptions of
methods for recovering from continuity errors; the description is
formal because of the aim for completeness. Though the notation is
superficially different from that used in Section 2.4, the processes
involved are still expressed in terms of production rules. The surface
differences reflect the sorts of difference one normally assumes between
peripheral visual processing and central cognitive processing. The aim,
as I have said repeatedly, is for completeness, but full conviction about
completeness can really only be had when the processes have been
shown to be effective. I have endeavoured to check the representation
thoroughly but as yet no attempt has been made to confirm its effectiveness in the best way, by computer simulation.

Before turning to describe the representation in detail one more
observation must be made. In order to express the mental processes
involved in reinterpretation of the visual input I have chosen to break
down the model of the system into a few major components. Such
concepts as "goals" or intentions and the goal "stack" or memory
have been distinguished from the Immediate Memory (*IM*), the latter
resembling Short-term Memory but perhaps with particularly visual
functions. Similarly I have chosen to make distinctions between such
concepts as noticing and scrutinizing because I feel that a coherent
account results. However, at the point at which one attempts to speak of
processes reminiscent of thinking one must be rather tentative because
obviously our perceptual and cognitive skills are extraordinarily
complex, continually undergoing change, differing from individual to
individual. I have no wish to reduce them to inert algorithms so the
particular processes I describe and the theoretical concepts that are
invoked should not be regarded as some sort of sacrosanct schema;
if the theory is to prove of any value it must be able to accommodate
change and extension. As Newell and Simon (1972) emphasize, the
method of analysis has more significance than any particular case.

The method used is based on *production systems* which consist of a set
of separate production rules. Each production rule has two components,
a *condition* written on the left, and an *action* on the right of the special
symbol ⇒ which can be read to mean "gives rise to" or "results in".
The condition specifies some state or event which, if it occurs, is to

result in the specified action. As an example we can write a simple production system as in PS1 which is designed for "knitting".

		Condition	*Action*
PS1:	PD1	IF GOAL = "START ROW"	⇒ KNIT ONE
	PD2	IF JUST(KNITTED ONE) AND	
		NUMBER(STITCHES) < 40	⇒ PEARL ONE
	PD3	IF JUST(PEARLED ONE)	⇒ KNIT ONE
	PD4	IF NUMBER(STITCHES) = 40	⇒ END ROW

As soon as the goal "START ROW" is acquired, production 1 (PD1) is activated because its condition becomes true, and the action, specified on the right-hand side of PD1, is executed, namely KNIT ONE. Having just knitted one the condition of PD2 becomes true and the action PEARL ONE is correspondingly taken. As a result of having pearled one PD3 fires, a stitch is knitted, and this reinstates the condition for PD2 to be activated, with the result that a stitch is pearled and so on. The production system continues with PD2 and PD3 being activated in alternation until forty stitches are complete at which point the condition of PD4 becomes true and the row is ended.

Production systems of this kind are a manageable, but nevertheless perfectly precise, way of expressing conjectures about the mental processes that might be implicated in any piece of behaviour. They are manageable because they allow one to explore the adequacy of a theory of mental activity without demanding specification of all the details—in PS1 for example it was unnecessary to specify the exact meaning of "KNIT", "PEARL" or "END ROW" to examine the adequacy of the scheme. It should also be noted that if the production system PS1 seems oddly mechanical this reflects firstly that the production system is abbreviated and secondly that knitting itself is indeed a mechanical activity! There is no reason why production systems should not embody the fluency and dexterity that is characteristic of human skills of greater sophistication.

I should draw attention to two additional points about PS1. First, the inclusion of "IF" in the conditions is not usual since it is redundant —it was added for those readers who have not encountered production systems before. Secondly, you will see that I have made GOAL = "START ROW" the condition for activation of PD1; in fact it is generally found to be more natural to keep GOALS distinct from the production rules themselves since they can serve a valuable control function. The concept of a goal in a production system is fairly sophisticated; it is the main mechanism by which control remains coherent during the execution of the production system. Goals make it possible, particularly, to have the concept of a subprocedure of skilled activity. For example the action of a production might be to change the current goal—"If you miss the bus to the airport then try to find someone to give you a lift"—without losing sight of the overall objective. In the example the overall objective is to get to the airport, but when something goes wrong one adopts a new objective of trying to hitch a ride, yet one doesn't want to forget why one is doing this. In a production system the previous goal is not lost because it is "pushed down on a stack". Whatever goal is on the top of the stack is the current goal, and when it is satisfied it is "popped off" the stack thus automatically reinstating the last goal which was not itself satisfied. Once one has obtained the necessary ride one returns to the business of catching the plane.

In the production systems outlined below the goals are kept separate from the productions on just such a goal stack; the evaluation of the conditions of all productions is carried out in the context of these goals.

3.3 Examples of reinterpretation methods

Perhaps one of the most important aspects of our perceptual flexibility and one that serves an enormous range of familiar habits and skills is our ability to *notice* things. We notice regular patterns against irregular backgrounds and vice versa; we notice abrupt appearances and disappearances and changes of direction; and if we look carefully we may notice slight discontinuities of detail or gradual changes of shape. I have suggested above that we may view cognitive processes as having access to a data structure composed of object-tokens assigned on the basis of continuities and discontinuities in the property map, primal sketch and proximity graph. If the optic array facing the observer changes radically then we may expect corresponding changes to the object-token data structure, and conversely if the optic array changes very little there will be little or no change in the object-tokens. By reapplying the continuity mechanism, this time to the object-token data, we can implement an operation called NOTICE:

PS2:   NOTICE

Goal	*Condition*	*Action*
Unspecified	$\mathrm{NOT}(E(OT_{t_i}^{L_j}, OT_{t_{i+1}}^{L_j})$	$\Rightarrow$ "NOTICE" $OT^{L_j} \to IM$

Which is to say that for any locality L_j, if the complement of object-tokens remains invariant from moment (t_i) to moment (t_{i+1}) then the cognitive effects are nil; if any change has taken place then symbols enter Immediate Memory (IM) to indicate the change and the object-tokens involved.

"NOTICE" is a symbol which, one might suppose, triggers a variety of cognitive productions. In the first instance these might be productions causing the perceiver to LOOKAT the new object:

PS3: LOOKAT

Goal	Condition	Action
Unspecified	$IM =$ "NOTICE"	$\Rightarrow$ SETGOAL(LOOKAT)
LOOKAT	$IM = (OT^{L_j})$	$\Rightarrow$ RECOVER(L_j) $\rightarrow IM$
LOOKAT	$IM = L_j$	$\Rightarrow$ POP GOALSTACK, SETGOAL(SACCADE)
SACCADE	$IM = L_j$	$\Rightarrow$ SACCADE(L_j)

This simple production system responds to the "NOTICE" symbol in IM by changing the current goal (whatever it is) to LOOKAT. In the context of the goal LOOKAT if there is no location specified in IM this is RECOVERed from the object-token in the immediate memory and this location replaces the token. The goal LOOKAT now controls the activation of a SACCADE goal and the appropriate saccade is made.

But notice what happens as a result of the SACCADE. One might imagine that on completion of LOOKAT and SACCADE these goals would be satisfied, and the perceiver would continue about his business. However, this would hardly be any use—one would be in the position of having noticed a source of danger, say, and then quite happily ignoring it! The system is, however, a little more subtle because having executed the SACCADE the property map of the retinal image is radically changed because of the acuity and other differences between retina and fovea. Such abrupt changes will of course result in the assembly of a new set of object-tokens which, quite remorselessly, will be NOTICEd by the system. The effect of this is to prevent our perceiver being so clumsy as to continue where he left off and an additional production coordinates a more useful activity, SCRUTINY:

Goal	Condition	Action
SACCADE	$IM =$ "NOTICE"	$\Rightarrow$ POP GOALSTACK, SETGOAL(SCRUTINIZE)

SCRUTINIZE is an important goal and will be encountered again, and explained, in a moment. The picture that I want to paint is one of many elementary processes being incorporated into a stream of generated behaviour. The stream being under the overall control of goals or intentions which, if all the necessary information can be supplied, provide the conditions under which other mental processes or productions can be activated. Such activated processes in turn produce direct effects, such as eye movements, and side-effects such as the availability of new object-tokens in immediate memory. So the process goes, sometimes punctuated by glazed stares but generally a fluent synchrony of relatively simple perceptual processes continually assembling new summaries of the visual world in the object-token data structure.

As has been discussed, one of the major purposes of such continual updating is to reveal structures that any single mechanism might not be competent to detect; but eye movements and overt changes of posture far from exhaust the repertoire of our abilities to make changes to the data structure compiled by early visual processes. A wealth of intuitive and experimental evidence demonstrates more covert abilities that serve to reveal objects that may not be evident at first glance. There are several such processes but I first want to single out one that may be the most important and is among the most familiar. I have chosen to call it SCRUTINIZE. It is a process by which we "pay attention to detail", the complement of "seeing things as a whole".

(These familiar phrases do not of course always refer to the visual sense; we can pay attention to the details of a piece of music or the details of an argument, but I don't wish to make anything here of any parallels that may exist.)

When we scrutinize an object or a place we generally apprehend only a relatively small part of it, seeing the local details of grain or texture while the overall shape or form seems to lose its clarity. When one looks at the texture in Fig. 9 the overall squareness of the figure recedes from awareness as we search locally for slight configuration differences and concealed region boundaries. (The same experience is evident when one tries to pick out a camouflaged animal.) As mentioned in the last section, we have found that the critical variable for the texture example can be identified with continuity of proximity relations in the region, and discontinuity of proximity relations at the region boundary. I used the analogy of a map-maker standing on a hill and measuring all the distances to neighbouring hills (the p-graph), and doing this for all hills. Similarly the p-graph of each texture assertion is assembled by measuring the proximity of all the assertions in its neighbourhood. In order to understand why the different textures in Fig. 9 vary in ease of discrimination, however, one has to understand the idea of *neighbourhood* rather more precisely. Returning to the map-maker again we must ask the question "Up to how far away does he measure the distance of hills?" Up to a kilometre? Five kilometres? The horizon? The probable answer is that it depends on what he is trying to do—if he wants to get a rough idea of the overall layout of the range of hills then it would be useful to measure peaks at great distances even though the measurements may be relatively inaccurate; on the other hand, if he wants a rather detailed analysis of the geography of the range then he would do well to confine himself to measuring the distance of immediately adjacent landmarks so that the details don't get lost in the mass of imprecise long-distance measurements. The same thing goes for the textures—in cases where the texture region is very easy to pick out, a computer simulation has shown that discontinuities of proximity relations are very marked at all distances—both in the immediate neighbourhood of the region boundary and if the neighbourhood is allowed to take in a large proportion of the pattern. In the case of the textures where it is hard to pick out a distinct region this is not the case, the boundary discontinuity is more localized and will be lost if measurements are taken over great distances. In the case of Fig. 9a then, p-graphs can be assembled over large neighbourhoods and the boundary discontinuity will still be considerable, while in the case of Fig. 9b very small neighbourhoods must be used. Figure 9c is intermediate.

Our experiments showed that the *time taken* by observers to identify the odd region was inversely related to the *neighbourhood size* at which the discontinuity should theoretically become visible. This together with introspective evidence, suggests that the time to find the concealed region is governed by the time taken to organize the visual system appropriately; that is to "tune" the neighbourhood size from its typical state in which gross layout is preferentially picked up to a state in which local configurational properties can be seen. Progressive retuning eventually reveals a region boundary if one is present, with the result that a NOTICEable set of new object-tokens corresponding to the regions and boundaries becomes available; cognitive productions are activated as a result and the appropriate response is made. Evidence for similar processes in which tuning from a state in which the observer is predisposed to pick up global structures to a state in which more localized relationships are emphasized is presented by Navon (1975) and Fox and Teicher (1976).

The process of SCRUTINIZEing by progressive modification of neighbourhood size (the variable *pmax*, *see* Section 2.4) can be expressed in the following production system:

PS4: SCRUTINIZE

Goal	Condition	Action
SCRUTINIZE	$E((OT_{t_i}), (OT_{t_{i+1}}))$	$\Rightarrow$ REDUCE($pmax$)
SCRUTINIZE	$NOT(E((OT_{t_i}), (OT_{t_{i+1}})))$	$\Rightarrow$ "NOTICE" $(OT_{t_{i+1}})$
		$\rightarrow IM$

This pair of productions simply continues reducing the neighbourhood size until a change in the object-token set occurs, else the search is abandoned due to a change of goal by other concurrent mental processes. When new object-tokens become available a NOTICEing condition occurs with a consequent activation of LOOKAT (*see above*).

After the details of the scene have been examined one might imagine that the intention to see the pattern "as a whole" will once again be established; this will result in the activation of an analogous production system which progressively increases *pmax*.

Although I have no evidence to hand, it seems to me that on introspective grounds there is also a temporal analogue of SCRUTINIZE, in which one carefully examines an object or place which one suspects may be undergoing some sort of slow change. The analogue of expansion and contraction of spatial neighbourhoods would presumably be extension and contraction of the period over which temporal relations like *just-before*, *same-speed-as* and of course *same-proximity-as* are recorded; i.e. some sort of control over the historical range of immediate memory. This seems to be an intriguing possibility whose implications are by no means clear, though of course at the present it has no more force than a conjecture.

An equally familiar method of covert control is "Broadbent's Filter" (Broadbent, 1958, 1971). According to Broadbent, the Filter acts to selectively enhance certain portions of the input, other portions are attenuated and will have less influence on cognitive decision processes as a result. Kahneman (1973) applies this idea to his theory of visual attention by proposing two distinct stages in visual processing. The first, unit or group formation, carries out the organization of the visual input in terms of "rules of grouping, similarity, proximity etc." The present account of object-token assignment offers a mechanism for this step. The second stage is a process of "figural emphasis" by which certain of the groups recovered in Stage 1 are selectively emphasized. However, on the present view, units or object-tokens that are recorded on the basis of spatial relations such as proximity relations only become available as a *result* of tuning; tuning does not have to emphasize them, for without the tuning the object-tokens cannot arise. With respect to sensory properties such as colour and brightness the position is different, as the measurement of these properties is not under central control, but the notion of "emphasis" may still be slightly misleading. I would prefer simply to suppose that if an object or pattern has an effect on central processes then that is because the object-token has been *referenced* by these central processes. The notion of emphasis may be redundant. For present purposes we might imagine the Filter (which references the object-token) being set under the control of a goal called LOOKFOR:

Goal	Condition	Action
LOOKFOR	IM = physical attribute ⇒	SETFILTER(attribute)

But to get a more interesting picture of this process we might think of it being embedded in a more complex process. Our present theme concerns the discovery of objects or patterns not previously seen; however, such discoveries are not always made by oneself alone. To take a somewhat light-hearted example, imagine hearing the command "Look at the blue Ford". One might suppose without too much implausibility that one of the effects of such an instruction would be the adoption of the goal LOOKAT together with the description BLUE FORD becoming available in immediate memory. A production system that might be activated in these circumstances is:

PS5: LOOKFOR*

Goal	Condition	Action
LOOKAT	IM = description	⇒ SETGOAL(LOOKFOR)
LOOKFOR	IM = description	⇒ GET-ATTRIBUTE(description) $\rightarrow IM$
LOOKFOR	IM = physical attribute	⇒ SETFILTER(attribute) POP GOALSTACK

This production system responds to the goal of LOOKAT in the presence of a *description* but no *location* by setting up conditions in which a location can be recovered. The first gambit is to try to obtain a physical attribute from the target description—this might presumably be a production system that recovers the attribute from the description—which becomes available in immediate memory if successful. LOOKFOR in the presence of an attribute or feature of this kind sets the filter which is applied to the property map and ignores those parts of the map which are not the same as the specified feature. The result is to make changes to the object-token set in turn, and the new set of tokens will be NOTICEd, and the LOOKAT goal adopted as described in PS3.

Before leaving the subject of LOOKFOR, an additional point should be mentioned; for simplicity we have considered a hypothetical situation in which a target specified by a simple colour attribute is being

---

* The terms LOOKFOR and LOOKAT are taken from the discussion by Newell (1972).

looked for. However, there is no reason that I can see to suppose that LOOKFOR should be limited to such targets in principle. After all it is well within our competence to look for conjunctive targets such as "something round and orange" or targets that are only poorly specified "rather big and long" or functionally specified "something to sit on". It is of course true that where time is severely limited as in tachisto-scopic studies it is very hard to search for targets on the basis of proper-ties that are more complex than simple physical attributes. There seems to be no in-principle reason, however, to suppose that this has more significance than that one is not allowing the observer enough time to sufficiently elaborate the object-tokens prior to the fading of the image. The processes of retrieving information from sensory memory, for example, are not necessarily limited to operations on simple attributes—it just takes longer if the task demands more complex descriptions. The scores in tachistoscopic studies reflect the time required to assemble complex object-tokens.

Hierarchical assembly of object-tokens can be expressed by a recursive production:

Goal	*Condition*		*Action*
Unspecified	$((OT_i) \langle \rangle (OT_j))$	$\Rightarrow$	OT_{ij}

which makes the characteristic (c) of the object-tokens in Section 2.3 precise. The symbol $\langle \rangle$ specifies that a relationship exists between object-tokens i and j which the perceptual system is capable of recog-nizing. For example, in Fig. 10, one can conceive of object-tokens being assigned to the "horizontal" and "vertical" groups of dots on the basis of continuity of *proximity* and *collinearity* relations. The result is two object-tokens that specify contours which, if the system is competent to recognize the relation *cuts*, can now be assembled into a complex object-token. In fact I have argued elsewhere that the continuity mechanism is capable of implementing a variety of relation-implement-ing mechanisms such as those for the relations *parallel* and *cuts*, together with more complex relations like *symmetrical*. Indeed it is possible to apply the continuity mechanisms repeatedly (hierarchically) in such a way that a competent production system for recognizing alphanumeric characters results (Fox, 1975b). I have assumed that object-tokens are prenominal but if one can get to the point where a TEE configuration has been specified as a single object-token then it would seem to be a relatively small step to assigning a name.

Given adequate time, therefore, object-tokens of arbitrary complexity can be assembled, and similarly can be matched by a variant of the continuity mechanism with a target description of similarly arbitrary complexity. I am optimistic that our manifest ability to search for objects as complexly defined as "something to sit on" will not constitute an insurmountable difficulty for the present approach.

Returning to my theme, the final covert control process for dealing with concealment structures that I would like to discuss is illustrated in Fig. 11. The example in Fig. 11a is taken from Attneave (1968) and is a striking example of multiple stability—an array that can be interpreted in different ways. With an effort that is completely conscious we can choose to perceive the set of triangles as oriented in any one of several directions. Similarly in Fig. 11b we can mentally select the pair of vertical columns of dots or the horizontal pair; and this can be achieved without shifting one's gaze from the central dot. There also appears to be some evidence that the process by which a particular axis of a pattern is selected can be initiated prior to the onset of a stimulus, at least in the case of axes of symmetry (Fox, 1977). My own view is that these are not merely laboratory amusements but reflect a process that is fundamental for discovering slight, but potentially important axial relationships in the world. It is often said, for example, that stripes roughly perpendicular to the body axis of an animal serve to "break up the contours" of the body. A predator requires mechanisms for seeing through the subterfuge.

A production system to implement this kind of selective set or attention would in many ways resemble Broadbent's Filter and need not be repeated; it suffices to note that the "attribute" which is the variable required by Broadbent's Filter is not a "physical feature" in

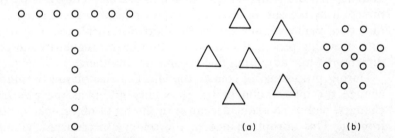

(a)   (b)

Fig. 10. A configuration whose analysis could lead to the assignment of two object-tokens, one for the horizontally aligned elements, one for the vertically aligned elements. The *cuts* relationship between the two tokens could then be identified and the two tokens combined into a single "TEE" token.

Fig. 11. Examples of multistability: (a) after Attneave (1968), (b) demonstrating that the effect is not critically dependent on eye movements—changes in perceived organization can be obtained with the eye constantly fixated on the central element.

the sense that Broadbent has outlined but a configurational property such as an axis of symmetry. The production system involved would not therefore act as a filter on the property map of the stimulus but act to bias the analysis of spatial relationships such as those represented in the proximity graph. However, unlike the case of the Filter it does appear to be possible to say something about a possible selective mechanism. It appears to be possible to relate this to the mechanism SCRUTINIZE which, it will be remembered, modifies the range or neighbourhood over which proximity relations are measured. But rather than modifying the neighbourhood size by the same amount in all directions from the assertions a bias is placed on the analyses to produce a neighbourhood whose shape might resemble an ellipse.

To illustrate this let us return to the analogy of the map-maker. Suppose the map-maker wanted to get some idea of the lay-out of a particular feature of the terrain, such as a river or valley; to do this it would be useful to do two things. Firstly, to get a rough idea of the lay-out of the valley all along its length while, secondly, keeping track of the details of the terrain within the valley. From his hill a natural way for the map-maker to achieve this is to take rough distance measurements of landmarks at considerable distances *along* the valley while recording accurate distances of landmarks *within* the valley in his neighbourhood. Repeating this procedure at several sites along the valley and combining the sets of information can provide a good compromise between the need for an overall picture of the lay-out of the valley and the need to be selective about details. Similarly one might imagine that the visual system can get an overall picture in a particular direction by measuring proximity over a relatively great range in that direction, while keeping the range short on other axes. The result of such a biasing process would be to admit coarse regularities in certain directions while admitting fine regularities in others.

During processing, of course, the effect of this biasing would be to change the information in the proximity graph as the axis of bias changes, with a consequent change in the set of object-tokens derived from it. This abrupt change in the set of object-tokens, as axes of regularity become "tuned in", would result in the familiar activation of the NOTICEing system, and the axis of regularity would become available at the cognitive level.

4. SUMMARY

In this chapter I have tried to make a start on the knotty problem of process and control in visual perception. The problem area chosen for this is that of concealment and I have tried to shed some light on why concealment occurs as a result of the way the visual system operates. This necessitated the introduction of a partial theory of visual information processing, which drew upon the important account recently published by Marr (1975). In the emphasis on continuity, and the object-tokens that result from the several kinds of continuity, I have been forced to depart substantially from Marr's original course but I believe that it has been possible to motivate these changes since they assist considerably in the account of concealment. The concept of the object-token is described in detail.

Sections 1 and 2 provided a basis for understanding how concealment takes place, given the way the visual system acts to take advantage of optical structure. Section 3 emphasizes the inevitability of continuity errors under these circumstances, and the importance of recovering from them. Several mechanisms for such recovery are outlined and their selective character suggests that they all be regarded as part of the repertoire of *attentive* processes. Such processes include overt changes of posture including eye movements, and more subtle covert changes in which pattern attributes such as colour and orientation, and structural regularities such as symmetry, serve as a basis for referencing and modifying the object-tokens.

The theory developed is broadly compatible with the views of recent reviewers of theories of visual attention. The concept of a "filter" developed by Broadbent is preserved throughout the account as are the stages of perceptual processing discussed by Kahneman (1973)— sensory registration, unit formation, figural emphasis and activation of recognition units. However, while the processes *controlling* unit formation and figural emphasis are distinguished in the present account, in some cases at least it seems more natural to think of the *action* of figural emphasis as constraining the units (object-tokens) .that are formed. Kahneman's theory assumes that all perceptual groups that might be detected *are* detected, but only some are emphasized. The present theory on the other hand suggests that the state of apprehension of the perceptual system at any moment limits the kinds of structure that it is competent to detect.

An additional aspect of the present approach is the extension of the theory into the *procedural* domain. The production system approach is used to provide a basis for understanding the moment-to-moment events in perception and for understanding the processes by which problems posed by the visual world, such as the concealment problem, can be ameliorated. One of the major requirements of a successful reconciliation of the apparatus of early visual processing and the strategic aspects of cognition is a procedural account of the mediating control mechanisms.

ACKNOWLEDGEMENTS

My thanks to Vicki Bruce and Richard Young for their comments on an earlier draft of this chapter.

REFERENCES

Attneave, F. (1968). Triangles as ambiguous figures. *American Journal of Psychology* **81**, 447–453.

Beck, J. (1966). Effect of orientation and of shape similarity on peripheral grouping. *Perception and Psychophysics* **1**, 300–302.

Blakemore, C. and Campbell, F. W. (1969). On the existence in the human visual system of neurons selectively sensitive to the orientation and size of retinal images. *Journal of Psychology* **203**, 237–260.

Broadbent, D. E. (1958). "Perception and Communication". Pergamon Press, London.

Broadbent, D. E. (1971). "Decision and Stress". Academic Press, London and New York.

Bruce, V. G. and Morgan, M. J. (1975). Violations of symmetry and repetition in visual patterns. *Perception* **4**, 239–249.

Bryant, P. (1974). "Perception and Understanding in Young Children: An Experimental Approach". Basic Books, New York.

Campbell, F. W., Cooper, G. F. and Enroth-Cugell, C. (1968). The spatial selectivity of the visual cells of the cat. *Journal of Physiology* **103**, 223–225.

Clark, S. E. (1969). Retrieval of colour information from pre-perceptual memory. *Journal of Experimental Psychology* **82** (2), 263–266.

Corballis, M. C. and Roldan, C. E. (1974). On the perception of symmetrical and repeated patterns. *Perception and Psychophysics* **16** (1), 136–142.

Dick, A. O. (1969). Relations between the sensory register and short-term storage in tachistoscopic recognition. *Journal of Experimental Psychology* **82**, 279–284.

Fox, J. (1975a). The use of structural diagnostics in recognition. *Journal of Experimental Psychology: Human Perception and Performance* **104** (1), 57–67.

Fox, J. (1975b). Towards a reconciliation of the mechanisms and methods of visual perception. *MRC Social and Applied Psychology Unit*, Memo No. 84.

Fox, J. (1977). An observation on set and visual comparison processes. *Quarterly Journal of Experimental Psychology* **29**, 267–276.

Fox, J. and Mayhew, J. E. W. (1977). Region suppression sheds light on information processing in texture discrimination (unpublished).

Fox, J. and Teicher, R. D. (1977). Holistic processes, correlation and structure in identity perception (unpublished).

Gibson, E. J., Gibson, J. J., Smith, O. W. and Flock, H. R. (1959). Motion parallax as a determinant of perceived depth. *Journal of Experimental Psychology* **58**, 40–51.

Huttenlocher, J. (1967). Children's ability to orient and order objects. *Child Development* **38**, 1169–1176.

Johannson, G. (1971). Visual perception of biological motion and a model for its analysis. Dept. of Psychology, Report 100, University of Uppsala.

Julesz, B. (1975). Experiments in the visual perception of texture. *Scientific American* **232**, 34–43.

Kahneman, D. (1973). "Attention and Effort". Prentice-Hall, Englewood Cliffs, N.J.

Marr, D. (1976). Early processing of visual information. *Philosophical Transactions of the Royal Society B* **275**, 483–524.

Miller, G. A. and Johnson-Laird, P. N. (1976). "Language and Perception". Cambridge University Press, Cambridge.

Musatti, C. L. (1931). Forma e assimiliazione. *Archivio Italiano di psicologia* **9**, 61–156.

Navon, D. (1975). Forest before trees: the precedence of global features in visual perception. Dept. of Psychology, University of Haifa.

Newell, A. (1972). A theoretical exploration of mechanisms for coding the stimulus. Dept. of Computer Science, Carnegie-Mellon University, Pittsburgh.

Newell, A. (1973). You can't play twenty questions with nature and win. *In* "Visual Information Processing" (W. G. Chase, ed.). Academic Press, New York and London.

Newell, A. and Simon, H. A. (1972). "Human Problem-Solving". Prentice-Hall, Englewood Cliffs, N.J.

Norman, D. A. and Bobrow, D. G. (1975). On data-limited and resource-limited processes. *Cognitive Psychology* **7**, 44–64.

O'Callaghan, J. F. (1974). Human perception of homogeneous dot patterns. *Perception*, **3**, 33–45.

Olson, R. K. and Attneave, F. (1970). What variables produce smilarity grouping? *American Journal of Psychology* **83**, 1–21.

Triesman, A., Russell, R. and Green, J. (1975). Brief visual storage of shape and movement. *In* "Attention and Performance V" (P. M. A. Rabbitt and S. Dornic, eds), pp. 699–721. Academic Press, London and New York.

Von Wright, J. M. (1968). Selection in visual immediate memory. *Quarterly Journal of Experimental Psychology* **20**, 62–68.

Von Wright, J. M. (1970). On selection in visual immediate memory. *Acta Psychologica* **33**, 280–292.

Williams, L. G. (1966). The effect of target specification on objects fixated during visual search. *Perception and Psychophysics* **1**, 315–318.

APPENDIX

Notation

∀ "for all"—the universal quantifier

∀̃ "for most"—the imperfect quantifier which allows, in this context, some degradation of perfect continuity

∃ "there exists"—the existential quantifier
⇒ gives-rise-to, results-in—the activation of a production
⟨⟩ an unspecified relation
∈ is-an-element-of
$|x|$ means the *magnitude* of x
OT Object-token
(OT) Set of object-tokens
→ assign-to or become-available-in

Three

Understanding Speech: How Words are Heard

Ronald A. Cole and Jola Jakimik

Carnegie–Mellon University

This chapter is concerned with the problem of how we recognize words from fluent speech. Our research into this problem was originally motivated by a desire to learn how discrete percepts are derived from a continuously varying signal. Our research soon led us to believe that word recognition is the most fundamental problem in speech perception. Recognizing words from fluent speech involves the total linguistic (and sometimes intellectual) repertoire of the perceiver. As we will demonstrate below, a word's recognition provides the meeting place for the interaction of all of the conceptual structures that we use to understand language. The study of word recognition therefore includes most other problems in psycholinguistics. To put it bluntly, words are where the action is.

The thesis of this chapter is that a word's recognition from fluent speech requires the use of many different sources of knowledge. Any constraint on the structure of a spoken language is a potential source of knowledge. Words in an utterance are constrained by, among other factors, acoustic, syntactic, semantic, logical and thematic structure, as well as the larger situational context in which the utterance is produced. In a given utterance, any or all of these factors may provide constraints on a word's identity. The research described in this chapter suggests that a word is recognized when it is sufficiently constrained by all of the available sources of knowledge. It is proposed that a word is recognized *during* the interaction of input and knowledge-directed constraints.

Section 1 details the nature of the problem. It is argued that the structure of the physical stimulus effectively rules out pattern-matching accounts of word recognition from fluent speech. It is shown that the two major problems involved in word recognition are (1) locating appropriate word boundaries in a continuously varying signal, and (2) identifying intended words from a highly variable and often incomplete phonetic representation.

Section 2 examines the other side of the coin. Under certain circumstances, words are spoken fairly precisely. In addition, some aspects of speech are relatively immune to the blurring of boundaries and identity. In this section, we examine evidence that the listener pays special attention to stop consonants in stressed syllables. These sounds are least affected by their fluent speech context, and therefore are highly informative.

Section 3 presents a model of word recognition which states that (1) each word in an utterance is constrained both by its acoustic structure and by the context in which it occurs, (2) a word's recognition occurs during the interaction of these two sources of constraint, (3) an utterance is processed, as far as possible, syllable by syllable and word by word, and (4) recognition of one word locates the beginning of the following word and may constrain its identity—acoustically, syntactically or semantically. Two experiments are described which test several assumptions of the model.

Section 4 describes a series of experiments which demonstrate some of the sources of knowledge which are used during word recognition from fluent speech. The experiments suggest that word recognition is influenced by quite abstract sources of knowledge, such as a title of a story.

1. LISTENING TO FLUENT SPEECH

How do we recognize words from fluent speech? At first glance, it is not clear that this question presents an interesting problem. When we reflect on the experience of listening to speech, intuition tells us that we hear a series of discrete and separate words, one at a time, just after the speaker produces them. Because individual words are perceived clearly and rapidly, it seems obvious that we recognize a word as we identify its auditory pattern. In this view, the listener is assumed to have in memory a stored representation or template of the sound pattern of each word in his or her language. A word is recognized when its template is activated by the appropriate pattern of sound. The fact that words are recognized more efficiently (i.e. faster or with less energy input) when they are contextually appropriate can be readily explained by assuming that a template can be "primed" (partially activated) by prior information. For example, the template for "apple" might be primed when a listener heard the word "fruit" or saw an apple.

1.1. Words as stable patterns

Pattern-matching models require detectable patterns. Do spoken words have a stable acoustic structure?

It is an axiom of acoustic phonetics that no two utterances are ever identical. No two vocal tracts are exactly the same, and even when the same monosyllabic word is repeated by the same speaker, small differences in the microstructure of the acoustic signal—such as the structure of the waveform in successive glottal pulses—can always be observed.

Despite these sources of variation, words spoken *in isolation* display relatively stable auditory patterns. If we ask an informant to read a list of separate words, we note that he or she articulates each of the words in a fairly precise manner. Because of this careful articulation, words spoken in isolation exhibit a great deal of stability at the acoustic/phonetic level, in that the same set of acoustic features signal the same phonetic segments whenever a given word is spoken. This point has been demonstrated by Peterson and Barney (1952) who found 95% correct identification of randomly presented vowels produced by different talkers in /hVd/ syllables, and by Miller and

Nicely (1955) who found equally high recognition rates for naturally spoken consonants presented in CV syllables under quiet conditions. Listeners rarely misperceive words or syllables spoken in isolation.

In his excellent review paper on machine recognition of speech, Reddy (1976) notes that computer systems are able to achieve recognition of words spoken *in isolation* using classical pattern-matching techniques. In these systems,

> the general paradigm involves comparing the parameter or feature representation of the incoming utterance with the prototype reference patterns of each of the words in the vocabulary. . . . Given a known vocabulary (of about 30 to 200 words) and a known speaker, these systems can recognize a word spoken in isolation with accuracies around 99 percent.

These results demonstrate that carefully articulated words *spoken in isolation* are characterized by a great deal of invariant information.*

1.2. Words in fluent speech

On the other hand, attempts to recognize words from *fluent* speech using pattern-matching techniques have resulted in failure. As 5 years of intensive research and development on speech understanding systems have revealed, fluent speech cannot be recognized by computers using word-level pattern-matching techniques. According to Reddy (1976, p. 509):

> The answers are not difficult to find. In connected speech it is difficult to determine where one word ends and another begins. In addition, acoustic characteristics of sounds and words exhibit much greater

---

* It is well known that the acoustic cues for certain phonemes are structured by their environment. Thus, the same acoustic feature—such as the frequency of the release burst or the second formant transition—may be quite different for the same phoneme in different syllables. We term this phenomenon *cue variation* to distinguish it from *phonological variation*. The point we want to emphasize here is that, while the problem of how phonemes are perceived in the face of cue variation is an interesting problem in its own right, it is largely irrelevant to the problem of how words are recognized from fluent speech. *Given the appropriate sound pattern*— whether produced by man or speech synthesizer, and whether composed entirely of context-conditioned transitional or invariant cues—listeners are able to unambiguously perceive the phonetic message. The question of how words are recognized from fluent speech does not centre on the issue of the kinds of cues that are present in the signal; rather the important issue is whether or not the cues which are needed to unambiguously perceive a word are actually present in the signal. The problem of word recognition from fluent speech *is* largely one of variation, but it is phonological variation, in which the continuous nature of fluent speech alters the acoustic/phonetic structure of a word from its citation form.

variability in connected speech, depending on the context, compared with words spoken in isolation.

The problems of *segmentation* (locating word boundaries) and *variation* (lack of stable patterns) identified by Reddy can be illustrated by analogy to printed text. Words in printed text are characterized by two invariant properties. First, they are separated from each other by spaces. Secondly, in the same text, a word looks the same whenever it appears. A word typically has only one spelling, and variation in the physical stimulus is usually limited to case alteration (when a word is capitalized) or changes in type font (when a word is italicized). By contrast, words in spoken language have neither of these properties.

1.3. The problem of segmentation

In order to understand word recognition from fluent speech, it is essential to understand the nature of the stimulus. Words in fluent speech are not reliably separated by pauses or indicated by any other physical parameter. Periods of relative silence in fluent speech accompany the production of stop (/b/, /d/, /g/, /p/, /t/, /k/) and affricate (/č/, /ǰ/) consonants, so the acoustic representation of the phrase "acoustic signal" looks something like "a cous ti csi gnal". Thus, words do not exist in the speech wave as discrete and separate events.

The fact that words in fluent speech are not separated by pauses is reflected in the principle of *geminate reduction*, which holds that "two identical consonants reduce to one across a syllable, morpheme or word boundary" (Oshika *et al.*, 1975, p. 110). For example, whenever two nasals occur at a word boundary, a single nasal murmur is likely to occur. In combinations such as "some more" or "Tom makes" there is no point at which a word-final or word-initial [m] can be identified in the speechwave. Similarly, geminate reduction is observed in "cab bill", "bad drape", "big gate", "lip play", "that train", "attack corps", "half fast", "save votes", "Cliff's store", "was zoned", "fresh shout", "real love", "more rice", "say yes" and "grew wise".

Because the physical signal is continuous across word boundaries, a particular sound sequence can usually be meaningfully segmented in more than one way. For example, all of the examples of geminate reduction provided in the previous paragraph have alternative segmentations: "some ore", "Tom aches", "cab ill", "bad rape", "big eight", "lip lay", "that rain" and "that drain", "attack or" and "a tack or", "half assed", "save oats" and "say votes", "Cliff's door", "was owned", "fresh out", "reel of", "more ice", "say s", and "grew eyes". Most spoken sequences of two or more words can be segmented in more than one way, although the unintended segmentation may not always make sense.

Unless one is listening to an unfamiliar language, it is difficult to appreciate that individual words are decoded from a continuous signal. Our intuition while listening to someone talk is that words are recognized, one after the other, soon after they are spoken. It is possible, however, to construct English sentences that listeners have great difficulty segmenting into words. The most famous example is the nursery rhyme "Mares eat oats and does eat oats and little lambs eat ivy. A kid'll eat ivy too, wouldn't you?" Other examples are the sentence pairs, "In mud eels are, in clay none are", and "In pine tar is, in oak none is". The responses of four subjects who listened to these sentences, taken from Reddy (1976, p. 504) are given below:

In mud eels are	*in clay none are*
in muddies sar	in clay nanar
in my deals are	en clainanar
in my ders	en clain
in model sar	in claynanar

In pine tar is,	*in oak none is*
in pine tarrar	in oak? es
in pyntar es	in oak nonus
in pine tar is	in ocnonin
en pine tar is	in oak is

The errors subjects make on these sentences are instructive. According to Reddy (1976, p. 504):

> The responses show that the listener forces his own interpretation of what he hears, and not necessarily what may have been intended by the speaker. Because the subjects do not have the contextual framework to expect the words "mud eels" together, they write more likely sounding combinations such as "my deals" or "models". We find the same problem with words such as "oak none is". Notice that they failed to detect where one word ends and another begins. It is not uncommon for machine recognition systems to have similar problems with word segmentation.

Perceptual segmentation errors in conversational speech have been reported by Garnes and Bond (1975), who have collected about 900 examples of spontaneous "slips of the ear". In their words: "Examples of word-boundary deletions dominate our data". For example, listeners reported hearing "tenure" for "ten years", "coconut Danish" for "coke and a Danish", and "chocolate" for "chalk dust.".

1.4. Phonological variation

We have noted that words in isolation are characterized by relatively stable auditory patterns. One reason for this stability is that speakers are careful to articulate individual words—especially when they are speaking into a microphone. In conversational speech, articulation is not nearly so precise, and the acoustic structure of a word may be altered substantially from its citation form.

The extent of phonological variation that may be observed in fluent speech is shown in Fig. 1, which compares speech spectrograms of the utterance "Did you want to see his shoes?" with spectrograms of each of the words spoken in isolation. Examination of the spectrograms reveals a number of obvious differences. The utterance, realized phonetically as [jǝwʌnǝsiyIšuz], contains no silent intervals and is therefore continuous—there are no pauses between words. The phrase "Did you" is realized as [jǝ]; "want to" has been reduced to [wʌnǝ], and the [h] and [z] have been deleted from "his".

Ross (1975) suggests that phonological variation can be understood in terms of the principle of the "Lazy Tongue". According to Ross:

> most types of phonological processes . . . are to be explained on the basis of a need to adapt what we have to communicate to the structure of what we have to wiggle. . . . There are some things that our vocal tract can do easily (like producing a sequence of obstruents which are either all voiced or all unvoiced), and some things that it either cannot do, or can do only with great effort (like producing a string of obstruents of alternating voicelessness) (p. 284).

and,

> it is clear that the deletions and shortenings stemming from the Lazy Tongue . . . are aids to pronounceability—the less said, the easier (p. 291).

The most comprehensive study of phonological variation in natural continuous speech has been performed by Oshika et al. (1975). Many of the examples provided below were taken from their article. According to Oshika et al. (1975, p. 104):

> there is a great deal of phonological variation in natural continuous speech. A word does not have the same phonemic shape when pronounced in citation form as it does in normal running speech . . .

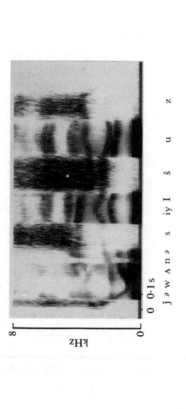

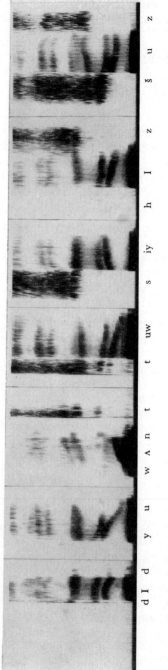

Fig. 1. Speech spectrograms of the same words spoken in the utterance "Did you want to see his shoes?" and in isolation.

It is also clear that much of this variation is governed by phonological environments, such as the influence of surrounding vowels or consonants or stress patterns, and that many of the systematic relationships can be captured in general phonological rules.

Perhaps the most pervasive form of phonological variation is *vowel reduction*, in which vowels carrying reduced stress are realized as [ə] (as in "the"). Examples are *spectrəgram* (spectrogram), *prətect* (protect), *phonəlogical* (phonological), *go ən see* (go and see) and *less thən five* (less than five).

In some environments segments are deleted entirely. The vowel deletion rule described by Oshika *et al.* (1975) states that certain three-syllable words are reduced to two syllables when the first syllable carries the main stress, as in *crim'nal* (criminal), *choc'late* (chocolate) and *ars'nal* (arsenal). This rule applies when the second syllable is followed by ə single sonorant consonant, such as [l], [r], [m] or [n].

Other vowel deletion rules drop the vowel schwa ([ə]). Schwa is deleted between two voiceless stops, as in *mult'ply* (multiply) and *p'tassium* (potassium), and in a word-initial syllable if preceded by a consonant and followed by a stressed syllable, as in *p'lice* (police) and *d'stroy* (destroy).

Consonant segments are also reduced or deleted. *Alveolar flapping*, in which [d] or [t] are realized as a flap (acoustically often only a small drop in vowel amplitude) is observed in a number of environments. An alveolar flap usually occurs following [r] in a falling stress pattern, as in "party". Flapping also occurs between reduced stress syllables as in "ability" or "purity".

Stop consonants are deleted in a number of environments. Stops are often deleted following a nasal having the same place of articulation, and followed by another consonant, as in *kin'ness* (kindness), *kin'ly* (kindly) and *ben's* (bends). This rule also applies to [t] and [d] before reduced vowels, as in *hun'er* (hunter) and *twen'y* (twenty).

The alveolar stops are deleted in other contexts as well. In word final position [t] and [d] may be deleted following [l], as in *tol'* (told) or *mel'* (melt). Alveolar stops may be deleted following [f], [v] or [s] at word or morpheme boundaries, as in *mos'ly* (mostly) and *cos'ly* (costly).

Stop consonants may also be *inserted* into speech. For example, a stop may be inserted between a nasal and a fricative, as in con*t*sonant, warm*p*th, and leng*k*th, or between a nasal and a stop with different places or articulation, as in dream*p*t.

Phonological variation in single words is not the crux of the problem however. There is no reason to reject pattern matching theories of word recognition from fluent speech solely on the basis of *within-word* variation.

The same word may be realized in fluent speech in a number of different ways; but the number is finite. Thus, although several templates would be needed for each word, within-word phonological variation does not *by itself* present insurmountable problems for pattern-matching theories of word recognition.

The problem, of course, is that the greatest effect of phonological variation occurs not within words, but across word boundaries. Within words, the sound pattern of a given language prohibits the occurrence of sequences of phonemes that are difficult to produce. In continuous speech, segments at word junctures often present difficult or unnatural articulatory gestures, which are then simplified. The result of these articulatory short-cuts is that phonetic segments are most often altered, deleted, or inserted at word boundaries. When such variation occurs, word boundaries are no longer marked phonetically.

What are the sources of between-word variation? We have already discussed several. All of the rules described above operate across word boundaries, and thereby obscure them. For example, by applying the stop deletion rules previously described to fluent speech, it can be seen that word final [d] may be dropped in "bend steel", "kind of" and "told me". In addition, word final [d] and [t] are often deleted when the following word begins with another stop consonant, as in "good boy", "bad girl", "good pie", "bad cake", "best buy", "just great", "best pie" and "best car".

We conclude our discussion of phonological variation with a consideration of palatalization, which is one of the most psychologically interesting sources of variation in speech. According to Oshika *et al.* (1975), the alveolar obstruents [d], [t], [s] and [z] are palatalized when followed by a palatal and an optional intervening boundary. Common examples of palatalization are [dIǰyu] (did you), [pʊčyr] (put your), [mIšyr] (miss your), [hIšuz] (his shoes). It can be seen that [d] becomes [ǰ] and [t] becomes [č] before [y]. In expressions such as "did you" where vowel reduction occurs, [y] is usually deleted and the utterance is realized as [dIjə]. Palatalization occurs extensively in normal speech.

Palatalization is one of the most interesting sources of phonological variation because it is influenced by the syntactic structure of an utterance. This was demonstrated by Cooper *et al.* (1977) who asked speakers to say the following two sentences:

1. We haven't broken the code yet, but we hope to soon.
2. We haven't broken the code, yet we hope to soon.

The question was whether speakers would palatalize the word final [d] of "code" and the word initial [y] of "yet"; that is, would they say "cojet". In the first sentence, the major syntactic boundary occurs following "yet", and palatalization was observed. In the second sentence, the major syntactic break occurs between "code" and "yet", and in this sentence palatalization was blocked. The results demonstrate that the phonetic realization of an utterance is influenced by higher-order linguistic variables. This means that a listener cannot segment an utterance into words solely on the basis of his (intuitive) knowledge of articulatory rules; he must take into account higher-level structure.

1.5. Summary

Our examination of the stimulus suggests that words are both overspecified and underspecified in fluent speech. On the one hand, the listener is typically presented with many more words than the speaker intended to produce. Because speech is continuous across word boundaries, almost any utterance can be segmented in many alternate ways. Thus, the sequence "which states" contains many potential words— "which", "itch", "states", "dates", "ate" and "eights". The utterance "He gave the example" can be parsed as "He gave the eggs ample", and so forth.

On the other hand, because speech is produced with a Lazy Tongue, the phonetic representation of an intended word may be vastly underspecified. This point has been demonstrated in a classic series of experiments by Pickett and Pollack (1963, 1964) and Pollack and Pickett (1963), who examined the intelligibility of words excised from fluent speech.

In one experiment (Pollack and Pickett, 1963), the speech of four female speakers was surreptitiously recorded while they were engaged in conversation. Portions of the speech containing one or more words were excised (by means of an electronic gate) and presented to listeners for identification. There was tremendous variability in identification scores for different words and for different speakers. For example, excised samples of 300-ms duration varied from near zero to near perfect intelligibility. For the four female speakers, listeners identified isolated words with 62, 38, 53 and 35% accuracy. But when these same words were presented in two-word samples—that is, followed by another word—identification scores rose to 83, 59, 65 and 65%. This study demonstrates that it is often difficult to recognize words in fluent speech solely on the basis of their acoustic representation. The phonetic representation of a word spoken in conversation may provide insufficient information *by itself* to uniquely specify its identity.

2. INVARIANT FEATURES IN FLUENT SPEECH

Are there conditions of invariance in fluent speech? Are certain words, syllables, or segments immune to phonological variation?* The research reviewed in this section suggests that speakers carefully articulate (1) important and/or informative words, and (2) consonants in stressed syllables, especially in word-initial position.

2.1. Invariance in important and informative words

There are at least two general factors which influence the precision with which the speaker produces an utterance. One factor is the overall "situational context" of the communication act. According to Lieberman (1967, p. 166):

> the speaker must weigh the anticipated linguistic competence of the hearer as well as the linguistic context furnished by the entire sentence, the semantic context of the conversation, and the total context of the social situation. A speaker may, for example, talk more distinctly to a foreign student when he believes that the listener is unfamiliar with the grammar of the language. A husband may talk less distinctly to his wife when he knows that she is familiar with his particular dialect.

Thus, the overall intelligibility of the speech produced by a given speaker depends upon the speaker's perception of his environment (e.g. is it quiet or noisy) and his intuitions about the listener's competence—linguistic and otherwise. It is interesting to note that a listener is often quite sensitive to a speaker's assumptions about his or her competence. We can communicate sarcasm and scorn with overly precise articulation.

Articulatory precision is also determined by a word's *importance* or *information value*. Words which are most informative tend to be articulated

---

* Unfortunately, little is known about the *limits* of variation in fluent speech. There are a number of reasons for this state of affairs. Psychologists and acoustic phoneticians interested in speech perception have directed their attention, with few exceptions, to the cues for phonemes in isolated syllables. Researchers working with synthetic speech, with a few notable exceptions (e.g. Stevens, 1975), have elected to stress the importance of cues which vary with context, rather than those cues which are relatively invariant. The field of linguistics also offers little help in defining invariant structures in fluent speech. In fact, generative phonology is almost entirely concerned with defining and representing conditions of phonetic and phonological *change*, and most of the effort in this area has been directed to within-word changes (e.g. Chomsky and Halle, 1968). There has been no general attempt in linguistic theory to define the *limits* of phonological change, and thereby define the invariant structure of fluent speech.

most carefully. This point was clearly demonstrated by Lieberman (1963), who showed that a listener's ability to identify words excised from fluent speech and presented in isolation was determined by the predictability of the word in the original utterance. For example, the word "nine" was correctly recognized 90% of the time when excised from the utterance "The number you will hear is nine", but 50% of the time when excised from the utterance "A stitch in time saves nine". Similarly, "borrower" and "lender" were recognized 80 and 40% of the time, respectively, when excised from the sentence "The (borrowers) (lenders) were all imprisoned" compared to 45 and 10% recognition when removed from the sentence "Neither a borrower nor a lender be". The results clearly show that a speaker will carefully articulate a word when he knows that it cannot be inferred from the context in which it occurs.

Speakers often convey important information by placing stress on a particular word in a sentence. To use Cutler's (1976b) example, "FELICITY eats caviar for breakfast" focuses attention on Felicity, and presupposes that caviar has already been established as the breakfast food. By comparison, "Felicity eats CAVIAR for breakfast" focuses attention on caviar, and presupposes that Felicity's identity has been established. Thus, by placing stress on a word, the speaker focuses the listener's attention to new or important information in a sentence.

We might expect, therefore, that listeners will be most accurate in identifying stressed words in fluent speech. Research by Cutler and Foss (1977) has demonstrated that reaction times are significantly faster to word-initial target phonemes in stressed words. In the sentences "I'm not sure Shakespeare's plays are even BY Shakespeare" and "I'm not sure that Shakespeare's plays are even by SHAKEspeare", subjects were faster detecting the /b/ in "by" when it was stressed.

In a subsequent study, Cutler (1976a) showed that the reaction time advantage to a target phoneme in a stressed word is not due solely to the acoustic structure of the word. Cutler first recorded sentence pairs like those below:

1. She managed to remove the dirt from the rug, but not the berry stains.
2. She managed to remove the dirt from the rug, but not from their clothes.

The dependent clause at the end of the sentence determined that "dirt" received the main stress in (1) but not in (2). As previously shown by Cutler and Foss (1977), subjects were significantly faster detecting the target phoneme /d/ in sentence (1).

In addition to these two versions, a neutral version was recorded: "She managed to remove the dirt from the rug". This sentence was duplicated and the neutral version of "dirt" was then spliced into sentences (1) and (2). The result of this manipulation was that exactly the same target word occurred in the two experimental sentences. The sentences differed, however, in that the intonation contour prior to the target word predicted that stress would fall on "dirt" in (1), but not on "dirt" in (2). The results showed that, although the reaction time difference was smaller than in the unspliced sentences, subjects were still significantly faster detecting the target phoneme in "dirt" when the preceding intonation contour *predicted* that it was stressed. Thus, Cutler (1976a, p. 58) concludes that:

> An acoustically identical word was perceived faster when embedded in a suprasegmental context which predicted that it would bear high sentence stress than in a context which predicted that it would bear reduced stress. . . . We are led then, to the inescapable conclusion that prediction of upcoming stress is an integral part of the sentence comprehension process. Further, this prediction is undertaken for the apparent end of focusing attention on the highly stressed portions of the sentence— since these are perceived more rapidly than the less stressed portions.

In an important experiment, Cooper *et al.* (1978) have provided direct evidence that phonological variation is blocked when the speaker considers a word to be important or informative. Subjects were instructed to read aloud a sentence such as "Peter said that he stood your bottles on the fire". The sentence was read without emphatic stress, or with emphatic stress placed on "stood" or on "your". When the sentence was read without emphatic stress, palatalization of the word-final [d] in "stood" and the word-initial [y] of "your" ([d] + [y] → [j]) was observed. Placing emphatic stress on "your" substantially reduced palatalization. There was significantly *less* blocking of palatalization when emphatic stress was assigned to "stood", showing that speakers are careful to articulate the first but not the final segment of an important word. Analogous results were obtained when word frequency was manipulated.

Direct acoustic evidence that phonological variation is limited in certain environments has been provided by Umeda (1977) who examined the temporal behaviour of "all measurable consonants, detailed in all possible conditions" in 20 minutes of recorded speech. Umeda found that word-initial consonants have longer durations in content words than in function words. Umeda's data are displayed in Fig. 2, which (Umeda, 1977, p. 850):

shows the durational difference between word-initial stressed consonants in content words and those in function words, both in vowel
environments. Comparisons are made in the figure between closure
duration of /t/ in content words and that in "to"; aspiration time in
these two cases; duration of /f/ in content words and in the function
words "for" and "from"; duration of /b/ in content words and in "be"
verbs (be, been, and being); duration of /d/ in content words and in
"do" verbs (do, did, does, and done); and duration of /m/ in content
words and in "may", "might", and "must". There is a 20- to more
than 40-msec difference in the mean duration of initial consonants in
terms of content–function distinction. The data distributions of these
two situations—content and function—are clearly distinguished.

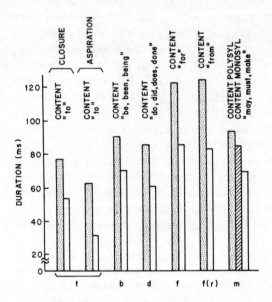

FIG. 2. Consonant durations in content and function words (from Umeda, 1977)

Umeda (1977, p. 850) explains the results in terms of the relative
information value supplied by content *vs.* function words:

Content words usually carry important information concerning the
content of the message, and so they are pronounced with considerable
care, whereas function words are easy to guess from the context and
pronounced with minimum effort. Therefore it is not surprising to find
that this difference between content words and function words is
reflected in the duration of the consonant at the edge of the word as
well as in vowel duration and other acoustic parameters. Our data show
that there is always a significant difference between the two situations

in terms of the duration of the word-initial consonant, but the word-final consonant (except /n/) does not show a consistent difference.

Umeda's data suggest that, within an utterance, the precision with which a word is articulated may be influenced by its importance or information value.

2.2. Perceptual anchors

Our own research suggests that, under specifiable conditions of syllable position and stress, certain consonant features are largely immune to variation in fluent speech. We have found that the listener pays special attention to these segments and syllables. We propose that these invariant features play a major role in word recognition; they serve as *perceptual anchors* which constrain the word recognition process. Perceptual anchors (1) provide the most direct and reliable input about the identity of words in fluent speech, (2) play a major role in guiding the segmentation process, and (3) provide information about syllable stress within a word *in addition to* information about syllable stress carried by the vowel. Thus, certain features provide information about both the phonetic identity of a segment *and* the stress of the syllable in which it occurs; together these factors provide considerable constraint on the identity of a particular word in a particular utterance.

Invariant features can be identified in the consonant portion of stressed consonant-vowel syllables. As Stevens (1975, pp. 314–315) points out, the CV syllable seems to play a special role in language:

> Syllables of this type occur universally in language, and children appear to learn first to discriminate between different consonant places of articulation when the consonant is in this environment. The implications are (i) that children are, in some sense, predisposed to respond to the acoustic properties that indicate place of articulation in this environment, and furthermore, (ii) that ability to discriminate different places of articulation in stressed CV syllables is a prerequisite for learning to extract the features in other phonetic environments.

We are arguing that the phonetic features that accompany consonants in stressed CV syllables are largely immune to the sources of variation described above. One line of support for this position is provided by Umeda's (1977) results on consonant durations in different environments in fluent speech. Umeda reports that:

> Major factors that determine the duration of a consonant in a vowel environment (i.e. located between two vowels) are (1) the position of

the word boundary—whether the consonant is immediately after a word boundary, before the boundary, or inside a word; and (2) the position of stress—whether or not the consonant is at the head of a stressed syllable.

Consonant durations reported by Umeda in vowel environments reveal that word-initial stressed CV syllables have the longest durations, virtually without exception, and that consonants in stressed CV syllables *not* in word-initial position have the next longest durations. Umeda also shows that the duration of the burst and aspiration portion of a stop consonant is positively correlated with the duration of the closure interval. It is on the basis of Umeda's data that we argue that listeners can compute syllable stress from the durational information provided by the consonant.

Our own observations confirm that phonological variation is limited in stressed CV syllables. Features describing a consonant's *manner of articulation* appear to be present for all English consonants in stressed CV syllables. *Stop* consonants—/b/, /d/, /g/, /p/, /t/, /k/ in English— are produced with total occlusion in the oral cavity and with the velum raised to block the escape of air through the nasal passage. Stop consonants in CV syllables are characterized by a period of relative silence during the closure interval (during which glottal pulsing is sometimes observed for voiced stops preceded by a voiced segment) and an abrupt onset or burst produced by the explosive release of the consonant. *Fricatives*—/s/, /š/, /z/, /ž/, /f/, /θ/, /v/, /ð/ in English—involve extreme narrowing of the oral cavity. Air forced through this opening produces a characteristic hissing or friction noise known as frication. The *affricates*—/č/ and /ǰ/ in English—are produced with an initial occlusion, like the stops, but are released with frication, like the fricatives. Affricates are thus characterized by a period of relative silence followed by frication having an abrupt onset. Finally, *nasals*—/m/ and /n/ in English—are produced with occlusion of the oral cavity and a lowered velum, so that air is forced through the nasal passage. The resonant properties of the nasal cavity produce a clearly detectable "nasal murmur".

Examination of spectrograms of fluent speech reveals that manner of articulation features for consonants in CV syllables are rarely if ever deleted. Our own research supports this observation. In the experiments described below, our methodology required that tones be placed on magnetic tape near the onset of stop, fricative, affricate and nasal consonants in CV syllables. It was therefore necessary to find reliable acoustic markers for these consonants in fluent speech. For each class of consonant, we chose an acoustic event corresponding to

,the consonant's manner of articulation; the abrupt onset following the closure interval for stops and affricates, the onset of frication for fricatives, and the onset of the low amplitude nasal murmur for nasals. To date, we have performed over 1000 tone placements in both stressed and unstressed CV syllables, spanning several hours of recorded speech produced by different speakers. There have been less than half a dozen instances in which tone placement was made impossible by the absence of the necessary acoustic event.

Recently, Goldberg and Reddy (1977) have provided a more elegant demonstration that consonants in stressed syllables are accompanied by invariant features of manner of articulation. Their computer controlled speech recognition system correctly identified manner of articulation over 90% of the time in stressed syllables.

2.3. Listening for mispronunciations

Our conclusion that listeners are most sensitive to consonant features in stressed CV syllables is based on the results of a series of experiments in which we asked subjects to detect the occurrence of mispronounced words in fluent speech. We are using this procedure, developed by Cole (1973), to measure a perceiver's sensitivity to phonetic features in fluent speech *during* the process of word recognition.

It is possible to mispronounce almost any word in English by changing a single segment to produce a non-word. For example, mispronouncing "boy" as "moy", "doy", "poy", or "voy" involves, in each case, a change of a single distinctive feature in a single segment. By asking listeners to detect the presence of such mispronunciations in fluent speech, we can examine the relative perceptibility of these features. We can also determine the perceiver's sensitivity to phonetic features as a function of syllable or word position, stress and surrounding phonetic environment.

In the experiments reported below, subjects listened to a short story by Kurt Vonnegut entitled *Next Door*. This story was chosen because it is easy to follow, entertaining, contains few unusual words, and takes about 20 minutes to read. The story was usually recorded by the first author, although in two of the experiments described below female speakers were used.

On the average, about 100 mispronounced words occurred in each story, so that subjects heard between four and five mispronunciations per minute, or about one every three sentences. Mispronunciations were always produced by changing one consonant segment in a word to produce a non-English word (e.g. *boy* to *poy*, *good* to *dood*, *five* to *vive*) which did not violate phoneme sequence constraints in English.

Thus *b*lue would not be changed to *d*lue, since /dl/ is not a permissible English sequence. We were careful to pronounce the altered word as it would normally be spoken in the story, except for the altered consonant. With a little practice, it was possible to produce mispronounced words in a completely natural manner without interfering with the prosodic structure of the story.

In all of the experiments, subjects listened to naturally recorded speech binaurally through headphones at a comfortable listening level. Subjects were instructed to listen to the story, and to push a response button whenever they detected a mispronounced word.

Finally, we want to stress that mispronunciations were detected as a natural consequence of listening to the story. Our subjects reported that they became involved in the plot of the story and that mispronunciations "presented themselves" as they listened to the story.

The LM task provides two dependent measures: (1) the number of detected mispronunciations, and (2) the speed with which mispronunciations are detected. A brief tone (inaudible to the subject) was placed on the alternate channel of the recording tape at the onset of each altered segment. It triggered a millisecond timer, which was stopped by the subject's detection response. As the experiments reveal, the two dependent variables can provide different measures of information processing in the same task.

In the remainder of this section we describe a series of experiments that examine the perceptibility of phonetic features during word recognition from fluent speech. The experiments suggest that stop consonants in stressed CV syllables enjoy a special status as perceptual anchors.

2.3.1. Experiment 1: Voicing changes in English consonants

Except for the nasals, all of the true consonant phonemes in English can be arranged into pairs—or cognates—which differ by the voicing feature. Experiment 1 examined listeners' sensitivity to changes in the *voicing* feature for the set of English consonants in stressed syllables in word-initial position.

The fourteen consonant phonemes /b/, /d/, /g/, /p/, /t/, /k/, /ǰ/, /č/, /z/, /v/, /ð/, /s/, /f/, /θ/ occurred eight times each in word-initial position; four times in a one-syllable word and four times in a two-syllable word with stress on the first syllable. The resulting 112 words were mispronounced in the story by changing the voicing of the initial consonant (e.g. *s*outh to *z*outh; *z*ero to *s*ero; *f*un to *v*un; *v*ote to *f*ote).

The results, shown in Fig. 3 and Table I, were extremely consistent for phonemes within each class of sound (i.e. stop, affricate, fricative). Voicing changes were detected most often for stops (70%), next most often for affricates (64%), and least often for fricatives (38%), $F(2,28) = 81 \cdot 1$, $p < 0 \cdot 001$. Examination of Table I reveals only one exception to this pattern—a change from /t/ to /d/ was detected less often than a voicing change among the affricates. For stops and affricates, there was no overall effect of the direction of feature change. For fricatives, a change from voiceless to voiced was detected more often than a change from voiced to voiceless, $F(2,28) = 3 \cdot 85$, $p < 0 \cdot 05$.

The results of Experiment 1 demonstrate that listeners are quite sensitive to voicing changes in stop and affricate consonants, and relatively insensitive to voicing changes in fricatives. We suspect that our

TABLE I. Percent detections of voicing changes.

	Voiced to voiceless		Voiceless to voiced	
Stops	/b/ to /p/	77	/p/ to /b/	72
	/d/ to /t/	65	/t/ to /d/	55
	/g/ to /k/	70	/k/ to /g/	79
Affricates	/ǰ/ to /č/	65	/č/ to /ǰ/	64
Fricatives	/v/ to /f/	36	/f/ to /v/	42
	/z/ to /s/	40	/s/ to /z/	49
	/ð/ to /θ/	22	/θ/ to /ð/	34

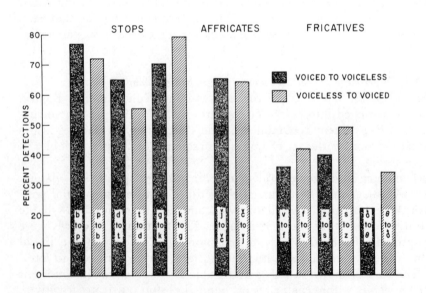

Fig. 3. Detection of voicing changes in stops, affricates and fricatives.

subjects did not attend to this feature because it carries little perceptual weight in English. There are few word pairs in English which differ only by the voicing of the initial fricative.

2.3.2 Experiments 2–4: Place vs. voicing changes for stop consonants

The results of Experiment 1 suggested to us that stop consonants (and perhaps affricates in CV syllables) may enjoy a special status as perceptual anchors in fluent speech. Unlike fricatives, which are continuous with adjacent segments, stop consonants in CV syllables are separated from preceding segments in fluent speech by a period of relative silence (the closure interval) which occurs prior to the release of the stop. Umeda (1977, her Fig. 2) has shown that the duration of the closure interval is almost identical for voiced and voiceless stops; the significant cues for voicing and place of articulation occur after the release of the consonant.

We believe that stop consonants in CV syllables present the listener with a remarkably stable set of cues. The presence of a closure interval of between 50 and 80 ms (Umeda, 1977) serves as a reliable signal that a stop or affricate is about to occur. The closure interval may also provide the vocal tract sufficient time to reach the target place of articulation for the consonant. Therefore, the acoustic cues associated with voicing and place of articulation may be the most reliable for stop consonants in CV syllables. If this is so, listeners should be quite sensitive to changes involving these features.

Experiments 2–4 compared changes in place of articulation and voicing for stop consonants. In each of these experiments, mispronunciations were produced by changing a word-initial stop consonant in a stressed syllable to a new stop consonant differing from the original by place of articulation or voicing. Half of the mispronunciations occurred in one-syllable and half in two-syllable words, but stress was always on the first syllable (the results were identical for one- and two-syllable words and data are combined across this variable).

To control for all contextual factors, two versions of the story were recorded and exactly the same words were mispronounced in each version. Thus, changes in place of articulation in one version (e.g. *b*oy to *d*oy) were compared to changes in voicing in the same words in the other version (e.g. *b*oy to *p*oy).

Experiment 2 compared the two possible changes in place of articulation for each stop (e.g. /b/ to /d/ or /b/ to /g/) to changes in voicing for that stop (e.g. /b/ to /p/). The comparison of place *vs.* voicing changes, shown in Table II, revealed one interesting difference— changing a voiceless stop to its voiced cognate (e.g. *p*ot to *b*ot, *t*able to *d*able, *c*up to *g*up) produced fewer detections than changing the stop from voiced to voiceless or changing the place of articulation. There was no difference in the two place changes for any of the stops, so these data are combined in Table II.

TABLE II. Percentage of detected mispronunciations.

/b/ to /p/	80	/b/ to /d/ or /g/	83
/d/ to /t/	86	/d/ to /b/ or /g/	92
/g/ to /k/	87	/g/ to /b/ or /d/	82
/p/ to /b/	66	/p/ to /t/ or /k/	86
/t/ to /d/	71	/t/ to /p/ or /k/	89
/k/ to /g/	79	/k/ to /p/ or /t/	89

Experiments 3 and 4 sought to replicate this result using two different speakers. In these experiments the stimulus set was reduced to the stops /b/, /d/, /p/ and /t/. As in the previous experiment, words changed by place of articulation in one version of the story (e.g. /b/ to /d/) were changed by voicing in the other version (e.g. /b/ to /p/). There were ten voicing and ten place changes for each stop consonant in each version of the story, so that subjects were presented with a total of eighty mispronunciations in each version of the story.

Exactly the same words were mispronounced in Experiments 3 and 4; the only difference between the two experiments was the speakers. In Experiment 3 the speaker was a native Texan. However, this female speaker was a drama major with extensive voice training and her accent was, if anything, pseudo-British. This speaker read the story with a great deal of dramatic expression. The speaker in Experiment 4 was a native of Montreal, Canada. Speaker 1 (Experiment 2) read the story in about 20 minutes; Speaker 2 read the story in about 19 minutes; while Speaker 3 had a slightly faster speech rate and read the story in 16 minutes. For each speaker, the two versions of each story were within 60 seconds total duration of each other.

The results are presented in Fig. 4, along with the comparable data for Speaker 1 from Experiment 2. The overall detections for Speakers 1, 2 and 3, respectively, were 82, 78 and 69%.

For all three speakers, place changes were detected more often than voicing changes. This main effect was significant for Speakers 1 and 3 ($F(1,72) = 14 \cdot 50$, $p < 0 \cdot 001$; and $F(1,64) = 8 \cdot 55$, $p < 0 \cdot 01$), but not for Speaker 2 ($F(1,64) = 1 \cdot 66$). Examination of detections as a function of the direction of voicing change (i.e. voiced to voiceless vs. voiceless to voiced) revealed interesting differences among the three speakers. For Speaker 1 (Experiment 2) a voiceless to voiced change

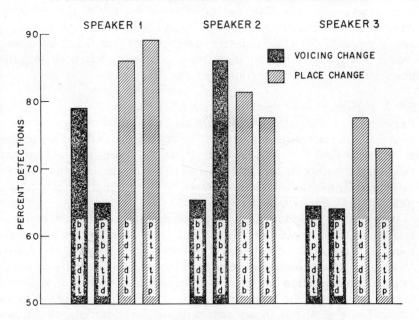

FIG. 4. Detection of voicing and place changes in stops.

was most difficult to detect $(F(1,72) = 13·83, p < 0·001)$. For Speaker 2, a voiced to voiceless change was most difficult to detect $(F(1,64) = 23·58, p < 0·001)$. For Speakers 1 and 2, a significant interaction was observed between direction of change and type of feature change $(F(1,72) = 10·07, p < 0·001;$ and $F(1,64) = 18·42, p < 0·001)$. For Speaker 3, voicing changes in *either* direction were more difficult to detect than changes in place of articulation. Thus, across all speakers, changes in place of articulation were detected more often than changes in voicing, although the effect is sensitive to the *direction* of feature change along the voicing dimension for the different speakers.

The main point to be noted in these experiments is that changes in a single feature of a stop consonant are readily detectable in connected speech—about 75% of the time across the three speakers. As was seen in Experiment 1, mispronunciations involving stop consonants are readily detected compared to mispronunciations of other English consonants. We would thus prefer to emphasize the overall similarity of place and voicing changes in stop consonants, and the high detectability of either type of change, rather than the difference between them.

Finally, it may be noted that no differences in reaction times to detected mispronunciations (measured from the onset of the stop burst) were observed for place *vs.* voicing changes for any of the speakers. Average reaction times were 925, 946 and 955 ms for Speakers 1, 2 and 3, respectively. It takes listeners slightly less than 1 s to recognize that a word containing an initial stop consonant has been mispronounced while listening to connected speech.

2.3.3. Experiment 5: Word-initial vs. word-final changes

Experiment 5 compared word-initial and word-final changes of place of articulation in nasals (e.g. *make* to *nake vs.* drum to dru*n*; *not* to *mot vs.* gone to go*me*) as well as word-initial *vs.* word-final changes of voicing in the stops /t/ and /d/ (e.g. *d*ish to *t*ish *vs.* crie*d* to crie*t*; *t*aste to *d*aste *vs.* spli*t* to spli*d*). Changes always involved either the first or last phoneme in a one-syllable word.

We expected to find many more detections in word-initial than word-final stops, since word-initial stops in a stressed syllable are accompanied by a fairly well defined set of features, such as the stop burst, VOT and vowel onset characteristics following the stop. By contrast, stops in final position may not be released, and voicing is signalled by the duration of the preceding vowel. For nasal consonants, Umeda (1977, her Fig. 4) has shown that nasals in word-initial position are approximately 40 ms longer than nasals in word-final position. However, place of articulation in nasals is signalled by formant transitions to and from an adjacent vowel, and *not* by the nasal murmur. It is not clear to what extent the perceptibility of formant transitions is affected by word or syllable position.

Each feature change occurred in ten words in initial position and ten words in final position. The eighty words were presented in a single story to ten subjects.

The results are displayed in Table III. Over twice as many detections occurred in word-initial position (72%) than in word-final position (33%) ($F(1,9) = 157\cdot89, p < 0\cdot001$). As expected, word-final changes in voicing for the stops were extremely difficult to detect, and

TABLE III. Percentage of detected mispronunciations in word-initial *vs.* word-final position.

	Initial	Final
/m/ to /n/	66	29
/n/ to /m/	72	52
/d/ to /t/	75	33
/t/ to /d/	75	12

only 13% of word-final changes from /t/ to /d/ were detected. Large differences were also observed between word-initial and word-final nasals. The results for nasals show that listeners may selectively attend to the beginnings of one-syllable words. These results are paralleled by the finding of Cooper *et al.* (1978) that speakers are careful to articulate a consonant segment at the beginning but not at the end of a word.

2.3.4. *Experiment 6: Stress*

Experiment 6 directly examines the effect of syllable stress on detection of mispronunciations. In this experiment, mispronunciations always involved changing a voiceless stop to its voiced cognate in a CV syllable. Word position and syllable stress were varied in a 2×2 factorial design. Thus, twenty-four two-syllable words (eight for each voiceless stop) contained an altered segment in the first syllable when it was stressed (e.g. cáncel to gáncel), while twenty-four words contained an altered segment in the first syllable when it was not stressed (e.g. concérn to goncérn). Similarly twenty-four words contained a change in the voiceless stop in the second syllable when it was stressed (e.g. inclíned to inglíned), while twenty-four words contained exactly the same feature changes in the second syllable when it was not stressed (e.g. bróken to brógen). The resulting ninety-six words were mispronounced in the same 20-minute short story, which was presented to ten subjects.

The results, shown in Table IV and Fig. 5, revealed a strong effect of syllable stress on detections. Mispronunciations were detected more often when the altered segment occurred in the stressed syllable ($F(1,9) = 112 \cdot 15$, $p < 0 \cdot 001$). Changes in stressed syllables were detected equally well in the first or second syllable of a word. A significant interaction ($F(1,9) = 35 \cdot 00$, $p < 0 \cdot 01$) between syllable stress and syllable position was due entirely to changes involving /t/ to /d/ in unstressed syllables; in initial position, /t/ to /d/ changes in unstressed syllables were detected much more often than changes involving either /p/ or /k/, and in medial position, /t/ to /d/ changes were detected less often than those involving /p/ or /k/. The extremely low detection rate for /t/ to /d/ in unstressed medial syllables occurred despite the fact that we carefully chose words in which the /t/ at the onset of the unstressed second syllable is not usually flapped (in seven of eight words the /t/ followed a nasal, which causes the /t/ to be released). Apparently the frequency with which /t/ is flapped in medial position in normal speech in *other* phonetic environments caused subjects to ignore the /t/ to /d/ change as a mispronunciation.

Mispronunciations in stressed syllables were detected almost twice

TABLE IV. Percent detections of mispronunciations as a function of syllable stress and syllable
position.

	Stressed	Unstressed
First syllable		
/p/ to /b/	84	54
/t/ to /d/	62	85
/k/ to /g/	86	45
Second syllable		
/p/ to /b/	76	41
/t/ to /d/	76	15
/k/ to /g/	84	46

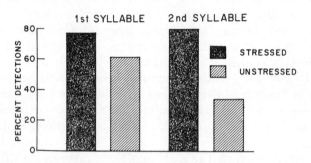

FIG. 5. Detections of mispronunciations as a function of syllable position and stress.

as often as mispronunciations in unstressed syllables. The higher
detection of mispronunciations of stop consonants in stressed syllables
supports our claim that stressed syllables receive special attention from
the listener. Since unstressed syllables are most vulnerable to phonological variation (such as vowel reduction), deviations from the correct
form are likely to be discounted. Stressed syllables, on the other hand,
present reliable information, and the listener attends to them.

2.3.5. Summary: Experiments 1–6
Experiments examining the perceptibility of consonant features
suggest that: (1) stop consonants are more perceptible than other consonants, (2) consonants in stressed syllables are more perceptible than
consonants in unstressed syllables, and (3) consonants at the beginnings of words are more perceptible than consonants at the ends of
words. Taken together, the results support the claim that consonant
features in stressed CV syllables are highly perceptible in fluent speech.

The results demonstrate not only that certain consonant features are highly perceptible in fluent speech, but that these features provide the most reliable and important information about a word's identity. This conclusion is based on the nature of the experimental task—feature changes were perceived *as mispronunciations of words* in fluent speech.

3. A MODEL OF WORD RECOGNITION

Let us set the stage for the modest theory of word recognition presented below by reviewing the main points we have tried to establish. We began by asking why speech understanding systems have failed to recognize words from fluent speech using pattern-matching procedures. An examination of the stimulus revealed two related problems: segmentation and phonological variation. Because of phonological variation, words in fluent speech often vary substantially from their citation form. The extent of this variation is great enough so that perceivers are often unable to identify a spoken word when it is removed from its fluent context and presented in isolation. Moreover, because segments are combined or altered at the word boundaries, it is difficult to segment fluent speech into words using pattern-matching techniques—there are usually alternate ways to parse any portion of a spoken utterance.

On the other hand, we saw in the previous section that conditions of invariance can be identified in natural continuous speech. Speakers are careful to articulate important words. Infrequent, informative and important (e.g. stressed) words are produced more precisely and are therefore more distinct acoustically than frequent or uninformative words. On a more general level, we have found that some consonant features are more perceptible than others in natural continuous speech. Experiments with mispronunciations have shown that features of consonants at the beginnings of stressed syllables or one-syllable words are used to recognize words from fluent speech.

3.1. The model

In its barest outline, the model has two basic assumptions. First, words in an utterance are recognized in a strict serial fashion. We assume that the phonetic input is processed syllable by syllable and word by word. Under normal listening conditions, the listener can begin to recognize a word as soon as he is able to process its phonetic input—decisions about a word's identity are *not* deferred until an entire phrase or clause has been completed. Secondly, each word in an utterance is constrained both by the phonetic input and its prior context. The notion of prior context, as used here, is meant to be very powerful. Prior context is defined as any source of knowledge about the structure of spoken language that can be used to constrain word choice; we assume that listeners use different sources of knowledge—prosodic, phonological, lexical, syntactic, semantic, thematic, situational—to constrain word choice. For example, recognizing a word X that ends with /d/ includes the knowledge that the following word may be palatalized (contain an initial [j] if it begins with /y/ in its underlying form) as well as the knowledge that palatalization will not occur if word X completes a clause (Cooper *et al.*, 1977).

This model states that speech perception is both a serial and a parallel process. It is a serial process because the words (and syllables) in a sentence are recognized in order. This assumption allows us to make a number of specific (and testable) predictions about word recognition. For example, if words are recognized in order, then one word's recognition automatically directs segmentation of the immediately following word. Assuming a syllable-by-syllable analysis, we can predict that, in the case of multisyllable words, the first syllable of a word can be used to constrain word choice to any and all contextually appropriate words. We thus predict that a syllable is recognized faster within a word than at the beginning of a word, since syllables within a word are constrained by the first syllable.

Word recognition is also an "interactive parallel process" (Marslen-Wilson, 1975) since a word is mutually specified by its phonetic structure and prior context. A word's recognition occurs *during* the interaction of input and knowledge-directed constraints. We believe that contextual information is extracted very rapidly. In fact, we postulate that a word's recognition carries with it the immediate knowledge of constraints it provides on other words (such as selectional rules described by Chomsky, 1965). Thus, we predict that a word is recognized faster when it is constrained in some way by an immediately preceding word.

To summarize, our model of word recognition claims that:

1. An utterance is analysed syllable by syllable and word by word.
2. All syllables and all words are constrained by their acoustic structure and the context in which they occur.
3. Context includes many different sources of knowledge.
4. A word's recognition (a) locates the beginning of the next word, (b) provides knowledge about phonological variation that can affect the next word, and (c) carries with it the immediate knowledge of constraints on (immediately) following words.

5. The first syllable following a recognized word is identified either as: (a) a contextually appropriate complete word, or (failing that) (b) is used to access multisyllable words beginning with that syllable.

3.2. Tests of the model

3.2.1. Experiment 7

Consider the sentence "They saw the cargo on the ferry" in which "go" is mispronounced as "ko". This sentence has two possible segmentations—the mispronunciation may be perceived as occurring within the word "cargo" or at the beginning of "go" in the sequence "car go". We now splice a recording of this sentence into two different stories. One story containing the "cargo" sentence is about two men sent to the docks to pick up a shipment of cargo arriving on a ferry. This story directs a one-word segmentation of the sound sequence containing the mispronunciation—i.e. "cargo". The other story is about a young man's parents who arrive at the dock to watch their son drive his car on to the ferry for the start of his summer vacation. This story directs a two-word segmentation, i.e. "car go". In both stories, the mispronunciation occurs in the sentence "Looking down from the pier, they saw the cargo (car go) on the ferry."

We have assumed that (1) listeners sequentially process the phonetic input syllable by syllable, and (2) contextual information—such as that provided by the theme of a story—is actively used to segment and recognize words from the syllables under analysis. The model further predicts that reaction times will be faster when the mispronunciation occurs *within* a word, that is, in "cargo". When the story is about two men looking for a shipment of cargo, the word "cargo" is highly constrained given the prior context "Looking down from the pier, they saw the car . . .". Recognition of "car" predicts that the next syllable is "go", and "ko" is rapidly recognized as a mispronunciation of "cargo". When the story is about a young man's parents waiting to see their son's car go on the ferry, the same sequence of words, ending with "they saw the . . ." causes "car" to be recognized as a complete word. Given that "car" is recognized as a word, the listener must wait for subsequent phonetic information to recognize that "ko" is a mispronunciation of "go" and not the start of a new word actually beginning with "ko" (e.g. "collide"). Thus, given the identical acoustic input, reaction times should be faster to mispronunciations occurring within a word than at the beginning of a word if (1) prior contextual information is used to constrain word choice, and (2) syllables and words are recognized in a rapid serial fashion.

To test this hypothesis, six stories were written so as to demand either a one- or a two-word segmentation of "snowdrift", "address" and "cargo" in the following sentences:

1. They saw the snowdrift (snow drift) by the window.
2. He gave her address (a dress) with pleasure.
3. They saw the cargo (car go) on the ferry.

Each story contained four mispronounced words prior to the critical mispronunciation. Two of these occurred in word-initial position, while two occurred in syllable-initial position in the second syllable of a word. In addition, each story contained at least one prior occurrence of the word(s) used for the critical mispronunciation. Thus, the words "a dress" were mentioned prior to the mispronunciation of "dress" in one story, while in the other story the word "address" was presented prior to its mispronunciation. The stories were recorded at a conversational speaking rate by a male speaker and had an average duration of about 3 minutes.

To control for acoustic factors, the three target sentences were each recorded *a single time* (with the mispronunciation), duplicated, and then spliced into the appropriate stories. Splices were not detectable. Thus, exactly the same mispronunciation was presented in the same acoustic environment in two different stories. Mispronunciations were produced by changing /d/ to /t/ in "snowdrift" and "address", and /g/ to /k/ in "cargo". A tone was placed on the alternate channel of the recording tape at the onset of the stop burst of the altered segment. Tone placement was performed before the sentences were duplicated, so tone placement was identical for the duplicated versions. The onset of the tone triggered a millisecond timer that was stopped when the subject pushed a response button indicating the detection of a mispronunciation.

Subjects were randomly assigned to two groups of thirteen subjects each. They were told that they would hear short stories in which some of the words were mispronounced and that they should press the button in front of them as quickly as possible whenever they detected a mispronunciation.

The mean reaction times to the one- and two-word segmentations of "snowdrift", "address" and "cargo" are presented below in Table V. It can be seen that the reaction times are considerably faster when the story directed a one-word segmentation—i.e. when the mispronunciation was perceived as occurring within a two-syllable word rather than at the beginning of a word. Mean reaction times were about 350 ms faster when the stories required perception of "cargo", "address" and "snowdrift" as single words, $t(2) = 6 \cdot 88$, $p < 0 \cdot 02$.

To summarize, prior context produced large differences in reaction times to detected mispronunciations. When the story dictated a one-word segmentation, so that mispronunciations were perceived as occurring in the second syllable of a word, the mean reaction time to detect the mispronunciation was 685 ms. When the story dictated a two-word segmentation of the utterance, the mean reaction time was 1054 ms. We thus have a clear demonstration that listeners use information provided by the thematic content of a story to segment and recognize words from fluent speech.

TABLE V. Mean reaction times to one- and two-word segmentations of the same phonological sequence.

snowdrift ($N = 6$)	address ($N = 6$)	cargo ($N = 7$)
772	679	604

snow drift ($N = 11$)	a dress ($N = 5$)	car go ($N = 7$)
1039	1128	994

3.2.2. Experiment 8

In Experiment 7, the segmentation of the acoustic sequence as one or two words was highly constrained, since the stories were written expressly for the purpose of directing one of the alternative segmentations. Experiment 8 was designed to determine whether segmentation of the same phonological sequence could be guided by the first few words of a single sentence.

Consider the following pair of sentences:
1. The doctor said that nosedrops will help the cold.
2. The doctor said he knows drops will help the cold.

Starting with the syllable [noz], the two sentences are phonologically identical, and the mispronunciation occurs in drops (pronounced trops). By splicing a recording of the first four words of each sentence ("the doctor said that" and "the doctor said he") on to a duplicated recording of "nosetrops will help the cold", we create a pair of sentences in which the first few words of each sentence direct a one- or two-word segmentation of the same physical stimulus.

If subjects are able to use contextual information provided by the first few words of a sentence to constrain word choice, we should again find faster reaction times when the mispronunciation is perceived as occurring within a word. For example, the occurrence of the complementizer "that" in sentence (1) predicts that [noz] is likely to be the first syllable of a nominal compound (e.g. nosebleeds, nosedrops) or perhaps the first word in an adjective–noun phrase (e.g. nose infection). Since word choice is highly constrained, when "*t*rops" is heard, the listener should be very fast in determining that it is a mispronunciation of "drops" in "nosedrops".

By comparison, in a sentence beginning "The doctor said he", the pronoun "he" specifies that [noz] must be "knows". Recognition of "knows" as a word automatically determines that "trops" begins a new word. When a mispronunciation occurs in the beginning of a word, the listener must wait for *subsequent* phonetic information to determine that "trop" does not begin a legitimate word (e.g. tropical). Thus, if word recognition occurs in a rapid serial fashion, where recognition of one word constrains recognition of the next, reaction times to a mispronunciation of "drops" should be faster in (1) than (2).

The twelve pairs of experimental sentences are shown in Table VI. Examination of Table VI reveals that, within each pair, the two sentences end with exactly the same sequence of words, and that the first few words in each sentence determine whether the mispronunciation occurs at the beginning of a syllable *within* a nominal compound, or in the first segment of a one-syllable word.

In order to control for acoustic factors, the two sentences in each pair were recorded and duplicated a number of times. The sentences were spoken so as to neutralize any inherent differences between them, such as the phrase final lengthening of segments in the if–then constructions. The initial portion of each sentence in a pair was then spliced on to the same final phrase taken from one of the sentences. Thus, the segments of tape containing, "The doctor said he" and "The doctor said that" were spliced on to, "nose *t*rops will help the cold". The resulting sentences sounded perfectly natural (although in a few cases constructing the sentences required several attempts). The tape splicing manipulation produced pairs of sentences that contained exactly the same acoustic information in the latter portion of the sentence. In each sentence pair when the initial portion of the sentence determined a one-word segmentation (e.g. "nosedrops"), the mispronunciation was located *within* a word, in syllable-initial position. When the initial portion of the sentence required a two-word segmentation of the phonological sequence (e.g. "for getting"), the mispronunciation

TABLE VI. Sentences requiring one- and two-word segmentation of the same phonological string[a].

---

1. The judge went to the fair*g*rounds for a divorce.
   The judge said he saw fair *g*rounds for a divorce.   (/g/ to /k/)
2. He just hated for*g*etting the right number.
   He was noted for *g*etting the right number.   (/g/ to /k/)
3. The doctor said that nose*d*rops will help the cold.
   The doctor said he knows *d*rops will help the cold.   (/d/ to /t/)
4. The truck ploughed the growing snow*d*rift into the street.
   The wind made the falling snow *d*rift into the street.   (/d/ to /t/)
5. The colour of the house*p*aint was rare.
   When I lived at the house *p*aint was rare.   (/p/ to /b/)
6. Antoinette watched the Corvette over*t*ake the bus.
   If you have to bring Annette over *t*ake the bus.   (/t/ to /d/)
7. The coach watched his quarter*b*ack go to the office.
   When Don gets his quarter *b*ack go to the office.   (/b/ to /d/)
8. My grandma's making home*m*ade preserves.
   The people staying home *m*ade preserves.   (/m/ to /b/)
9. Homework was the draw*b*ack in high school.
   Randy learned to draw *b*ack in high school.   (/b/ to /d/)
10. She wrote her a*dd*ress with pleasure.
    He made her a *d*ress with pleasure.   (/d/ to /t/)
11. I will help them load car*g*o on the ferry.
    If you want the old car *g*o on the ferry.   (/g/ to /k/)
12. She saw some hand*s*ome statues through the window.
    She saw him hand *s*ome statues through the window.   (/s/ to /z/)

---

[a] Note: The mispronounced segments are italicized.

always occurred at the beginning of the second word.

The mean reaction time for each sentence is shown in Table VII. The mean reaction time when the mispronunciation occurred within a word (one-word segmentation) was 948 ms, compared to 1120 ms when the same mispronunciation occurred in word-initial position (two-word segmentation), $F(1,11) = 17.93$; $p < 0.005$. There was thus a 170-ms reaction time advantage for the sentences in which the first few words demanded a one-word segmentation of the phonological sequence in which the mispronunciation occurred.

These experiments show that when the acoustic input can be parsed in different ways, listeners produce a segmentation that is consistent with their expectations about what the speaker is trying to say. The reaction time advantage for mispronunciations within words (one-

TABLE VII. Accuracy and speed of detections for one- and two-word segmentations of the same phonological sequence.

	Detections	RT		Detections	RT
fairgrounds	18	910	fair grounds	16	1418
forgetting	18	954	for getting	18	1290
nosedrops	11	874	knows drops	14	1150
snowdrift	20	836	snow drift	17	1016
housepaint	15	974	house paint	14	1170
overtake	19	876	over take	19	1000
quarterback	18	885	quarter back	18	995
homemade	17	965	home made	18	1069
drawback	18	879	draw back	16	994
address	13	1264	a dress	8	1280
cargo	17	1054	car go	16	1105
handsome	16	902	hand some	18	954
Mean	16·7	948	Mean	16·0	1120

word segmentations) is readily explained if it is assumed that, from the first word of a sentence, the listener attempts to construct a meaningful representation on a word-by-word basis. As each word is recognized, the next syllable is identified as either (1) a contextually appropriate one-syllable word, or (2) the first syllable of a multisyllable word. If the syllable does not specify a complete word, it is used to direct word access to appropriate words beginning with that syllable. Thus, mispronunciations are detected faster within words because the phonetic input is highly constrained. Note that this explanation involves considerable "top-down" (i.e. knowledge-driven) processing, since phonetic structure is predicted from an ongoing analysis of word choice, which is in turn guided by the active use of prior context.

Experiment 7 showed that listeners can use information from the theme of a story to constrain word choice. The main point of Experiment 7 is that segmentation and word recognition are very fast when word choice is highly constrained. As pointed out previously, the stories in Experiment 7 were written for the express purpose of directing a one- or two-word segmentation of the same phonological sequence. Thus, when the sentence "They saw the carko on the ferry" occurred in a story about a shipment of cargo, listeners were very fast in deciding that "ko" was a mispronunciation of "go" in "cargo". By contrast, when the same sentence occurred in a story about a car, "ko" was perceived as beginning a new word, and the listener had to wait for additional syllables before being able to decide that "ko" did not begin a multisyllable word.

Experiment 8 showed that segmentation can be guided by words occurring just before the ambiguous sequence. For example, "The doctor said he" and "The doctor said that" produced alternate segmentations of "knows drops (nosedrops) will help the cold". The faster reaction times for the mispronunciation in "nosedrops" suggest that information provided by one word can be used to constrain recognition of a subsequent word. It appears that a word's recognition carries with it the immediate knowledge of certain constraints provided by the word. This possibility is not too surprising if one accepts the notion that a word is itself recognized within a contextually appropriate framework. A word's recognition therefore elaborates this framework and further constrains subsequent word choice.

A comparison of the results of Experiments 7 and 8 reveals that the *amount* of constraint provided by prior context determined the magnitude of the reaction time difference for one- *vs.* two-word segmentations of the same stimulus. In Experiment 7, the one-word segmentations of "address", "cargo" and "snowdrift" were highly constrained by the theme of a story, and reaction times were over 300 ms faster for the one-word segmentations. In Experiment 8, where segmentation and actual word choice were not so highly constrained, the reaction time difference was 150 ms. A dramatic demonstration of this point is that "address", which produced a large reaction-time difference in the stories when the alternate segmentations were highly constrained, produced no reaction time difference in single sentences.

4. SOURCES OF KNOWLEDGE IN WORD RECOGNITION

Research described in this section is based on the notion that word recognition requires the use of various sources of knowledge. The concept of sources of knowledge has been used with great success by computer scientists in the design of speech understanding systems (see Reddy, 1976, for a review). Cutler's (1976a) finding that listeners use the prosodic contour of a sentence to predict (and focus attention on) the temporal location of a stressed word is an excellent demonstration that listeners use a particular source of knowledge—prosody—during speech perception.

4.1. Context and noisy (or ambiguous) input

Sources of knowledge in speech perception have generally been studied under the heading of *context*. The facilitating effect of linguistic context on speech perception was first demonstrated by Miller *et al.* (1951). These authors found that words presented in a background of noise were identified more accurately in the context of a grammatical sentence than when the words were scrambled and presented in isolation. In a further experiment, Miller and Isard (1963) demonstrated that word recognition was influenced by both syntactic and semantic factors. Subjects identified a higher percentage of words in a background of noise in syntactically well formed but meaningless sentences such as "Hunters spend work from the highways" than in ungrammatical strings composed of the same words, thus demonstrating the importance of syntax for word recognition. Performance was best for normal sentences, demonstrating that word recognition is aided by semantic as well as syntactic information. These experiments convincingly demonstrated that a listener can utilize syntactic and semantic constraints to identify (or accurately guess at) a word that is partially or totally obscured by noise.

Perhaps the most dramatic effect of context in speech perception is Warren's (1970) phonemic restoration effect. Warren erased a single phoneme from the middle of a word in a sentence (e.g. the first /s/ in "legislators") and replaced the missing /s/ with a coughing sound of about the same intensity. Warren's subjects had great difficulty in locating the actual site of the cough and were generally unaware that a consonant phoneme had been removed from the speech wave. Warren's demonstration of phonemic restorations suggests that a listener can generate phonemic information in the complete absence of phonetic information, given sufficient linguistic context.

Garnes and Bond (1976) investigated the relationship between constraint provided by the semantic structure of a sentence and the phonetic input. Subjects were presented with the synthesized sentences:

1. Here's the fishing gear and the ———.
2. Check the time and the ———.
3. Paint the fence and the ———.

Each sentence ended with one of sixteen words drawn from an acoustic continuum which spanned the distinction between the words "bait", "date" and "gate". When the acoustic information corresponding to the last word in the sentence was unambiguous, the semantic structure of the sentence did not affect its perception. However, when the acoustic information fell in the cross-over range between [b]–[d] or [d]–[g], perception was determined by the semantic structure of the sentence.

Thus, a word usually perceived as "bait" in a neutral sentence (The word is ——) was now perceived as "date" when preceded by the carrier "Check the time and the ——". The results demonstrate that, under ideal listening conditions, when the phonetic input is unambiguous subjects do report hearing semantically unusual sentences, such as "Check the time and the bait". However, when the phonetic input is open to interpretation, perception is determined by context.

In a subsequent experiment, Garnes and Bond (1977a) showed that context has a more potent effect when speech is heard under noisy conditions. In this experiment *naturally* recorded sentences such as (1) Check the *time* and the *date*, (2) Check the *dime* and the *date*, and (3) Check the *time* and the *bait*, were presented in noise. The results showed that under ideal listening conditions, listeners again identified the critical words correctly, even when they occurred in semantically inappropriate sentences. However, when these same sentences were presented in noise ($-$ 3 dB signal to noise ratio) subjects responded with the semantically appropriate word rather than the actual, inappropriate word 33% of the time.

Bond and Garnes (1975) and Garnes and Bond (1975, 1977b) have analysed 900 instances of "slips of the ear"—misperceptions observed first-hand during perception of conversational speech. Although a detailed analysis of their corpus is beyond the scope of the present chapter, two aspects of their analysis are relevant to the present discussion (the predominance of errors involving word boundaries was discussed in Section 1). First, misperceptions of conversational speech commonly involve the application of phonological rules observed in speech production. For example, misperceptions involving consonant deletion (e.g. "nodes" misperceived as "nose") and insertion, and syllable deletion and insertion account for over 10% of the misperceptions. Secondly, their analysis indicates that "speech perception is a primarily active, rather than passive, process. . . . No other explanation is possible for misperceptions which quite radically restructure the message, e.g., *Say, there's Pier I imports* [heard as] *Beer wine imports?*" (Garnes and Bond, 1977b, pp. 10 and 11). According to Garnes and Bond (1977b, p. 10):

> Some perceptual errors suggest that the listener is scanning the signal for possible lexical items. In the example, *I had this appointment* . . .— (interrupting) *disappointment?* the listener reacts appropriately to a message he believes is going to convey something quite serious. He does this on the basis of a hypothesized lexical item; in this case, however, his hypothesis is erroneous. The irresistible impression is that the lexical

item arrived as soon as the speaker's phrase *this appointment* was available.

4.2. Shadowing

The model of word recognition proposed in this chapter was partially motivated by Marslen-Wilson's research with "fast shadowers". Marslen-Wilson's (1973, 1975) experiments demonstrate that syntactic and/or semantic constraints are rapidly used to recognize words from fluent speech. Marslen-Wilson tested sixty-five subjects for their ability to shadow (repeat verbatim) connected prose. From this group, seven "close" shadowers were found who could maintain the intelligibility of their speech while shadowing at mean delays of about 270 ms. Close shadowers were thus able to remain little more than a syllable behind the incoming speech. These subjects (along with more "distant" shadowers with latencies between 500 and 800 ms) were asked to shadow two 300-word prose passages presented at a conversational speaking rate (160 words min^{-1}).

Marslen-Wilson's analysis of the speech errors made while shadowing demonstrates that subjects were using both syntactic and semantic information while shadowing. Of the 402 errors made by the fourteen subjects, most were delivery errors (slurring, hesitations) or word omissions. The remaining errors were *constructive errors*, "in which subjects either added or changed entire words, or changed part of a word so as to make it into a different word". Of the 111 constructive errors, only three were structurally inappropriate. Errors made during shadowing, even at very short latencies, were both syntactically and semantically appropriate to the material being shadowed. According to Marslen-Wilson (1973, p. 523):

> The constructive errors of close and distant shadowers are also qualitatively very similar, and indeed the same errors were sometimes made by subjects in both groups. For example, in the sentence "It was beginning to be light enough so I could see . . .", two subjects inserted the deleted "that" following "so": one shadowing at 254 ms, the other at 559 ms. In the sentence beginning "He had heard at the brigade . . .", five subjects replaced "heard at" with "heard that": their latencies were 264, 287, 862, 444, and 553 ms. Nor do these errors occur only when the subject's shadowing delay is longer than usual. These errors, especially in the case of the closest shadowers, usually occur when the subjects' latencies are shorter than average, as if they are placing more reliance on the predictive properties of the higher order context.
> These examples, and the errors in general, also show that the subjects'

output can be constrained by the preceding context up to and including the word immediately before the error. The error "that" in the first example is clearly contingent on knowing that the preceding word is "so". Similarly, in the second example, the subjects would need to have extracted the structural implications of "heard" to make the grammatically appropriate error of saying "that" instead of "at".

In a more recent experiment, Marslen-Wilson and Welsh (1978) have provided further evidence that the phonetic processing of a word is determined by its preceding context. In this experiment, subjects shadowed a prose passage in which various three-syllable words were mispronounced by changing a single phonetic segment to produce a non-word. Mispronunciations occurred either in the first or last syllable of a word, and phonetic segments were changed by either one or three distinctive features. In addition, the mispronounced words were either highly constrained by (i.e. predictable from) the preceding context, or were relatively unconstrained (e.g. ". . . he wanted to smoke a . . ." vs. "It was his . . ."). Marslen-Wilson and Welsh were interested in the occurrence of "fluent restorations", in which the shadower produced the altered word *without* the mispronunciation. Fluent restorations occurred in over 80% of highly constrained words mispronounced by a single feature and in 65% of words that were not highly constrained. These results suggest a trade-off between contextual constraint and reliance on the acoustic input during word recognition from fluent speech. An analysis of shadowing latencies prior to the fluent restorations revealed no increase in latencies; the evidence suggests that the subject never heard the mispronunciation.

4.3. Experiments with mispronunciations

The mispronunciation detection task offers one convenient method for examining the sources of knowledge that listeners use to recognize words from fluent speech. In the experiments reported in this section, we provide the subjects with a potential source of knowledge in experimental, but not control, sentences. We assume that, if subjects are able to use a particular source of knowledge during word recognition, then reaction times to mispronounced words will be faster when that knowledge source is available.

The explicit assumption behind the experiments reported below is that the amount of time it takes to recognize a word is directly related to the amount of time it takes to detect that the word was mispronounced. In order for this to be true, it must hold that a mispronunciation is perceived as a natural consequence of attempting to recognize words from both context and input. An *a priori*, logical analysis of the task reveals two ways in which a listener can detect a mispronunciation. One, the listener can know what the word should be, and notice a mismatch between the input string of sounds, and his hypothesis. Two, the listener can know that the string is not a word at all, although he does not know what word should be there. Our subjects report that both occur, although we have found that subjects given a sentence containing a mispronounced word accurately identify the original word over 90% of the time.

4.3.1. Experiment 9: Transitional probability

The transitional probability of a word in a sentence is its probability of occurrence given a string of preceding words. It seems likely that a word with a high transitional probability would be recognized more efficiently than a word with a low transitional probability in a spoken sentence. Morton and Long (1976) have recently confirmed this intuition using a phoneme monitoring task. Subjects heard sentences which differed only in the transitional probability of the word containing the target phoneme, e.g. "A sparrow sat on the branch/bed whistling a few shrill notes to welcome the dawn". The words containing the target phoneme (branch or bed) were balanced for their frequency of occurrence in the language.

The results showed that subjects were approximately 50 ms faster detecting the target phoneme in high transitional probability words. Since the sentence pairs in the Morton and Long experiment were matched for syntactic structure, the transitional probability effect must have been based on semantic (real-world) constraints. The results demonstrate that subjects use such constraints to recognize words from continuous speech.

We used twenty of the sentences employed by Morton and Long (1976). We used all of their sentences in which the high and low transitional probability words in each sentence began with either a stop, affricate or nasal consonant. Examples of sentences containing high and low transitional probability words are provided in Table VIII. The altered segment is underlined in each sentence, and the phonetic change is indicated in parentheses following each sentence. Across the entire set of sentences, high and low transitional probability words were matched for number of syllables and frequency of occurrence in the language, and the mispronounced words within each sentence were matched for initial phoneme and phonemic alteration. The twenty sentences were embedded in short (five- or six-sentence) paragraphs which included at least two other mispronunciations. A separate paragraph was recorded for the two versions of each sentence. Each subject heard an equal number of each sentence type, and only one of

TABLE VIII. Sentences with high *vs.* low transitional probability target words.

---

1. Happily they listened to the *music/machine* until it was time for them to go out. (/m/ to /n/)

2. He sat reading a *book/bill* until it was time to go home for his tea. (/b/ to /v/)

3. Passing overhead was a *bird/ball* which stood out starkly against the redness of the sky. (/b/ to /p/)

4. A sparrow sat on the *branch/bed* whistling a few shrill notes to welcome the dawn. (/b/ to /p/)

5. Slowly he opened the *door/dance* for it was an occasion which required a little formality. (/d/ to /t/)

---

the two versions of each sentence. Reaction times were measured from the onset of the nasal murmur or the onset of the stop burst. Subjects were instructed to listen to each paragraph and push a button whenever they detected a mispronounced word.

Subjects were 150 ms faster detecting mispronunciations in high transitional probability words. The mean of the median reaction times for sixteen subjects was 770 ms for probable words, and 919 ms for improbable words ($F(1,15) = 27 \cdot 4$, $p < 0 \cdot 001$). The effect was provided by sixteen of the twenty sentences. The mean number of detections was exactly the same in the two sentence types.

Listeners are able to use semantic and/or pragmatic information to facilitate a word's recognition. We suspect that the large reaction time difference found here (compared to the 50 ms difference found by Morton and Long) is partly due to the nature of our experimental task. When a probable word is mispronounced, listeners may quickly identify the mispronunciation as they recognize what the word was intended to be. When an improbable word is mispronounced, the subject may be unable to determine the identity of the intended word. Whatever the specific mechanism, it is clear that a word's appropriateness to prior semantic context is a powerful determinant of its recognition.

4.3.2. Experiment 10: One word's recognition is the next word's context

An assumption of the model is that a word's recognition carries with it the immediate knowledge of constraints on other words. Evidence in support of this claim was provided by a few of the "segmentation" sentences used in Experiment 8, and by Marslen-Wilson's analysis of constructive errors made by fast shadowers. Experiment 10 was performed as a direct test of the hypothesis.

Examples of the sentences we used are shown in Table IX. As can be seen from the table, sentences in each pair differed by a single word—matched for number of syllables and final segment—which occurred immediately before the mispronounced word. In one case, the critical word constrained the identity of the mispronounced word (e.g. *mink* coat), and in the other it provided minimal constraint (e.g. *pink* coat).

Two groups of ten subjects listened to thirty sentences: ten experimental sentences, ten controls and ten fillers with no mispronunciations. Each subject heard either the experimental or the control version of each sentence.

TABLE IX. Examples of sentences in which the mispronounced word was or was not constrained by an immediately preceding word.

---

1. She wanted a mink/pink *c*oat to go with the Rolls-Royce her husband had left her.   (/k/ to /p/)
2. He wore a gold/old *r*ing on the little finger of his left hand.
                                                                          (/r/ to /l/)
3. Mrs Jones was pleased to see that the broom/groom *s*wept the floor very thoroughly.   (/s/ to /š/)
4. His knife/wife *c*ut the bread neatly, and then he buttered the slices.
                                                                          (/k/ to /t/)
5. The fans applauded as the boxer/actor *p*unched a man in the first row.
                                                                          (/p/ to /k/)

The results showed that listeners detected a mispronunciation 99 ms faster (776 *vs.* 875 ms) when the word was constrained by an immediately preceding word ($F(1,18) = 15 \cdot 5$, $p < 0 \cdot 01$). The results demonstrate that semantic constraints provided by one word are used during recognition of an immediately following word.

4.3.3 Experiment 11: Implication

In a study by Johnson *et al.* (1973), subjects were presented with stories in which an instrument of action was or was not implied by a verb in the story. For example, subjects heard the following story:

John was trying to fix the birdhouse. He was pounding (looking for) the nail when his father came out to watch him and to help him do the work.

Half of the subjects heard "pounding the nail" and half heard "looking for the nail" in the story. In a subsequent recognition test, subjects were asked to decide whether the sentence "John was using the hammer to fix the birdhouse . . ." had occurred in the original story. More false recognitions to this sentence were made by subjects who had heard the story containing "pounding the nail". The implied instrument—hammer—had been encoded into the memorial representation of the story.

In the present experiment we examine reaction times to mispronunciations in words which were or were not implied by a word in a previous sentence.* Consider the following pair of sentences:

It was a stormy night when the phonetician was murdered.
It was the middle of the next day before the *k*iller was caught.

Since the mispronounced word "killer" is implied by the fact that the phonetician was murdered, subjects should be relatively fast at detecting the mispronunciation, compared to the case in which the first sentence states that the phonetician merely died.

Twenty-five sentence pairs were used, and there were two versions of each pair. In one version, the mispronounced word (which always occurred in the second sentence) was implied by a word in the first sentence; in the other version the mispronounced word was not implied. As Table X shows, the second sentence in each pair was the same in the two versions, and by cross-recording the original sentence, we ensured that it was acoustically the same.

The sentence pairs, along with filler sentences which contained no mispronunciations, were presented to twenty-six subjects. Half of the

TABLE X. Examples of sentences in which the mispronounced word either was or was not implied in the first sentence.

---

1. The maid swept/cleaned the hallway.
   She used a *b*room that was old and worn.   (/b/ to /p/)
2. The student flew/went home for Christmas loaded with gifts.
   The *p*lane was full of people returning for the holidays.   (/p/ to /b/)
3. The tourist drove/travelled all over the city.
   He used the *c*ar for a whole week.   (/k/ to /g/)
4. The children glued/fastened the pictures to the wall.
   They were covered with *p*aste.   (/p/ to /b/)
5. The girl was chased/ran through the field.
   Her boyfriend could not *c*atch her although he ran as fast as he could.
   (/k/ to /g/)

---

* This experiment was suggested to us by Marcel Just and Pat Carpenter, who graciously supplied many of the sentences used in our study.

subjects heard the implied version of each pair, while half heard the non-implied version.

The results revealed that mispronunciations were detected 80 ms faster when the mispronounced word was implied in the previous sentence ($F(1,25) = 9\cdot41$, $p < 0\cdot01$). The mean of the median reaction times to implied words was 912 ms, and 997 ms to words not implied. The effect was observed for sixteen of the twenty-five pairs. There was no difference in the number of detections to implied *vs.* non-implied words.

4.3.4 Experiment 12: Thematic organization and word recognition

Bransford and Johnson (1973) presented subjects with a story which, when read by itself, made no sense whatsoever. But when the same story was accompanied by the appropriate picture, it was readily understood. In an experiment run in collaboration with Sarah Goldin, we attempted to determine whether thematic organization supplied to

TABLE XI. Balloon story (thematic words are asterisked, and mispronounced phonemes are italicized.

It certainly is a novel and romantic idea, sort of like a modern *b*allet of Romeo and Juliet. The whole idea is pretty weird, however, and there is no guarantee that the *w*oman will be impressed. My *g*uess is that she will be incredibly flattered. In fact she will probably be left *sp*eechless by the whole thing. The problem is that there are just so many things that could go wrong. If he has a bad *v*oice* the effect will be ruined. Also, I'm not sure how well he is able to play his *g*uitar*. I happen to know that he just hauled it out of his *g*arage where it has been sitting for about four years. On the technical side there are a number of possible problems that can arise. Of course the *f*irst problem is the problem of getting the current. There are also a number of problems that could arise with the *b*alloons*. If he uses too much or too little *g*as* the whole operation will be a failure. In order to get the height right, he had better consider two things: the weight of the *sp*eaker* and the fact that the apartment is on the *f*ifth* floor. It is a good thing that the girl will be part way out the *w*indow* or else she wouldn't hear a thing because buildings are so well insulated these days. In any case, he had better stand with his *m*outh as close as he possibly can to the *m*icrophone* or else the sound will not carry. Fortunately, the apartment faces the *s*t*reet right above where he is standing so she will have a good *v*iew of the whole set-up. Lighting may be a problem since judging by the size of the *m*oon*, it will be pretty dark. On the other hand the moonlight should provide the *m*aximum effect. Finally, let's hope the speaker is held by heavy duty *s*t*ring* or he is in danger for his life. By some miracle, if everything works, he should give her a memory she will never forget.

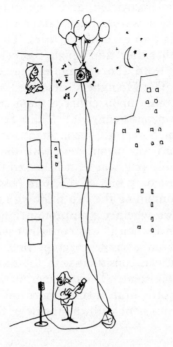

Fig. 6. Picture context for "Balloon" story.

a story by either a picture or a title would facilitate recognition of words related to the theme of the story.

The "balloon" story, altered substantially from the version which was used by Bransford and Johnson (1972), was recorded on tape with the mispronunciations shown in Table XI. Half of the subjects were shown the picture in Fig. 6, which provides a meaningful context through which one can interpret the story. Half of the mispronounced words in each story were related to the theme implied by the picture, while the remaining half, matched according to initial phoneme, number of syllables and stress were unrelated to the theme of the story.

When subjects saw the picture before listening to the story, the mean reaction time was 726 ms to thematically related words, and 866 ms to thematically unrelated words. When no picture was provided reaction times were 831 and 843 ms to thematic and non-thematic words, respectively. Thus, reaction times were over 100 ms faster to thematically related words when subjects saw the picture.

In a second experiment, we examined reaction times to a single target word in a story. The independent variable was whether this word was consistent or inconsistent with the title of the story. Six different stories were constructed, and each story contained two titles and two possible target words. Each target word was either appropriate or inappropriate to each of the titles. The stories were written to be consistent with either title up to the occurrence of the (mispronounced) target word. For example, one story, entitled either "The Sorcerer" or "The Moonmen" described a man walking over a rocky terrain who comes upon either a giant crater (consistent with "The Moonmen", inconsistent with "The Sorcerer") or a castle (consistent with "The Sorcerer", inconsistent with "The Moonmen"). When the target word was inconsistent with the title, the subsequent sentence justified its use (e.g. "at least it looked like a castle . . .").

Each subject heard only one of the four possible versions of each story produced by combining the two titles with the two target words. The main question was whether a mispronunciation would be detected faster in a target word when it was consistent with the title. Over all stories, we observed an average reaction time of 921 ms when the mispronounced word was consistent with the title, and 1063 ms when the word was inconsistent. These experiments demonstrate that listeners recognize words from a story more quickly when the word is appropriate and consistent with the theme of the story.

5. SUMMARY AND CONCLUSIONS

We have tried to show that word recognition from fluent speech can be best understood by viewing the problem from the perspective of the total communication act. Words are encoded into a continuous signal because of the manner in which they are produced. Because man speaks with a Lazy Tongue, the listener is presented with the problem of recognizing a discrete set of words from a continuously varying signal in which words are altered substantially through phonological variation.

Problems introduced by phonological variation are at least partially counteracted by conditions of invariance. The speaker appears to be at least partially sensitive to the problems caused by his Lazy Tongue, and aids the listener in understanding his or her speech both by investing more time and effort in the articulation of important and/or informative words, and by directing the listener's attention to these words through the use of prosodic, syntactic or discourse structure.

The research described in this chapter supports three observations about word recognition from fluent speech. First, listeners are most sensitive to phonetic features that are not normally affected by phonological variation. Our research suggests that consonant features are (1) more perceptible in word-initial than in word-final position in one-syllable words, (2) more perceptible in stressed than unstressed CV syllables, and (3) more perceptible in stop consonants than other consonants. We view consonant features in stressed CV syllables as perceptual anchors which provide the listener with the most powerful and reliable information for segmenting and recognizing words from fluent speech.

Secondly, word recognition is fast. The listener is probably not more than one or possibly two words behind the speaker. Our own research with mispronunciations and Marslen-Wilson's research with close shadowers suggests that recognition of one word constrains recognition of an immediately following word.

Thirdly, our results suggest that word recognition occurs during the interaction of input and knowledge-directed constraints. The listener uses all available information to recognize a word from fluent speech. We found that listeners will make use of quite abstract sources of knowledge—such as the title or theme of a story—to recognize a word.

The model of word recognition proposed in Section 3 incorporates the last two observations. We hypothesized that word recognition proceeds syllable by syllable and word by word, making use of constraints on word choice as soon as they become available. Our definition of contextual constraints was very broad, encompassing many sources of knowledge.

According to the model, the listener attempts to recognize an incoming syllable as a contextually appropriate word. If he can do so, he can segment the next word. If the syllable under analysis cannot be a complete word, it is used to direct access to appropriate words beginning with that syllable. In support of this assumption we found (Experiments 7 and 8) that the time to detect a mispronunciation was shorter when the context dictated that the mispronunciation occurred within a word, rather than at the beginning of a word.

Our model assumes that a word's recognition carries with it immediate knowledge of constraints on following words. As direct evidence for this claim, we found that word recognition was facilitated when the word was constrained by an immediately preceding word (Experiment 10).

The collection of experiments in Section 4 supports our generous definition of context. For example, we found faster recognition of words implied by a verb in the previous sentence (Experiment 11) and words related to the theme of a story (Experiment 12), both subtle and abstract sources of constraint.

The message of Sections 3 and 4 is that a considerable amount of active comprehension is involved in word recognition. We can conclude then, that it is not only what we hear that tells us what we know; what we know tells us what we hear.

ACKNOWLEDGEMENTS

We would like to thank Bill Cooper, Christine Glenn, Marcel Just and Raj Reddy for their comments on a previous version of this chapter.

REFERENCES

Bond, Z. S. and Garnes, S. (1975). Implications of misperceptions in conversational speech. Proceedings of the Eighth International Congress of the Phonetic Sciences, Leeds.

Bransford, J. D. and Johnson, M. K. (1973). Considerations of some problems of comprehension. In "Visual Information Processing" (W. G. Chase, ed.). Academic Press, New York and London.

Chomsky, N. (1965). "Aspects of the Theory of Syntax". MIT Press, Cambridge, Massachusetts.

Chomsky, N. and Halle, M. (1968). "The Sound Pattern of English". Harper and Row, New York.

Cole, R. A. (1973). Listening for mispronunciations: A measure of what we hear during speech. Perception and Psychophysics 1, 153–156.

Cooper, W. E., Lapointe, S. G. and Paccia, J. M. (1977). Syntactic blocking of phonological rules in speech production. Journal of the Acoustical Society of America 61, 1314–1320.

Cooper, W. E., Egido, C. and Paccia, J. M. (1978). Grammatical conditioning of a phonological rule: Palatalization. Journal of Experimental Psychology: Human Perception and Performance (in press).

Cutler, A. (1976a). Phoneme-monitoring reaction time as a function of preceding intonation contour. Perception and Psychophysics 20, 55–60.

Cutler, A. (1976b). Beyond parsing and lexical look-up: An enriched description of auditory sentence comprehension. In "New Approaches to Language Mechanisms" (R. J. Wales and E. C. T. Walker, eds). North-Holland, Amsterdam.

Cutler, A. and Foss, D. J. (1977). On the role of sentence stress in sentence processing. Language and Speech 20, 1–10.

Garnes, S. and Bond, Z. S. (1975). Slips of the ear: Errors in perception of casual speech. Proceedings of the Eleventh Regional Meeting of the Chicago Linguistic Society, 214–225.

Garnes, S. and Bond, Z. S. (1976). The relationship between semantic expectation and acoustic information. Proceedings of the Third International Phonology Meeting, Vienna.

Garnes, S. and Bond, Z. S. (1977a). The influence of semantics on speech perception. Journal of the Acoustical Society of America 61, S65 (A).

Garnes, S. and Bond, Z. S. (1977b). A slip of the ear: A snip of the ear?, A slip of the year? Paper prepared for the Working Group on "Slips of the Tongue and Ear" at ICL XII, Vienna.

Goldberg, H. G. and Reddy, R. (1977). Phonetic labelling by template matching. *Journal of the Acoustical Society of America* **61**, S69 (A).

Johnson, M. K., Bransford, J. D. and Solomon, S. K. (1973). Memory for tacit implications of sentences. *Journal of Experimental Psychology* **98**, 203–205.

Lieberman, P. (1963). Some effects of semantic and grammatical context on the production and perception of speech. *Language and Speech* **6**, 172–187.

Lieberman, P. (1967). "Intonation, perception, and language". MIT Press, Cambridge, Massachusetts.

Marslen-Wilson, W. D. (1973). Linguistic structure and speech shadowing at very short latencies. *Nature, Lond.* **244**, 522–523.

Marslen-Wilson, W. D. (1975). Sentence perception as an interactive parallel process. *Science, N.Y.* **189**, 226–228.

Marslen-Wilson, W. D. and Welsh, A. (1978). Processing interactions and lexical access during word recognition in continuous speech. *Cognitive Psychology* **10**, 29–63.

Miller, G. A. and Isard, S. (1963). Some perceptual consequences of linguistic rules. *Journal of Verbal Learning and Verbal Behavior* **2**, 217–218.

Miller, G. A. and Nicely, P. (1955). An analysis of perceptual confusions among some English consonants. *Journal of the Acoustical Society of America* **27**, 338–352.

Miller, G. A., Heise, G. A. and Lichten, W. (1951). The intelligibility of speech as a function of the context of the test materials. *Journal of Experimental Psychology* **41**, 329–335.

Morton, J. and Long, J. (1976). Effect of word transitional probability on phoneme identification. *Journal of Verbal Learning and Verbal Behavior* **15**, 43–51.

Oshika, B. T., Zue, V. W., Weeks, R. V., Nue, H. and Aurbach, J. (1975). The role of phonological rules in speech understanding research. *IEEE Trans. Acoust., Speech, Signal Processing* ASSP-23, 104–112.

Peterson, G. E. and Barney, H. L. (1952). Control methods used in a study of the vowels. *Journal of the Acoustical Society of America* **24**, 175–184.

Pickett, J. M. and Pollack, I. (1963). Intelligibility of excerpts from fluent speech: Effects of rate of utterance and duration of excerpt. *Language and Speech* **6**, 151–164.

Pickett, J. M. and Pollack, I. (1964). Intelligibility of excerpts from fluent speech: Auditory *vs.* structural context. *Journal of Verbal Learning and Verbal Behavior* **3**, 79–84.

Pollack, I. and Pickett, J. M. (1963). Intelligibility of excepts from conversation. *Language and Speech* **6**, 165–171.

Reddy, R. (1976). Speech recognition by machine: A review. *Proceedings of the IEEE* **64**, 501–531.

Ross, J. R. (1975). Parallels in phonological and semantactic organisation. *In* "The Role of Speech in Language" (J. F. Kavanagh and J. E. Cutting, eds). MIT Press, Cambridge, Massachusetts.

Stevens, K. N. (1975). Potential role of property detectors in the perception of consonants. *In* "Auditory Analysis and Perception of Speech" (G. Fant and M. A. A. Tathan, eds). Academic Press, New York and London.

Umeda, N. (1977). Consonant duration in American English. *Journal of the Acoustical Society of America* **61**, 846–858.

Warren, R. M. (1970). Perceptual restoration of missing speech sounds. *Science, N.Y.* **167**, 393–395.

Four

Strategy Effects in the Assessment of Hemispheric Asymmetry

M. P. Bryden
University of Waterloo

1. INTRODUCTION

Work such as that of Kimura (1973) with normal adults and of Sperry (Sperry, 1974; Sperry *et al.*, 1969) with commissurotomized patients has stimulated interest in lateral asymmetries and how they relate to the functions of the cerebral hemispheres. As early as 1960, Kimura showed that performance on a verbal dichotic listening test was related to cerebral speech lateralization: subjects with left-hemispheric speech representation were more accurate on material presented to the right ear, while those with right-hemispheric speech representation showed the opposite effect. Other dichotic listening procedures were soon developed that yielded a left-ear advantage in normal right-handed adults, thus presumably tapping the functions of the right hemisphere. Thus left-ear advantages have been reported for the recognition of such material as melodies (Kimura, 1964), environmental sounds (Curry, 1967), emotional tone (Haggard and Parkinson, 1971; Carmon and Nachson, 1973), sonar signals (Chaney and Webster, 1966) and intonation pattern (Blumstein and Cooper, 1974).

Research with visual procedures has followed a very similar pattern. Thus a number of tachistoscopic procedures have been developed on which normal adults show a right visual field advantage in the recognition of letters (e.g. Bryden, 1965) or words (McKeever and Huling, 1970). Left visual field superiorities have been reported for such tasks as dot localization (Kimura, 1969), stereoscopic depth (Durnford and Kimura, 1971), line orientation (Umilta et al., 1974), face recognition (Geffen et al., 1971), and Gestalt completion (Nebes, 1973). Reviews of this work have been published by White (1969, 1972).

In general, this work has been corroborated by the research on commissurotomized patients (Sperry, 1974; Gazzaniga, 1970; Nebes, 1974). Thus, the general picture which emerges is of a left hemisphere specialized for speech, and a right hemisphere that is concerned with music, spatial relations, and more generally holistic functions.

Initially, there was considerable resistance to interpreting these lateral differences to an asymmetry of cerebral function (Harcum, 1964; Inglis, 1962). More recently, however, the idea of a relationship between lateral asymmetries in perception and motor behaviour and cerebral organization has become generally accepted. Indeed, virtually any lateral asymmetry is now interpreted as indicating something about cerebral organization. Thus we have seen an increasing number of studies in which some lateral difference in performance is taken as a manifestation of differences in cerebral organization. Increasingly, simple dichotic, tachistoscopic and motor tasks are being used to make inferences about brain processes. There have been reports of sex differences in cerebral lateralization (Lake and Bryden, 1976) and of age differences (Geffner and Hochberg, 1971; Bryden and Allard, 1977), and abnormal patterns of lateralization have been reported in poor readers (Bryden, 1970; Marcel et al., 1974; Zurif and Carson, 1970), stutterers (Curry and Gregory, 1969) and in virtually every other special group one can imagine. Indeed, patterns of lateralization have been related to hypnotizability, the choice of one's profession and a wide variety of personality characteristics (Bakan and Strayer, 1973; Ornstein, 1972; Galin and Ornstein, 1974).

It is the contention of the present chapter that we have become too accepting of the relation between behavioural laterality and cerebral organization. We have too often forgotten that our tasks are administered to active, thinking subjects, who have their own particular strategies for dealing with the demands that are put upon them. Thus many of the differences that have been attributed to differing patterns of cerebral organization may, in fact, be manifestations of different ways of dealing with the tasks. Such an argument does not deny the existence of hemispheric asymmetry; rather, it claims that many of the procedures used for assessing asymmetry are subject to other sources of variation.

2. CONCEPTUALIZATIONS OF HEMISPHERIC ASYMMETRY

2.1. Structural

At present, there seem to be two major theoretical conceptions of hemispheric asymmetry, a *structural* approach, which originates with Kimura (1966, 1967), and an *attentional* approach, which derives from Kinsbourne (1973, 1975). While many versions have been offered of both viewpoints, there are certain fundamental distinctions between them.

In essence, a structural model proposes that laterality effects exist because one hemisphere is more proficient than the other at dealing with certain types of material or at carrying out certain processes. Stimuli impinging on the right side of the body—the right ear, hand or visual field—have more direct access to the left hemisphere, and thus there is a right-side superiority for tasks involving the materials that the left hemisphere deals with more proficiently. Conversely, stimuli arriving on the left have better access to the right hemisphere, and a left-side superiority exists for tasks involving stimuli that the right hemisphere is more suited for treating.

At a very elementary level, such a model provides a convenient mnemonic for laterality effects. We know that most people show a left-hemispheric lateralization of speech, and, in general, tasks that involve verbal material or verbal processes show a right-side superiority. Thus, there is a right-ear superiority for verbal material in dichotic listening (Kimura, 1961b; Studdert-Kennedy and Shankweiler, 1970), a right visual field superiority for words (Mishkin and Forgays, 1952) or letters (Bryden, 1965) presented randomly in the left or right visual fields at tachistoscopic durations, and a right field superiority for bilaterally presented words under certain conditions (McKeever and Huling, 1971). The right hemisphere is more implicated than the left in spatial processes and in music perception, and it is tasks involving such material that show a left ear or left visual field superiority.

More recently, structural conceptions of hemispheric functioning have become more process-oriented than stimulus-oriented. It has become much more common to attribute perceptual laterality effects to the manner in which stimuli are processed rather than to the nature of the stimuli *per se*. Thus, Levy (1971) and Nebes (1974) see the right hemisphere as carrying out integrative, Gestalt-like operations, while the left hemisphere is more analytic. Cohen (1973) argues that the left hemisphere is a serial processor, and the right a parallel processor. Such an idea also finds expression in Carmon and Nachson's notion that the left hemisphere is more involved in sequential discriminations (Halperin *et al.*, 1973; Nachson and Carmon, 1975), and in Kimura's linking of speech lateralization to sequential motor control (Kimura, 1976).

Unfortunately, it is not always obvious whether a particular task involves simultaneous and integrative processes, or successive and analytic processes. Thus the specific predictions to be made from such an approach are not always clear. Furthermore, it is uncertain to what extent these different modes of processing are under optional control, and to what extent they are obligatory and dictated by the specific task.

2.2. Attentional

An alternative approach that takes more cognizance of the ways in which strategies are controlled has been offered by Kinsbourne (1970, 1973, 1975). He may be considered to have an attentional theory of laterality. According to his arguments, whenever a person is engaged in verbal thought, the left hemisphere is activated and the right suppressed. This activation of the left hemisphere leads to a directing of attention to the right side of space, head and eye turning to the right, and an increased sensitivity of the left hemisphere to incoming stimulation. Conversely, when one is thinking in a non-verbal mode, the right hemisphere is activated, the left suppressed, and the reverse effects occur. These attentional or pre-stimulus effects are dictated by the set which is given to the subject and the subject's own thought processes. They serve to bias the subject's attention to the left or right, and lead to left- or right-side superiorities. In addition, Kinsbourne

(1973) recognizes the existence of what he calls post-stimulus effects: regardless of the initial bias, the left hemisphere is more efficient at processing verbal material and the right at processing spatial material. Thus, even when attentional biases have been controlled, a right-side superiority will be observed with verbal material because the left hemisphere is more efficient at processing the verbal stimulus once it has arrived.

One of the attractions of Kinsbourne's argument is that it offers an explanation for the fact that non-verbal laterality effects are much smaller and less consistent than verbal effects. If we assume that subjects are more likely to engage in verbal thought than in non-verbal thought, and that in the course of a lengthy psychological experiment they are more likely than not to think about irrelevant activities, then it becomes very difficult to avoid some kind of left-hemisphere bias. When the material is verbal, the set for verbal material, the verbal superiority of the left hemisphere, and the likely verbal bias of irrelevant thought will all summate to produce a strong right-ear or right visual field effect. With non-verbal material, the initial set and the right hemispheric spatial superiority will be at least partially counteracted by the verbal nature of the irrelevant thought, and the left superiority will be reduced. Of course, the weaker non-verbal effects may also be attributed to the fact that the right hemisphere spatial superiority is not as marked as the left hemisphere verbal superiority.

It is not, however, the intent of the present chapter to provide a detailed review of Kinsbourne's theory and the evidence relating to it. It is sufficient to note that Kinsbourne has provided convincing evidence that attentional factors can contribute to the laterality effect, at least under some conditions. On the other hand, there are some experiments, such as that of Gardner and Branski (1976), that fail to find attentional effects when they might logically be expected to appear. At present it is best to conclude that Kinsbourne's theory does not have unequivocal support.

While it may not be possible to settle the argument between structural and attentional theorists, it does seem that the experimental procedures used to demonstrate laterality effects in normal subjects are not without flaw. With many procedures, factors that have nothing to do with cerebral asymmetry may influence the results, and lead unwary investigators into false claims. To take a ridiculous example, it would be foolish to test a pre-reading child on a word identification task and conclude that he lacks normal cerebral organization because he does not show the usual right visual field superiority. If the child cannot read the material, he can hardly be expected to do the task.

Before we turn to a more detailed consideration of how subject's biases and strategies may affect performance in laterality experiments, it is necessary to comment briefly on the measurement of laterality and on techniques for comparing one study with another.

3. ON COMPARING LATERALITY EFFECTS

It is frequently desirable to compare the magnitude of laterality effects obtained with different procedures or in different studies. This requires a measure of laterality that will permit comparisons between studies. Accuracy in different experiments varies from extremely low to extremely high, and a simple percentage difference score does not take this into account. Krashen and Harshman (1972) have suggested "per cent of error" (POE) as an appropriate measure, where

$$POE = \frac{R \text{ (errors)} - L \text{ (errors)}}{R \text{ (errors)} + L \text{ (errors)}}$$

However, as Marshall *et al.* (1975) have indicated, this measure has difficulties with low levels of overall accuracy. Kuhn (1973) has recommended the phi-coefficient, but this does not have the same limits for all levels of accuracy. In the present chapter, a laterality coefficient (LC) proposed by Halwes (1969), and advocated by Bryden (1975) and Marshall *et al.* (1975), will be used when it is desired to compare different studies or different treatments. Essentially, this statistic expresses the observed degree of laterality as a percentage of the maximum possible difference that could have occurred given that particular level of overall accuracy. At all levels of accuracy, it has a range from -1 to $+1$, with an expected value of 0. By convention, positive scores will indicate a right superiority, and negative scores a left superiority. The statistic is equivalent to calculating a POE for accuracy levels above 50% and a similar "per cent of correct" (POC) measure for accuracy levels below 50%.

Like other statistics, the LC is not without its difficulties. First, it is applicable only to accuracy measures, and not to response time measures, and is therefore inappropriate to some studies. Secondly, it is often necessary to calculate the LC from the means given in published reports. Unfortunately, since subjects differ in their accuracy, this is not equivalent to calculating LCs for individual subjects and averaging them. Despite these problems, however, it does provide a convenient way of comparing the magnitude of laterality effects obtained in different conditions.

4. POSSIBLE SOURCES OF LATERALITY EFFECTS

There can be little doubt that there are laterality effects in a wide variety of situations. Our concern in the present chapter is how these might arise. There seem to be five rather general ways in which laterality effects might occur: they might be produced by the distribution of attention, by set, by individual differences in strategy, by the sequence of analysis, or by the true hemispheric asymmetry.

4.1. Distribution of attention in space

Laterality experiments involve the comparison of stimuli presented to the left side of the body with those presented, either simultaneously or successively, to an homologous area on the right side of the body. With virtually every procedure that has been employed, the subject is free to bias his attention to one side or the other. If, in a dichotic situation, a subject pays more attention to items arriving at the right ear than to those arriving at the left, it should not be very surprising if he does better with right-ear items.

It is clear that the way in which attention is deployed is at least partially under voluntary control, and some attentional biases result from conscious strategies adopted by subjects. In a verbal dichotic listening experiment, for example, the subject may realize that he is doing poorly on the left-ear items, and consciously direct more attention to the left ear than the right in an attempt to compensate. Such a strategy is, in fact, commonly reported by subjects.

The problems produced by such attentional biases are, if anything, even more obvious in tachistoscopic studies. To make a proper comparison between left and right visual fields, it is necessary to ensure that stimuli fall on homologous retinal areas, and to do this, one must know where the subject is fixating at the time of exposure. Because of this issue, most tachistoscopic studies (e.g. Bryden, 1965; Kimura, 1966) have involved the random presentation of stimuli in the left or right visual fields, a procedure that has become known as unilateral presentation. Since the subject cannot predict whether the next stimulus will appear in the left or the right visual field, there is no obvious reason to bias attention to one side or to fixate eccentrically. Most experimenters have been satisfied with this as a control for fixation bias, and have left it at that.

One investigator concerned with fixation control is McKeever. He and his colleagues (e.g. McKeever and Huling, 1971; McKeever, 1974) have had great success in obtaining large right visual field superiorities with a bilateral presentation procedure. In a typical experiment, two words are presented simultaneously, one in each visual field, with a small number at fixation. The subject must first identify the fixation number, thus demonstrating that he was fixating, before reporting the peripheral items. While such a procedure may well provide a better control of fixation, it may also introduce other contaminating factors (cf. White, 1973).

Even if one succeeds in controlling fixation, one may not have controlled attentional biases, and visual studies have shown remarkably little concern for this problem. As is the case with dichotic listening, subjects may well attend to one visual field more than the other, and this deployment of attention is certainly under voluntary control to some extent.

Even instructions to attend to or monitor one ear or visual field to the exclusion of the other may not be entirely adequate as a control over attentional biases, for it may well be easier to attend to one ear than to the other (cf. Treisman and Geffen, 1968).

Of course, to have major explanatory value, attentional biases would have to be task or stimulus-specific. That is, they would have to show right-side biases for verbal tasks, and left-side biases for non-verbal tasks. This is the essence of Kinsbourne's (1970, 1973, 1975) theory. However, while Kinsbourne's model requires that attentional biases exist, their existence does not require his model.

First of all, attentional biases may exist quite independently of hemispheric asymmetry. To speculate, the very fact that one is right-handed may lead one to bias attention to the right, quite independent of the cortical processes controlling speech and handedness. Some hint that this possibility should be taken seriously is contained in the original Kimura (1961b) study. This study involved the free recall of dichotically presented lists of numbers, three to each ear. The subjects were clinical patients of known cerebral lateralization, as determined by the sodium amytal test (Wada and Rasmussen, 1960). Although individual data and error estimates are not available, it is possible to calculate group laterality coefficients (*see above*) for each combination of handedness and speech lateralization. The results of such computations are shown in Table I. As Kimura claimed, subjects with left hemispheric speech are better at identifying right-ear numbers, while the reverse is true for those with right hemispheric speech. However, quite independent of this hemispheric asymmetry effect, there is a *handedness* effect: right-handers within either speech subgroup are more right-dominant than left-handers. One need not resort to laterality coefficients to see this: the same trend is apparent in Kimura's (1961b) original table. This analysis indicates that handedness has an effect on dichotic listening performance over and above that of speech lateralization. Of course, this effect may be related to hemispheric asymmetries that are not detected by the sodium amytal test, but it is entirely possible that they are produced by asymmetric biases related more to body tonus than to hemispheres.

Such an observation is rather disturbing, in that it suggests that the comparison of left- and right-handed subjects is not so powerful a means of determining whether a task is related to hemispheric asymmetry as many experimenters have thought (e.g. Bryden, 1965; Curry, 1967; Kinsbourne, 1972; Zurif and Bryden, 1969).

TABLE I. Laterality coefficients for groups differing in handedness and speech lateralization (data from Kimura, 1961b) (sample size in brackets).

| Handedness | Speech lateralization | | |
	Left	Right	Average
Left	0·106 (10)	−0·298 (9)	−0·096
Right	0·214 (93)	−0·075 (3)	0·070
Average	0·160	−0·187	−0·013

In addition, attentional biases may be quite idiosyncratic. Subjects may well try out different ways of distributing their attention, either to improve their performance or to see what will happen. While the results of such wanderings may not be systematic, they will certainly have an effect on performance. So long as we permit attentional biases to occur without trying to understand or control them, we run the risk that our measures of laterality will turn out to be measures of bias rather than of hemispheric asymmetry.

It is also worth pointing out that an attentional bias to the left or right could occur because of the type of task being performed (e.g. as in Kinsbourne's model), because of the characteristics of the subject (e.g. right-handedness), or because the subject consciously chose to bias his attention.

4.2. Set effects

A second possibility is that laterality effects are produced by the way in which the subject is set to perform the task that he is supposed to do. Again, this forms an integral part of Kinsbourne's theory: he would argue that the left hemisphere is primed when one is set to perform a verbal task, and the right primed when one is set for musical or spatial tasks. Although set is related to the deployment of attention in Kinsbourne's model, this need not be the case. It is possible, for instance, that a verbal set could prime the left hemisphere for right-side input without producing any real bias of fixation or attention to the right. Of course, in order to have any effect on laterality measures, the relevant processes must somehow be related to cerebral asymmetry.

One example of set effects is Spellacy and Blumstein's (1970) demonstration that a right-ear effect can be obtained for vowels if the subject expects to hear language material, while a left-ear effect is obtained with the same material in non-language context. Unfortunately, this study does not tell us whether the set had an influence by altering attentional biases to the left or right, or by changing the manner in which the material was processed.

If the expectancy of the task to be done sets a subject to use one mode of processing rather than another, and one hemisphere carries out one type of processing more efficiently than another, then it is clear that set can affect measured laterality. In so far as the subject can instruct himself to use a particular manner of processing, rather unexpected effects may appear. Sidtis and Bryden (1975) and Perl and Haggard (1975) have, for example, noted practice effects in dichotic listening that may be due to the subject learning a more optimal strategy.

4.3. Individual differences in processing strategy

There is a long history of attempts to classify people according to particular perceptual or cognitive styles (e.g. Gardner *et al.*, 1959; Witkin, 1949). There has recently been a renewed interest in individual differences in perceptual strategies (e.g. Hock *et al.*, 1974; Cooper, 1976). If people vary systematically in the way in which they process particular stimuli, and if the manner of processing affects laterality, then individual differences become of critical import in studies of laterality.

This issue has led to a confusion of interpretation that has yet to be resolved. Suppose we find (cf. Lake and Bryden, 1976) that men are more lateralized on a verbal dichotic listening task than are women. Does this mean that linguistic processes are more fully lateralized in the left hemisphere in men than in women, or, alternately, that men are more likely to approach the task as a linguistic one, while women are more likely to use non-linguistic strategies? At present, the interpretation offered seems to be dictated more by one's theoretical pre-conceptions than by any serious attempt to solve the problem.

4.4. The sequence of analysis

In some of the more common laterality procedures, some characteristic of the stimulus display may lead the subject to analyse the material in a particular sequence that produces a spurious laterality effect. Thus, it has sometimes been argued that laterality effects are due to order of report rather than to hemispheric asymmetry (Harcum, 1964; Inglis, 1962).

The relevance of the sequence of processing is particularly evident in tachistoscopic recognition studies. Heron (1957) and Bryden (1960, 1967a) have shown that tachistoscopically exposed letter rows are normally processed from left to right, and that this order of processing affects the pattern of recognition. Items on the left of the display, processed first and reported first, are identified with greater accuracy than items on the right of the display. Such directional scanning and report processes are certainly affected by reading experience (Mishkin and Forgays, 1952; Orbach, 1967), and can be controlled by the subject to some extent (Bryden *et al.*, 1968). According to Heron's (1957) arguments, the left-to-right scan gives an advantage to the left visual field with bilateral presentation, and to the right visual field with unilateral presentation.

Although any directional scan may be much faster with words than with letter rows, similar effects almost certainly occur. Furthermore, there is probably more information in the first letter of a word (nearest fixation in the right visual field) than in the last letter (nearest fixation in the left visual field), at least under conditions in which the stimulus set is limited: it is easier to think of an animal name beginning with T than to think of one ending in R.

Much the same approach can be seen in Inglis' (1962) critique of Kimura's original dichotic work. Bryden (1963) noted that, in free recall, most subjects choose to initiate their report with an item from the right ear, and that most subjects give first the items from one ear and then those from the other. Inglis pointed out that the items reported first have an advantage in short-term memory, since there is not so long between presentation and recall for them as for later reported items. The right-ear effect, he argued, could then be simply the result of reporting the items from the right ear first. Although much subsequent research has been devoted to eliminating this as a factor, it continues to be ignored by many workers attempting to show differences in cerebral organization between different groups, and is rediscovered with boring regularity.

4.5. Hemispheric asymmetry

Finally, the current vogue may well be perfectly correct, and laterality effects may arise from the differing properties of the two hemispheres, and the relative ease of transmitting information from one side of the body to the contralateral hemisphere. The fact that Kimura (1961b) found a highly significant difference in dichotic listening performance between subjects known to have left hemispheric speech representation and those known to have right hemispheric speech, is clear evidence that functional asymmetry is related to at least some aspect of dichotic listening. It is unfortunately far less clear whether the same statement can be made about the plethora of other tasks that show laterality effects.

While other factors undoubtedly influence the results obtained with specific procedures, the above considerations seem to be most pertinent to the majority of laterality studies. If one accepts the idea that a wide variety of factors can influence the results of a specific experiment, it is easy to see that relatively few, if any, studies have completely isolated the relevant variables. Since we are still groping towards an understanding of hemispheric asymmetry, such negligence is forgivable in those studies that are primarily concerned with mechanism. However, recent years have seen a greater interest in the relation of hemispheric functioning to typological and pathological variables, and it is here that over-enthusiasm is at its worst. Many experimenters are guilty of taking a laterality procedure that shows consistent results, administering it to groups that differ in some way, and concluding that the groups differ in cerebral organization, with no consideration for the other factors that might lead to performance differences.

5. COMMENTS ON SOME EXPERIMENTAL PROCEDURES

To develop the argument more fully, let us examine in detail some of the more commonly used experimental procedures for studying laterality effects. These procedures are precisely the ones that are most likely to be employed by investigators from other subfields interested in particular pathologies, and thus are the ones most likely to appear in work making extravagant claims about differences in hemispheric organization.

Of all the techniques for investigating laterality effects in normals, the dichotic listening procedure is the oldest and most commonly used. It is fitting that a commentary on the way in which voluntary strategies could affect performance in laterality experiments should begin with this procedure.

5.1. Dichotic listening procedures

Many of the studies of dichotic listening have followed the procedures developed by Kimura for studying speech lateralization (Kimura, 1961a, b) and non-verbal laterality (Kimura, 1964). It is therefore well worth taking a careful look at these procedures to see what kinds of variables might affect performance.

Kimura's (1961a) verbal procedure involved the presentation of one list of three numbers to the left ear, and, at the same time, a second list of three different numbers to the right ear. Subjects were told to listen to the material and to report as many of the numbers as they could, in any order they chose.

At the rate of presentation used, one pair of numbers every half second, the majority of subjects report first the three numbers from one ear, and then the three from the other ear. Errors tend to appear on the second ear reported (Bryden, 1962). Subjects are also rather more likely to give the right ear first than the left (Bryden, 1963).

In adult right-handed subjects—those presumably having left-hemispheric speech representation—a right-ear superiority is normally observed. However, while virtually all right-handers have left-hemispheric speech (Milner et al., 1964; Rossi and Rosadini, 1967), only about 85% of normal subjects show a right-ear advantage in the dichotic task. Obviously, there is not a one-to-one correspondence between ear advantage and speech lateralization. Other factors must enter to determine the final scores.

What might these other factors be? Not all subjects report the items from one ear and then the other (Bryden, 1962), and perhaps those who use other strategies do not show the right-ear advantage. Perhaps the choice of starting ear is important. Certainly, reporting the right ear first puts the left ear at a disadvantage, and Bryden (1963) has reported a significant correlation between starting ear and the laterality effect. Furthermore, the task is one in which the subject has freedom in how to deploy his attention: he can attend to one ear and hope to get items from the other, or he can try to divide attention equally between the two ears. Final performance on the task can be determined by factors of attention, perception, memory, order of report and starting bias. Kimura's (1961b) results make it evident that overall performance is correlated with speech lateralization, but this correlation can arise for many reasons. While all of the above factors might be related to cerebral lateralization, it is equally possible that only one or a few are involved in the correlation, and others simply serve to introduce error variance. The fact that some presumably left-hemispheric subjects fail to show the right-ear advantage makes the latter explanation more likely.

The approach employed by dichotic listening experimenters has been one of simplifying the task, removing one or more of the possible sources of error, and seeing if the right-ear advantage remains. Thus Bryden (1963) employed an instructed order of report, requiring subjects to give the right ear before the left on half the trials, and the left before the right on the other half. A right-ear advantage was observed, and in about the same proportion of subjects as is found with the free recall procedure. From this, one can conclude that starting bias and report strategy are sources of error that are probably unrelated to speech lateralization.

The relevance of the memory component is less clearly understood. Some investigators (e.g. Satz et al., 1965; Blumstein et al., 1975) are quite convinced that laterality effects are much more pronounced on the second ear than on the first. However, accuracy is very much higher on the first ear than on the second, and the seeming difference in the absolute laterality effect may be the result of right-ear scores being so close to ceiling (cf. Bryden, 1967b). An examination of those studies using lists of words or numbers suggests that large laterality effects are just as likely to occur on the first ear recalled as on the second.

Nevertheless, procedures have been developed to reduce the in-fluence of memory factors. One method is to use only a single pair of items, frequently CV or CVC syllables (Studdert-Kennedy and Shank-weiler, 1970). This has the additional advantage of permitting more precise control over the onset times, durations and intensities of the stimuli. However, so long as both items are to be reported, one must be given first and the other second, and some small memory component still exists. Studies in my own laboratory indicate that accuracy is very much poorer on the second item given than on the first, when the stimuli are single pairs of CV syllables. Presumably the way to control this is to have the subjects report only a single stimulus on any given trial, as did Haggard and Parkinson (1971).

Another procedure to reduce the memory factor was introduced by Springer (1971). Subjects listen to a continuous stream of speech arriving at both ears, and are asked to press a response key whenever a particular target sound or syllable occurs. With this procedure, response times are faster to targets presented to the right ear than to those presented to the left.

Even with control over memory factors, some investigators believe that short-term memory factors are critical in producing the laterality effect (Darwin and Baddeley, 1974; Yeni-Komshian and Gordon,

1974). Darwin and Baddeley, for example, argue that large laterality effects are observed for material that is difficult to store in echoic memory, such as stop consonants, while little laterality is found with material such as vowels.

While the distinction between memory and perceptual factors as determinants of the laterality effects is an interesting and unresolved issue, there is little data on how strategies of perceiving or remembering relate to verbal dichotic listening tasks. The role of attention is an even more critical issue. In the experimental situation, the subject can choose to deploy his attention in a number of ways: he can attend to one ear, he can divide attention equally between the two ears, or he can bias it in favour of one side. The significance of possible attentional biases has become a critical one. If one takes the position that the right-ear advantage arises because of the superior ability of the left hemisphere to process verbal signals (Kimura, 1967; Studdert-Kennedy and Shankweiler, 1970), then attentional biases are something to be controlled. On the other hand, Kinsbourne (1970, 1975) has made attentional bias the basis for much of the laterality effect. According to his model, attending to speech signals or being set to deal with speech signals activates the left hemisphere and produces an attentional bias towards the right. This is manifested by a shift of eyes and head towards the right, and by an increased sensitivity of the left hemisphere to incoming stimulation. At its strongest, Kinsbourne's model would lead us to predict that the right-ear advantage for verbal material would disappear if all attentional factors were properly controlled. This would require, first, that the subject was not set for verbal material, since the verbal set introduces a bias towards the right, and second, that accuracy on the two ears was measured under identical attentional conditions. This latter requirement is somewhat more difficult to achieve than seems at first glance.

Clearly any instructions that permit the subject to select the manner in which attention is deployed open the gates for a bias to one side or the other. Thus, for instance, in Springer's (1971) reaction time procedure, the subject may very well bias his attention to one side or the other. A partial solution to this is to get the subject to monitor one channel to the exclusion of the other. Thus, one may include a condition in which the subject is required to attend to the right ear and ignore the left, and a second condition in which the reverse is true (e.g. Schwartz, 1970). Even this has its difficulties. If Kinsbourne's model is right, it may well be easier to attend to verbal material arriving at the right ear than that arriving at the left ear. Certainly, the subjective experience of monitoring dichotic lists would suggest that this is true.

If verbal dichotic procedures have so many possible sources of bias, what about the non-verbal procedures? Again, experimenters have tended to copy Kimura's initial procedure (Kimura, 1964). In this experiment, subjects heard two passages of music, one at each ear. These two samples were followed by a sequence of four binaurally presented alternatives. The subject had to choose which two of these alternatives matched the two that had been presented dichotically. While some of the problems associated with the free recall of dichotic lists are avoided with this procedure, there are still several possible sources for any observed ear effect. There may be, as Kimura (1964, 1966) has argued, a perceptual difference between the left and right hemispheres for musical stimuli. On the other hand, some of the attentional factors suggested by Kinsbourne (1970, 1975) may also be of import. The procedure does not make any attempt to determine how the subject deploys his attention, and the subject may consciously attend to the left ear in preference to the right. More subtly, it may be easier to attend to musical stimuli arriving at the left ear than at the right. Finally, because the procedure involves the presentation of four separate alternatives, spread out over some 8 to 10 seconds, that are physical matches to the original dichotic stimuli, complex echoic and short-term memory effects may be involved.

Some attempts have been made to rectify some of these problems. Spellacy (1970) and Sidtis and Bryden (1975) have employed A–B–X paradigms, in which a single foil is presented following the dichotic pair, which either matches one of the pair or does not. Kallman and Corballis (1975) have used a monitoring task, in which the subject listens for a particular signal and responds to it as rapidly as possible. While these may eliminate possible memory factors, they do not solve the attention problem. Although there have been many reports of non-verbal dichotic effects, we can say remarkably little about the relative significance of attentional and perceptual factors.

What is clear, however, is that non-verbal dichotic effects do not give a left-ear advantage of nearly the magnitude of the verbal right-ear effect. This seems to be generally true for musical stimuli (Kimura, 1964; Kallman and Corballis, 1975; Spellacy, 1970; Spreen et al., 1970), environmental sounds (Curry, 1967, 1968), singing (Bartholomeus, 1974a, b), musical chords (Gordon, 1970), emotional tone (Haggard and Parkinson, 1971; Carmon and Nachson, 1973), hummed melodies (King and Kimura, 1972) and sonar signals (Chaney and Webster,1966).

5.2. Visual procedures

As well as the large body of knowledge concerning dichotic listening, there is an immense literature on visual laterality. In general, a right visual field superiority is found for the recognition of letters or words, and a left visual field superiority for various non-verbal or spatial tasks. Virtually all of this literature has employed procedures of tachistoscopic presentation, in which the stimulus material is exposed for 150 ms or less. Such a procedure has been used to reduce or eliminate the possibility of eye movements taking place during stimulus presentation, but it does represent a fundamental difference between the visual and auditory procedures. Furthermore, in dichotic listening, the individual stimuli would be clearly intelligible if they were presented alone without competing material; in a tachistoscopic task, the stimuli are degraded by the very brief presentation.

Much of the literature on visual laterality has its origins in early experiments by Mishkin and Forgays (1952) and Heron (1957), although neither paper addressed the question of cerebral asymmetry. Mishkin and Forgays (1952) found that words were more readily identified when they appeared to the right, rather than to the left, of a central fixation point. They also found that readers of Hebrew tended to favour the left visual field rather than the right, suggesting a directional scanning interpretation rather than a cerebral asymmetry effect. Later, Heron (1957) showed that a right visual field superiority was obtained with single letters or rows of letters when they were exposed unilaterally, that is, with items only in the left visual field on some trials, and only in the right visual field on other trials. In contrast, a left visual field superiority was found when the material extended across the fixation point and appeared in both visual fields simultaneously (bilateral presentation).

Heron (1957) argued that this pattern of results could be accounted for by post-exposural scanning processes. With bilateral presentation, the row of letters was scanned from left to right in accordance with English reading habits: since the items on the left were scanned first, they could be processed and recalled, while by the time the scanning process had reached the items on the right, trace strength had decayed below that necessary for recognition. Thus, a left visual field superiority was found with bilateral presentation. In contrast, with unilateral presentation, the subject was already fixated at the beginning of the line when the items were in the right visual field, but had to shift attention to the left when items appeared in the left visual field: thus, the right visual field superiority for unilateral presentation.

Because of Heron's (1957) work, much of the early research on visual laterality with verbal material employed unilateral presentation, and virtually all of the non-verbal work has done so. While Heron's specific arguments about the processes involved in unilateral recognition may hold for horizontal rows of letters, it is somewhat more difficult to accept the relevance of a left-to-right scan in studies involving single letters (Bryden, 1964, 1965), or vertical arrays of letters (Barton *et al.*, 1965; Bryden, 1969). For example, Bryden (1965) showed that a right visual field superiority for single letters was much more readily obtained in right-handers than in left-handers; that is, those subjects who would be expected to be left-hemispheric for speech were more likely to be right visual field superior than those whose speech lateralization was more uncertain.

Following this, many verbal experiments and a vast majority of the non-verbal experiments employed procedures designed to eliminate scanning effects by presenting stimuli unilaterally (e.g. Kimura, 1966, 1969; Durnford and Kimura, 1971; Cohen, 1972, 1973).

More recently, other procedures have become popular. Impressed with the success of dichotic listening procedures, many investigators have attempted to produce competitive situations which are the visual analogue of the dichotic task. For instance, Zurif and Bryden (1969) and Hines *et al.* (1969) have produced visual tasks that are similar to dichotic lists. In the Hines *et al.* procedure, for example, a film strip is used to present a series of pairs of letters, with one letter appearing in each visual field, followed by a second letter in each visual field, and so on. Not only does this procedure yield a right visual field superiority (Hines *et al.*, 1969) but Hines (1972) reports that it correlates well with dichotic results. This is perhaps not as compelling as it might seem at first glance, since many of the same strategy options affect both visual and dichotic lists.

A third approach has been advocated by McKeever (1971; McKeever and Huling, 1970, 1971), employing bilateral presentation. Heron's (1957) work made it clear that one of the advantages of unilateral presentation was that the subject did not know on any given trial whether the stimulus would appear in the left or the right visual field. Thus, at least from the experimenter's point of view, there was nothing to be gained by biasing fixation to one side or the other. In contrast, with bilateral presentation, the subject always knew where the material would appear, and could employ a fixation strategy that would optimize his performance. McKeever has attempted to circumvent this difficulty by introducing a new technique for controlling fixation. He presents words bilaterally, one on each side of fixation. At fixation, a small number appears at the same time as the stimulus material. The subject is required to identify the digit before reporting the words. Such a procedure leads to a right visual field superiority for words far in excess of that obtained with unilateral presentation (McKeever, 1971; McKeever and Huling, 1971; Hines, 1972).

Hines (1975) argues that the McKeever procedure, by employing competition like the dichotic listening procedure, sets up conditions in which the left hemisphere processes right visual field material, while the right hemisphere processes left visual field material. Thus, bilateral presentation permits one to assess the capacities of each hemisphere independently. In contrast, unilateral presentation involves no competition, and thus permits left visual field material to be shunted by the right hemisphere to the left, and processed there. Unilateral presentation, therefore, is more appropriate for assessing callosal transmission time and loss than for determining the functions of the right hemisphere.

McKeever's bilateral presentation procedure is not without its critics. One possibility, for instance, is that by forcing recall of the centre digit first, one led subjects to report the item to the right of the digit. However, the right visual field superiority is maintained with ordered recall (McKeever and Huling, 1971), and with other methods of fixation control (McKeever et al., 1972; Olsen, 1973; Kershner and Jeng, 1972).

More recently, Hirata and Bryden (1976) have found that the right visual field superiority with bilateral presentation is dependent on the presence of a gap between the left and right halves of the display. This suggests that scanning factors or localization of the beginning of the display is critical even when order of report is controlled. Along these lines, one should remember that McKeever's experiments involve words of four or more letters, and that internal scanning processes may be relevant within these words.

It is evident, then, that the visual procedures used to study laterality may well involve components that have little or nothing to do with hemispheric functioning. It has become far too commonplace for researchers to assume that any observed laterality effect indicates something about brain processes and cerebral specialization. Controlling fixation has proved to be difficult. With unilateral presentation, most experimenters have been rather cavalier in the control of fixation, assuming that randomizing trials between left and right fields is sufficient to ensure that subjects fixate the central spot. That such may not be the case is suggested by the results of Bryden and Rainey (1963), who found that the magnitude of the right visual field superiority for single letters depended on how strongly fixation instructions were emphasized. With bilateral presentation, fixation control has been somewhat more adequate, but even here it is not clear how such procedures as using a central digit may affect performance. Even if fixation is controlled, more attention may be given to one side than to the other (Kinsbourne, 1975), and this has proven even more difficult to control.

Two other observations about visual laterality studies should be made. First, it is rather surprising how rarely any attempt is made to link visual field effects to hemispheric functioning either directly or indirectly. The relation to hemispheric asymmetry is assumed rather than demonstrated. Even the demonstration that left-handers differ from right-handers has rarely been made, although Bryden (1965) and Zurif and Bryden (1969) have done so for unilaterally presented single letters. In addition, there have been remarkably few attempts to control the processing strategies involved in dealing with a single task. Almost invariably, a subject is given a single task, and may adopt virtually any strategy he chooses for dealing with it. The results are then compared to other visual tasks, administered to different subjects with potentially different sets. Rarely, for instance, have both verbal and non-verbal materials been intermingled in the same experiment (*but see* Terrace, 1959). This is critical, for if processing strategies affect the results, foreknowledge of the type of material to be shown permits the subject to adopt a strategy appropriate to the material. Given a different type of material, the subject may choose to behave in a totally different fashion. To infer differences in brain organization from such data is rashness indeed.

5.3. An illustrative experiment

Even with the refinement of using only a single dichotic pair, the specific instructions may influence the way in which the subject behaves and thus may affect the observed laterality effect. To examine the effects of instructions in detail, we carried out an experiment in which a group of sixteen right-handed subjects were tested under each of four different conditions.

The materials for this experiment were pairs of CV syllables, using the six stop consonants paired with the vowel /a/. There were a total of 30 different stimulus pairs. Following an initial practice session, all subjects were given 60 trials under each of the four instructions, in counterbalanced order, a total of 240 trials per subject. Order effects in the experiment were minimal.

Two of the instructions may be considered to have demanded divided attention. In one condition, the subjects were told to listen to the stimulus pairs, and to identify the two that were presented, giving the one about which they were most certain first, and then the other. Subjects were required to give two responses on each trial, even though one may have been a guess. Because our previous experience had been that accuracy on the second response was very poor, we used a second condition in which the subjects were told to give the one response of which they were most certain, and to give a second response only if they thought they were right. These two conditions will be referred to as the "Give 2" and the "Give 1+" conditions. Both permitted the subject to deploy his attention in any way he chose, although the instructions encouraged a division of attention between the ears.

The other two conditions required a focusing of attention to one ear or the other. In one case, subjects were told to listen to the right ear and to report only the items that arrived at that ear. A single response was required on every trial. In a further condition, subjects were required to attend to the left ear rather than the right.

The results of this experiment are shown in Table II. Since our experience had been that the second response was very inaccurate, the Give 2 and Give 1+ data were scored for the first response only as well as for total accuracy. This first table indicates that a right-ear superiority was observed in all of the conditions.

TABLE II. Mean accuracy on dichotic pairs under different instructions.

	Left ear	Right ear	t	Laterality coefficient
Give 2				
First response	24·50	30·06	1·72	0·102
Total	39·94	45·31	3·54[b]	0·158
Give 1+				
First response	24·25	31·56	2·14[a]	0·132
Total	34·81	39·75	2·12	0·107
Attend	34·44	41·25	4·26[c]	0·150

[a] $p < 0.05$.
[b] $p < 0.01$.
[c] $p < 0.001$.

Perhaps the most meaningful point about these data is that, while the laterality effect is of about the same magnitude in all conditions, it is somewhat more stable in the Attend conditions than in the two divided attention conditions. Thus, the t value for correct responses in the Attend condition is much larger than that in the Give 2 or Give 1+ conditions. This would suggest that the control of attention provided by the Attend instructions reduces an extraneous error factor that is present in the divided attention conditions. In this sense, the Attend instructions yield data that are less likely to be influenced by the idiosyncratic decisions of the subject as to how to distribute his attention, and thus provide a better test of cerebral lateralization.

5.3.1. Scoring the Attend condition

The interpretation of these results is not without its difficulties. In the Attend condition, the right-ear score is based on one block of sixty trials, while the left-ear score is based on a different set of sixty trials. On the other hand, in the divided attention conditions, both left and right ear scores are based on the same sixty trials. Furthermore, two responses are scored on every trial in the divided attention conditions, while only one is permitted in the focused conditions. Finally, and most critically, subjects need not specify the ear of arrival in the divided attention conditions, while they must do so, at least implicitly, in the Attend conditions. In effect, then, the Attend data are based on information that provides both correct identity and correct location, while the divided attention data require only correct identity.

There are several approaches to this problem, none of which are entirely satisfactory. One might argue that the right ear should be credited with every right-ear item that managed to get through, regardless of the attentional instructions, and similarly for the left ear. This would lead to a left-ear score that was the sum of the Attend left corrects and the Attend right intrusions, and vice versa for the right ear. If one does this, the overall laterality effect does not change appreciably ($t = 3 \cdot 93$, $p < 0 \cdot 01$). Mathematically, it is equivalent to subtracting one item from the correct score for each intrusion.

Likewise, it is difficult to decide whether the Attend conditions should be compared to the total data for the divided attention conditions, or to the first response data only. If one opts for the first response, then the Attend conditions clearly give a more stable laterality effect. The increase in laterality seen in the Give 2 condition when the second response data are included may be another manifestation of what has been termed the "second ear effect" (Blumstein et al., 1975).

5.3.2. Attentional biases

While there may be greater stability with Attend instructions than with divided attention instructions, it remains possible that it is easier to attend to the right ear than to the left. Certainly, Kinsbourne (1975) would argue that this is the case for verbal material.

One measure of how successful the subject was in following the Attend instructions is the number of intrusions he makes (see Table III). Since one cannot tell anything about what the subject was doing from an error, we computed an attentional index by dividing the number of intrusions by the number of responses to items that were actually presented, i.e. intrusions/(intrusions + corrects). Under Attend Left instructions, 32·5% of the responses were intrusions, while only 24·3% were intrusions under Attend Right instructions ($t = 3·41$, $p < 0·01$). This analysis indicates that it is, in fact, easier for subjects to attend to the right ear than to the left.

TABLE III. Mean scores for different responses under Attend instructions.

	Attend left	Attend right	t
Correct responses	34·44	41·25	4·26[a]
Intrusions	16·56	13·19	
Errors	9·00	5·56	

[a] $p < 0·001$.

Among our sixteen subjects, some showed rather gross differences between left and right ears in intrusion rates, while others did not. We divided these subjects into two subgroups of eight. One of these groups may be called biased attenders, showing a mean of 40·3% intrusions when attending left, and only 23·7% when attending to the right ear. The others were unbiased attenders, with intrusion rates of 24·7% and 24·8% for the left and right ears respectively. We then compared these two groups on our other dichotic measures of laterality. A summary of the findings is shown in Table IV. Remember that the definition of biased and unbiased attenders is based solely on the two Attend conditions, and does not employ information from the two divided attention conditions.

The results are striking in that a significant laterality effect exists for the biased attention group in all comparisons, while it appears in none for the unbiased group. Assuming that subjects who are biased attenders in the Attend conditions are also biased when they are free to deploy their attention the way they choose, then virtually all of the laterality effects in these data can be attributed to the biased attenders.

At one level, then, Kinsbourne is correct. It is easier to attend to the right ear in a verbal dichotic experiment, and this fact leads to a significant right-ear advantage. It does not necessarily follow, however, that the rest of Kinsbourne's model is correct. It is necessary to see if the opposite effect occurs with non-verbal material.

Does this imply that all of the right-ear advantage is attributable to

TABLE IV. Summary of differences between biased and unbiased attenders.

| | Mean difference between left and right ears | | |
	Unbiased attenders ($N = 8$)	Biased attenders ($N = 8$)	Difference between groups (t)
Give 2			
First response	− 0·50	11·62[b]	2·07[a]
Total	2·00	8·75[c]	2·62[b]
Give 1+			
First response	0·75	13·88[b]	2·16[b]
Total	−0·50	10·38[c]	2·89[b]
Attend			
Correct responses	2·75	10·88[c]	3·25[c]
Ignoring intrusions[d] $\left\{ \dfrac{\text{Correct}}{\text{Correct} + \text{error}} \right\}$	0·083[a]	0·101[a]	0·55

[a] $p < 0.10$.
[b] $p < 0.05$.
[c] $p < 0.01$.
[d] This difference is expressed as a difference in proportions, rather than as a difference in mean items identified.

an attentional bias? We think not, although the present data make it very clear that such bias has a powerful effect. One other analysis reveals an accuracy difference that is unrelated to attentional bias. When a subject gives an intrusion response, we know relatively little about his ability to detect the target stimulus: we know only that the strength of the unattended item was greater. To obtain a measure of accuracy uncontaminated by attentional errors and biases, then, it is perhaps important to see what happens when intrusions do not occur. An accuracy index based on such trials is corrects/(corrects + errors). When this index is computed, we find an overall right-ear superiority (79·3% left ear, 88·5% right ear, $t = 3·25$, $p < 0·01$), and no difference at all between unbiased and biased attenders, with both groups showing differences at the 0·10 level because of the small N values (see Table IV, last line).

This analysis indicates that there is a right-ear advantage independent of attentional bias. Such a superiority is presumably attributable to the easier access that right-ear material has to the left hemisphere language processing centres (Kimura, 1967).

This experiment has led us a long way. For many reasons, the Attend instructions give more useful results than do divided attention instructions, even though the latter have been much more commonly employed in the past. Attend instructions give more stable laterality effects, better control of the distribution of attention, and, as we have seen, make it possible to separate attentional biases and identification accuracy.

In addition, the present experiment provides very strong support for Kinsbourne's position that attentional biases have a very profound influence on dichotic laterality effects. However, there is also evidence that there is a right-ear superiority in identification that is independent of attentional bias. It remains to be seen how these two factors relate to cerebral mechanisms.

5.4. Implications

In the preceding pages, we have seen that the commonly used experimental procedures for assessing laterality effects in normals permit many possible factors to control the magnitude of the laterality effect observed. Some of these are directly related to cerebral function, others, like the deployment of attention, may be, and still others may well have nothing at all to do with cerebral asymmetry. Adequate procedures for separating out all the factors are only now being developed.

Such an analysis has far-reaching implications for the interpretation of laterality studies. Most studies speculating about abnormalities in cerebral organization as a result of some particular pathology, such as dyslexia, or about the development of cerebral asymmetry, have used one of the more common procedures discussed above. But if these procedures fail to distinguish between true laterality, attentional bias, and strategy effects, then to what can we attribute the reported differences? Is it not just as likely that all of the differences between groups are due to one of the confounding factors we have isolated as that they are attributable to true differences in cerebral organization?

Let us consider a few examples. Lake and Bryden (1976), as one instance, reported a sex difference in dichotic listening performance, such that men were more likely to show the right-ear effect than were women. However, in their task they presented pairs of CV syllables, with instructions for their subjects to report both if they could. By the arguments above, this procedure fails to control the deployment of attention to one side or the other, and permits a bias in the order of responding to the two items. Thus the sex differences reported may well be a function of some factor other than cerebral organization.

An instance of a similar difficulty in tachistoscopic studies can be seen in the work of Marcel *et al.* (1974) and Marcel and Rajan (1975). These workers have reported a relationship between reading ability and right visual field superiority for word recognition. Their test procedure involves standard unilateral presentation, with the addition of a post-exposure mask. However, these studies did not involve any fixation control other than instruction and the unpredictability of unilateral presentation. Even with such control, there was no measure of the deployment of attention: subjects may very well have been biased towards the left or the right. Finally, the study does not permit an assessment of the interaction of reading strategies with cerebral laterality. If Heron's (1957) arguments have any merit, some of the right visual field superiority can be attributed to the normal strategy of scanning from left to right. To the extent that this affects the results, the two Marcel experiments may do little more than to show that good readers read more efficiently than poor readers.

A third example is provided by Witelson (1976). She found that the normal left-hand (right hemisphere) superiority on a bimanual analogue of a non-verbal dichotic listening task was absent in poor readers. She concluded that poor readers showed a deficit in right hemispheric function. If one can criticize the original Kimura (1961a, b) experiments for opening the way to many different sources of variation, the same faults are even more obvious in tactual work. Witelson presented a series of pairs of forms, for simultaneous palpation, then required free recall of the identity of these forms. Possible influences of order of recall, the deployment of attention, memory factors, and even the simple strategy of being more active with one hand that the other are all confounded with any influence of cerebral asymmetry. With a rate of presentation far slower than that commonly used in dichotic listening, the opportunity for conscious manipulations of recall are magnified. There may be a difference between good and poor readers on the task, but it is not certain that this difference has anything to do with cerebral organization.

6. IN CONCLUSION

In the preceding pages, we have examined some of the procedures employed in the investigation of perceptual laterality effects. It is now commonplace to interpret the laterality effects obtained with these procedures as arising from the differing capacities of the two hemispheres.

Yet, as we have seen, there is a plethora of other factors that may contribute to the laterality effect observed in any given experiment. To some extent, performance is dictated by the task that is set to the subject, and to some extent by the way in which the subject chooses to do the task. Very critically, laterality effects can be determined by the way in which the subject deploys his attention. These points make it evident that perceptual laterality experiments often measure something more than cerebral lateralization: the results are profoundly affected by the way in which the subject approaches the task.

If one is concerned primarily with the investigation of cerebral asymmetries in the normal subject, then we must take every precaution to minimize the subject's control over the situation. In particular, the subject cannot be left free to deploy his attention as he chooses, but some formal control must be employed. Otherwise, we run the danger of measuring not cerebral lateralization, but how the subject responds to the situation.

On the other hand, it is entirely possible that the particular strategies that a subject employs in a laterality experiment are not determined adventitiously, but are determined, at least in part, by the cerebral organization. Thus, a subject may choose to attend to the right ear in a dichotic listening experiment not simply because of some strategy to improve performance, but because his brain is organized with the speech functions lateralized in the left hemisphere. At present, hard evidence relating cerebral lateralization to the choice of strategy is lacking, and this is one issue to which future experimentation should be addressed.

ACKNOWLEDGEMENTS

This work was supported by Grant No. A–95 from the National Research Council of Canada. Kevin Munhall collected the data reported in Section 5.3. The author is indebted to P. M. Rowe, S. M. Tapley and T. G. Waller for their critical commentaries on content and style.

REFERENCES

Bakan, P. and Strayer, F. F. (1973). On reliability of conjugate lateral eye movements. *Perceptual and Motor Skills* **36**, 429–430.
Bartholomeus, B. (1974a). Effects of task requirements on ear superiority for sung speech. *Cortex* **10**, 215–223.

Bartholomeus, B. (1974b). Dichotic singer and speaker recognition. *Bulletin of the Psychonomic Society* **2**, 407–408.

Barton, M. I., Goodglass, H. and Shai, A. (1965). The differential recognition of tachistoscopically presented English and Hebrew words in the right and left visual fields. *Perceptual and Motor Skills* **21**, 431–437.

Blumstein, S. and Cooper, W. E. (1974). Hemispheric processing of intonation contours. *Cortex* **10**, 146–158.

Blumstein, S., Goodglass, H. and Tartter, J. (1975). The reliability of ear advantage in dichotic listening. *Brain and Language*, **2**, 226–236.

Bryden, M. P. (1960). Tachistoscopic recognition of non-alphabetical material. *Canadian Journal of Psychology* **14**, 78–86.

Bryden, M. P. (1962). Order of report in dichotic listening. *Canadian Journal of Psychology* **16**, 291–299.

Bryden, M. P. (1963). Ear preference in auditory perception. *Journal of Experimental Psychology* **65**, 103–105.

Bryden, M. P. (1964). Tachistoscopic recognition and cerebral dominance. *Perceptual and Motor Skills* **19**, 686.

Bryden, M. P. (1965). Tachistoscopic recognition, handedness, and cerebral dominance. *Neuropsychologia* **3**, 1–8.

Bryden, M. P. (1967a). A model for the sequential organization of behavior. *Canadian Journal of Psychology* **21**, 36–56.

Bryden, M. P. (1967b). An evaluation of some models of laterality effects in dichotic listening. *Acta Oto-laryngologica* **63**, 595–604.

Bryden, M. P. (1969). Binaural competition and division of attention as determinants of the laterality effect in dichotic listening. *Canadian Journal of Psychology* **23**, 101–113.

Bryden, M. P. (1970). Laterality effects in dichotic listening: Relations with handedness and reading ability in children. *Neuropsychologia* **8**, 443–450.

Bryden, M. P. (1975). Speech lateralization in families: A preliminary study using dichotic listening. *Brain and Language* **2**, 201–211.

Bryden, M. P. and Allard, F. (1978). Dichotic listening and the development of linguistic processes. *In* "Asymmetrical Functions of the Brain" (M. Kinsbourne, ed.). Cambridge University Press, Cambridge.

Bryden, M. P. and Rainey, C. A. (1963). Left–right differences in tachistoscopic recognition. *Journal of Experimental Psychology* **66**, 568–571.

Bryden, M. P., Dick, A. O. and Mewhort, D. J. K. (1968). Tachistoscopic recognition of number sequences. *Canadian Journal of Psychology* **22**, 52–59.

Carmon, A. and Nachson, I. (1973). Ear asymmetry in perception of emotional non-verbal stimuli. *Acta Psychologia* **37**, 351–357.

Chaney, R. and Webster, J. C. (1966). Information in certain multidimensional sounds. *The Journal of the Acoustical Society of America* **40**, 447–455.

Cohen, G. (1972). Hemispheric differences in a letter classification task. *Perception and Psychophysics* **11**, 139–142.

Cohen, G. (1973). Hemispheric differences in serial versus parallel processing. *Journal of Experimental Psychology* **97**, 349–356.

Cooper, L. A. (1976). Individual differences in visual comparison processes. *Perception and Psychophysics* **19**, 433–444.

Curry, F. K. W. (1967). A comparison of left-handed and right-handed subjects on verbal and nonverbal dichotic listening tasks. *Cortex* **3**, 343–352.

Curry, F. K. W. (1968). A comparison of the performances of a right hemispherectomized subject and 25 normals on four dichotic listening tasks. *Cortex* **4**, 144–153.

Curry, F. K. W. and Gregory, H. H. (1969). The performance of stutterers in dichotic listening tasks thought to reflect cerebral dominance. *Journal of Speech and Hearing Research* **12**, 73–82.

Darwin, C. J. and Baddeley, A. D. (1974). Acoustic memory and the perception of speech. *Cognitive Psychology* **6**, 41–60.

Durnford, M. and Kimura, D. (1971). Right hemisphere specialization for depth perception reflected in visual field differences. *Nature* **231**, 394–395.

Galin, D. and Ornstein, R. (1974). Individual differences in cognitive style: 1. Reflective eye movements. *Neuropsychologia* **12**, 367–376.

Gardner, E. B. and Branski, D. M. (1976). Unilateral cerebral activation and perception of gaps: A signal detection analysis. *Neuropsychologia* **14**, 43–53.

Gardner, R. W., Holzman, P. S., Klein, G. S., Linton, H. B. and Spence, D. P. (1959). Cognitive control: A study of individual consistencies in cognitive behavior. *Psychological Issues* **1**, No. 4.

Gazzaniga, M. S. (1970). "The Bisected Brain". Appleton-Century-Crofts, New York.

Geffen, G., Bradshaw, J. L. and Wallace, G. (1971). Interhemispheric effects on reaction time to verbal and nonverbal visual stimuli. *Journal of Experimental Psychology* **87**, 415–422.

Geffner, D. S. and Hochberg, I. (1971). Ear laterality performance of children from low and middle socioeconomic levels on a verbal dichotic listening task. *Cortex* **7**, 193–203.

Gordon, H. W. (1970). Hemispheric asymmetries in the perception of musical chords. *Cortex* **6**, 387–398.

Haggard, M. P. and Parkinson, A. M. (1971). Stimulus and task factors as determinants of ear advantage. *Quarterly Journal of Experimental Psychology* **23**, 168–177.

Halperin, Y., Nachson, I. and Carmon, A. (1973). Shift of ear superiority in dichotic listening to temporarily patterned nonverbal stimuli. *The Journal of the Acoustical Society of America* **53**, 46–50.

Halwes, T. G. (1969). Effects of dichotic fusion on the perception of speech. *Supplement to Status Report on Speech Research*, Haskins Laboratories, New Haven, Connecticut.

Harcum E. R. (1964). Effects of symmetry on the perception of tachistoscopic patterns. *The American Journal of Psychology* **77**, 600–606.

Heron, W. (1957). Perception as a function of retinal locus and attention. *The American Journal of Psychology* **70**, 38–48.

Hines, D. (1972). Bilateral tachistoscope recognition of verbal and nonverbal stimuli. *Cortex* **8**, 315–322.

Hines, D. (1975). Independent functioning of the two cerebral hemispheres for recognizing bilaterally presented tachistoscopic visual half-field stimuli. *Cortex* **11**, 132–143.

Hines, D., Satz, P., Schell, B. and Schmidlin, S. (1969). Differential recall of digits in the left and right visual half-fields under free and fixed order of recall. *Neuropsychologia* **7**, 13–22.

Hirata, K. and Bryden, M. P. (1976). Right visual field superiority for letter recognition with partial report. *Canadian Journal of Psychology* **30**, 134–139.

Hock, H. S., Gordon, G. P. and Marcus, N. (1974). Individual differences in the detection of embedded figures. *Perception and Psychophysics* **15**, 47–52.

Inglis, J. (1962). Dichotic stimulation, temporal-lobe damage, and the perception and storage of auditory stimuli—a note on Kimura's findings. *Canadian Journal of Psychology* **16**, 11–17.

Kallman, H. J. and Corballis, M. C. (1975). Ear asymmetry in reaction time to musical sounds. *Perception and Psychophysics* **17**, 368–370.

Kershner, J. R. and Jeng, A. G. R. (1972). Dual functional hemispheric asymmetry in visual perception: Effects of ocular dominance and post-exposural processes. *Neuropsychologia* **10**, 437–445.

Kimura, D. (1961a). Some effects of temporal-lobe damage on auditory perception. *Canadian Journal of Psychology* **15**, 156–165.

Kimura, D. (1961b). Cerebral dominance and the perception of verbal stimuli. *Canadian Journal of Psychology* **15**, 166–171.

Kimura, D. (1964). Left–right differences in the perception of melodies. *Quarterly Journal of Psychology* **16**, 355–358.

Kimura, D. (1966). Dual functional asymmetry of the brain in visual perception. *Neuropsychologia* **4**, 275–285.

Kimura, D. (1967). Functional asymmetry of the brain in dichotic listening. *Cortex* **3**, 163–178.

Kimura, D. (1969). Spatial localization in left and right visual fields. *Canadian Journal of Psychology* **23**, 445–448.

Kimura, D. (1973). The asymmetry of the human brain. *Scientific American* **228**, 70–78.

Kimura, D. (1976). The neural basis of language qua gesture. In "Current Trends in Neurolinguistics" (H. Avakian-Whitaker and H. A. Whitaker, eds). Academic Press, New York and London.

King, F. L. and Kimura, D. (1972). Left-ear superiority in dichotic perception of vocal nonverbal sounds. *Canadian Journal of Psychology* **26**, 111–116.

Kinsbourne, M. (1970). The cerebral basis of lateral asymmetries in attention. *Acta Psychologia* **33**, 193–201.

Kinsbourne, M. (1972). Eye and head turning indicates cerebral lateralization. *Science* **176**, 539–541.

Kinsbourne, M. (1973). The control of attention by interaction between the cerebral hemispheres. In "Attention and Performance IV" (S. Kornblum, ed.). Academic Press, New York and London.

Kinsbourne, M. (1975). The mechanism of hemispheric control of the lateral gradient of attention. In "Attention and Performance V" (P.M.A. Rabbitt and S. Dornic, eds). Academic Press, London and New York.

Krashen, S. and Harshman, R. (1972). An "unbiased" procedure for comparing degree of lateralization of dichotically presented stimuli. *UCLA Working Papers in Phonetics* **23**, 3–12.

Kuhn, G. (1973). The phi-coefficient as an index of ear differences in dichotic listening. *Cortex* **9**, 447–457.

Lake, D. A. and Bryden, M. P. (1976). Handedness and sex differences in hemispheric asymmetry. *Brain and Language* **3**, 266–282.

Levy, J. (1971). Lateral specialization of the human brain: Behavioral manifestations and possible evolutionary basis. Paper presented at the Thirty-second Annual Biology Colloquium on the Biology of Behavior, Oregon State University, Corvallis, Oregon.

Marcel, T. and Rajan, P. (1975). Lateral specialization for recognition of words and faces in good and poor readers. *Neuropsychologia* **13**, 489–497.

Marcel, T., Katz, L. and Smith, M. (1974). Laterality and reading proficiency. *Neuropsychologia* **12**, 131–139.

Marshall, J. C., Caplan, D. and Holmes, J. M. (1975). The measure of laterality. *Neuropsychologia* **13**, 315–322.

McKeever, W. F. (1971). Lateral word recognition: Effects of unilateral and bilateral presentation, asynchrony of bilateral presentation, and forced order of report. *Quarterly Journal of Experimental Psychology* **23**, 410–416.

McKeever, W. F. (1974). Does post-exposural directional scanning offer a sufficient explanation for lateral differences in tachistoscopic recognition? *Perceptual and Motor Skills* **38**, 43–50.

McKeever, W. F. and Huling, M. D. (1970). Left cerebral hemisphere superiority in tachistoscopic word recognition performance. *Perceptual and Motor Skills* **30**, 763–766.

McKeever, W. F. and Huling, M. D. (1971). Lateral dominance in tachistoscopic word recognition performance obtained with simultaneous bilateral input. *Neuropsychologia* **9**, 15–20.

McKeever, W. F., Suberi, M. and VanDeventer, A. D. (1972). Fixation control in tachistoscopic studies of laterality effects: Comment and data relevant to Hines' experiment. *Cortex* **8**, 473–479.

Milner, B., Branch, C. and Rasmussen, T. (1964). Observations on cerebral dominance. *In* "CIBA Symposium on Disorders of Language" (A. V. S. de Reuck and M. O'Connor, eds). J. and A. Churchill, London.

Mishkin, M. and Forgays, D. G. (1952). Word recognition as a function of retinal locus. *Journal of Experimental Psychology* **43**, 43–48.

Nachson, I. and Carmon, A. (1975). Hand preference in sequential and spatial discrimination tasks. *Cortex* **11**, 123–131.

Nebes, R. D. (1973). Perception of spatial relationships by the right and left hemispheres in commissurotomized man. *Neuropsychologia* **11**, 285–289.

Nebes, R. D. (1974). Hemispheric specialization in commissurotomized man. *Psychological Bulletin* **81**, 1–14.

Olsen, M. E. (1973). Laterality differences in tachistoscopic word recognition in normal and delayed readers in elementary school. *Neuropsychologia* **10**, 437–445.

Orbach, J. (1967). Differential recognition of Hebrew and English words in right and left visual fields as a function of cerebral dominance and reading habits. *Neuropsychologia* **5**, 127–134.

Ornstein, R. E. (1972). "The Psychology of Consciousness". W. H. Freeman, San Francisco.

Perl, N. and Haggard, M. (1975). Practice and strategy in a measure of cerebral dominance. *Neuropsychologia* **13**, 347–352.

Rossi, G. F. and Rosadini, G. (1967). Experimental analysis of cerebral dominance in man. *In* "Brain Mechanisms Underlying Speech and Language" (F. L. Darley, ed.). Grune and Stratton, New York.

Satz, P., Achenbach, K., Pattishall, E. and Fennell, E. (1965). Order of report, ear asymmetry and handedness in dichotic listening. *Cortex* **1**, 377–396.

Schwartz, M. (1970). Competition in dichotic listening. PhD thesis, University of Waterloo.

Sidtis, J. and Bryden, M. P. (1975). Differential practice effects in dichotic listening. Paper presented at Canadian Psychological Association meeting, Quebec City.

Spellacy, F. (1970). Lateral preferences in the identification of patterned stimuli. *The Journal of the Acoustical Society of America* **47**, 574–578.

Spellacy, F. and Blumstein, S. (1970). The influence of language set on ear preference in phoneme recognition. *Cortex* **6**, 430–439.

Sperry, R. W. (1974). Lateral specialization in the surgically separated hemispheres. *In* "The Neurosciences: Third Study Program" (F. O. Schmitt and F. G. Worden, eds). MIT Press, Cambridge, Massachusetts.

Sperry, R. W., Gazzaniga, M. S. and Bogen, J. E. (1969). Interhemispheric relationships: The neocortical commisures syndromes of hemisphere disconnection. *In* "Handbook of Clinical Neurology" (P. J. Vinken and G. W. Bruyn, eds), Vol. IV. North-Holland Press, Amsterdam.

Spreen, O., Spellacy, F. J. and Reid, J. R. (1970). The effect of interstimulus interval and intensity on ear asymmetry for nonverbal stimuli in dichotic listening. *Neuropsychologia* **8**, 245–250.

Springer, S. P. (1971). Ear asymmetry in a dichotic detection task. *Perception and Psychophysics* **10**, 239–241.

Studdert-Kennedy, M. and Shankweiler, D. (1970). Hemispheric specialization for speech perception. *The Journal of the Acoustical Society of America* **48**, 579–594.

Terrace, H. (1959). The effects of retinal locus and attention on the perception of words. *Journal of Experimental Psychology* **58**, 382–385.

Treisman, A. and Geffen, G. (1968). Selective attention and cerebral dominance in perceiving and responding to speech messages. *Quarterly Journal of Experimental Psychology* **20**, 139–150.

Umilta, G., Rizzolatti, G., Marzi, C. A., Zamboni, G., Franzini, C., Carmada, R. and Berlucchi, G. (1974). Hemispheric differences in the discrimination of line orientation. *Neuropsychologia* **12**, 165–174.

Wada, J. A. and Rasmussen, T. (1960). Intracarotid injection of sodium amytal for the lateralization of cerebral speech dominance. *Journal of Neurosurgery* **17**, 266–282.

White, M. J. (1969). Laterality differences in perception: A review. *Psychological Bulletin* **72**, 387–405.

White, M. J. (1972). Hemispheric asymmetries in tachistoscopic information processing. *British Journal of Psychology* **63**, 497–508.

White, M. J. (1973). Does cerebral dominance offer a sufficient explanation for laterality differences in tachistoscopic recognition? *Perceptual and Motor Skills* **36**, 479–485.

Witelson, S. F. (1976). Abnormal right hemisphere functional specialization in developmental dyslexia. *In* "The Neuropsychology of Learning Disorders: Theoretical Approaches" (R. M. Knights and D. J. Bakker, eds). University Park Press, Baltimore, Maryland.

Witkin, H. A. (1949). Sex differences in perception. *Transactions of the New York Academy of Science* **12**, 22–26.

Yeni-Komshian, G. H. and Gordon, J. F. (1974). The effect of memory load on the right ear advantage in dichotic listening. *Brain and Language* **1**, 375–381.

Zurif, E. B. and Bryden, M. P. (1969). Familial handedness and left–right differences in auditory and visual perception. *Neuropsychologia* **7**, 179–187.

Zurif, E. B. and Carson, C. (1970). Dyslexia in relation to cerebral dominance and temporal analysis. *Neuropsychologia* **8**, 351–361.

Five

Lexical Access in Simple Reading Tasks

Max Coltheart
University of London

1. INTRODUCTION

Throughout this chapter I will adopt the view that a reader's knowledge of the words of his language is embodied in an internal lexicon. Each word the reader knows is represented in this internal lexicon as a lexical entry, where is stored information about the word's meaning, pronunciation and spelling. He understands what a printed word means by gaining access to its lexical entry and hence to the semantic information represented in this entry; and it is this process, lexical access, with which the chapter is mainly concerned. In particular, the issue of the mode in which a printed word is internally represented for the purposes of gaining access to its lexical entry will be of central interest.

This issue can conveniently be introduced by considering non-alphabetic as well as alphabetic forms of script. When a reader encounters a printed word which he has never seen or heard before, he will be unable to understand it; it will not have an entry in his internal lexicon. However, if the word is printed in an alphabetic or syllabic script, he may be able to pronounce it. This would not be possible if it were printed in an ideographic or pictographic script. Thus one property of alphabetic and syllabic scripts, a property which distinguishes them from ideographic and pictographic scripts, is that it is in principle possible for a reader of an alphabetic or syllabic script to obtain a word's phonological representation from the word's printed form without reference to the word's lexical entry. In contrast, the word's *semantic* representation can only be obtained by consultation of its lexical entry. Since, for these scripts, a phonological representation of a word can be obtained without access to the word's lexical entry, such a representation might be available prior to the occurrence of such lexical access; and it is therefore logically possible that this mode of internal representation of a word is used for the purpose of gaining access to the word's lexical entry.

Such a possibility is embodied in a number of theories of lexical access. Some of these theories (e.g. those proposed by Rubenstein *et al.*, 1971, and by Gough, 1972) in fact propose that the *only* mode of internal representation used for lexical access during reading is the phonological representation. Others (e.g. Meyer *et al.*, 1974) take the view that this is one of two modes of representation used for lexical access, the other mode being a representation in terms of a word's visual form.

It is crucial for these theories that the logical possibility of converting a printed word to its phonological representation without using the lexicon be more than just a logical possibility, since if such non-lexical phonological encoding cannot occur in practice, or if it always occurs more slowly than does lexical access, then theories claiming that l access is sometimes or always achieved by using a phonological enc of a printed word can be rejected immediately. In Section 2 o chapter, therefore, I discuss some of the possible ways in which a reader might be able in practice to obtain such phonological encodings of alphabetically printed words in the absence of lexical access.

If it can be shown that lexical access using phonological encoding is a practical possibility, one can then consider whether there is any evidence that lexical access actually *is* sometimes achieved by phonological encoding. This is the subject of Section 3 of the chapter.

The last section deals with the possibility that the processes underlying lexical access are not immutable and automatic. Perhaps subjects are capable of exerting optional control over these processes; in other words, perhaps there are strategy effects occurring during lexical access, subjects choosing sometimes this strategy, sometimes that strategy, to achieve such access.

2. PHONOLOGICAL ENCODING WITHOUT LEXICAL ACCESS

In this section I consider three possible methods by which a reader might derive a phonological representation from the printed form of a word in such a way that this representation could be used to gain access to the meaning of the word. These three possible methods differ with respect to the units into which the letter string representing a word is analysed during this derivation. The first possibility is that a reader possesses an internal system of grapheme-phoneme correspondences (GPCs), and that a letter string is analysed into its constituent graphemes (single letters or letter clusters), after which the GPC system is used to assign a phoneme to each grapheme, thereby converting a string of letters into a string of phonemes. The second possibility is that a letter string is analysed into those groups of letters which represent single *syllables*, rather than phonemes; then the syllable corresponding to each syllabic letter group is obtained (perhaps by consultation of an internal syllabary), thereby converting a string of letters into a string of syllables. The third possibility is a radical one, since it rejects the view that there exists an internal lexicon in which semantic, phonological and orthographic information about a word is all contained in a unified lexical entry; instead, it is supposed that there are at least two separate and independent lexicons, a semantic lexicon containing only semantic information and a phonological lexicon containing only phonological information. The unit of analysis here is the *whole word*, rather than the syllable or the phoneme. The letter string as a whole is looked up in the phonological lexicon, and this lookup provides a phonological representation of the word, a representation which could then be used to gain access to the word's entry in the semantic lexicon. The intention of Section 2 is to consider which (if any) of these three proposals can provide a satisfactory account of how a reader might proceed from a printed to a phonological representation without using the internal lexicon.

2.1. The GPC procedure

If for every letter in the printed form of an English word there existed a corresponding phoneme in its phonological form, and vice versa (that is, if the relationship of letters to phonemes were one-to-one), and if for any letter the phoneme corresponding to it were always the same phoneme (that is, if the relationship of letters to phonemes were invariant), then deriving a phonological representation from a printed letter string by means of GPCs would be fairly simple. The relationship of letters to phonemes is, however, neither one-to-one nor invariant in English.

Departures from a one-to-one relationship usually take the form of there being two or more letters corresponding to a single phoneme (for example, SHEEP has five letters but only three phonemes), though the reverse can occur (for example, the letter X corresponds to the phoneme sequence /ks/). This requires that a printed word be first divided up into those single letters or letter sequences which correspond to single phonemes, before the GPC procedure could be used to assign phonemes. Thus SHEEP would need to be analysed into SH/EE/P before the three phonemes corresponding to these three letter units could be obtained from a system of GPCs. This analysis of a letter string into those letters or letter groups which correspond to single phonemes will be referred to as *graphemic parsing*. The units yielded by the graphemic parsing will have a one-to-one relationship with the phonemes of the letter string's phonological representation, and thus a phoneme can be assigned to each of these units.

Thus, if we are considering how a GPC procedure could allow the derivation of phonological representations from printed letter strings, it appears necessary to propose that this derivation consists of two stages. First, the letter string is *parsed* into those letters or letter groups which correspond to phonemes. Then the system of GPCs is used to *assign* a phoneme to each of the units produced by the parsing. These two stages, graphemic parsing and phoneme assignment, will now be considered separately.

2.1.1. Graphemic parsing
Some work by Venezky (1970) is useful here. He introduced the term "functional spelling unit" to describe the letter or letter group in a

letter string which corresponds to each phoneme in that string's phonological representation. Such letter combinations as OO, SH or NG, and numerous others, are functional spelling units in English, as are the individual letters of the alphabet. Graphemic parsing consists of converting a string of letters into a string of functional spelling units; there is a one-to-one relationship between functional spelling units and phonemes.

We are concerned here with how a reader could perform graphemic parsings without making use of his internal lexicon, since this parsing is part of any GPC-based phonological encoding procedure, and Section 2 is concerned with non-lexical procedures for phonological encoding. One of the ways in which English spelling is irregular is at the level of the relationship between letters and functional spelling units; this irregularity is sufficiently widespread to suggest that no parsing procedure exists which correctly analyses every English word into its functional spelling units without using lexical knowledge. There are many forms of this irregularity; the vowel digraphs provide a convenient example (taken from Wijk, 1966). In English, AI, EA, OA, OE, UE and UI usually correspond to single vowel phonemes, and hence each of these letter pairs is usually a single functional spelling unit. Usually, but not always: consider DAIS, REAL, BOA, CRUEL and RUIN. These variations cannot be resolved by seeking rules of the form "OA is one unit except at the end of a word, where it is two", since exceptions can always be found to *these* rules too (COCOA).

Venezky (1970) has demonstrated that morphophonemic considerations can make predictable some of the apparent inconsistencies in the relationships between letters and functional spelling units in English. For example, the letter sequence PH sometimes corresponds to one phoneme and sometimes to two; but this variation can be predicted exactly by the rule "PH is one functional spelling unit when it occurs within a morpheme, and two when it spans a morpheme boundary"— cf. GOPHER, PHASE, GRAPHIC *vs.* SHEPHERD, TOPHEAVY, UPHILL. Other examples in which morphemic considerations eliminate parsing ambiguity are SIGNPOST/IGNOBLE, COMBING/COMBINE, or, for that matter, MATHEWS/COLTHEART (*see* Redmonds, 1973). However, though rules of this kind may provide satisfying regularities for the descriptive linguist, they are of no use to a reader attempting to convert print to phonology without using lexical knowledge. A reader must gain access to the lexical entries for COMBING and COMBINE before he could discover that there is a morpheme boundary between the M and the B in the second word, but not in the first. Therefore no non-lexical phonological-encoding procedure could exist, if correct phonological encoding depended upon such morphemic knowledge.

These and many other such examples show that there is no procedure which, applied to all English words, produces a correct parsing of every word into its constituent functional spelling units without any use of lexical knowledge. If such graphemic parsing is an essential part of any GPC procedure, then no such procedure can yield a correct phonological representation for every English word. If this is so, how can any theory which proposes that the non-lexical derivation of a phonological representation from a printed representation is accomplished by GPCs be maintained? This is considered further in Section 2.1.3, but before pursuing it I would like to consider the second stage of the GPC procedure, the assignment of phonemes to functional spelling units.

2.1.2. *Phoneme assignment*

Suppose for the moment that the problem of graphemic parsing had been solved: someone had found a set of procedures which correctly parsed every English word into its functional spelling units. Correct functioning of the GPC procedure would then simply depend upon correct assignment of phonemes to spelling units.

English spelling is irregular at this level too, as well as at the parsing level, since the relationships of phonemes to spelling units is not invariant. As Venezky (1970) notes, the spelling unit O has 17 possible phonemic assignments; A has 10; E has 9; the five vowels have a total of 48. Although context-sensitivity reduces this variability, much of it still remains. Some of it is eliminated by lexical considerations (TH → /ð/ when at the beginning of function words, → /θ/ at the beginning of content words; in homographs such as DUPLICATE the A in -ATE is /ə/ at the end of nouns, and /ei/ at the end of verbs), but this is irrelevant if we are interested only in what a reader can do without his lexicon.

Thus even when a letter string has been correctly parsed, there will often be many different legitimate ways of assigning phonemes to the functional spelling units. How can a reader choose between these? Given that BREAD has been correctly parsed as B/R/EA/D, the digraph EA could be assigned the phoneme /i:/ (cf. VEAL) or /ei/ (cf. STEAK) or /e/ (cf. HEAD). All three assignments produce phonological representations which are words, so it is not even possible to use, as a criterion for the correct assignment, that the result must be an English word rather than a neologism.

Consequently, there are grave problems for any GPC procedure at both the parsing stage (alternative parsings are often possible, with no non-lexical method available for choosing from them) and at the phoneme assignment stage (alternative assignments are usually possible, again with no non-lexical method available for choosing from them). It is scarcely surprising, then, that the view is often taken that the GPC procedure is not a workable means for deriving pronunciation from print, since it is certainly the case that no such procedure exists which will provide a correct phonological representation for every English word. Does this mean we must look elsewhere for an answer to the question of how phonological encoding could be achieved without use of the lexicon?

2.1.3. Regular words and exceptions

For any proposed parsing procedure, it is easy to find examples of English words which are incorrectly parsed by the procedure. For any set of assignments of phonemes to functional spelling units, it is easy to find examples of English words for which the set yields incorrect assignments. Various examples of these kinds have already been given. But this should not be allowed to obscure the fact that one can devise a GPC procedure (that is, a set of parsing procedures plus a set of phoneme assignments) which yields a correct phonological representation for *most* of the words of English. This is what Wijk (1966) and Venezky (1970) have done. In fact, the words of English can be divided into two mutually exclusive and exhaustive classes: a large class of *regular words* (those for which the Wijk-Venezky procedures yield a correct phonological representation) and a smaller class of *exceptions* (those for which the procedures yield an incorrect phonological representation). Various estimates have been given as to the percentage of English words which are exceptions: 20% (Hanna and Hanna, 1959), 13% (Forbes, 1964), 10% (Hanna and Hanna, 1965) and 5–10% (Wijk, 1966).

This means that, although we will never find a GPC procedure which works for all English words, procedures do exist which work for most words. As an example, consider the vowel digraph EA. Suppose the parsing procedures include a statement that EA is a single functional spelling unit, and the phoneme assignment procedures assign the phoneme /i:/ to this unit. Now a GPC procedure will fail at the parsing level for such words as REAL, CREATE or BEATITUDE, and will fail at the phoneme assignment level for such words as DEAF or STEAK; but since in most English words containing this digraph it is a single functional spelling unit pronounced /i:/, the correct phonological representation of most English words containing -EA- will be obtained.

When a particular letter sequence can be parsed in more than one way in English, the *regular parsing* for this sequence is the parsing which occurs in the largest number of those words containing the letter sequence. Similarly, when there is more than one legitimate assignment of a phoneme to a particular functional spelling unit, the *regular assignment* is that which occurs in the largest number of those words containing the functional spelling unit. Note that this definition of regularity ignores the frequency of occurrence of *words*. It could be that, in most of the words containing EA, the digraph is pronounced /i:/, but that the relatively few words in which it is pronounced /e/ happen to have relatively high frequencies of occurrence, so that in fact most of the time when one sees EA it is pronounced /e/ even though this is the pronunciation in relatively few words. A serious discrepancy between the proportion of occasions in a corpus of text in which a certain phoneme assignment occurred, and the proportion of words of English in which it occurs, could only arise if exception words were of higher frequency of occurrence than regular words. I know of no evidence that this is so, but it is not implausible. The pronunciation of a word often changes over the centuries, but, since the development of dictionaries, spelling is frozen. Sometimes this has the effect that pronunciation converges on spelling. For example, FALCON was spelt FAUCON and pronounced as such up until the sixteenth century. Then, for etymological reasons, its spelling changed to FALCON, and as dictionaries came into existence soon afterwards, this spelling was fixed. Gradually, the L present in the spelling crept into the pronunciation. Thus the word was regular in the fifteenth century, experienced some centuries as an exception word, and now is regular again. Scragg (1974) gives other examples of this sort; but also many where pronunciation has *diverged* from spelling. If it is the case that the older a word is, the more likely it is to have a pronunciation which has diverged from its spelling, and if it is also the case that there is a positive correlation between a word's age and its frequency, then it is likely that exception words will be of higher frequency than regular words. What implication this actually has for the definitions of regularity given at the beginning of this paragraph remains to be seen. I am going to assume that these definitions would not be altered even if the frequency of occurrence of words were taken into account.

The existence of exception words means that we are confronted with this choice: either we dismiss the GPC procedure as a method for non-lexical phonological encoding and look elsewhere for some method which will work for all rather than only most words, or else we accept that non-lexical phonological encoding is possible only for most words (regular words) but not for the remainder (exceptions). My choice will be the latter one, for two reasons. First, the other two possible methods for non-lexical phonological encoding (syllabary, phonological lexicon) encounter much more severe difficulties than the GPC method—this is discussed in Sections 2.3 and 2.4. Secondly, current work suggests that the classification of words as regular or exceptions actually has "psychological reality"; subjects behave differently with the two types of word. This is strong evidence in favour of the view that non-lexical phonological encoding uses a GPC procedure, since other methods for such encoding do not distinguish between regular words and exceptions, and hence cannot explain why this distinction is reflected in behaviour.

Baron and Strawson (1976) investigated the possibility that the distinction between regular words and exceptions is psychological rather than merely linguistic. The task they gave their subjects was to read aloud a list of ten items as fast as possible. The lists were of three kinds: lists of ten regular words, lists of ten exception words, and lists of ten pronounceable non-words (which were all pseudohomophones).* They found that subjects read aloud regular lists faster than exception lists, and exception lists faster than non-word lists, the mean times per list being 4·28 s, 5·94 s and 8·18 s respectively. This finding has been confirmed by L. Midgley-West (unpublished) with naming latencies for singly presented words rather than word lists; her work is discussed in Section 4.2. Baron and Strawson interpreted their findings by proposing that there are two strategies which may be used by a reader when he is pronouncing printed text:

1. An *orthographic* strategy (i.e. use of GPCs). This succeeds for regular words and for pronounceable non-words. It fails for exception words, because the GPC procedure yields incorrect pronunciations for exception words.

2. A *lexical lookup* strategy: here the reader gains access to a lexical entry, and extracts from this entry the information necessary to generate an articulation of the word corresponding to that entry. This succeeds for regular words and exceptions (equally well, we presume). It fails for non-words, because they do not have lexical entries.

In these terms, the reason why a list of regular words can be uttered in a shorter time than a list of exception words is that exception words can only use the lexical lookup strategy, whereas regular words can be dealt with by either strategy. If subjects can operate the two strategies in parallel and without interference, and if on some occasions the orthographic strategy produces a pronunciation more quickly than the lexical lookup strategy, whereas the reverse is true on other

---

* By "pseudohomophone" I mean a non-word whose pronunciation is identical to the pronunciation of some English word. Examples of pseudohomophones are BRANE, MEEN, WURD etc.

occasions, then words whose utterance is generated by whichever of the two strategies happens to finish earlier (regular words) will on the average be uttered earlier than words which must wait for the lexical lookup strategy to finish (exception words).

This interpretation raises a number of questions. First, does the orthographic strategy actually *fail* with exception words, or do they suffer merely because their parsings or phonemic assignments, being less common, are tried out *after* the more common ones have failed? If the orthographic strategy does fail and an incorrect phonological representation is produced, how does the reader know it is incorrect, and what does he do about it? These and other similar questions are discussed at various points throughout the chapter; all I wish to do for the moment with Baron and Strawson's findings is to note that they suggest that the distinction between regular words and exceptions is a genuine one. If so, the difficulty created for a GPC-based theory by exception words is not a defect of such a theory, but a virtue, since readers experience this difficulty too.

2.1.4. Surface dyslexia

A second line of evidence implying that GPC procedures have psychological reality is provided by the clinical studies of Marshall and Newcombe (1973), Newcombe and Marshall (1973) and Holmes (1973). These authors describe two patients whose reading and writing had been seriously impaired by injury to the temporoparietal region of the left hemisphere, resulting in the syndrome "surface dyslexia". When these patients are asked to read aloud single printed words, many of their pronunciations are incorrect. Some examples of these incorrect pronunciations are given in Table I.

The authors point out that many of the patients' errors can be ascribed to impaired application of GPC procedures. For example, failure to apply the phoneme assignment procedure "For vowel + consonant + final e, the vowel is long" could be the basis of such incorrect pronunciations as BIKE → "bik", UNITE → "unit" and DESCRIBE → "describ". Failure to apply the assignment "G or C are soft before E or I, otherwise hard" produces such errors as GUEST → "just", INCENSE → "increase", RECENT → "rikunt", GAUGE → "jug". Other errors appear to arise at the graphemic parsing stage, since the patients have great difficulty with vowel digraphs, usually pronouncing one vowel and ignoring the other (NIECE → "nice", GUEST → "just", GAUGE → "jug", BOIL → "bowl", REIGN → "region").

Holmes (1973) studied three dyslexic children, in addition to the two adults with brain damage. The errors produced by these children

TABLE I. Some examples of the errors made by surface
dyslexics
(from Marshall and Newcombe, 1973).

Case JC	Case ST
INSECT → insist	RESENT → rissend
BARGE → bargain	RECENT → rikunt
LISTEN → liston	GAUGE → jug
BIKE → bik	REIGN → region
NIECE → nice	LACE → lass
INCENSE → increase	REAPPLY → reply
GUEST → just	PHASE → face
OF → off	DESCRIBE→describ
ISLAND → izland	BOIL → bowl
UNITE → unit	
VIOLENT → volent	
MONARCH→monaruch	

when reading aloud bore some striking similarities to the errors made by
the adults; the children, like the adults, appeared to be making errors
because they were misapplying or failing to apply common GPCs.

2.1.5. Summary

Demonstrations that exception words are pronounced with longer
latencies than regular words, and examination of the types of error
made by surface dyslexics (whether their dyslexia be acquired or
developmental), support the view that GPC procedures for pronouncing
printed words do exist and are used. Thus a theoretical approach based
upon GPCs seems a promising way of explaining how printed letter
strings might be pronounced without use of the internal lexicon,
despite the existence of a class of English word for which a GPC
procedure cannot be used. There remain, however, the two other
possible theoretical approaches briefly mentioned earlier, and I would
now like to consider each of these.

2.2. The internal syllabary

Some theoretical advantage might be gained by supposing that the
units used during the process of converting a printed to a phonological
representation are syllables, rather than phonemes. Highly-encoded
phonemes such as stop consonants cannot be produced in isolation:

they can only be pronounced when accompanied by a vowel. Given this, it is not clear what view we are to take of the nature of the phonemes involved in grapheme–phoneme conversion. If they are in a pronounceable form, there is the problem of *blending*. The GPC procedure will return the phonemic sequence /bə/ + /æ/ + /tə/ for BAT. How is the reader to strip the vowels from the two consonant phonemes so as to arrive at the correct phonological form /b æ t/? The problem is avoided if one thinks of the consonant phonemes as being unaccompanied by vowels in the first place, but now they are abstract entities: linguists are not perturbed by the postulation of abstract constituents of language, but perhaps psychologists should be. The whole problem does not even arise if the basic units are syllables rather than phonemes; syllables *can* be pronounced in isolation, and the transition from a sequence of isolated syllables to an integrated phonological representation is straightforward.

A procedure for phonological encoding based on the syllable as a unit requires that a letter string first be parsed into syllabic letter groups in such a way that there is a one-to-one relationship between letter groups and syllables; once this parsing is completed, the appropriate syllable can be assigned to each letter group. One attempt (Hansen and Rodgers, 1973) has been made to devise a procedure which would parse a letter string into syllabic letter groups without the use of lexical knowledge.

2.2.1. The Hansen–Rodgers theory of lexical access

Hansen and Rodgers preferred to avoid the term "syllable" because of difficulties which have been encountered in attempts to define this term. Instead, the unit they use is the Vocalic Centre Group or VCG. As will be seen from the definition of the VCG, the terms "VCG" and "syllable" may be regarded as synonymous for the purposes of this discussion. The VCG is

> the optimally minimum sequence within which all necessary rules of phonemic co-occurrence (phonotactic rules) can be stated. The VCG is marked by one vocalic element (which is not necessarily a vowel). Non-vocalic (consonantal) or semi-vocalic elements may occur preceding or following the vocal center (Hansen and Rodgers, 1973, p. 74).

Hansen and Rodgers set out a detailed procedure for parsing letter strings into constituent VCGs without using lexical knowledge. This parsing procedure is the first of three stages in their model of lexical access. The second stage is decoding (obtaining a phonological representation for each VCG, and integrating these to produce a phonological representation for the whole letter string). The third and final stage is lexical search: the phonological representation yielded by the second stage is used in a search of the internal lexicon, and lexical access has been achieved when a match is obtained between this representation and some lexical entry. This three-stage procedure can be recursive; if no lexical match is obtained by the third stage, an alternative (lower priority) parsing is then carried out, and stages 2 and 3 are repeated.

The adequacy of an approach based on an internal syllabary can be assessed by considering the Hansen and Rodgers model in some detail. My conclusion will be that the model fails both at the parsing-decoding stages and at the lexical search stage, and that these failures can be demonstrated *a priori*, without recourse to experimental evidence. If this is so, it is not necessary to investigate the model experimentally, as was done by Spoehr and Smith (1973, 1975; *see also* Smith and Spoehr, 1974), nor can any agreement between their results and predictions from the model save the model.

2.2.1.1. The parsing-decoding stages. Even if the remainder of the Hansen–Rodgers model was unsatisfactory, their parsing procedures could still be important, since if these procedures worked they would enable a printed word to be parsed into letter groups in such a way that each letter group constitutes a syllable (or VCG); and *any* theory of lexical access based on a syllabary will need as its first stage this kind of parsing procedure. Thus it seems worth while to consider the Hansen–Rodgers procedure in some detail and to determine how good a job it actually does of deriving syllabic letter groups from a letter string.

The parsing begins by marking each vowel in the letter string. If the string contains more than one vowel, and the vowels are not consecutive in the string, then there is more than one VCG in the string, and so parsing is required. If there is only one vowel, or if all the vowels are consecutive, there is only one VCG, hence no parsing is required. The procedure therefore fails straight away for all words in which a sequence of two vowels corresponds to two phonemes (LION, CHAOS, DUAL, VIAL etc.) because for all such words there is a syllable boundary between the two vowels which the parsing procedure will not detect. It also fails immediately with all words ending in a vowel followed by a consonant followed by an E, since it parses this three-letter sequence as two VCGs instead of one.

If parsing is required, it is carried out by applying the following parsing rules to the segments of the letter string where one or more consonants occur between vowels:

$$\begin{aligned} \ldots \text{VCV} \ldots \quad &\to \text{V} + \text{CV} \quad &(1\text{A})\\ \ldots \text{VCCV} \ldots \quad &\to \text{VC} + \text{CV} \quad &(2\text{A})\\ \ldots \text{VCCCV} \ldots \quad &\to \text{VC} + \text{CCV} \quad &(3\text{A}) \end{aligned}$$

Hansen and Rodgers give as an example the word FASTING. Rule 2A parses this into FAS + TING. The decoding stage derives, from these two VCGs, the syllables /f æ s/ + /t i ŋ/. When integrated, these two syllables produce the correct phonological representation for FASTING. Hence a lexical search using this phonological representation will succeed in locating the correct lexical entry, and lexical access will then have been achieved.

A second example they give is the word PASTING. This is parsed as PAS + TING and so decoded into /p æ s/ + t i ŋ/. No word has this pronunciation, so the lexical search will be unsuccessful. Whenever this happens, the initial letter string is reparsed, using a different set of rules.

$$\begin{aligned} \ldots \text{VCV} \ldots \quad &\to \text{VC} + \text{V} \quad &(1\text{B})\\ \ldots \text{VCCV} \ldots \quad &\to \text{V} + \text{CCV} \quad &(2\text{B})\\ \ldots \text{VCCCV} \ldots \quad &\to \text{V} + \text{CCCV} \quad &(3\text{B}) \end{aligned}$$

Application of these second-priority rules to PASTING produces PA + STING, which is decoded as /pei/ + /stiŋ/. This is the correct pronunciation, so this time the lexical search will succeed, and lexical access will have been achieved, at the second attempt.

Although the Hansen–Rodgers model of lexical access is syllabic (or rather, VCG-oriented) in that it begins by parsing letter strings into VCGs, and ends by chaining the phonological representation of individual VCGs into an integrated phonological representation of an entire letter string, the decoding stage operates at the individual-letter level for individual VCGs:

> We conceive of the actual processing within [the decoding stage] in terms of a recursive generator which, taking one graphic element at a time, assigns a set of phonetic features to that element (Hansen and Rodgers, 1973, p. 87).

A wholly syllabic procedure would instead obtain the phonological representation of a syllabic letter group by looking it up in a syllabary. I will argue that whether one thinks of VCGs as being decoded at the individual-letter level, as proposed by Hansen and Rodgers, or as whole units referred to an internal syllabary, attempts to discover a means for VCG decoding encounter insuperable problems.

The problems can be illustrated by using as examples the 28 five-letter words used by Spoehr and Smith (1973) in the first of their experimental investigations of the Hansen–Rodgers theory. Ten of these words have the consonant–vowel structure CVCVC, which is parsed as CV + CVC. The difficulty here is that the phonological representation of the initial VCG in each of these ten words is ambiguous, the number of possible pronunciations ranging from two (for the PA of PAPER) to five (for the CO of COVER and COLOUR and the LO of LOWER). How can the correct phonological representation be selected? Note that if an incorrect representation is selected, and a non-word results, the next step is to reparse the word as CVC + VC, not to try a different phonological representation for the initial CV. This is not simply the familiar problem of the irregularity of English grapheme–phoneme relationships, but a much more severe problem, because many of the ambiguities present at the syllabic level are resolved at the grapheme–phoneme level. For example, in English words containing a double G followed by I or E, the double G is invariably pronounced as a single hard G; but the Hansen–Rodgers procedures will parse such words as DAGGER or DRUGGIST into two VCGs with a division between the two Gs. If so, the second G will be soft, since followed by an E or an I, and so the double G will become a hard G followed by a soft G. What results are non-words; so a reparsing is carried out, and this produces a VCG beginning with a double GG, which is illegal in English.

Medial NG is also mishandled by the Hansen–Rodgers procedure. When followed by A, O or U in English, it is almost always pronounced /ŋ g/, but a word like FUNGUS will first be parsed in such a way as to produce an incorrect phonological representation (FUN/GUS) and then to produce an illegal VCG (FU/NGUS).

These two examples show that there are words which are regular at the grapheme–phoneme level but are given incorrect phonological representations by a procedure which treats the VCG or syllable as an indivisible unit, or even by a procedure which decodes syllables at the grapheme–phoneme level but treats each syllable independently of other syllables in the same word. The vowel digraphs offer a third example. The Hansen–Rodgers model assumes that all vowel digraphs constitute a single phoneme. This is false for many digraphs which at the grapheme–phoneme level display considerable regularity: a graphemic parsing using the rule "EO, IA, IO and UA are always two phonemes, whilst OE, AI, OI and AU are always one" works for nearly all the English words containing one or other of these vowel digraphs.

As I have noted, ten of the words used by Spoehr and Smith have ambiguous initial VCGs, and no mechanism is provided within the

Hansen–Rodgers procedure for resolving this ambiguity. Seven of their words end with a consonant followed by a final E. This is an extremely common ending for English words, and one whose pronunciation is highly regular. Nevertheless, the Hansen–Rodgers procedure cannot cope with it. The initial parse produces a disyllable (since there are two vowels and they are not adjacent) which is incorrect for six of the words (FAL/SE, FOR/CE, TAS/TE, LAR/GE, HOR/SE, FRA/ME). These will therefore need a second parsing, which is no better: either it produces unpronounceable VCGs (LSE, RCE, RGE, RSE) or else the disyllable still occurs (TA/STE, FRAM/E). The seventh word in this group, TABLE, *is* a disyllable, but neither of its parsings (TAB/LE, then TA/BLE) could lead to the correct phonological representation. As with the examples given earlier, these are words which can be correctly dealt with by a context-sensitive GPC procedure but not by a syllabic procedure.

Three of the words used by Spoehr and Smith end in a consonant followed by a Y. Here the final VCG is CY, TY or PY, and each one has three possible different pronunciations in English. Only one is permissible in final position, but there is no provision in the Hansen–Rodgers scheme for such sensitivity to VCG position.

The remaining eight words used by Spoehr and Smith are of the form CVVCC or CCVCC. None of these engage the parsing procedure, since their vowels are adjacent.

In sum, then, the Hansen–Rodgers parsing-decoding procedure fails for twenty of the twenty-eight words used by Spoehr and Smith, and is not needed for the remaining eight; so it can scarcely be argued that their procedure is a satisfactory answer to the question of how prelexical phonological encoding could be performed.

2.2.1.2. The lexical search stage. Consider NOBLY. The first parse gives NOB + LY, which is decoded to /nob/ + /li:/. When a lexical search is carried out using this phonological representation, a lexical match will occur—with the lexical entry for KNOBBLY. The procedure will then terminate, since its goal is to find a lexical match. This termination is, of course, incorrect, since the lexical entry located is the wrong one; but there is no way in which such errors can be detected. It is not difficult to find words for which the wrong lexical entry will always be reached—WORKING, LOVES and GAUGED are examples. There is not even any way in which distinctions between homophones can be made: any homophone will produce more than one lexical match, and no basis exists in the theory for determining which is correct. Thus the lexical search stage of this theory is no more satisfactory than the parsing and decoding stages.

2.2.2 Problems for syllabaries

Since the Hansen–Rodgers syllabic procedure appears to be unworkable, it remains to be seen whether any procedure for parsing letter strings into syllabic letter groups can be invented; if non-lexical phonological encoding is accomplished by operating at the syllabic level, it must begin by this kind of parsing, so the absence of any satisfactory proposals as to how this might be done is a serious one. Problems also exist in connection with the derivation of a pronunciation for each of the parsed syllabic letter groups; these problems are more extensive than those which arise in connection with deriving pronunciation at a grapheme–phoneme level, since there are some useful forms of regularity in English which cannot be used if the syllable is treated as an unanalysable unit. Furthermore, if this derivation of pronunciation uses an internal syllabary, there seems no reason why such a syllabary would contain any of the large number of syllables which are pronounceable but do not occur in English—examples are ZUJ, QUEV or WUX. There are many more possible syllables than actually occur in English (Fudge, 1970). If such non-occurring syllables are absent from the internal syllabary, how is it that we can pronounce them?

As well as these theoretical points, there is evidence which is difficult to reconcile with a syllabic-level theory of phonological encoding. First, such a theory cannot explain why a subject's ability to pronounce a word is influenced by whether it is a regular word or an exception: why should such syllables as SORT, CAPE, TOOTH or COUCH have more rapid access to their entries in an internal syllabary than such syllables as PINT, SURE, BLOOD or TOUCH? Secondly, such a theory offers no account of the particular characteristics of the errors made in surface dyslexia, errors which can easily be understood as failures to apply context-sensitive GPCs.

2.3. The phonological lexicon

A radical possibility is to suggest that the internal lexicon is not a unified body of knowledge concerning the meanings, spellings and pronunciations of words, and that we must instead distinguish between a phonological lexicon (a dictionary of pronunciations) and a semantic lexicon (a dictionary of meanings). These are independent, and access to a word's entry in one of them does not provide immediate access to the corresponding entry in the other. If these two lexicons are distinct, then it is still possible to suppose that one method of gaining access to the semantic lexicon is to use the phonological lexicon to obtain the appropriate phonological representation of a printed word, and then to use this phonological representation to gain access to the word's entry in the semantic lexicon. Consequently, if it is argued that words are pronounced by looking them up in a phonological lexicon, it still makes sense to propose that their meanings can be accessed in either of two ways: by direct access to the semantic lexicon, or by using a phonological representation obtained from the phonological lexicon.

As a general proposal for explaining how a reader obtains a phonological representation for any pronounceable letter string without accessing the letter string's entry in the (semantic) lexicon, this obviously fails, since it cannot explain how non-words can be pronounced. It could scarcely be argued that the phonological lexicon contains entries for every possible pronounceable non-word. Thus at best this kind of theory is incomplete. Even if we consider only the pronunciation of words, however, the theory runs into difficulties. It offers no explanation of the patterns of pronouncing errors which occur in surface dyslexia. Why, for example, should these patients pronounce LISTEN as "liston" or ISLAND as "izland" if these letter strings are simply being looked up, as whole-word units, in a phonological lexicon? Why should there be particular difficulty with the ambiguous consonants C and G, or with vowels when they are consecutive? Nor can the results of experiments comparing regular and exception words be explained in terms of a theory based upon a phonological lexicon. One could not even explain Baron and Strawson's results by claiming that, for some unexplained reason, exception words have less effective access to their entries in a phonological lexicon than do regular words, since L. Midgley-West (unpublished) has shown that the difference in naming latency between these two classes of word diminishes when subjects cannot predict whether the words they see will be regular words or exceptions; this is discussed in Section 4.2.

2.4. Conclusions

Of the three theoretical approaches to the question of how a reader converts a printed representation to a phonological representation without using his internal lexicon, the approaches which postulate an internal syllabary or an internal phonological lexicon are difficult to reconcile with our ability to pronounce non-words, with the symptoms of surface dyslexia, and with differences observed between subjects' responses to regular and to exception words, whereas the approach based on GPCs deals well with all three of these. Furthermore, though a GPC approach is not entirely free of theoretical difficulties, such difficulties are much more severe for the other two approaches. It is of course possible that a reader uses more than one, or possibly all three, of these methods for non-lexical phonological encoding; but since there is no evidence implicating the use of an internal syllabary or phonological lexicon, and no evidence that cannot be explained in terms of the use of a GPC procedure, I will take the view that, if non-lexical phonological encoding of printed letter strings occurs, it is achieved by using a GPC procedure. Thus the question of whether a phonological representation of a printed word is sometimes or always used for lexical access during reading reduces to the question of whether such access is sometimes or always a consequence of applying a GPC procedure to a printed word. This allows us to reject *solely* phonological theories of lexical access, because there are some words (exceptions) which cannot be dealt with by GPC procedures. A second reason for rejecting such theories is that a substantial number of printed symbols in English text are ideographs: examples are numerals, punctuation marks, mathematical signs, abbreviations such as lb or cwt, words whose meaning has been modified by italicization or capitalization, £ and $, and many others. A GPC procedure could not be used to obtain a phonological representation for such ideographs, since the visual pattern representing an ideograph is not comprised of subunits (graphemes) corresponding to subunits in its phonological representation (phonemes). There must therefore exist a method of lexical access which does not employ an intermediate phonological encoding—the "direct route" to the lexicon—and since this works for regular words, exception words and ideographs, it is theoretically possible that it is the only route used. Thus the general topic of phonological encoding and lexical access can be narrowed down to the specific question of whether there are occasions on which lexical access is achieved by using a phonological representation (produced by application of GPCs)—this being the "indirect route" to the lexicon. If we conclude that there are such occasions, then we want to know under what circumstances they arise. Thus the next issue I would like to discuss is whether GPC-produced phonological representations of printed letter strings are ever used for lexical access during reading, and, if so, under what circumstances. Skilled readers, unskilled readers and those learning to read might not all make the same use of such representations; I will consider only skilled readers here.

3. THE USE OF PHONOLOGICAL ENCODING IN SKILLED LEXICAL ACCESS

3.1. Methods of investigation

This chapter is concerned with a rather limited aspect of the activity of reading: the process by which a reader gains access to the lexical

entry corresponding to a single printed word. A wide variety of information-processing tasks has been used over the past decade for investigating this and other aspects of reading. The suitability of many of
these tasks for investigating lexical access can, however, be questioned.
Some tasks can be criticized because they do not necessarily involve
lexical access. Others can be criticized because they necessarily involve
more than lexical access.

Examples of the first kind of task are tachistoscopic report, the
Reicher–Wheeler forced-choice task, visual search, same–different
judgement, the Sternberg memory-search task and reading aloud. All
six of these tasks can be performed with letter strings which are not
words. It is therefore possible in principle that when the stimuli used
for such tasks actually are words, the subjects do not treat them as such
—that is, do not make use of an internal lexicon when carrying out the
task. Whether lexical access is used in these tasks is a matter for investigation, not something which can be assumed. This makes the tasks
unsuitable for investigating lexical access. If one finds that effect X
occurs in say, tachistoscopic recognition, one cannot conclude that
lexical access involves effect X; an alternative explanation is that X
is *not* involved in lexical access, and lexical access is not involved in
tachistoscopic recognition.*

Tasks which require more than just lexical access are, for example,
reading a passage of text in anticipation of being asked questions about
what it means, or reading a sentence and deciding whether it is semantically anomalous. In addition to lexical access, the former task requires
the reader to construct, retain and interrogate an internal representation of the meaning of the text as a whole, whilst the latter task requires
the reader to integrate the words in a sentence after accessing their
lexical entries, and then to evaluate the degree to which this integrated
representation makes sense. Effects observed in such experiments may
pertain to those processes which must be carried out after lexical access,
rather than to lexical access itself.

If we take the view that reading a word consists of gaining access
to its entry in the internal lexicon, and if we wish to discover how
lexical access is achieved, it seems advisable to use experimental tasks
which cannot be performed in the absence of lexical access, but which
require little else. Such tasks do exist. One example is semantic classification (e.g. Landauer and Freedman, 1968). Another is "phrase

---

* Demonstrations that certain effects occur which imply the occurrence of lexical
 access—for example, word frequency effects—are not sufficient to validate any of
 these tasks. Such effects indicate at most that lexical access *sometimes* occurs. On
 other occasions, words might be treated as if they were non-words, and it could be
 that it is these non-lexical occasions which generate effect X.

evaluation"—judging whether a short phrase makes sense (e.g. Baron, 1973). Neither task is ideal, since in addition to lexical access, they require some form of judgement concerning the semantic representation yielded by such access. Nevertheless, these additional processes are so clearly delineated that there are reasonable prospects of deciding whether it is these postlexical processes, or lexical access itself, which is the source of any experimental effect.

A third example of a task which requires lexical access but little (perhaps nothing) else is judging whether a letter string is a word of English or not—the lexical decision task. Non-lexical methods for making such decisions are available in certain instances—for example, if the non-words in a lexical decision task always contain letter sequences which never occur in English, one can determine that CHEESE is a word merely by verifying that it contains no illegal letter sequences. However, if all the non-words used in a lexical decision task are well formed, in the sense that they do not contain such illegal letter sequences, then this non-lexical strategy cannot be used. In this case, it is difficult to see how a reader could determine whether a well formed letter string is or is not a word except by consulting his internal lexicon. How else could one decide that MANLINESS is a word whereas MANTINESS is not, except by finding that MANLINESS is present in one's internal lexicon whereas MANTINESS is absent? If there is no other way, then the lexical decision task does necessarily require lexical access, and therefore may be used to provide information about how such access is achieved.

Section 3 of this chapter is concerned with the role of phonological encoding in skilled lexical access. It was argued in Section 2 that if visually presented letter strings are converted to phonological representations prior to lexical access, this is achieved by the application of GPC procedures. Therefore, where it is important in the rest of the chapter to be specific about the actual method by which phonological encoding is achieved, it will be assumed that this occurs by using GPC procedures. Furthermore, the remainder of this section will be concerned mainly with three experimental tasks which avoid the objections just discussed—that is, the lexical decision task, the semantic classification task, and the phrase-evaluation task.

3.2. Phonological encoding and lexical decision

This topic was first investigated by Rubenstein *et al.* (1971). They observed two effects which suggested that their subjects were converting visually presented letter strings into phonological representations prior to lexical access. First, pseudohomophones (such as BURD, BLUD or

GROE) produced slower NO latencies than non-words (such as ROLT, HOSK or WESP). Secondly, homophonic words produced slower YES latencies than non-homophonic words, provided that the homophonic words were the less frequent members of homophone pairs. This second result need not detain us; it was only detected in a *post hoc* analysis of YES times, and in the comparison of homophones to non-homophones there was no matching on such variables as word frequency or part of speech, which influences YES latency in lexical decision tasks (Scarborough and Springer, 1973). In an experiment which did control for such factors, no difference was found between YES latencies to the less frequent members of homophone pairs and YES latencies to matched non-homophones (Coltheart *et al.*, 1977).

The pseudohomophone effect observed by Rubenstein *et al.* (1971), however, has been confirmed by Meyer and Ruddy (1973), Coltheart *et al.* (1977) and Patterson and Marcel (1977). Furthermore, Patterson and Marcel investigated this effect in two patients who had suffered injuries to the left hemisphere resulting in the syndrome of "deep dyslexia" (Marshall and Newcombe, 1973), also known as "phonemic dyslexia" (Shallice and Warrington, 1975). One symptom of this syndrome is an inability to accomplish phonological encoding of visually presented letter strings. These patients cannot pronounce aloud simple non-words such as RUD or GLEM, though they can pronounce some words (presumably solely by using the lexical lookup strategy). If the Rubenstein *et al.* effect is genuinely due to the occurrence of phonological encoding, it should be absent in these patients; and this is what Patterson and Marcel (1977) found. The patients were able to perform the lexical decision tasks with a high degree of accuracy, but neither their reaction times nor their error rates for NO responses were influenced by whether or not non-words were phonologically identical to English words. A group of control subjects judging the same set of words and non-words were, however, slower with pseudohomophones than with non-words.

Although the original pseudohomophone effect has been confirmed in the three subsequent studies referred to above, some doubts concerning this effect have been expressed. First, Meyer *et al.* (1974) and Meyer and Gutschera (1975) have argued that pseudohomophones and non-words may differ in their visual similarity to English words, and hence the difference in NO latencies for these two types of letter string may be an artefact of this visual similarity difference, rather than evidence for phonological encoding. It seems unlikely that this could be the explanation of the pseudohomophone effect found by Coltheart *et al.* (1977), in view of the closeness with which they matched each of their pseudohomophones to a non-word; but conclusive evidence that the effect is not due to differential visual similarity is provided by the absence of the pseudohomophone effect in phonemic dyslexics. These patients rely exclusively on visual similarities to English words in their (largely unsuccessful) attempts to deal with non-words (Marin *et al.*, 1975; Patterson and Marcel, 1977). If the pseudohomophone effect is a visual effect, it should thus be magnified in phonemic dyslexia. If it is a phonological effect, it should be absent in phonemic dyslexia; and it is the latter result which Patterson and Marcel obtained.

The other difficulty in connection with this effect is that it was not obtained in three experiments (Meyer and Gutschera, 1975; Cohen and Freeman, 1976, Experiment III (b); Frederiksen and Kroll, 1976). However, in all three experiments, the effect (53 ms, 17 ms and 20 ms, respectively) was in the expected direction. The effect has occurred in seven independent experiments; the fact that it was not statistically significant, though of reasonable magnitude, in the three of these experiments (which were not solely intended for investigations of the effect) scarcely justifies doubting the existence of the effect. In what follows, then, I assume that the pseudohomophone effect is a genuine one, and furthermore, that it is due to phonological encoding of non-word letter strings, rather than being an artefact of differential visual similarity.

These findings with normal and with brain-damaged readers, then, show that phonological encoding of visually presented letter strings does occur during the lexical decision task. I have argued in Section 2 that such encoding occurs by means of GPC procedures, and hence can only be performed for regular words and for non-words—not for exception words. Thus if lexical access via phonological encoding occurs in the lexical decision task, this should benefit regular words. Coltheart *et al.* (1978) compared YES latencies to regular and exception words in a lexical decision task; they found a 1-ms difference (in favour of exception words). In a second experiment, using only one class of exception word (words containing vowel digraphs with an irregular pronunciation assigned to them), the difference was 2 ms (in favour of regular words). So in these lexical decision experiments there was no trace of an advantage of regular words over exceptions, which implies that GPC processing (which would benefit regular words) is not involved in lexical access in these experiments; and if the GPC procedure is the only method for deriving phonological representation pre-lexically, this means that lexical access based on phonological encoding is not occurring in this experiment. Yet the finding that subjects in lexical decision experiments are slower to respond NO to pseudohomophones than to non-words indicates that letter strings *are* being phonologically encoded prior to lexical access.

The possible occurrence of this paradox was considered by Coltheart *et al.* (1977). They pointed out that demonstrations of phonological encoding for the NO response in a lexical decision task do not necessarily imply that access to the lexical entry of a word is ever achieved via phonological encoding. It is logically possible that phonological encoding is so slow that access based on a visual representation is always achieved before the phonological encoding process has produced a phonological representation of the letter string. When lexical access cannot be achieved (that is, when a non-word has been presented), the unsuccessful attempt at lexical access may consume a considerable time, enough to allow phonological encoding to be completed; hence effects due to phonological properties will be able to emerge. This suggestion is consistent with the absence of any effect on YES times of whether phonological encoding of a word is possible (regular words) or not possible (exceptions), whilst an effect of phonological encoding is nevertheless evident in NO responses.

This reasoning suggests that it might be possible to demonstrate a difference between regular and exception words in the lexical decision task if it were possible to impair visual encoding of letter strings whilst leaving phonological encoding unaffected, since this might slow down lexical access based on visual representations sufficiently to allow phonological encoding of a word sometimes to be completed before access to the word's lexical entry via a visual representation had occurred. Coltheart *et al.* (1978) presented letter strings vertically in one lexical decision experiment, and right-to-left (with individual letter orientation normal) in another, in an attempt to distort the visual appearances of words and hence impair visual encoding. Still no advantage of regular over exception words occurred, but perhaps this was because phonological encoding was also slowed by the unfamiliar orientations, even though each individual letter's orientation was normal.

It may thus be argued that phonological encoding of visually presented letter strings is occurring in the various lexical decision experiments mentioned in this section, but that such encoding is purely epiphenomenal as far as the YES response is concerned, since access to a lexical entry by means of visual representations of letter strings is always achieved before phonological encoding is completed. One reason for arguing in this way is that effects due to phonological encoding are evident on NO responses (where visual access to a lexical entry cannot occur) but not on YES responses. A second reason for taking this kind of view is provided by the results of Experiment 2 of Meyer and Gutschera (1975).

They used three types of letter string: real words (e.g. NAIL), pseudohomophones (e.g. NALE) and non-words (e.g. HEAK). Subjects had two different tasks to perform with these letter strings. On some trials, their task was straightforward lexical decision: they responded YES if the letter string was a word, otherwise NO. On the remaining trials, their task was to respond YES if the letter string was *pronounced* like an English word, otherwise NO. Thus the two tasks differed with respect to the response to pseudohomophones; the former task (Task S, for "spelling") required a NO response, whilst the latter (Task P, for "pronunciation") required a YES response.

Consider how the S and P tasks might be done on those occasions when the letter string presented is a word. I have argued that in Task S (lexical decision) lexical access via a visual word representation is always achieved before access via a phonological representation. Thus YES responses in Task S will always be produced by using a visual encoding, never by using a phonological encoding. In this way, difficulties potentially present with pseudohomophones (they become words once they are phonologically encoded, which would lead to an incorrect YES response) are avoided. These difficulties are not present, however, for Task P. If the phonological encoding produces a word, the response is YES, whether the original letter string was a word or not. Thus two methods for deciding upon a response are available in Task P: respond YES if lexical access occurs via a visual encoding, and respond YES if lexical access occurs via a phonological encoding. Only the former of these methods is appropriate for responding YES in Task S; the occurrence of pseudohomophones prevents the use of the latter method. One might therefore expect YES responses to words to be faster for Task P than for Task S. This was not so; the mean RTs for the two kinds of YES response differed by only 4 ms. The equality of these two YES responses suggests that in Task P, which *could* be performed correctly by using a phonological encoding, nevertheless was always performed by means of a visual encoding on those trials where the letter string presented was a word. This is to be expected if lexical access via a visual encoding is always faster than access via a phonological encoding in lexical decision experiments of the kind I have been discussing. Whether this difference between the two encoding procedures is an immutable characteristic of the visual information-processing system, or whether it can be influenced by experimental manipulations or subjects' strategies, is discussed in Section 4.

3.3. Naming latency and lexical decision time

There have been two investigations (Forster and Chambers, 1973; Frederiksen and Kroll, 1976) which attempted to discover something about how lexical decisions are made by measuring both naming latency and lexical decision time for the same set of words and non-words.

Forster and Chambers (1973) measured the correlation between naming latency and lexical decision time, separately for non-words and words. They argued that naming printed non-words depends entirely upon phonological encoding, and therefore that the possible role of phonological encoding in lexical decision could be explored, at least for non-words, by determining whether there was a positive correlation between naming latency and lexical decision time, across a group of non-words.

One type of letter string they used was so-called "unfamiliar words"; examples are SCISSEL, UMBO and ARIL. All of their unfamiliar words, though present in (large) dictionaries, were unanimously considered to be non-words by a panel of judges; furthermore, these "unfamiliar words" ($N = 15$) yielded naming latencies and lexical decision NO times equivalent to those for genuine non-words ($N = 30$). Clearly, then, for the purposes of the two experiments, the "unfamiliar words" should be classed as non-words. When all 45 of these items are treated as non-words, the correlation between naming latency and lexical decision NO time was significantly positive ($r = + 0.327$, $t_{44} = 2.269$, $p < 0.05$). When the correlations are computed separately for the 15 "unfamiliar words" and 30 non-words, they are similar in magnitude to this value, but because of the reductions in sample size the former correlation is insignificant ($r = + 0.39$) and the latter significant only with a one-tailed test ($r = + 0.32$, $p < 0.05$); but such separate analyses would seem to be unjustified.

One cannot take this positive correlation as an indication that phonological encoding is playing some role in the lexical decision task, however, since phonological encoding is not the only possible source of the correlation. The correlation could arise at an individual letter-identification stage, or at a stage at which letter sequences are identified as units, for example: either or both of these stages would precede a phonological encoding stage and also a lexical access stage, and so would introduce a correlation between the latter two stages even if there were no involvement of phonological encoding in lexical access. Nor is the correlation between naming latencies and lexical decision times for words (this was $+ 0.545$) relevant to the question of the role of phonological encoding in lexical access. A positive correlation could occur either (1) because phonological encoding is involved both in lexical decision and in the naming task; or (2) because *lexical access* is involved both in lexical decision and in the naming task, since, as Forster and Chambers argue, words can be named via their lexical entries rather than via phonological encoding. The first interpretation of the correlation implies that YES responses in a lexical decision task sometimes occur via a phonological encoding, but the second interpretation has no such implication. Hence the occurrence of this correlation cannot be taken as evidence for an involvement of phonological encoding in lexical access.

Frederiksen and Kroll (1976) also measured naming latencies and lexical decision times for a set of words and non-words. They found that naming latency increased with the number of letters in the string to be named. They also found that this increase (about 28 ms per letter) was the same for words and non-words, and was the same when words and non-words were presented in random order as when a subject received only words or only non-words, to name aloud. They argued that this string-length effect is a characteristic of the process by which phonological recoding is achieved, and therefore that one can investigate whether phonological recoding occurs in the lexical decision task by determining whether the string-length effect occurs when lexical decisions are being made. In a lexical decision experiment using the same words and non-words as the naming-latency experiment, there was no trace of an effect of number of letters on the YES response. Latency of the NO response increased monotonically with number of letters, both for one-syllable and two-syllable words, but these effects were not significant.

They therefore concluded (Frederiksen and Kroll, 1976, p. 373) that:

> there is no evidence to support the idea that phonological translation must be performed prior to accessing the internal lexicon. The results suggest instead that, at least in this case, lexical access is based upon the distribution of visual features in the array.

This conclusion depends upon the assumption that the string-length effect observed in the naming-latency experiment reflects the operation of the process by which a string of letters is converted into a phonological code. I will argue that this assumption is not obligatory, and in fact is not even completely consistent with Frederiksen and Kroll's naming-latency data.

If one distinguishes between the terms *phonological code* (the form of code resulting from the application of GPCs to a letter string) and *articulatory code* (the form of code which is the immediate precursor of an overt pronunciation), one could argue that the string-length effect may be a property of the process by which an articulatory code is generated, and so its occurrence is irrelevant to the question of whether or not a phonological code is being used. Thus Frederiksen and Kroll's

argument rests on a repudiation of the distinction between phonological code and articulatory code, and although they give reasons for
such a repudiation, these reasons have been challenged (Coltheart *et al.*,
1978).

A more serious problem exists, here, however. Frederiksen and Kroll
argue that, in a naming-latency experiment, non-words are always
named by application of the GPC procedure, whereas words are
sometimes named by this method and sometimes by using the internal
lexicon; and they provide evidence for this view, as do Forster and
Chambers (1973). This point is discussed later, in Section 4.3. Its
relevance here is that, if a string-length effect on naming latency occurs
whenever a phonological code is generated by application of GPCs
to a letter string, whereas naming via the lexicon does not generate
such an effect, then the slope of the function relating naming latency
to number of letters in a string should be steeper for non-words than
for words. This is so because the effect occurs every time a non-word is
named, but only on some of the occasions on which a word is named.
This difference in slope did not occur in Frederiksen and Kroll's
experiment; words and non-words yielded the same slope.

Furthermore, Frederiksen and Kroll argue that the lexicon is more
often used for naming words in a blocked condition (where only words
are presented) than in the mixed condition (where a random sequence
of words and non-words was presented). If so, the effect of number of
letters on naming latency for words should be attenuated in the
blocked condition compared to the mixed condition. This effect too
was absent from Frederiksen and Kroll's data: the slope of the relationship between number of letters and naming latency for words was the
same in the blocked as in the mixed condition.*

Thus there are difficulties in arguing that the effect of number of
letters on naming latency is a property of the procedure by which letter
strings are converted to phonological representations without lexical
involvement; but if this argument cannot be accepted then the failure
to find any effect of number of letters on lexical decision time does not
imply that lexical access is never based on phonological encoding.
Consequently, neither of the studies of the relationship between
naming latency and lexical decision time discussed in this section
provide unequivocal evidence concerning the role of phonological

---

* The absence of interactions between the string-length effect and the word/non-
  word and blocked/mixed variables could be explained by viewing the effect as an
  attribute of an articulatory coding system which is required for pronunciation
  equally when an item is a non-word, a mixed word or a blocked word. Thus one
  could take the view that the absence of these interactions is evidence for a distinction between phonological and articulatory codes.

encoding in lexical access, though the conclusions reached were consistent with the general argument of this chapter concerning phonological encoding and lexical access.

3.4. Phonological encoding in semantic tasks

This has been investigated by Meyer and Ruddy (1973) whose experiment was repeated by Meyer and Gutschera (1975, Experiment I) with the same results. On each trial in these experiments, the subject was presented visually with a category question (e.g. IS A KIND OF FRUIT?), followed, after a brief delay, by a test word. Three types of test word were used: category members (e.g. PEAR) pseudomembers (e.g. PAIR—these were non-members which were homophones of members) and non-members (e.g. TAIL). Half of a subject's trials were run under Task S (for "spelling"—respond YES only if the test word is a category member) and half were Task P (for "pronunciation"—respond YES if the test word is pronounced like a category member). Thus pseudomembers required a NO response for Task S and a YES response for Task P.

Let us refer to this as the categorization experiment. Meyer and Gutschera also carried out a lexical decision experiment (their Experiment 2, mentioned briefly in Section 3.2). This paralleled the categorization experiment in that three types of letter string were used (words, pseudohomophones, and non-words) and in that half the trials required the subject to deal with a letter string in terms of its spelling (Task S—here the correct response to a pseudohomophone is NO) and half in terms of how it is pronounced (Task P—here the correct response to a pseudohomophone is YES). I would like first of all to consider the results of this lexical decision task, and then to return to the categorization task.

3.4.1. The NO response in lexical decision experiments

A difficulty which sometimes occurs when lexical decision tasks are being discussed is that, although it can be plausibly argued that a subject makes the YES response by detecting that lexical access has occurred, it is unclear how he makes the NO response. One suggestion, made by Rubenstein et al. (1971), is that there is a serial search of lexical entries, and that when this exhausts the lexicon without locating a lexical entry appropriate to the letter string which has been presented to the subject, the response NO is made. Evidence against this view has been provided by Coltheart et al. (1977). They proposed instead that the NO response is made by means of a deadline. The subject merely waits until some time t has elapsed since stimulus onset, and if at that point no lexical entry has been located, he decides that no entry is ever going to be located, so responds NO. Clearly he could choose a value of t such that even the slowest lexical access would occur in less than this time, and such a value would provide perfectly accurate (though slow) NO responses. If these responses are unacceptably slow, t could be reduced (which would introduce incorrect NO responding) until the desired speed–accuracy relationship is reached. In these terms, the pseudohomophone effect in the lexical decision task occurs because phonological encoding is sometimes completed in less than t ms, so that on these occasions a lexical entry is accessed incorrectly before the deadline is reached. If a subject attempts to circumvent this difficulty by reducing the value of t to prevent phonological encoding *ever* being completed earlier than the deadline he may encounter a new difficulty: this value may now be so small that the deadline often expires before visual lexical access to genuine words can be completed, so that an unacceptably large error rate on word trials would result. The two difficulties could only be avoided if two things were jointly true. First, lexical access via a visual encoding would have to be fast enough, and lexical access via a phonological encoding slow enough, so that the fastest phonological access was slower than the slowest visual access. Secondly, a value of t would have to be chosen which lay between the slowest visual access time and the fastest phonological access time. Under these circumstances, there would be no pseudohomophone effect and yet no incorrect NO responses to genuine words. Since a pseudohomophone effect *does* occur in lexical decision experiments, this ideal situation does not obtain. Therefore, either subjects choose unnecessarily large values of t, or else the distribution of times required for visual lexical access overlaps with the distribution of times required for phonological access, or both. It is argued later that, in these kinds of experiments, the two distributions do not overlap.

3.4.2. *Meyer and Gutschera's lexical decision experiment*

In Task S of Meyer and Gutschera's lexical decision experiment, NO responses were 53 ms slower to pseudohomophones than to non-words, and although this effect was not significant in their experiment, reasons for regarding it as a genuine effect were advanced in Section 3.2. Thus I will take the view that on a small proportion of occasions in this experiment, phonological lexical access occurred before the deadline elapsed.

Consider now what the subject has to do in Task P of the lexical decision experiment. He is now required to respond YES to pseudo-homophones instead of NO. Therefore he must now arrange matters so that phonological lexical access occurs *before* the deadline elapses, since it is only by means of phonological lexical access that he can produce a YES response to pseudohomophones. There are two ways in which he might do this. First, he could use the same value for the deadline as he used in Task S, but carry out phonological encoding and phonological lexical access much faster, so that it is always, rather than never, completed before the deadline. Alternatively, the times needed for phonological encoding and phonological lexical access could be left as they were for Task S, but the deadline value increased enough so that phonological access always occurred earlier than the deadline.

One can assess these possibilities by comparing reaction times in Task S and in Task P. If the subject deals with Task P simply by adopting a much larger deadline value, the NO responses to non-words, which are made when the deadline elapses, will take much longer in Task P than Task S. If the subject deals with Task P instead by leaving the deadline value unaltered and carrying out phonological access much faster, so that it is completed before the deadline elapses, then non-words will yield equivalent NO responses in the two tasks (since the deadline is unchanged) and furthermore YES responses to pseudowords in Task P will be faster than NO responses to non-words in Task S (since the latter responses provide a measure of the average deadline value, and the former responses must be made before the deadline elapses).

What Meyer and Gutschera found was that NO responses to non-words took 270 ms longer in Task P than in Task S, and that YES responses to pseudowords in Task P took more than 100 ms longer than NO responses to non-words in Task S. Thus subjects did adopt a much larger deadline value in Task P than in Task S; they did not deal with Task P solely by increasing the speed of phonological lexical access. They may *also* have adopted the strategy of accelerating phonological access; it may be possible to detect whether this occurred by fitting a model involving the distributions of visual and phonological access times and a deadline to the Task S and Task P data.

A possible line of argument here is that, if the subject does carry out phonological access more rapidly in Task P than in Task S (as well as using a longer deadline in Task P) this should produce a difference in YES responses to words, since in Task S these responses can only be produced by visual access, whereas in Task P either form of access can produce such responses. Certainly, if YES responses to words were faster in Task P than Task S, this would suggest more rapid phonological access in the former task. However, if YES responses to words were equally fast in Task P and in Task S (which is what Meyer and Gutschera found) this does not rule out an increase in the speed of phonological access in Task P. It could be that in Task S there is no overlap between the distribution of visual access times and the distribution of phonological access times. If so, and if phonological access is made more rapid in Task P than it was in Task S, there *still* need be no overlap between the two distributions and hence no difference between YES responses to words in the S and P conditions, since in this situation such responses are always made via visual access in both conditions. If it were demonstrated that visual and phonological access times do have overlapping distributions in Task S, then the equality of YES responses to words in Task P and Task S would demonstrate that the mean time for phonological lexical access was not reduced in Task P relative to Task S. However, it has not been shown that these distributions of times do overlap. The existence of the pseudohomophone effect in lexical decision time does not imply any overlap. What it implies is that phonological lexical access sometimes occurs prior to the *deadline*, not that it sometimes occurs prior to visual lexical access.

3.4.3. Regular words and exceptions again

Inspection of the words used in Meyer and Gutschera's experiment reveals that approximately 23% of them were exceptions to the grapheme–phoneme correspondence rules provided by Wijk (1966) and Venezky (1970).* Furthermore, application of the rules to each of these exception words produced a non-word in almost every case, rather than simply a different word. It was argued in Section 2 that, if phonological lexical access occurs, it is achieved by applying GPC procedures to letter strings, and hence that such access can only occur for regular words. If so, phonological lexical access is impossible for almost a quarter of the words used in Meyer and Gutschera's lexical decision experiment. What implications does this have for the foregoing analysis of Task S and Task P results?

For Task S, the presence of exception words is irrelevant if, as has been argued earlier, YES responses in this task are made on the basis of visual lexical access. The fact that some of the words will be given a correct phonological code (the regular words) whereas others will be given phonological codes which are non-words (the exceptions) cannot benefit regular words or cause errors with non-words, because phonological access to a lexical entry is never the basis of the YES response. Occasionally phonological access does beat the deadline (hence the pseudohomophone effect), but, when the letter string present is a word, occasions when phonological access precedes the deadline will not affect behaviour because visual lexical access will already have occurred and the YES response made. Thus any potential difficulties for exception

---

* I am grateful to Dr. Meyer for providing a listing of his stimuli.

words or benefits for regular words will be concealed by the relative slowness of phonological lexical access and by the particular choice of deadline value.

For Task P, the presence of exception words is irrelevant too. The crucial point is that NO responses are made by a deadline. Thus when CHOIR is encoded as the non-word /tʃɔijə/ by the GPC procedure, this does not generate incorrect tendencies towards responding NO, it simply has no effect. Very soon afterwards, if not before, access to the lexical entry for CHOIR by means of a visual word representation will occur, and a correct YES response is thus produced. What *could* happen here is an advantage for regular words over exceptions in the latency of YES responses; this would occur if there is a significant proportion of occasions on which phonological lexical access precedes visual lexical access in Task P. Such comparisons between YES times to regular and to exception words in Tasks S and P might allow us to discover something about the overlap between the distributions of visual and phonological access times in these tasks, since an advantage for regular words demonstrates an overlap of the distributions.

The presence of a substantial proportion of exception words in this experiment, then, provides no difficulties for the account being given of how subjects perform Task P and Task S, since visual access is sufficient for dealing with words in both tasks, and since the incorrect phonological codes derived from exception words will not lead the subject to produce an incorrect NO response.

3.4.4. The NO response in semantic categorization experiments
As was the case for the lexical decision experiment, we need to decide how NO responses are made in semantic categorization experiments before drawing conclusions about phonological encoding from the results of such experiments. A deadline model for the NO response is much less attractive when the task is semantic categorization than when it is lexical decision. In Meyer and Gutschera's semantic categorization experiment described at the beginning of Section 3.4, the letter string to which a response is being made is always a word, and so lexical access will always occur, whether the correct response is YES or NO. Thus one cannot make NO responses contingent upon the non-occurrence of lexical access within some time t since stimulus onset, because within any such time access will occur just as often when NO is the correct response as when YES is. There are two considerably more plausible suggestions as to how the NO response could be made. The first is that the subject accesses the lexical entry of the target word, retrieves its semantic representation, and interrogates this representation to determine whether the target word is or is not a

member of the semantic category. The other possibility is that the target word is encoded (this encoding could be visual, or phonological; or both encodings could be used) and then a search of the members of the semantic category is made. The YES response is produced if the encoded target word matches any of these category members; if no match is found, then the subject response is NO. Here the lexical entry of the target word is not used.

A decision between these two possibilities can be made provided we once again assume that phonological encoding prior to lexical access is achieved by application of GPC procedures and hence is available only for regular words. Approximately 14% of each of the three categories of words used by Meyer and Gutschera are exception words, and for nearly all of them the incorrect phonological representation produced by GPCs is a non-word (e.g. SOUL → /saul/). Now, let us assume that semantic categorization is done by searching the relevant semantic category. If a phonological encoding of the target word is ever used for the category search, the search will fail for all those category members which are exception words (14% of them) because no match for the phonologically encoded exception words will be found. Thus in Task S, when the phonological search fails, the subject cannot tell whether this is because the word he is looking at is a non-member (to which he should respond NO) or a member which is also an exception word (to which he should respond YES). Furthermore, if the phonological search succeeds and a lexical match occurs, the subject cannot tell whether this is because the word he is looking at is a regularly spelled member (to which he should respond YES) or a regularly spelled pseudomember (to which he should respond NO).

Thus, unless the phonological search is rarely faster than the visual search (and, as we shall see, the opposite is implied by Meyer and Gutschera's data if one assumes a search model), the result of the phonological search will produce many NO and YES errors. The phonological search is even less useful for the P task. Here a visual search cannot be used to produce a NO response, because such a search fails equally with non-members (to which the response should be NO) and pseudomembers (to which the response should be YES). The alternative, a phonological search, will fail with non-members (thus correctly producing a NO response) but also with members and pseudomembers which are exception words (thus incorrectly producing a NO response). Thus, even when *both* searches fail to locate a lexical entry the correct response may still be YES. How then can a subject know when he ought to respond NO? This argument leads to the conclusion that, if semantic categorization is done by serial search, only a visual search would be of use in the S task, and neither visual nor phonological search could allow subjects to cope with the P task. Since there were clear phonological effects in the S task, and since subjects were actually faster in the P task than the S task with members and pseudomembers, Meyer and Gutschera's data are difficult to reconcile with a search model of semantic categorization.

There is a second form of conflict between their data and a search model, one which does not assume that phonological search is based upon GPC encoding. In the S task, a phonological search can at best only be used for the NO response, since if YES responses are generated by it, the subject will incorrectly respond YES to pseudomembers. In the P task, visual search can at best only be used for the YES response, since if it is allowed to produce NO responses, the subject will incorrectly respond NO to pseudomembers. Meyer and Gutschera therefore proposed that both forms of search operate independently and in parallel in both forms of task, but that in Task S, location of a lexical entry by the phonological search has no effect (no response is made), and that in Task P, failure of the visual search has no effect (no response is made). In other words, phonological search is not allowed to produce a YES response in Task S, and visual search is not allowed to produce a NO response in Task P.

Define V as the time needed for an exhaustive visual search, and P as the time needed for an exhaustive phonological search. Given a search model with the two additions proposed by Meyer and Gutschera, we can express in terms of V and P the mean search times required for each of the three types of word in each of the two types of task. These expressions are given in Table II. They assume that when a search succeeds, the time consumed by the search is on the average half that needed for an exhaustive search. Note that YES responses to members in the P task and NO responses to non-members in the S task can be produced by either form of search; the other four types of response are based on a single search mode.

One can estimate the values of V and P from Meyer and Gutschera's data, since V is equal to twice the difference between mean NO time to pseudomembers and mean YES time to members in Task S, and P is equal to twice the difference between mean NO time to non-members and mean YES time to pseudomembers in Task P. Estimating from Meyer and Gutschera's Figs 6a and 6b produces a value of roughly 200 ms for V and roughly 100 ms for P. This is the first surprise—phonological search is twice as fast as visual search, rather than being slower, as has consistently been implied by earlier work. A comparison between mean NO latency to non-members in the S task and mean YES latency to members in the P task produces a further surprise. These means differ by roughly 60 ms. This means, according to

TABLE II. Mean search times required when a search model is applied to the data of Meyer and Gutschera (1975).

	Member	Pseudomember	Non-member
Task S	$V/2$	V	min (V, P)
Task P	min $(V/2, P/2)$	$P/2$	P

Table II, that the minimum of P and V is on average 120 ms. Of course, on a search model, the mean value of min (P, V) cannot be larger than the mean value of P, nor larger than the mean value of V. Since min (P, V) has an average which is no smaller than the mean value of P, this implies that P is *always* faster than V, not just faster on the average. Such an implication is inconsistent with two major features of Meyer and Gutschera's data. Firstly, YES responses in Task P are faster to members (where both visual and phonological search can produce a YES response) than to pseudomembers (where only phonological search can produce a YES response). Secondly, NO responses to non-members are faster in Task S (where both searches can produce a NO response) than in Task P (where only phonological search can produce a NO response). In both cases, responses are made more rapidly when a phonological search is supplemented by a parallel independent visual search than when only a phonological search is used; and this could not be so if visual search were slower than phonological search on every occasion. Yet application of a search model to Meyer and Gutschera's data yields this conclusion concerning the two forms of search.

I have thus suggested two reasons for doubting the applicability of a search model to this semantic categorization experiment. First, the existence of exception words makes it difficult to see how a phonological search could be used; yet phonological effects are evident in the data. Secondly, the analysis of reaction times by the search model produces internal inconsistencies. The alternative view suggested earlier was that the task is accomplished by accessing the lexical entry of the target word, examining the semantic representation of the word provided by such access, and determining in this way whether the target word belongs to the specified semantic category. I will argue that this view can account for the results of Meyer and Gutschera's semantic categorization experiment, and that applying it to these results provides information about the roles of phonological and visual encoding in semantic categorization.

3.4.5. Meyer and Gutschera's semantic categorization experiment
This is described in Table III, which shows the three types of stimulus used in this experiment, with examples relating to the question IS A KIND OF FRUIT? All stimuli used in this experiment were not only words, but homophones, and so, when phonologically encoded, were potentially capable of exciting two different lexical entries, one of which is incorrect.

TABLE III. An outline of Meyer and Gutschera's semantic categorization experiment.

Class of item	Example	Form of access	Entry accessed	Task S decision
Member	PEAR	visual	pear	Yes
			pear	Yes
		phonological	pair	No (error)
Pseudomember	PAIR	visual	pair	No
			pair	No
		phonological	pear	Yes (error)
Non-member	TAIL	visual	tail	No
			tail	No
		phonological	tale	No

Meyer and Gutschera propose that subjects avoid responding YES to PAIR in this experiment by refusing to make YES responses when these are arrived at via phonological access; such access is only permitted to produce NO responses. Thus the response of YES to PEAR when PAIR was presented (and also, though they do not consider this, the response of YES to PEAR when PEAR was presented and a YES decision reached via phonological access) cannot be made; the subject simply waits until a decision based on visual access is made. This answer to the question of how subjects avoid responding YES to pseudo-items in Type S experiments seems to me not entirely satisfactory, for three reasons:

1. If this form of strategy (do not respond YES if access is phonological) is available to subjects, why don't they use it in the lexical decision task to avoid the difficulties caused by pseudohomophones?

2. As a matter of fact, subjects *did* respond YES to pseudohomophones quite often in Meyer and Gutschera's Task S, this error rate being 15%. If the subject does not permit the production of a YES response consequent upon phonological encoding, where do these errors come from?

3. Errors occur, according to Table III, when a decision is made via phonological access, and when the wrong lexical entry is accessed first (PAIR rather than PEAR for members; PEAR rather than PAIR for pseudomembers). The strategy of not responding YES via phonological access eliminates the errors with pseudomembers, but not the errors with members. One would therefore expect incorrect NO responses to members to be more frequent than incorrect YES responses to pseudomembers. The reverse was true; the error rate for members was 10·5%, and for pseudomembers it was 15%.

These three objections to Meyer and Gutschera's proposal may not be conclusive, but they do suggest that it might be worth looking for an alternative account of how a subject performs semantic categorization under Task S conditions. The account I want to suggest begins by assuming that, although as argued earlier lexical *access* via a visual code is always faster than lexical access via a phonological code, nevertheless a semantic categorization *decision* can sometimes be reached earlier via a phonological code than via a visual code. That this can be so may be demonstrated as follows.

The categorization task consists of two serially ordered stages: lexical access and semantic interrogation. Suppose that the distribution of visual lexical access times has a maximum of max (VA) and a minimum of min (VA), the distribution of phonological access times has the limits max (PA) and min (PA), and the distribution of times taken by semantic interrogation has the limits max (I) and min (I). Now the overlap of the P and V access–time distributions is max (VA) − min (PA), positive values representing overlap, negative values indicating that the slowest visual access is faster than the fastest phonological access (no overlap).

Consider now the distribution of *decision* times (times between stimulus onset and result of semantic interrogation). There will be two such distributions, one for decisions using visual access and one for decisions using phonological access. The maximum of the visual distribution will be [max (VA) + max (I)] and the minimum of the phonological distribution will be [min (PA) + min (I)]. Therefore the overlap between the distribution of decision times based on visual access and the distribution of decision times based on phonological access is:

$$[\max (VA) + \max (I)] - [\min (PA) + \min (I)].$$

Again, positive values indicate overlap. This can be rearranged thus:

$$[\max (VA) - \min (PA)] + [\max (I) - \min (I)].$$

Note that the first half of this expression gives the overlap between the visual and phonological access–time distributions. Unless the distribution of semantic interrogation times has zero variance, $\max (I) > \min (I)$, and hence $[\max (I) - \min (I)] > 0$. Thus the overlap between the distributions of phonological and visual *decision* times is larger than the overlap between the distributions of phonological and visual *access* times. In fact, whatever is the case for the overlap of the access time distributions, there will be an overlap of the decision time distributions unless

$$\min (PA) - \max (VA) > \max (I) - \min (I),$$

i.e. unless the range of interrogation times is smaller than the difference between the fastest phonological access time and the slowest visual access time.

Thus it is not implausible to take the view that, even if there is no overlap between the two access time distributions, the proportion of occasions on which a decision is based upon phonological access in semantic categorization tasks is large enough to produce phonological effects on the speed and/or accuracy of such decisions.

The second point I wish to make before offering an alternative explanation of Meyer and Gutschera's results concerns lexical priming. The accessibility of a lexical entry is increased if a word semantically related to this entry has just been encountered by the subject (*see* Section 4.3). Since, for the example given in Table III, the subject has just seen the word FRUIT, access time for the lexical entry for PEAR will have been made shorter than normal, whereas access times for the entries for PAIR, TALE and TAIL will not have been affected by the just-presented category name.

My proposal is that the subject can perform this Type S semantic categorization task in a satisfactory way, despite the presence of pseudomembers, without needing to adopt any special strategies such as refusing to respond YES when access was phonological. As in lexical decision tasks, parallel and independent access procedures are being operated (one visual, one phonological). Decisions based on visual access present no problem, since such access deals correctly with members, pseudomembers and non-members. On a small but not negligible proportion of trials, however, a decision based upon phonological access is made. For non-members, this decision will be a correct NO, even if it was produced by accessing the wrong lexical entry (TALE instead of TAIL). Note that, in the absence of priming, the lexical entries for the correct and incorrect entries for a non-member should be equally accessible, taking all non-members into account, so within the small proportion of occasions when decisions are based upon phonological access, the entry accessed will be the correct one half the time.

On occasions when a decision via phonological access is made in response to a pseudomember, the wrong entry (PEAR) will be more likely to be accessed than the correct one (PAIR) because the former entry is primed by the previously presented category name. When PEAR is accessed and this access serves as the basis for a decision, the subject will simply make an error—he will respond YES. This will not happen every time a phonologically based decision is made, since sometimes the entry yielding the decision is PAIR; but an error will be made on more than 50% of these occasions, since priming has made PEAR more accessible than PAIR. The proportion of incorrect YES responses to pseudomembers, which was 15% in Meyer and Gutschera's experiment, is an upper bound on the proportion of occasions on which a decision was based upon phonological access to the entry PEAR.

On occasions when a decision via phonological access is made to a member, the right entry, PEAR, since it is primed, is more likely to have been accessed than the wrong entry, PAIR. Thus incorrect NO responses to members should be less common than incorrect YES responses to pseudomembers, since the former error is produced via an unprimed entry whilst the latter is produced via a primed entry. This difference in error rates held in Meyer and Gutschera's experiment, the error rates being 10·5% and 15%, respectively. Furthermore, incorrect NO responses to non-members should be made much less often than these other two types of error, since even when a decision is based upon the wrong lexical entry, the decision itself is still correct; and it was the case in Meyer and Gutschera's experiment that non-members yielded a lower error rate than members or pseudomembers.

This account also describes correctly the reaction time data of Meyer and Gutschera. There are three ways in which a NO response can occur to a non-member such as TAIL: visual access to TAIL, phonological access to TAIL or phonological access to TALE. This is not true for a pseudomember such as PAIR; only two ways are available, since the last possibility (phonological access to an incorrect lexical entry) generates an error. Thus NO responses to non-members occur by whichever of three independent processes finishes first, whereas only two of these contribute to NO responses to pseudo-members. Therefore, as was found, the NO response to pseudo-members will be slower than the NO response to non-members.

The YES response to members should be faster than the NO response to pseudomembers, because when these responses are based on visual access, the lexical entry involved in the YES response is primed whereas the lexical entry involved in the NO response is not, and this is also true for correct responses based on phonological access. This YES–NO difference did occur (though of course it could also simply be a feature of the procedure used for interrogating the semantic representation yielded by lexical access).

Thus an account can be given of the error rate and reaction time data of Meyer and Gutschera's Type S semantic categorization task without supposing that subjects introduce any unusual strategies to cope with this task. The answer to the question "What does the subject do about pseudomembers?" is "Nothing". Decisions based on phonological access do not occur very often, and even when they do, sometimes the entry accessed is the correct one; when it is not, the subject makes an error. The only differences between what a subject does in a Type S lexical decision task and what he does in a Type S semantic categorization task are that (1) a deadline is used for responding NO to non-words in lexical decision, since these have no lexical entries; and (2) after lexical access has occurred, the semantic categorization task requires a second stage (semantic interrogation) before the subject can decide how to respond, whereas in lexical decision the response YES is made as soon as lexical access occurs.

Consider now the Type P semantic categorization task. The subject must do something different here, compared to what he does in a Type S task, because now he must respond YES to pseudomembers nearly all the time, instead of hardly ever.

First of all, how might exception words be dealt with in Type S and Type P tasks? In Type S tasks, the incorrect phonological representations they are given by the GPC procedure will prevent them from reaching their lexical entries via phonological encoding, but *wrong* entries will rarely be accessed, since these incorrect phonological representations are rarely words. Exceptions will simply not enjoy any benefits produced by phonological access; they will be dealt with solely by visual access. Matters are more serious in Type P tasks. In response to IS A PART OF A SHOE?, neither visual access nor GPC-based phonological access permit the correct YES response to SOUL (since, by the GPC procedure, its pronunciation is /saul/). The only way to produce a correct YES response in a Type P task to a pseudomember which is also an exception word is to gain access to its lexical entry by a visual code, obtain its phonological representation from this entry, and use this for further lexical access. If this is what subjects decide to do in Type P tasks, it not only provides them with a way of dealing with exception words, but it allows them to avoid incorrectly responding NO on the basis of visual access. When semantic interrogation following visual access yields positive evidence, a YES response can of course be made; but when it yields negative evidence, the subject obtains a phonological representation from the lexical entry and uses this for accessing the lexicon again. The entry located in this way is then interrogated and a YES or NO response made.

This proposal, however, is insufficient to explain Meyer and Gutschera's results, because it predicts that YES latencies to members will be the same in Task P and Task S. This was not so; these responses were faster in Task P. I cannot see how else to explain this except by proposing that subjects carry out phonological encoding and subsequent phonologically based lexical access more rapidly in Task P than in Task S. Whether subjects are capable of exerting such control over their phonological encoding systems is discussed in more detail in Section 4. If this is possible, it does explain the superiority of Task P over Task S in responses to genuine members.

Meyer and Gutschera's Task P results can thus be accounted for if one supposes that, when subjects are asked whether a word *sounds like*, rather than merely *is*, a category member, they modify their usual mode of processing in two ways. First, they carry out phonological recoding and phonological lexical access more rapidly than usual. Secondly, when they discover that a visually accessed lexical entry is not that of a category member, they obtain from this entry a phonological representation and use this for further lexical access.

According to this account, YES responses to members are faster in Task P than Task S because phonological access is faster, visual access taking the same amount of time. With non-members, NO responses are slower in Task P than in Task S because, although phonological access is faster at producing a NO response in Task P than in Task S, most of the responses in Task S were based on visual access, which is the faster mode, and this mode is greatly slowed in Task P by the necessity of carrying out the subsidiary phonological access (after visual access has suggested a NO response) before a NO response can be made.

Within the P task, YES responses will be faster to members than to pseudomembers. Although such responses can be based on visual access for either form of word, the procedure of obtaining a phonological representation from a visually accessed lexical entry and then using this for subsequent access is needed when visual access occurs for pseudomembers but not when it occurs for members; hence the additional time required to respond YES to pseudomembers.

Stringent investigations of the psychological reality of the distinction between exception words and regular words are possible when Task P semantic categorization is used. The YES response to a pseudomember should take much more time when it is an exception word, since it will require the elaborate procedure of visual access, followed by subsequent phonological access; regular pseudomembers can be dealt with simply by phonological access. Similarly the NO response to non-members should be much slower for exception words than for regular words.

3.4.6. Baron's experiments on phrase evaluation

Baron (1973) asked his subjects to classify short visually presented phrases as making sense or being nonsensical. Three types of item were used: genuine phrases (e.g. TIE THE KNOT), pseudophrases (e.g. ITS KNOT SO—these make sense when represented phonologically) and non-phrases (e.g. I AM KILL, which are nonsense even when spoken). These items were used in two experiments; the first a Task S experiment (respond YES if this item is correct, i.e. the phrase makes sense, in terms of how it is spelled) and the second a Task P experiment (respond YES if this item is correct, i.e. the phrase makes sense in terms of how it is pronounced).

For Task S, the mean latency of NO responses was slightly greater to pseudophrases than to non-phrases in both sessions of the experiment but these differences were small (10 ms and 15 ms, respectively) and not statistically significant. However, subjects did make significantly more errors (incorrect YES responses) to pseudophrases than to non-phrases (5·1% vs. 2·4%). The YES response to genuine phrases was faster in Task P than in Task S.

These phrase-evaluation experiments are precisely parallel to the experiments of Meyer and Gutschera on semantic categorization and lexical decision. All three forms of experiment used "items" (phonologically and visually correct), "pseudo-items" (phonologically correct but visually incorrect) and "non-items" (phonologically and visually incorrect); and all three forms of experiment were carried out under Task S conditions (operating in terms of the item's spelling) and Task P conditions (operating in terms of the item's pronunciation). Whether the subject's task is lexical decision, semantic categorization, or judgement of sense/nonsense, the subject is worse at responding NO to pseudo-items than to non-items in Task S (though in Baron's experiment this was a significant effect only on error rate, not on latency), and he is better at responding YES to genuine items in Task P than in

Task S. These two effects, one with NO and one with YES, imply the occurrence of phonological encoding.

The explanation of Meyer and Gutschera's semantic categorization experiments offered earlier provides a satisfactory account of the results of Baron's phrase-evaluation experiments. Under Task S conditions, performance is superior with non-items than with pseudo-items because, of the three ways of dealing with pseudo-items and non-items shown in Table III, all lead to a correct NO for non-items, whereas one leads to an incorrect YES for pseudo-items. There is one difference between the Baron experiment and the Meyer and Gutschera experiment, which is that priming does not occur in Baron's experiment. Since it was priming which was proposed as an explanation of higher error rates for pseudo-items than genuine items in Meyer and Gutschera's experiment, one would expect this difference to be absent in Baron's experiment; and one finds that these error rates were similar (5·1% and 4·3%, respectively) and did not differ significantly.

For the Task P version of Baron's experiment, as in the Task P version of Meyer and Gutschera's experiment, it is suggested that subjects (1) carry out phonological access more rapidly than they did in Task S; and (2) do not respond NO when negative evidence is obtained via visual access, but instead obtain, from this access, a phonological representation which is used for subsequent lexical access; interrogation of the semantic representation thus obtained yields a YES or NO response. This correctly describes Baron's Task P results. Genuine items produced faster YES responses in Task P than Task S. Responses to non-items were slower, and much less accurate, in Task P than Task S. Within the P task, YES responses were faster to genuine items than to pseudo-items.

It thus appears that the account proposed for Meyer and Gut-schera's Type S and Type P semantic categorization experiments is also adequate to account for the results of Baron's Type S and Type P phrase-evaluation experiments.

3.4.7. Individual differences

Baron and McKillop (1975) investigated the occurrence of individual differences in the relative speeds of visual and phonological lexical access. On each trial in this experiment the subject was given a list of phrases, half of which required a YES response and half a NO response. Three types of trial were used:

1. SH—here each item was a genuine phrase (respond YES) or a pseudophrase (respond NO),

2. HN—here each item was a pseudophrase (respond YES) or a non-phrase (respond NO),

3. SN—each item was a genuine phrase (respond YES) or a non-phrase (respond NO).

Thus SH lists could only be dealt with by visual access, HN lists only by phonological access, and SN lists by either form of access. A total of forty subjects was run. The speed of visual access relative to phonological access was measured for each subject by calculating the ratio of his SH time (that is, the time he needed to perform a task solely via visual access) to his HN time (the time he needed to perform a task solely via phonological access). When this ratio is low, the subject is unusually fast at visual access relative to phonological access; when this ratio is high, the subject is unusually slow at visual access relative to phonological access. Those five subjects with the lowest ratio(call them Group V) and those five with the highest ratio (call them Group P) were selected from the original forty subjects. With the SN lists, where correct responses can be produced by either form of lexical access, Group V subjects were significantly faster than Group P subjects. This is consistent with the view that, even when both forms of access can be used to make a response, visual access is on the average faster than phonological access. Further analysis indicated that Group P subjects actually used phonological access more than Group V subjects in the SN task (rather than the difference between the groups merely being in the speed of visual lexical access).

These data repay still closer inspection. The two groups yielded almost identical times and error rates for the HN lists (those which could only be dealt with by phonological access). Thus the difference between the two groups is not in mean phonological access time; therefore, since the groups differed in the ratio of visual access time to phonological access time, it must be that the difference between the groups is due to a difference in their visual access times. Group P has slow visual access; in fact, since performance in this group was no better on SN lists (where either form of access works) than on HN lists (where only phonological access works), one could conclude that, for Group P subjects, phonological access is always faster than visual access. Group V has fast visual access; in fact, since performance in this group was no better on SN lists than on SH lists (where only visual access works) one could conclude that, for Group V subjects, visual access is always faster than phonological access. If this is so, then responses to SN lists are produced purely by phonological access for Group P and purely by visual access for Group V; and since Group P was slower than Group V on SN lists, phonological lexical access in those subjects for whom it is the faster access mode is slower than visual lexical access in those subjects for whom it is the faster access mode. Furthermore, the equality of the two groups on HN lists shows that phonological lexical access time is no faster in those subjects for whom it is the faster access mode than in these subjects for whom it is the slower access mode. In sum, then, general conclusions of the form "Visual lexical access is faster than phonological lexical access" may not hold for all adult subjects, merely for the majority; such conclusions may be reached only because Group V individuals predominate in the population from which subjects are drawn.

Frederiksen (1976) has studied such individual differences by measuring the relationship between naming latency for words or non-words and a subject's reading ability as measured by the Nelson–Denny Reading Test; his subjects were twenty high-school students. Naming latency was inversely related to reading ability, this relationship being more marked for non-words than for words. Naming latencies were longer for two-syllable items, and this was a larger effect for poorer readers; here it should be noted that Frederiksen and Kroll (1976) found no syllable effects on naming latency with college-student subjects. Poor readers also showed more marked effects on naming latency of numbers of letters in a string than did good readers.*

3.5. Conclusions

One thing is quite clear from the experiments discussed in Section 3. Subjects presented visually with a string of letters in a task requiring lexical decision, semantic categorization or phrase evaluation do derive a phonological recoding of the letter string, even when the task does not require this, and even when this can make the task more difficult. Evidence that this occurs includes the pseudohomophone effect in the lexical decision task, the difficulties caused by pseudomembers in a Type S semantic categorization task, the increased error rates for pseudo-phrases relative to non-phrases in a Type S phrase-evaluation task, the reaction-time advantage of genuine phrases over pseudophrases in a Type P phrase-evaluation task, and the faster YES responses to genuine items in Type P tasks compared to Type S tasks. Perhaps relevant also is the finding of Bakan and Alperson (1967) that naming the ink colour of a stimulus is slower when that stimulus is a pronounceable non-word (DAP, ISH, LAR or FON) than when it is unpronounceable

---

* Studies of individual differences in naming latency reported by Baron and Strawson (1976) will not be discussed here since somewhat conflicting results have been obtained by L. Midgley-West (unpublished).

(FJQ, RZQ, VGJ or XFH). If subjects were not sometimes obtaining phonological codes for the letter strings whose colour they were supposed to name, there is no reason why colour-naming latency should be influenced by whether or not such strings are pronounceable.

Thus phonological codes can be, and are, obtained from visually presented letter strings in various experimental situations. What is more, such codes can be used for accessing the internal lexicon. If this were not so, Type P tasks could not be performed with pseudo-items—that is, one could not judge that WURD sounds identical to an English word, REN sounds identical to a type of bird, and TIE THE NOT sounds as if it makes sense. Furthermore, if the phonological code derived from a visually presented letter string were unsuitable for accessing the internal lexicon, pseudo-items would not be more difficult than non-items to reject in Type S tasks.

However, reading, with rare exceptions (such as proof-reading or reading poetry) is a Type S task, and one in which pseudo-items and non-items do not occur. Demonstrations of effects of phonological recoding on Type P tasks, or on responses to pseudo-items and non-items in Type S tasks, though they provide a great deal of information about how lexical access can occur, do not tell us whether responses to genuine items in a Type S task are ever generated via a phonologically mediated lexical access. Since reading, with few exceptions, corresponds to making responses to genuine items in a Type S task, it is this form of response in which we are especially interested. This interest can be formulated as two questions. First, is there overlap between the distribution of visual access times and the distribution of phonological access times? I have argued that there is no evidence for such an overlap, and that the failure to find advantage for regular over exception words in lexical decision tasks is evidence against the existence of such an overlap, though the latter argument relies on the assumption that phonological access is achieved by use of the GPC procedure. The second question is, does the distribution of times needed to retrieve a semantic representation by means of *visual* lexical access and to interrogate it overlap with the distribution of times needed to retrieve and to interrogate a semantic representation by means of *phonological* lexical access? I have argued that the results of Meyer and Gutschera's semantic-categorization experiments and of Baron's phrase-evaluation experiments indicate that these distributions do overlap. Hence, at least in these experimental situations, the meaning of a printed word or phrase is on some occasions attained via a phonological recoding *earlier* than it is attained via a visual recoding; and therefore understanding the meaning of a printed word or phrase is not exclusively achieved via visual recoding.

Occasionally throughout this section mention has been made of the possibility that such statements about the relative speeds of visual and phonological processing may not hold for every subject in a given situation (individual differences may be important), and also the possibility that such statements may not hold for a given subject in every situation (a subject's strategies may be important). The latter possibility is emphasized by the fact that it was found necessary, when attempting to explain Meyer and Gutschera's and Baron's experiments, to assume that a subject is capable of influencing the time required for lexical access to occur via phonological recoding. Such phonological access is of greater value in Type P than in Type S tasks, so that, if subjects *could* accelerate it, they should do so in Type P tasks relative to Type S tasks; and some aspects of the data of semantic-categorization and phrase-evaluation tasks can be understood on the assumption that subjects do adopt this strategy.

Thus I would now like to turn to the topic of subject's strategies in simple reading tasks. Have subjects any control over the extent to which lexical access is produced via phonological *vs.* visual encoding? Can they control the extent to which they use lexical access at all when processing visually presented letter strings in a task which does not require lexical access? Do the beneficial effects of context on reading occur automatically, or can a subject decide whether or not to take account of contextual information? These and other similar questions are discussed in Section 4.

4. STRATEGIES AND LEXICAL ACCESS

4.1. Introduction

One theoretical trend which is obvious in the cognitive psychology of the past 20 years is a progression from attempting to discover the method by which subjects perform Task X, through attempting to discover how many different methods are used by subjects for performing Task X, to attempting to discover when subjects use Method A and when Method B for performing Task X. An example of this trend emerges from comparing Sperling (1963), Coltheart (1972) and Hawkins *et al.* (1976). All three deal with the task of observing a brief display of letters and subsequently reporting the contents of this display. Sperling proposed that subjects performed this task by storing as much as possible of the display contents in a storage mode he referred to as AIS (auditory information storage), equivalent to the phonologically coded STM investigated extensively in recent years. Coltheart argued that there are other modes of storage which can also be used to perform this task—for example, storage of a visual representation of the display contents, or storage of a semantic representation. Hawkins *et al.* showed that both visual and phonological storage are used, and that subjects can decide for themselves which storage strategy they will mainly rely on. It seems highly likely that the next 20 years of cognitive psychology will be as dominated by the concept of "strategy" as the past 20 years have been dominated by the concept of "code". Consequently in this section I would like to discuss evidence, as yet rather fragmentary since this is a fairly novel area of research, concerning the extent to which the various procedures which can be involved in lexical access are strategic procedures—that is, procedures whose adoption are under the subject's control, rather than being automatic.

4.2. Strategies for pronouncing

As was pointed out in Section 2.2.3, there are at least two strategies available to a reader when he is attempting to pronounce a printed letter string. One is to consult his internal lexicon; if he can find an entry there corresponding to the letter string, he can retrieve the string's phonological representation from this entry, and can use this representation to generate an articulation. This *lexical lookup strategy* is available for all words (since all words have lexical entries) but not for non-words.* The other strategy for pronouncing does not use the lexicon, but instead derives a phonological representation directly from the letter string: this *orthographic strategy* uses GPCs, if the argument of Section 2 is correct, and hence is available for pronounceable non-words and regular words, but not for exceptions.† It should be noted that it may be necessary to subdivide the lexical lookup strategy into two: a lexical strategy based on lexical lookup via visual access (available for regular words and exceptions) and a lexical strategy based on lexical lookup via phonological access. One could object to this proposed subdivision on the ground that once a subject has obtained a phonological representation, he can then pronounce the item, so lexical access is unnecessary. This objection however, assumes that there is no distinction between "phonological representation" and "articulatory

---

* Except for pseudohomophones, perhaps?
† If by "exception" we mean a letter string whose dictionary pronunciation differs from the pronunciation given it by the GPC procedure, then of course there cannot be "exception non-words", since non-words have no dictionary pronunciations. Nevertheless, some pronounceable non-words contain letter sequences which have alternative pronunciations and some do not (e.g. PEAD *vs.* PELD), and so, in a sense, the former are "exception non-words".

representation". Such a distinction may be necessary, as has been pointed out by Forster and Chambers (1973, p. 633):*

> ... it is not necessary to equate the output of phonemic recoding with the information necessary for pronunciation. . . . One possibility is that the lexical entry contains stored motor commands, which permit much faster naming than a conversion from phonemes to motor commands.

Where this possible subdivision of the lexical lookup strategy is not important, I will neglect it, and simply consider a lexical and a non-lexical strategy for pronouncing print. That subjects do use both strategies for pronouncing printed items has been demonstrated in several different ways. For example, Baron and Strawson (1976) have shown that subjects read aloud a list of regular words (for which both strategies can be used) faster than they read a list of exception words (for which only the lexical strategy is usable).† A second demonstration can be obtained from the results of Forster and Chambers (1973). In their lexical decision experiment, using a random sequence of words and pronounceable non-words, the difference between mean YES latencies for high-frequency and low-frequency words was 196 ms. In their naming latency experiment, using a random sequence of the same words and pronounceable non-words, the difference between mean naming latencies for high- and low-frequency words was 71 ms. The YES response in a lexical decision task is always produced by lexical access. Given that the effect of word frequency on YES responses may be attributed to the relationship between a word's frequency and the time needed to access its lexical entry, it follows that if in the naming latency experiment words were always uttered via their lexical entries, the frequency effect should be of the same magnitude as it was in the lexical decision experiment. If, on the other hand, a non-lexical strategy was always used for uttering words, there should be no frequency effect. Neither of these outcomes was observed; there was a frequency effect, but it was smaller in the naming latency experiment than in the lexical decision experiment. This was also found by Frederiksen and Kroll (1976), and it indicates that sometimes words are named by the lexical lookup strategy, and sometimes by the non-lexical orthographic strategy. This mixture of strategies generates an attenuated but nevertheless a measurable frequency effect.

Frederiksen and Kroll (1976) carried out their naming latency experiment in two ways: *mixed* (a random sequence of words and non-words was used) or *blocked* (half of the subjects in this condition saw

* *See also* Section 3.2.
† *See* Section 2.2.3.

only words and were told that this would be so; the other half saw only non-words and were informed of this). If subjects are capable of altering the relative extent to which they use the lexical and orthographic strategies, such a capability should emerge here, because the word/blocked condition guarantees that the lexical strategy will always succeed, whereas the non-word/blocked condition guarantees that the lexical strategy will always fail. Furthermore, if the orthographic strategy fails with exception words, then the mixed condition will require both strategies, since the lexical strategy is needed for exception words and the orthographic strategy for non-words.

Two features of Frederiksen and Kroll's results suggest that subjects did manipulate their relative uses of the two strategies. First, there was a stronger relationship between word frequency and naming latency for words in the blocked condition compared to words in the mixed condition, suggesting, as Frederiksen and Kroll note, that the lexical strategy is used more extensively in the word/blocked condition than in the mixed condition. Secondly, the difference in naming latencies between words and non-words was twice as large in the blocked as in the mixed condition,* which also suggests that the lexical strategy is used more in the word/blocked condition than in the mixed condition. Now, if these two strategies operate independently and in parallel, rather than competing for use of "central processing capacity", there would be no reason not to operate both of them at full steam all the time. Subjects appear not to do this, since they use the lexical strategy less in the mixed than in the blocked condition. Thus one is led to consider the possibility that these strategies are operated less effectively together than singly. This possibility must be rejected, however, since it implies that naming latencies for non-words should be shorter in the non-word/blocked condition (where the subject should rely on the non-lexical, orthographic strategy) than in the mixed condition (where both strategies are being used), and this was not so: naming latencies for non-words were equal in the mixed and non-word/ blocked conditions. Thus adding the lexical strategy to the non-lexical strategy does not impair the operation of the non-lexical strategy. If so, it is implausible to argue that adding the non-lexical strategy to the lexical strategy impairs the operation of the lexical strategy. In that case, why does the subject not use the lexical strategy equally (that is, fully) in the mixed and word/blocked conditions? I suggest that he does and that the word frequency and word–non-word effects are more marked in the blocked condition because the *orthographic* strategy is

---

* This effect, however, though large, was not significant, which may have been, the authors suggest, because its statistical analysis involved a between-Ss comparison.

used less there. It is used less, not because it competes with the lexical strategy, but because it produces errors with exception words. It cannot be abandoned in the mixed condition because non-words, which require it, are present; but it can safely be abandoned in the word/blocked condition. Approximately 10·5% of the words used by Frederiksen and Kroll were exceptions. The non-lexical strategy will yield incorrect pronunciations for these if it uses the GPC procedure. The subject will have to do something about this, and whatever he does may be the reason for naming latencies being slower for words in the mixed than in the word/blocked condition; in the latter condition the difficulty is ameliorated to the extent to which the non-lexical strategy is abandoned.

Since in normal circumstances the words one reads consist of a mixture of regular words and exceptions, the user of GPC procedures will have to deal with the problem that for a significant proportion of words these procedures yield an incorrect phonological representation. How is a reader to cope with these? As a rule, he cannot predict whether the next word he sees will be a regular word or an exception. It is therefore not possible for him to apply the GPC strategy just to regular words and to avoid using it with exception words. Thus his choice is either to deploy the GPC strategy all the time (thereby producing incorrect pronunciations for exception words) or to relinquish it entirely. He cannot avoid the problems arising from applying the GPC strategy to exception words by assuming that this will result in neologisms, since, as I have pointed out earlier, some of the resulting incorrect pronunciations will themselves be words (GAUGE, COME, LOVES). Nor could it seriously be suggested that there are elementary visual features of words which permit an early pre-processing stage to decide whether a printed word is regular or an exception, hence permitting selective use of the GPC strategy.

This problem arises whether the reader's task is silent comprehension or reading aloud. However, because of the way in which Baron and Strawson desgined their experiment, it was possible for their subjects to evade the problem. Each list they used was either all regular words, all exceptions, or all non-words. This would allow the subject, at least in principle, to determine whether he could safely use the GPC strategy for a given list by determining whether the initial items in the list were regular words, exceptions or non-words. Subjects could, for example, start off by using both strategies (the GPC strategy and the lexical strategy); if they detect any incorrect pronunciations, these must come from application of the GPC strategy to exception words, so this strategy should be abandoned for the remainder of the current list. It should be noted that all the non-words used by Baron and

Strawson were pseudohomophones, so that if a subject generated a pronunciation which was not an English word this would strongly suggest that he was dealing with a list of exception words to which he had applied the GPC strategy. These suggestions are consistent with the error rates reported by Baron and Strawson; 4·5% of exception words were mispronounced, compared to 0·5% of regular words.

L. Midgley-West (unpublished) investigated this issue by comparing what happens when a subject can in principle predict whether the next word he has to name aloud will be regular or an exception with what happens when the category of the next word is completely unpredictable. She selected 39 regular words and a matched set of 39 exceptions. These words were presented one at a time on a visual display, and subjects were asked to say each word aloud as soon as possible after it appeared.

There were two conditions in this experiment: blocked and randomized. In the *blocked* condition, half of the subjects saw a practice series of regular words, then the 39 selected regular words, then a practice series of exception words, then the 39 selected exception words; the other half of the subjects saw all the exception words followed by all of the regular words. In this condition the subject can anticipate whether he will see a regular word or an exception with a high degree of certainty, as in Baron and Strawson's experiment; and as in their experiment regular words enjoyed significantly more rapid naming than exception words.

In the *randomized* condition, the order of presentation of the 78 selected words (39 regular and 39 exception) was completely random, so that it was impossible to predict whether the next word to be seen would be regular or an exception. Here the subject has no way of avoiding the problems which arise when the GPC strategy is applied to an exception word, except by relinquishing the GPC strategy entirely. If he does relinquish this strategy, the advantage enjoyed by regular words, which is caused by the use of the GPC strategy, will disappear.

In fact, the advantage of regular over exception words was significantly reduced here, but was still marginally significant. A further complexity in these results is that instead of regular words yielding faster latencies in the blocked compared to the randomized condition (as might have been expected if the GPC strategy were being used more in the blocked condition than in the randomized condition), the interaction between regular/exception and blocked/randomized was produced by the exception words being slower in the blocked than in the randomized conditions; regular words yielded similar mean latencies in the two conditions. It is difficult to explain this pattern of results in terms of differential strategies, though the results do confirm the view that the distinction between regular words and exceptions is a genuine one.

A miniature experiment also carried out by L. Midgley-West (unpublished) did however yield results suggesting that subjects have some control over the strategies they use for pronouncing print. In this experiment, the subject was asked to read aloud, as fast as possible, a list of 26 pronounceable letter strings arranged in a column. All were non-words excepts the 25th, which was the exception word WOLF. The idea here was to induce the subjects to abandon the lexical lookup strategy (which never produces a pronunciation for a non-word) and to rely solely on the GPC strategy (which always provides the correct pronunciation for a non-word). If they do this, they will pronounce WOLF to rhyme with GOLF, since that is the pronunciation which results when GPCs are applied to WOLF. A substantial proportion (7 of 18) of the subjects produced this mispronunciation, and none of these subjects noticed that the list had contained a word. Thus a steady diet of non-words induces subjects to rely extensively on the GPC strategy and abandon the lexical lookup strategy. The optional use of the GPC strategy in lexical decision tasks is suggested by the results of Davelaar et al. (1978) and its optional use in tachistoscopic recognition by the results of Hawkins et al. (1976); both experiments are discussed below.

The experiments described in Section 4.2, then, provide some evidence that subjects can control the extent to which they use the lexical lookup and non-lexical orthographic strategies in tasks requiring them to pronounce aloud words and/or non-words, and that they are also able to control the extent to which they employ GPC procedures in such tasks. The presence of non-words increases the use of the non-lexical orthographic strategy; the absence of exception words increases the use of GPC procedures.*

---

* Not only can subjects decide to what extent they will use the lexicon in a naming latency experiment; they may even be able to decide which region of the lexicon they will consult. In a naming latency experiment carried out by Berry (1971) there were three conditions: "Common" (subjects were truthfully informed that each of the twelve words they were to see were common words); "Rare" (here they were told that all twelve words were rather rare); and "Mixed" (both common and rare words would occur). For each of six key rare words, naming latency was shorter when the other six (filler) words used were rare too (the Rare condition) than when these six filler words were common (the Mixed condition). For each of six key common words, naming latency was shorter when the other six (filler) words were common (the Common condition) than when these six filler words were rare (the Mixed condition). Thus naming latency is faster when all the words a subject sees are drawn from a restricted frequency range than when they are drawn from a wide frequency range.

4.3. Strategies for lexical decision

If it were to be demonstrated that the presence of exception words discourages subjects from using GPC-based phonological access to the lexicon, it would then not be surprising that Coltheart et al. (1978) failed to find any difference between exception words and regular words in their YES latencies in a lexical decision task, since the two types of words were randomly mixed in their experiment. It is even conceivable that those experiments in which evidence of phonological encoding for lexical access was obtained by demonstrations of increased error rates and increasing latencies for NO responses to pseudohomophones compared to non-words obtained this evidence because exception words were rare in these experiments. For example, fewer than 15% of the words used by Rubenstein et al. (1971) were exceptions, and fewer than 10% of the words used by Coltheart et al. (1977) were exceptions. Perhaps one could abolish the pseudohomophone effect on NO responses if all the words in a lexical decision experiment were exceptions and so there was a substantial incentive for the subject to abandon phonological lexical access; this deserves investigation. Conversely, if exception words are rare in a lexical decision experiment, perhaps this will encourage GPC-based phonological access, and hence will produce an advantage for regular words over exceptions. A hint that this may occur is obtained by a *post hoc* analysis of the data of Coltheart et al. (1977). For five of the small number of exception words used in their lexical decision experiments, there was also a regular word matched on word frequency, number of letters, number of syllables and part of speech including inflections. In all five pairs, the YES response was slower to the exception word than to the regular word. Perhaps this is just a coincidence; perhaps it means that YES responses were sometimes based on phonological encoding in this experiment, because of the rarity of exception words. Clearly further work is needed here.

The question of whether subjects' use of phonological encoding for lexical access in a lexical decision experiment is under strategic control has been studied by Davelaar et al. (1978). She compared lexical decision YES times for the less frequent members of homophone pairs (e.g. WHINE, TAUT) to YES times to matched non-homophonic words. When the *non-words* in this experiment were all pseudohomophones, YES latency was not influenced by whether a word was a homophone or not, as was also found by Coltheart et al. (1977) in an experiment where 50% of non-words were phonologically identical to English words. However, when difficulties attendant upon the use of phonological encoding were reduced by using non-words which were *never* pseudohomophones, the YES response was slower to homophones than to non-homophones. This effect did not occur with homophones which were the more frequent members of homophone pairs.

A printed homophone becomes ambiguous when it is phonologically encoded. Readers may cope with this ambiguity by assuming that the more frequent of the two possible letter strings is the one which was presented, in which case difficulties will only arise when this assumption is incorrect, as Rubenstein et al. (1971) have argued. Davelaar et al. (1978) therefore interpreted her results thus: a phonological encoding strategy is adopted by subjects to a greater extent when the non-words are like SOAM or DORT than when they are like SOAL or CORT, because after such phonological encoding, non-words are still non-words in the former situation, whereas non-words are wrongly transformed into words in the latter situation. When a phonological encoding strategy is being used, difficulties will be experienced with words which are the less frequent members of homophone pairs; when the strategy is not being used, there can be no effect of whether a word is a homophone or not. This explains why there is a homophone effect for words when non-words never sound identical to English words, but no homophone effect for words when non-words always sound identical to English words. It is suggested that subjects can exert some control over the extent to which they use phonological access in lexical decision tasks, just as the evidence described in Section 4.2 suggested that subjects have some degree of control over the extent to which they use a GPC procedure for naming printed words. Also, the evidence described in Section 3.4 suggested that subjects carry out phonological lexical access in semantic categorization or phrase evaluation tasks more rapidly if they are carrying out these experiments under Task P conditions than if they are performing under Task S conditions with pseudo-items present.

A different kind of strategic effect in the lexical decision task is evident in results obtained by Tweedy et al. (1977). The YES response to a word in a lexical decision task is faster if this word is preceded by a semantically related word—thus the YES response to BUTTER is faster if the previous item seen by the subject was BREAD than if it was NURSE (Meyer and Schvaneveldt, 1971; Meyer et al., 1975). Tweedy et al. (1977) varied the proportion of occasions on which a word was preceded by a semantically related word: for one group of subjects this happened with 12·5% of words, for a second group it happened with 50% of words, and for a third group it happened with 87·5% of words. The size of the contextual facilitation effect on the YES response increased linearly as a function of the percentage of words for which context was provided. This suggests that the facilitation effect is not an automatic consequence of the way the internal lexicon is built, as has been a common interpretation (e.g. Meyer and Schvaneveldt, 1971; Collins and Loftus, 1975). Instead, it seems that making use of contextual information is a strategy, that subjects can choose the degree to which they use this strategy, and that the extent to which the strategy is used is influenced by the proportion of occasions on which it is useful. As Tweedy *et al.* (1977) point out, one cannot tell from their data whether the contextual effect could be eliminated entirely by using a sufficiently low proportion of contextually related word sequences, so we cannot tell from their experiment whether the whole of the context effect is under the subject's control, but it is clear from their results that at least part of the effect is produced by a strategy which subjects can choose to use or not to use.

This topic has also been investigated, independently, by Fischler (1977). In his lexical decision experiments, the 34th item the subject saw was a word. For half of the subjects (Group 1) the 33rd item was a word which was semantically related to the word following it; for the remainder of the subjects (Group 2) the 33rd item was a word which was semantically unrelated to the word following. Since semantic relatedness facilitates the YES response in lexical decision tasks, YES responses to the 34th item should be faster in Group 1 than in Group 2, and Fischler did find this. The point of his experiment, however, lay in the nature of Items 1–32. For half of the subjects in Group 1, these items included three words which were preceded by semantically related words; for the remainder of the subjects, no two consecutive words were semantically related. The subjects in Group 2 were similarly treated. For neither group was the magnitude of the semantic-facilitation effect on the latency of the response to the 34th item influenced by whether or not a semantic relationship had existed between any pair of items prior to this item. Furthermore, in a subsequent experiment in which subjects were *told* that such semantic relationships would occasionally hold for consecutive words, the facilitative effect of the semantically related preceding item on the YES response to the 34th item was not increased. Thus neither the presence of semantically related pairs on earlier trials, nor explicit instructions, increased the size of the context effect in this experiment. These results appear to be in direct conflict with those of Tweedy *et al.* (1977), since the latter found that the size of the facilitation produced by semantic relatedness varied directly with the proportion of word pairs which were semantically related, but in fact there is no conflict. Neely (1976) has shown that the degree to which a YES response in a lexical decision task is facilitated by a preceding semantically related word increases as the lexical decision experiment proceeds, though the effect is still present at the beginning of the experiment. It can therefore be argued that even without practice a subject will show an associative-facilitation effect, and that with extensive practice he can augment this effect, the extent to which he does so depending upon the proportion of occasions on which the effect is useful, i.e. the proportion of occasions on which a word is preceded by a semantically related word. Fischler's subjects were unable to adjust their strategies in this way since they were extremely unpractised (they saw only 32 items prior to the critical pair of items) whereas the subjects of Tweedy *et al.* were highly practised (they saw 18 practice items and 144 items in the main part of the experiment). Further work by Neely (1976, 1978) supports this view, since it suggests that one can distinguish an automatic and an optional component of the associative-facilitation effect. When the priming item occurs very shortly before the primed item (250 ms before), only the automatic component operates. This was shown in two ways. First, even when subjects are told that the prime will rarely be semantically related to the item following it, and this is in fact true, a semantic-facilitation effect occurs. Secondly, at this short interstimulus interval, no inhibition effect occurred when the primer was semantically unrelated to the following item. Such inhibition effects, measured by the difference between the response to a word preceded by an unrelated word and the (faster) response to a word preceded by a neutral (non-word) primer, do occur with longer intervals between primer and primed word, and the size of these inhibition effects increases with practice.* Furthermore, J. T. Jonasson (unpublished) has shown that such priming effects occur even when the primer is presented for such a short time, and masked sufficiently severely, that the subject cannot report its presence.

These results suggest that there is a basic associative-facilitation effect, which occurs automatically and without the subject needing to be aware that sometimes consecutive items are semantically related, which is not accompanied by an inhibition effect for unrelated item pairs, and which works even at very short time intervals; and, in addition to this automatic effect, there is an optional effect, which is under the control of the subject and therefore is influenced by the proportion of occasions on which consecutive items are semantically related. This optional, strategic effect requires some practice and can only influence response to a word when the interval between the primer and this word is not too short; furthermore, if the following word turns out *not* to be semantically related to the primer, this actually slows the response to this word.

---

* An inhibition effect of this kind was not significant in the data of Tweedy *et al.* (1977).

4.4. Strategies for tachistoscopic report

The two experiments discussed here are somewhat remote from the general theme of this chapter, since neither necessarily involves lexical access; nevertheless their results are relevant to the question of subjects' strategies in tasks concerned with visual information processing.

Hawkins et al. (1976) presented their subjects with a brief word display (e.g. RAIN) which was then masked. Above and below the mask were two alternative words (e.g. RAIN and RAIL), one of which was the original briefly presented word. The subject's task was to choose which of these alternatives had been the briefly presented word. Half of the subjects were encouraged to use phonological encoding of the brief display, because for them the two forced-choice alternatives were usually phonologically different (were rarely homophones). The remaining subjects were frequently given a pair of homophones as their forced choice alternatives, and were told that this would be so; thus these subjects were discouraged from using a phonological encoding strategy, since this strategy is ineffective when the forced choice is between two items which are phonologically identical.

Subjects encouraged to use a phonological strategy performed worse when the forced-choice alternatives were homophones than when they were not, suggesting that they were making some use of phonological encoding. Subjects discouraged from this strategy showed equal performance with these two types of forced-choice alternatives, suggesting that they were making no use at all of phonological encoding. When performance is averaged over the two types of trial, the two groups yield almost identical performance levels (65·4% vs. 67·2%), suggesting that the losses suffered by phonological encoders on homophone trials are compensated for by the gains they achieve on non-homophone trials by their use of a phonological strategy.

Corcoran and Rouse (1970) used both typewritten and handwritten words in a tachistoscopic recognition experiment. Accuracy for each type of presentation was approximately twice as high when this variable was blocked (i.e. when all the words shown to a subject were typed, or when they were all handwritten) than when it was randomized (a random sequence of typewritten or handwritten words was used). The effect was not obtained when two forms of handwriting were used, nor when upper-case and lower-case words were used. This suggests that different strategies are required for the identification of handwriting and for the identification of print, and that subjects can profit by the opportunity to prepare the appropriate strategy which is afforded by blocked presentation. Brooks (1973: cited by Bryden and Allard, 1976) found that handwritten words are recognized more accurately in the left visual hemifield, i.e. by the right hemisphere, which contrasts with the common finding of a right-hemifield (left-hemisphere) advantage for the recognition of printed words. Bryden and Allard (1976), using single letters as stimuli, and ten different typefaces, obtained left-hemisphere superiority for some typefaces and right-hemisphere superiority for others; the laterality difference for a typeface correlated $+ 0\cdot74$ with ratings of its similarity to script, with the more script-like typefaces showing right-hemisphere superiority or reduced left-hemisphere superiority. Thus print and writing appear to engage different hemispheres as well as different processing strategies.

4.5. Conclusions

Four of the many variables which influence the time a subject takes to deal with a letter string in simple reading tasks have been singled out in Section 4: whether the letter string is a word or not; whether, if it is a word, it has been preceded by a semantically related word; whether the subject carries out phonological encoding; and, again if the string is a word, what its frequency of occurrence in the language is. Evidence has been presented suggesting that at least part of the relationship between each of these four variables and the subject's performance is mediated by processes over which the subject has some control, and hence that the influence of these variables is not simply an automatic consequence of the structure of the system by which a reader deals with letter strings.

When a task can be done using, but does not require, lexical access, subjects can exercise at least a partial choice over whether they perform the task in the lexical or in the non-lexical way, this choice being influenced by the probability that the lexical way will be successful. The facilitative effect of prior presentation of a semantically related word appears to be partly automatic and partly under the subject's control, so that the effect is always present, but can be magnified if the subject so chooses. The degree to which a subject relies on a phonological representation of a visually presented letter string is also under his control: such representations are used much less when types of letter strings are present which cause difficulties when dealt with by phonological recoding (pseudohomophones in Davelaar's lexical-decision experiment; homophones in the tachistoscopic-recognition experiment of Hawkins et al.; and perhaps exception words in Midgley-West's pronouncing experiments). The slow responding which usually occurs with low frequency words is not so severe when the subject expects the words he sees to be of low frequency.

Such findings are important for two reasons. First, they demonstrate in fairly straightforward ways the flexibility of which subjects are capable when they are carrying out reading tasks. Secondly, these findings have considerable implications for the design of reading experiments. One of the major influences on a subject's choice of strategy is the nature of the letter strings with which he is confronted. A predominance of words encourages a lexical strategy; homophones, pseudohomophones and exception words discourage a phonological recoding strategy; prevalence of semantic relationships encourages a strategy which exploits such relationships. Thus the particular stimuli an experimenter chooses will be an important determinant of the kind of conclusions he will reach as to how subjects perform his experimental task.

5. SUMMARY

Two routes from a printed word to its entry in the internal lexicon have been distinguished: the "direct route", which uses a visual representation of the word, and the "indirect route", which uses a phonological encoding of the word. These terms may be somewhat inexact: the "direct" route relies on an encoding of the printed word (into its visual representation) just as the "indirect" route relies on an encoding (into a phonological representation), so it may be wrong to think of these routes as differing in how "direct" they are. Perhaps "visual" and "phonological" are preferable terms.

To speak of access to the internal lexicon via phonological encoding makes sense only if such encoding can be performed without reference to the contents of a word's lexical entry. Methods by which such phonological encoding could be performed without lexical access were discussed in Section 2, and it was concluded, both from theoretical considerations and from experimental evidence, that a grapheme–phoneme correspondence system is the means by which letter strings are converted to phonological representations without lexical access. Such a system operates in two stages. A letter string is first analysed into functional spelling units, i.e. into those letters or sets of letters which each correspond to a single phoneme ("graphemic parsing"). Then the appropriate phoneme for each spelling unit is obtained from a table of grapheme–phoneme correspondences ("phoneme assignment").

If this is the only method available for non-lexical phonological encoding of visually presented English words, it follows that some English words cannot be phonologically encoded without reference to the internal lexicon. There are two main classes of such words in English: exceptions (which are given incorrect parsings and/or incorrect phoneme assignments by the GPC procedure) and ideographs. Some ideographs cannot be parsed because they are not composed of letters, as is the case with numerals and other mathematical signs and various other symbols such as £ or $; some ideographs can be parsed, but the sequence of phonemes yielded by the GPC procedure disobeys the phonotactic rules of English and hence is "unpronounceable", as is the case with abbreviations such as lb or cwt.

For "regularly spelled" languages such as Italian, Finnish or Hungarian, there are no exception words (though ideographs still occur), and thus many of the experiments described in this chapter might yield interestingly different results if carried out using such regular languages, rather than English—perhaps readers use phonological encoding much more freely when reading such regularly spelled languages. By contrast, lexical access via phonological encoding is in principle impossible for an ideographic script such as that used for Chinese, since a reader can only obtain the phonological representations of an ideograph by gaining access to the ideograph's entry in an internal lexicon. Japan is currently attracting much attention amongst students of reading simply because Japanese uses a mixture of two forms of script—*kana* (a word written in kana is a sequence of symbols in which each symbol corresponds, invariantly and one-to-one, with one of the syllables occurring in Japanese, so that non-lexical phonological encoding could scarcely be simpler) and *kanji* (a purely ideographic script, and therefore one for which non-lexical phonological encoding is impossible).

One could write a chapter solely about visual access to the internal lexicon, though this has been investigated very little, and often by exclusion, i.e. by isolating instances where phonological access is not, or cannot be, used. Instead, this chapter has been about phonological access—or, more precisely, about access based on encoding using the GPC procedure, since Section 2 argued that, if phonological encoding occurs, it occurs by using such a procedure. One conclusion which was reached is that access to a lexical entry via phonological encoding is on the average slower in skilled readers than access via visual encoding; in fact, no evidence yet exists which is inconsistent with the claim that phonological access is *always* slower than visual access. Thus if one imagines a theoretical distribution of the times needed for visual access to lexical entries, and another distribution of the times needed for phonological access, not only is the mean of the visual distribution smaller than the mean of the phonological distribution, but there is no evidence that these distributions even overlap.

Reading, however, is more than lexical access—even the reading of a single isolated word. Having gained access to the lexical entry of a word, the reader needs to do something extra—usually, to retrieve semantic information from this entry and to "understand" it. Tasks requiring such understanding on the part of the reader (semantic categorization and phrase evaluation) yield data suggesting that the understanding of a word is sometimes generated from lexical access achieved via phonological encoding. Thus, at least in the case of isolated single words, reading for meaning is not achieved solely via visual representations of printed words.

Reading is thus sometimes visual and sometimes phonological. Furthermore, whether it is one or the other varies from person to person and from occasion to occasion. Some subjects rely heavily on phonological encoding in reading for meaning, others not at all. A subject can decide to what degree he will use phonological encoding, this decision being strongly influenced by the extent to which what he is being asked to do with the words he is seeing is helped or hindered by converting these words into their phonological representations. Similar flexibility exists with respect to the extent to which a reader chooses to use context, and even the extent to which he uses his internal lexicon at all.

As yet we know very little about such individual and situational differences, largely, I suspect, because we have been reluctant to accept that they are substantial. Reading is so much simpler to investigate if we assume that we may generalize from this subject to all subjects, and from this reading situation to all reading situations; and it is natural to feel that chaos would ensue if these assumptions were relinquished. The experimental work discussed in Section 4, however, shows not only that we must investigate strategic and individual-difference effects in reading tasks, but that we can do so successfully.

ACKNOWLEDGEMENTS

The preparation of this chapter, and some of the work reported in it, was supported by a grant from the Social Science Research Council. I thank V. Coltheart, J. T. Jonasson, D. Besner, E. Davelaar and N. S. Sutherland for helpful criticism of an earlier draft.

REFERENCES

Bakan, P. and Alperson, B. (1967). Pronounceability, attensity and inter-ference in the colour-word test. *American Journal of Psychology* **80**, 416–420.

Baron, J. (1973). Phonemic stage not necessary for reading. *Quarterly Journal of Experimental Psychology* **25**, 241–246.

Baron, J. and McKillop, B. J. (1975). Individual differences in speed of phonetic analysis, visual analysis, and reading. *Acta Psychologica* **39**, 91–96.

Baron, J. and Strawson, C. (1976). Use of orthographic and word-specific knowledge in reading words aloud. *Journal of Experimental Psychology: Human Perception and Performance* **2**, 386–393.

Berry, C. W. (1971). Advanced frequency information and verbal response times. *Psychonomic Science* **23**, 151–152.

Bryden, M. P. and Allard, F. (1976). Visual hemifield differences depend on typeface. *Brain and Language* **3**, 191–200.

Cohen, G. L. and Freeman, R. (1976). Individual differences in reading strategies in relation to handedness and cerebral asymmetry. Presented at Attention and Performance VII.

Coltheart, M. (1972). Visual information-processing. *In* "New Horizons in Psychology" (P. C. Dodwell, ed.). Penguin, Harmondsworth.

Coltheart, M., Davelaar, E., Jonasson, J. T. and Besner, D. (1977). Access to the internal lexicon. *In* "Attention and Performance VI" (S. Dornic, ed.). Academic Press, New York and London.

Coltheart, M., Jonasson, J. T., Davelaar, E. and Besner, D. (1978). Phonological encoding in the lexical decision task. Unpublished manuscript.

Collins, A. M. and Loftus, E. F. (1975). A spreading-activation theory of semantic processing. *Psychological Review* **82**, 407–423.

Corcoran, D. W. J. and Rouse, R. O. (1970). An aspect of perceptual organization involved in the perception of handwritten and printed words. *Quarterly Journal of Experimental Psychology* **22**, 526–530.

Davelaar, E., Coltheart, M., Besner, D. and Jonasson, J. T. (1978). Phonological recoding and lexical access. *Memory and Cognition* (in press).

Fischler, I. J. (1977). Associative facilitation without expectancy in a lexical decision task. *Journal of Experimental Psychology: Human Perception and Performance* **3**, 18–26.

Forbes, C. A. (1964). Why Roman Johnny *could* read. *In* "New Perspectives in Reading Instruction" (A. J. Mazurkiewicz, ed.). Pitman, New York.

Forster, K. I. and Chambers, S. M. (1973). Lexical access and naming time. *Journal of Verbal Learning and Verbal Behavior* **12**, 627–635.

Frederiksen, J. R. (1976). Decoding skills and lexical retrieval. Presented at Psychonomic Society Meeting, St. Louis.

Frederiksen, J. R. and Kroll, J. F. (1976). Spelling and sound: approaches to the internal lexicon. *Journal of Experimental Psychology: Human Perception and Performance* **2**, 361–379.

Fudge, E. (1970). Phonological structure and "expressiveness". *Journal of Linguistics* **6**, 161–188.

Gough, P. (1972). One second of reading. *In* "Language by Eye and by Ear" (J. P. Kavanagh and I. G. Mattingly, eds), M.I.T. Press, Cambridge, Massachusetts.

Hanna, J. S. and Hanna, P. R. (1959). Spelling as a school subject: a brief history. *National Elementary Principal* **38**, 8–23.

Hanna, J. S. and Hanna, P. R. (1965). The teaching of spelling. *National Elementary Principal* **45**, 19–28.

Hansen, D. and Rodgers, T. S. (1973). An exploration of psycholinguistic units in initial reading. *In* "The Psycholinguistic Nature of the Reading Process" (K. S. Goodman, ed.). Wayne State University Press, Detroit.

Hawkins, H. L., Reicher, G. M., Rodgers, M. and Peterson, L. (1976). Flexible coding in word recognition. *Journal of Experimental Psychology: Human Perception and Performance* **2**, 380–385.

Holmes, J. M. (1973). Dyslexia: a neurolinguistic study of traumatic and developmental disorders of reading. Ph.D. thesis, University of Edinburgh.

Landauer, T. K. and Freedman, J. L. (1968). Information retrieval from long-term memory: category size and recognition time. *Journal of Verbal Learning and Verbal Behavior* **7**, 291–295.

Marin, O. S. M., Saffran, E. M. and Schwartz, M. F. (1975). Dissociations of language in aphasia: implications for normal function. Presented at New York Academy of Sciences Conference on Origins and Evolution of Language and Speech, September 1975.

Marshall, J. C. and Newcombe, F. (1973). Patterns of Paralexia. *Journal of Psycholinguistic Research* **2**, 175–199.

Meyer, D. E. and Gutschera, K. (1975). Orthographic *vs.* phonemic processing of printed words. Presented at Psychonomic Society Meeting, Denver.

Meyer, D. E. and Ruddy, M. G. (1973). Lexical-memory retrieval based on graphemic and phonemic representations of printed words. Presented at Psychonomic Society Meeting, St. Louis.

Meyer, D. E. and Schvaneveldt, R. W. (1971). Facilitation in recognizing pairs of words: evidence of a dependence between retrieval operations. *Journal of Experimental Psychology* **90**, 227–234.

Meyer, D. E., Schvaneveldt, R. W. and Ruddy, M. G. (1974). Functions of graphemic and phonemic codes in visual word recognition. *Memory and Cognition* **2**, 309–321.

Meyer, D. E., Schvaneveldt, R. W. and Ruddy, M. G. (1975). Loci of contextual effects on visual word-recognition. *In* "Attention and Performance" (P. M. A. Rabbitt and S. Dornic, eds), pp. 98–118. Academic Press, London and New York.

Neely, J. H. (1976). Semantic priming and retrieval form lexical memory: evidence for facilitatory and inhibitory processes. *Memory and Cognition* **4**, 648–654.

Neely, J. H. (1978). Semantic priming and retrieval from lexical memory: the roles of inhibitionless spreading activation and limited-capacity attention. *Journal of Experimental Psychology: General* (in press).

Newcombe, F. and Marshall, J. C. (1973). Stages in recovery from dyslexia following a left cerebral abscess. *Cortex* **9**, 319–332.

Patterson, K. and Marcel, A. J. (1977). Aphasia, dyslexia, and the phonological coding of written words. *Quarterly Journal of Experimental Psychology* **29**, 307–312.

Redmonds, G. (1973). "Yorkshire West Riding (English Surnames Series, Volume 1)." Phillimore and Co., London.

Rubenstein, H., Lewis, S. S. and Rubenstein, M. A. (1977). Evidence for phonemic recoding in visual word recognition. *Journal of Verbal Learning and Verbal Behavior* **10**, 645–657.

Scarborough, D. L. and Springer, L. (1973). Noun-verb differences in word recognition. Presented at Psychonomic Society Meeting, St. Louis.

Scragg, D. G. (1974). "A History of English Spelling". Manchester University Press, Manchester.

Shallice, T. and Warrington, E. K. (1975). Word recognition in a phonemic dyslexic patient. *Quarterly Journal of Experimental Psychology* **27**, 187–199.

Smith, E. E. and Spoehr, K. T. (1974). The perception of printed English: a theoretical perspective. *In* "Human Information Processing: Tutorials in Performance and Cognition" (B. H. Kantowitz, ed.). Erlbaum, Hillsdale.

Sperling, G. (1963). A model for visual memory tasks. *Human Factors* **5**, 19–31.

Spoehr, K. T. and Smith, E. E. (1973). The role of syllables in perceptual processing. *Cognitive Psychology* **5**, 71–89.

Spoehr, K. T. and Smith, E. E. (1975). The role of orthographic and phonotactic rules in perceiving letter patterns. *Journal of Experimental Psychology: Human Perception and Performance* **1**, 21–34.

Tweedy, J. R., Lapinski, R. H. and Schvaneveldt, R. W. (1977). Semantic-context effects in word-recognition: influence of varying the proportion of items presented in an appropriate context. *Memory and Cognition* **5**, 84–89.

Venezky, R. L. (1970). "The Structure of English Orthography". Mouton, The Hague.

Wijk, O. (1966). "Rules of Pronunciation for the English Language". Oxford University Press, London.

Six

Reading Sentences: Some Observations on the Control of Eye Movements*

Alan Kennedy
University of Dundee

1. INTRODUCTION

When a subject reads aloud from a page of text his eyes show characteristic patterns of movement. These take the form of rapid horizontal saccades, five to fifteen letter spaces long, during which very little useful information is abstracted. The duration of saccades varies from 10 to 40 ms, from which it may be deduced that the eye moves with a

---

* A version of this paper was delivered in 1975 at a symposium on reading in the University of Stirling.

very high angular velocity (Tinker, 1958; Bouma and de Voogd, 1974). Saccades occupy only about 10% of total reading time, the remainder being spent in fixations of varying duration, averaging about a quarter of a second. There is some evidence that average fixation duration may alter as a function of the complexity of the material read (Tinker, 1958).

In silent reading much the same range of effects may be observed, but when the rate of reading is high it becomes less likely that subjects are tracking all (or even most) of the text in a line-by-line fashion. Thus, although estimates of the amount of text "taken in" per fixation are possible they may be misleading, not least because the temporal sequence of fixation may bear no very obvious relationship to features of the presented text. In fact, after many years of careful research it is still far from clear what, if any, relationship exists between components of the reading skill and concurrent patterns of eye movement. The question is nonetheless an important one since any analysis of reading demands a clear description of the manner in which information is gathered.

In the analysis of speech there is a rich diversity of possible signals which the hearer can use to achieve perceptual segmentation; many of these can be manipulated experimentally (e.g. the location of pause or stress position) and yield behavioural measures of the listener's strategies. The analysis of reading and writing is much more difficult. Measures of "comprehension" are often of low reliability and virtually the only potential behavioural index of the reader at work is the sequence and duration of his eye fixations. If these bear some significant relationship to the reader's segmentation of the presented text the possible theoretical rewards are very great, and it is largely for this reason that investigation has persisted since the time of Huey (1908), in spite of what has been at times a very unfavourable intellectual climate. For example, Tinker (1958) argued that research at that time had reached a point of diminishing returns. It appeared that saccadic eye movements during reading were autonomous (that is effectively "decoupled" from higher cognitive processes), highly regular, and of little or no relevance either to the development or practice of reading. This was a view accepted by Gough (1972) and which with only minor qualifications can find advocates at the present time (Kolers, 1976).

On the other hand it has become increasingly difficult to sustain such a point of view and at the same time acknowledge the very power-ful analytic use made of eye movement data in treating the way pictures and line drawings are encoded, memorized and recognized (Loftus, 1976). In certain specific respects the tasks of a reader and of someone looking at pictures are very similar; in fact the way highly practised "speed readers" appear to search the pages of a book is reminiscent of the scan-patterns found in scene analysis. These fixations are not regular, and while they might be random, they certainly serve the processes of comprehension in a way which makes entirely random control unlikely.

One of the more obvious reasons for this very unsatisfactory state of knowledge has been the lack of a significantly detailed theoretical account of the cognitive processes underlying the reading skill. Indeed, there is little evidence that "reading" can be looked at usefully as a single process at all. As Gibson (1972) points out, unless we know why a subject is reading (for example, whether he is skimming for the gist of a text or proof-reading it), then there is simply no way of assessing the priorities among the various strategies that he might be employing.

The position adopted here is that in some situations at least (the precise circumstances will be discussed later) reading can be looked on as a search process. Once the meaning of a particular printed word has been derived a number of other processes will occur simultaneously at several levels. At the lowest level, accessing a particular logogen will change the level of evidence required to trigger others (Morton, 1969). That is, reading a single word will alter, among other things, the threshold for recognition and the pronunciation latency of other words in an initially undifferentiated semantic field (Meyer and Schvaneveldt, 1971; Jacobson, 1973). At a somewhat higher level, lexical constraints will operate to limit this general "associative facilitation" to particular dimensions. Thus, Bradshaw (1974) showed that the interpretation placed on a single homograph (e.g. *palm*) following its tachistoscopic presentation will be systematically altered by the simultaneous presentation of a disambiguating context word. Subjects saw a word centrally located and sandwiched between a disambiguating word on one side in peripheral vision (e.g. *date* or *hand*) and a random letter string on the other. Even when subjects could not identify or report the items in peripheral vision their presence influenced the interpretation placed on the ambiguous lexical item.

Over and above purely lexical constraints, syntactic effects may be found which also influence associative priming. For example, in a recognition task it is commonly observed that false positive responses are made to both synonyms and antonyms of words presented in the test list. However, if the test list consists of simple adjective–noun pairs such as *black dress, open door* etc. (i.e. containing a minimal syntactic constraint), the false positive rate for antonyms drops to chance level (Anisfeld, 1970); the constraints imposed by the propositional form of the test list operate to limit associative priming to synonymous items. When whole sentences are used as context, as in the experiments by

Hall and Crown (1970, 1972) and Kennedy (1975), variations in priming appear to result from the operation of selectional restrictions between particular segments of the sentence frame. In particular, priming takes place in semantic fields congruent with the interpretation placed on a sentence, and its effects may be greater in relation to the logical subject rather than the object.

The realization of these processes of associative priming is, in other contexts, referred to as the construction of a hypothesis or the generation of expectations relating to the structure, meaning and continuation of a text (Hochberg, 1976). Their outcome is the construction of a mental representation of the meaning of the text, a "data base" which acts to modulate attention in such a way as to seek confirmatory evidence. If the text is highly predictable, confirmation of the interpretation placed upon it will be achieved on very little evidence—with as a consequence very high rates of reading if these are expressed in "words a minute". In other circumstances the construction of a mental representation may be difficult and involve painstaking processes of cross-reference. Confirmation of hypotheses as to the structure, thematic integration and meaning of a text may then be difficult to acquire. Rates of reading in such a situation may be lower, although there is no evidence that the representation, once achieved, is of lower "quality" (Kintsch and Monk, 1972).

Although this view of one aspect of the reading skill is general enough to operate as a working model, and can find some supportive evidence, it leaves quite unanswered a central question. Do these "constructive" cognitive processes show themselves in the eye movement behaviour of readers? Do people, in fact, look at text in a non-random fashion, launching successive fixations (or sequenced patterns of fixation) on the basis of the interpretation placed on it? The remainder of this chapter is an attempt to answer this question. It involves initially considering a variety of possible models of eye movement control; then turning to examine the degree of support which can be recruited for each; and finally outlining the results of an experiment designed to comment directly on one particular model.

2. THEORIES OF THE RELATIONSHIP BETWEEN EYE MOVEMENTS AND READING PROCESSES

2.1. Random control or no control

There have been a number of claims that eye movements are not related to other aspects of the reading process at all, or that there is, in the words of Rayner and McConkie (1976), "minimal control". Scanning movements are seen as purely automatic, not effective in regulating succeeding eye movements and not themselves under any "higher" cognitive control. Theories of this kind have laid particular emphasis on the apparent regularity of saccadic movements observed in the reader. This idiosyncratic reading style was for many years believed to be of some educational significance and susceptible to "training" and considerable research has been invested in training children with reading difficulties to adopt a particular form of rhythmical eye movement (see Tinker, 1958, 1965).

2.2. "Lax-control" theory

The term, taken from Bouma and de Voogd (1974), is equivalent to Hochberg's "peripheral guidance theory" (Hochberg, 1970). Theories of this type maintain that the ongoing sequence of eye movements is coupled at a peripheral level to comprehension, to ensure a steady and well modulated assimilation of information. Eye movements are guided to some degree by information in peripheral vision from an effective visual field which is (for English readers) asymmetrical and biased to the right. The size of the perceptual span in reading is a critical unit here in so far as it provides an estimate of the likely angular displacement over which effective discrimination might take place. There appears to be fairly general agreement that information relating to word shape, the location of the ends of words, spaces between words, their overall length and the presence of capital letters is available to skilled readers of normal text over about five degrees of visual angle, or seventeen character spaces (McConkie and Rayner, 1975; Hochberg, 1970; Levin and Kaplan, 1970; O'Regan, 1975). However, it is probably more appropriate to refer to a functional visual field since even with non-linguistic material subjects can capitalize on sequential redundancy to increase their effective span (Sanders, 1970).

It is important to see exactly what is claimed by a lax-control model. Since acuity in peripheral vision is low, only quite gross features can be detected: the length of a particular word perhaps; a double letter; some irregularity in the profile of a word; or an initial capital. This in itself might lead to directed eye movements, but only in an interesting way if in conjunction with other information. For example, it is difficult to see how peripheral guidance alone can be used as an explanation for the skipping of short words (if in fact this actually occurs) since the motivation for this must also depend on an understanding of the sentence, that is, the reader must have achieved an appropriate segmentation. Thus, low-grade information in peripheral vision becomes significant only when we admit the operation of other processes, and in particular hypotheses about the structure and meaning of the text being read. On this basis alone could peripheral information guide the reader's eye to search one potentially informative region rather than another. In an important sense, therefore, models of this kind may be difficult to distinguish from the "strong-control" theories discussed below.

2.3. "Strong-control" theory

This class of theories incorporates what Hochberg (1970) calls "cognitive search guidance". In a strong form such a theory might state that each and every eye movement is launched on the basis of centrally computed information regarding the linguistic and logical structure of the material being read. The control processes underlying eye movements are sensitive to the changing patterns of expectation in the reader arising from his linguistic knowledge and from inferences drawn from the data base constructed as a result of reading. In other words the reader looks at a particular point in the text because it is there that he expects to find confirmatory evidence. James, in his *Principles of Psychology* (1890) commented on the way lexical, syntactic and semantic constraints operated to allow for reading *without* understanding:

> If we read *no more*, we expect presently to come upon a *than;* if we read *however* at the outset of a sentence, it is a *yet*, a *still*, or a *nevertheless*, that we expect. A noun in a certain position demands a verb in a certain mood and number, in another position it expects a relative pronoun. Adjectives call for nouns, verbs for adverbs, etc. And this foreboding of the coming grammatical scheme combined with each successive uttered word is so practically accurate that a reader incapable of understanding four ideas of the book he is reading out aloud can nevertheless read it with the most delicately modulated expression of intelligence.

It is this "foreboding of the coming grammatical scheme" which acts in "strong-control" models such as that of Hochberg to guide eye movements:

> . . . the experienced reader must respond to the contents of one fixation by making plans as to where he will look next (Hochberg, 1970).

2.4. Process monitoring

Rayner and McConkie (1976) have pointed out that it is not necessary to assume that eye movements are under any form of direct control.

Rather, they could be steered by some mechanism which itself monitors the process of peripheral information extraction and comprehension. At a very simple level such a mechanism might operate to maintain a buffer store (or queue) of information with saccades adjusted to keep the buffer filled. Bouma and de Voogd (1974), and more recently Shebilske (1975), propose such a model. Obviously if the buffer is large the model reduces to the "minimal control" form with the possible addition of a gain control: the reader must simply ensure that his eyes move along the text in a more-or-less regular fashion at a rate adjusted by some overall index of the rate of comprehension. However, interesting implications arise from considering a small buffer capable, say, of integrating only the data from a very limited number of fixations. Shaffer and Hardwick (1970) offer a model of skilled typing which falls into this class. The movements of the fingers are looked on as being under the control of processes which act on a queue, or buffer, which the typist maintains by reading the material to be transcribed and organizing the input on the basis of linguistic rules. It is not clear as yet whether the stochastic latency theory developed by Shaffer can be usefully applied to eye movement data.

3. EVIDENCE ON THE RELATIONSHIP BETWEEN EYE MOVEMENTS AND LINGUISTIC PROCESSES

The available evidence suggests that a random control model, in its most extreme form, must be of very doubtful validity since it does not permit even the regulation of the fundamental scanning rate to suit changing rates of comprehension. Such a proposal is, to say the least, counter-intuitive: it is true that the reader occasionally becomes aware that his eyes have been moving although comprehension ceased some lines before, but what does not seem to happen is the act of comprehension being hampered by too fast or too slow an automatic scanning rate. In this strong form, then, theories of this kind are probably untenable. As Rayner and McConkie correctly point out, they must at the very least incorporate a form of simple gain control to account for the fact that both the length and duration of saccades can be varied directly by instructions, or indirectly by altering the nature of the material read. On the other hand, for some reading tasks, there does not appear to be any relationship between independent measures of such peripheral processes as scanning rate and the rate of uptake of letter and digit information and qualitative estimates of "good" and "poor" readers (Katz and Wicklund, 1971, 1972). Not much of the variance in measured reading ability, it would seem, is accounted for by qualitative variations in these peripheral processes.

Rayner and McConkie (1976) tried to assess the validity of random control models by examining the intercorrelations between various measures of eye movements. They showed that measures of fixation duration did not correlate with those of saccade length, which makes it likely that these two component processes are not under the direct control of a single mechanism. Thus, although reading rate might conceivably be adjusted by simultaneously increasing saccade length and decreasing fixation duration, and these two operations could be effected by a single gain control, in fact this appears not to be the case. Further, if saccades and fixations are under the control of a single mechanism, one would anticipate some positive correlation between the duration of successive fixations and successive saccades: this, too, is not the case. It would appear, therefore, that random control models, and process monitoring models which assume a very large buffer, are not viable. Clearly, however, this is very far from establishing the validity of the other models we have considered: to examine this we must first look at some of the available behavioural evidence linking comprehension and attention during reading.

If subjects are sensitive at all to information in peripheral vision and make use of this in guiding where they look one would expect this to be evident in situations where such information is misleading. In an unpublished paper, Neisser (1969) reported the results of an experiment in which subjects read lines of text printed in red ink and were asked to ignore an irrelevant message interleaved between the lines and printed in black. The task was a kind of visual analogue of the familiar auditory "shadowing" task (Treisman, 1964). The irrelevant message contained embedded in it the subject's own name or the repeated presentation of a particular word such as the name of a day of the week. Neisser showed that many of the effects found in dichotic listening situations were reproduced: overall reading speed was not apparently reduced, but in some circumstances the rejected "channel" would break through. The technique was exploited further by Willows (1974) who looked at two groups of children categorized as "good" or "poor" readers, in a situation where the interleaved text contained material associatively related to the main theme of what was being read. Her prediction was that good readers should show *less* susceptibility to interference. In fact, they showed considerably more. The interpretation placed on this result was that

> poor readers appeared to focus most of their processing capacity on visual aspects of the display . . . good readers on the other hand, have

automated the more basic visual skills involved in reading to the extent that they can be handled "pre-attentively".

The good reader, in other words, may adopt a sampling technique which if mediating eye movements will at times lead him to absorb related but inappropriate information. The difference between good and poor readers would thus not directly relate to the efficiency with which information in peripheral vision may be extracted. It would, rather, reflect the greater elaboration of the cognitive hypotheses formed by the better reader who will, paradoxically, be led in this highly artificial situation to find confirmatory evidence where it was not in fact on offer.

The influence of a coherent theme extracted from a linguistic input on the distribution of attention has also been shown in situations where eye movements have been measured directly. Carpenter and Just (1972) demonstrated that people scan and code pictures in a way that is congruent with their representation of a linguistic input. The experimental situation involved verifying short sentences like "Few of the dots are red" or "A minority of the dots are red" by reference to a pictorial display. In the first case the linguistic representation of the proposition is a denial that the major subset is red and subjects tended to scan this subset first. The second statement relates to the smaller subset in the pictorial display and here that was scanned first. Cooper (1974) produced a powerful elaboration of this technique in which subjects looked at a much more complex pictorial scene (a display containing a number of line drawings of objects) while listening at the same time to a story. There was a close link between the concurrent auditory input and the direction of gaze. In particular, eye movements appeared to reflect the interpretation placed on the speech since the auditorily presented sentences were at times ambiguous. For example, given the phrase "There would be lions and . . ." subjects would direct their gaze at the word "and" to another animal in the display *before* this auditory stimulus occurred. Hearing the word "striped" subjects scanned to a zebra in the display although in fact the words related at that point in the story to the lines on someone's forehead. It would appear therefore that there is an intimate coupling between one aspect of language processing and eye movements: the direction of gaze is "linguistically sensitive" at least in these situations. However, we are left with no more than a suggestion as to the form that eye movement control might take in reading. To examine this we must systematically manipulate features of text structure and measure eye movements directly. Experimental studies of this kind have been surprisingly few in number.

Typical of an indirect attempt to assess "peripheral search guidance"

is a study by Abrams and Zuber (1972). They distinguished between
two types of eye fixation, that relating to the control of eye position
alone and that reflecting the additional processing of textual information. Studies of the saccadic eye movement system reveal a minimum
"refractory" period of about 200 ms between two successive movements
of the eyes. Abrams and Zuber argue that, in reading, the oculomotor
system is occupied at times in the computation of eye position and
nothing more, whereas at other times it is involved in the processing
of both text and position information. Blank segments were inserted
randomly into passages of text to test the hypothesis that at these
positions (and at the ends of lines) primarily position-information
would be computed. This was supported to the extent that mean
fixation duration at these points fell from around 200–250 ms to about
170 ms. The conclusion was that these results showed unequivocally
that variations in the duration of fixations do reflect the type of processing occurring.

Using an ingenious computer-controlled system for acquiring eye
movement data during the reading of single sentences, O'Regan
(1975) provided direct evidence that information relating to word
length was available in peripheral vision and was used to guide the
location of fixations in normal reading. In particular, short words in
the periphery (e.g. the word "*the*") were systematically skipped in
reading. This result conflicts with previously published data appearing
to suggest that mean fixations per letter do not vary in normal reading
as a function of word length (Shebilske, 1975). However, there is
behavioural evidence (Healy, 1976) that detection errors in searching
for letters are higher in high-frequency words such as *the*, and the
question is obviously worthy of further examination.

McConkie (McConkie and Rayner, 1975; Rayner and McConkie,
1976) developed a technique similar to that of O'Regan which permitted the direct measurement of eye movements. The method used a
computer in real time and allowed the estimated line of regard to alter
characteristics of the computer-generated display being read. In a
typical experiment subjects read in effect a "window" of clear text
embedded in an array of lines of scrambled words. They were apparently unaware of this since the direction of gaze itself served to
determine the placing of the window, its location changing with eye
movements. Of primary interest here are alterations in fixation pattern
which occur when a word which is in the periphery on one fixation
changes to another word when brought into direct vision. McConkie
argued that if there is found to be a change in the duration of fixation
under such a condition, this would provide an estimate of the distance
into peripheral vision over which word length and semantic information

are available. For example, if the fixation duration varied with the kind of semantic relationship obtained between the initial and final form of a particular word, this would clearly provide evidence of the operation of some cognitive strategy which was making use of such information to guide eye movements. A lengthened fixation could then be used as an index of the additional processing incurred as a result of a disconfirmed "cognitive hypothesis". The results show conclusively that mean fixation duration is selectively changed on the basis of information in peripheral vision. For example, subjects launching a saccade from the letter *a* in the word *guarded* in the sentence: "The robbers guarded the pcluse with their guns", might find that when fixating the letter *p* the word had changed to read *palace*. Extended fixation durations in such circumstances indicated that subjects were capable of extracting some information from, in this case, ten letters out in peripheral vision. However, the size of the effective visual span was quite small (up to twelve characters), and the area within which purely *semantic* (as distinct from word-length) effects were found was even smaller (about four characters). Additional confirmation of these findings is provided by a study conducted by Marcel (1974) using a tachistoscopic presentation technique to provide an estimate of the effective visual field. His data suggest that "better" readers can devote more processing capacity to the events in peripheral vision and thus capitalize on contextual constraints when reading sentences.

This evidence is certainly not entirely conclusive, but we are left with enough support for a "minimal control" model to make it worth while examining in detail the much more complicated problem of "strong control". It might, of course, be argued at this stage that if usable semantic information is only available over a distance of about four character spaces this would not be adequate to guide eye movements in any useful fashion and consequently we could dispense with any kind of "cognitive search guidance" model; but the conclusion is not altogether warranted. The low-level information in peripheral vision may not be specific enough for the reader to identify meaning and look at one informative region rather than another on that basis alone. He will, however, if he is reading connected discourse, have developed hypotheses about the logical and syntactic structure of a sentence or sequence of sentences. It is these cognitive strategies which could capitalize on quite restricted information in peripheral vision, by constructing a plausible syntactic segmentation of the sentence being read or, through the attention-altering mechanisms already discussed, directing the eyes to points where semantic hypotheses may receive confirmation. The experiment described below was carried out to test this proposition directly.

4. SEMANTIC PRIMING AND EYE MOVEMENTS

Subjects read a series of short sequences of three sentences. They had no other instruction than to read and attempt to understand the material, which formed a natural descriptive or narrative sequence. In the experimental condition a single word in the first sentence of each group of three bore a strong semantic relationship to a word in the third sentence. In control sequences this was not the case, although the sentences read quite naturally. The critical question is what effect this "priming" word had on the way subjects read the third sentence of each set of three.

This experiment gives rise to two hypotheses and leaves open a number of interesting questions regarding the reader's behaviour. The two hypotheses are:

1. Words which are primed in the third sentence should be looked at earlier than the same words unprimed. This is the central hypothesis arising from the theory outlined above. Assuming that readers, asked simply to comprehend three sentences, engage in part in a search for cross-reference (Garrod and Sanford, 1977), then the experimental manipulation will act in such a way that the primed word should engage the reader's attention earlier.

2. Readers will fixate a primed word for a longer duration than the same word unprimed. This increased latency provides a measure in fact of the time taken to register the cross-reference.

Questions left open are:

1. The measurement of reading time (i.e. the time to comprehend the sentences) may be sensitive to priming. However, conflicting predictions can be derived from the literature: reading facilitation effects might lead one to expect shorter latency (Jacobson, 1973; Schvaneveldt et al., 1976); but Greeno and Noreen (1974) argue that times to read sentences which do not involve specific implications do not vary greatly, even when related sentences had been read earlier.

2. Given that associative priming acts to change the way in which readers search text, it is an open question whether this will be reflected in fixations on words other than the primed word. O'Regan's data (1975), for example, might lead to the expectation that in some circumstances short words or function words would be fixated less than content words, but as we have seen this finding conflicts with a great deal of earlier evidence.

4.1. Subjects

Sixteen undergraduate volunteers took part: they were paid 50p to participate. They knew that the purpose of the experiment was to investigate eye movements, but were instructed as far as possible to attempt to read in their usual manner. The subjects were unaware of the experimental hypotheses.

4.2. Materials

Fifteen sets of sentences were constructed. Each set consisted of three short sentences forming a natural narrative or descriptive sequence. From these sentences two experimental conditions were established by varying the relationship between a key word in the first and third sentence of each set. For one group there was always a strong associative relationship between these two words; for example (primed words are shown in upper case):

It is unwise to wander on a MOUNTAIN.
People can get lost there.
A HILL is not always easy to climb.

In the other group the key word in the first sentence of each set was replaced by a neutral item which nonetheless made sense in the context; for example:

It is unwise to wander on a track.
People can get lost there.
A hill is not always easy to climb.

The only difference between the two groups of fifteen sentence sets related to the presence or absence in the first sentence of each set of a synonym or near synonym of a word in the third sentence. The position of this primed word in the third sentence was varied between sets.

4.3. Procedure

Subjects were comfortably seated looking slightly upwards towards a CRT display with the head held rigidly by means of a dental composition bite bar fixed to a heavy metal frame. After calibration of the equipment subjects were told to read, in as natural a fashion as possible, the sentences which were to appear on the screen. Sentences were displayed for 2024 ms with an intersentence interval of 1 s. The subject had a button under the right-hand index finger and was asked to press it lightly as soon as he understood the meaning of the third sentence in each set. All subjects read the material in the same serial order. Subjects in Group 1 read fifteen sets of sentences with a priming relationship built in; subjects in Group 2 read control sentences. The first set of sentences was treated as a practice trial.

4.4. Data acquisition and analysis

Eye movements were measured using an infrared reflection technique which recorded horizontal movements of the left eye. The signal provided an analogue input to a PDP–12 computer which also generated text on a point-plotting CRT. The experiment was conducted in three stages.

1. *Optical and electronic calibration:* this involved lining up the infrared detectors and checking that a suitably large analogue voltage resulted from a horizontal excursion of the eyes across the (blank) CRT. The procedure normally took about 3 min.

2. *Self-calibration,* during which subjects, using a lever, moved a marker across the screen from left to right fixating it steadily at all times. The computer detected changes in a voltage controlled by the lever and used these to locate the marker on the display; at the same time it sampled eye movement signals. At the conclusion of the calibration (when the marker reached the extreme right edge of the screen) the computer had constructed a table of eye movement voltages and their equivalent screen positions. This self-calibration was based on the method employed by O'Regan (1975) and normally took about 1 min. It was repeated if the table of equivalent screen positions was unduly irregular or if the voltage difference generated in moving from the left margin to the right was too small to give a satisfactory resolution (defined as half a letter).

3. *Reading:* text was displayed using a standard character-generation program. Letters were in an upper case "font" formed by a matrix of 6 × 6 points. During the display eye movement data were sampled at a 1-ms rate with the mean of each eight samples being stored in the form of an estimated horizontal screen position. After 2048 ms or, in the case of the third sentence of each set, when the subject pressed the button, the display terminated. Between each set of three sentences a calibration display appeared, consisting of the letters A B C spaced across the screen. Subjects fixated each letter in turn briefly. Data from each sentence and from the calibration displays were stored on magnetic tape.

Analyses of the eye movement records were completed using a pattern-analysing computer program. A display was generated consisting of the sentence read and the eye movement track in the form of a graph (time being on the vertical coordinate). For each set of sentences the "calibration display" data were first examined and any discrepancy between characters and the displayed fixations was corrected by adding or subtracting a constant value through an analog channel. Once the calibration display was in perfect alignment the data from a set of three sentences were analysed. Output took the form of a print-out for each sentence of the point in time at which each word was first fixated; the total time spent fixating each word; and, in the case of the third sentence of each set, the reaction time to the button-press. In practice, the calibration displays showed very little drift and the measurement process was highly reliable.

4.5. Results

The time to press the button signalling comprehension of the third sentence differed in the two groups, Group 1 (the primed group) taking significantly longer (1547 ms $vs.$ 1366 ms, $p < 0.05$). It is likely that the greater thematic integration of the sets of sentences used in Group 1 led to this increase; however, without further experimentation the result is difficult to explain since it runs counter to some evidence suggesting that associative priming leads to an increase in reading speed.

The time elapsing before the eye first alighted on the critical word in the third sentence of each group of three was 372 ms for Group 1 (the primed group) and 482 ms for Group 2 ($p < 0.005$). The number of "fixations" on critical words (these were taken arbitrarily to be any continuous "look" in excess of 100 ms) was 0·88 per word in Group 1 and 0·77 per word in Group 2 ($p < 0.02$). The experimental hypotheses were therefore confirmed: subjects in Group 1 reached the critical word earlier and in general spent longer looking at it than subjects in Group 2. Since the design allowed for comparison of subject-group means for each word these were examained to provide an informal estimate of the generality of the results. In both cases (time to first fixation and fixation per word) the effect was found in thirteen out of fourteen sentences.

Since the overall number of fixations per letter did not differ between the two groups (0·12 fixations per letter in both), it is possible that some form of trade-off is taking place, and an analysis was carried out on the time spent looking at "function" words (defined as any short word of three or less letters which was neither a noun, a verb, nor an adjective). The number of fixations per letter in function words was 0·11 for

Group 1 and 0·16 for Group 2, $p < 0·01$. Subjects in Group 1 spent significantly less time looking at function words.

The point at which the eye first fixated the sentence was further to the right for Group 1 than Group 2 (2·6 *vs.* 2·1 words, $p < 0·05$), suggesting that the experimental condition led to a different reading strategy. However this was apparently unique to the reading of the third sentence. Analyses of the point of first fixation in the *second* sentence of each set of three, which were identical for both groups of subjects, showed no significant differences (1·9 *vs.* 1·7 words).

4.6. Discussion

This experiment attempted to simulate one significant property of continuous text and at the same time provide a manipulation of the cognitive hypotheses in which subjects engaged. The critical data are derived from subjects reading the same set of sentences and consequently any non-random differences may confidently be attributed to the only variable manipulated between the groups, namely the alteration of one word in the first sentence of each set of three.

The experiment lends further support to those models suggesting the operation of some form of cognitive control of eye movements in reading. Two important questions must wait on further experimentation. These are:

1. The degree to which the results can be generalized to other reading tasks, and
2. The possibility, which has frequently been raised, that some reading difficulties may relate to an ineffective use of information in peripheral vision and to failures in the construction of higher-level units, greater than the word, during reading.

The experimental techniques outlined here suggest how the interaction of these two processes might be studied.

REFERENCES

Abrams, S. G. and Zuber, B. L. (1972). Some temporal characteristics of information processing during reading. *Reading Research Quarterly* **8**, 40–51.
Anisfield, M. (1970). False recognition of adjective-noun phrases. *Journal of Experimental Psychology* **86**, 120–122.
Bouma, H. and de Voogd, A. H. (1974). On the control of eye saccades in reading. *Vision Research* **14**, 271–272.

Bradshaw, J. L. (1974). Peripherally presented and unreported words may bias the perceived meaning of a centrally fixated homograph. *Journal of Experimental Psychology* **103**, 1200–1202.

Carpenter, P. A. and Just, M. A. (1972). Semantic control of eye movements during picture scanning in a sentence-picture verification task. *Perception and Psychophysics* **12**, 61–64.

Cooper, R. M. (1974). The control of eye fixation by the meaning of spoken language. *Cognitive Psychology* **6**, 84–107.

Garrod, S. and Sanford, A. (1977). Interpreting anaphoric relations: the integration of semantic information while reading. *Journal of Verbal Learning and Verbal Behavior* **16**, 77–90.

Gibson, E. J. (1972). Reading for some purpose. *In* "Language by Ear and by Eye" (J. F. Kavanagh and I. G. Mattingly, eds). MIT, London.

Gough, P. B. (1972). One second of reading. *In* "Language by Ear and by Eye" (J. F. Kavanagh and I. G. Mattingly, eds). MIT, London.

Greeno, J. G. and Noreen, D. (1974). Time to read semantically related sentences. *Memory and Cognition* **2**, 117–120.

Hall, J. W. and Crown, I. (1970). Associative encoding of words in sentences. *Journal of Verbal Learning and Verbal Behavior* **9**, 92–95.

Hall, J. W. and Crown, I. (1972). Associative encoding of words in sentences by adults and children. *Journal of Verbal Learning and Verbal Behavior* **11**, 92–95.

Hochberg, J. (1970). Components of literacy: Speculations and exploratory research. *In* "Basic Studies on Reading" (H. Levin and J. P. Williams, eds.). Basic Books, New York.

Hochberg, J. (1976). Toward a speech-plan eye-movement model of reading. *In* "Eye Movements and Psychological Processes" (R. A. Monty and J. W. Senders, eds). Wiley, New York.

Healy, A. F. (1976). Detection errors on the word *the*: evidence for reading units larger than letters. *Journal of Experimental Psychology: Human Perception and Performance* **2**, 235–242.

Huey, E. B. (1908). "The Psychology and Pedagogy of Reading". MacMillan, New York.

Jacobson, J. Z. (1973). Effects of association upon masking and reading latency. *Canadian Journal of Psychology* **27**, 58–69.

James, W. (1890). "Principles of Psychology" Holt, New York.

Katz, L. and Wicklund, D. A. (1971). Word scanning rate for good and poor readers. *Journal of Educational Psychology* **62**, 138–140.

Katz, L. and Wicklund, D. A. (1972). Letter scanning rate for good and poor readers in grades two and six. *Journal of Educational Psychology* **63**, 363–367.

Kennedy, A. (1975). Contextual effects in reading and recognition. *In* "Studies in Long Term Memory" (A. Kennedy and A. Wilkes, eds). Wiley, London.

Kintsch, W. and Monk, D. (1972). Storage of complex information in memory: some implications of the speed with which inferences can be made. *Journal of Experimental Psychology* **94**, 25–32.

Kolers, P. A. (1976). Buswell's discoveries. *In* "Eye Movements and Psychological Processes" (R. A. Monty and J. W. Senders, eds). Wiley, New York.

Levin, H. and Kaplan, E. (1970). Grammatical structure and reading. *In* "Basic Studies on Reading" (H. Levin and J. P. Williams, eds). Basic Books, New York.

Loftus, G. R. (1976). A framework for a theory of picture recognition. *In* "Eye Movements and Psychological Processes" (R. A. Monty and J. W. Senders, eds). Wiley, New York.

Marcel, T. (1974). The effective visual field and the use of context in fast and slow readers of two ages. *British Journal of Psychology* **65**, 479–492.

McConkie, G. W. and Rayner, K. (1975). The span of the effective stimulus during a fixation in reading. *Perception and Psychophysics* **17**, 578–586.

Meyer, D. E. and Schvaneveldt, R. W. (1971). Facilitation in recognising pairs of words: evidence of a dependence between retrieval operations. *Journal of Experimental Psychology* **90**, 227–234.

Morton, J. (1969). Interaction of information in word recognition. *Psychological Review* **76**, 165–178.

Neisser, U. (1969). Selective reading: a method for the study of visual attention. Paper delivered to XIX International Congress of Psychology, London.

O'Regan, J. K. (1975). Structural and contextual constraints on eye movements in reading. Ph.D. thesis, University of Cambridge.

Rayner, K. and McConkie, G. W. (1976). What guides a reader's eye movements? *Vision Research* **16**, 829–837.

Sanders, A. F. (1970). Some aspects of the selective process in the functional visual field. *Ergonomics* **13**, 101–117.

Schvaneveldt, R. W., Meyer, D. E. and Becker, C. A. (1976). Lexical ambiguity, semantic context, and visual word recognition. *Journal of Experimental Psychology: Human Perception and Performance* **2**, 243–256.

Shaffer, L. H. and Hardwick, J. (1970). The basis of transcription skill. *Journal of Experimental Psychology* **84**, 424–440.

Shebilske, W. (1975). Reading eye movements from an information-processing point of view. *In* "Understanding Language" (D. W. Massaro, ed.). Academic Press, London and New York.

Tinker, M. A. (1958). Recent studies of eye movements in reading. *Psychological Bulletin* **55**, 215–231.

Tinker, M. A. (1965). "Bases for Effective Reading". University of Minnesota Press, Minneapolis, Minnesota.

Treisman, A. M. (1964). Contextual cues in selective listening. *Quarterly Journal of Experimental Psychology* **12**, 242–248.

Willows, D. M. (1974). Reading between the lines: selective attention in good and poor readers. *Child Development* **45**, 408–415.

Seven

Attentional Selectivity and Behavioural Control

Geoffrey Underwood

University of Nottingham

1. THE SELECTIVE CONTROL OF BEHAVIOUR

At one time in its career *Attention* was a central concept in psychology, and so it should have been. Wundt, Fechner, Titchener, Helmholtz and James were all very concerned with the phenomenon, but a healthy introduction in the early textbooks of psychology did little to resist dismissal by the radical behaviourists. The subjective behaviourists of the last few decades have, in contrast, been eager to reinstate this mentalistic and intangible concept to a position of respectability, and to reject the notion that because a process is not directly observable, it must be a pre-scientific concept. Indeed, to information processing theory, one of the more hard-nosed notions in contemporary psychology, attention and selectivity are central features. "Mind" has returned (*see* Joynson, 1972), and with it "Attention".

The problem as it stands is to integrate the intuitive concept of a state of mind into cognitive models of behaviour. Attention is an intuitive concept in the sense suggested by James (1890) that "everyone knows what attention is" and that "it is the taking possession by the mind, in clear and vivid form, of one out of what seems several simultaneously possible objects or trains of thought" (James, 1890, p. 403). Here we have two of the characteristics of the attention process which we must account for: the qualitative vividness of perception resulting from the directing of attention to information, and the operation of selectivity in the processing of one from a number of available sources of information. We select information for further processing, and implicit here is the notion of the limited capacity of the processor, and what is selected is perceived with greater clarity than that which is not selected. More generally, we must also explain why we need to attend to information at all. This question is again related to the issue of limited capacity on the one hand, and to the issue of the perceptual vividness of the contents of consciousness on the other. As well as describing the processes applied to that which is attended, it is of some interest to determine the effects of that which is unattended. Second only to perceptual vividness as a noticeable effect of attending to something is memorability, and the relationships between attention and memory are rich and binding. It is not possible to investigate any of the cognitive processes without being aware of the influences of other processes, and this is vitally true for the investigation of memory and the influence of attention. Attention may be viewed as the major control process in the passage of information into and out of the memory system (Underwood, 1976a, after Atkinson and Shiffrin, 1968), and indeed, through the human information processing system as a whole.

One of the functions of memory is, of course, to enable us to learn from past experience, and thus behave adaptively in novel situations. The first time we are introduced to a bicycle, or the driving seat of an automobile, the necessity of attending to so many sources of information may overwhelm the performer: the available processing capacity is insufficient to handle all of the information which is presented. Yet after a little experience of the situation the performer may be riding or driving quite competently, and even accepting further information at the same time by talking with an associate. Attention would no longer appear to be essential. The performer's memories of the situation are now sufficient to guide his behaviour without reference to a system involving the vividness of an attended activity. Skilled activities performed without the performer attending continuously to the input or to the organization and execution of the response are said to be automatized. During the acquisition of a skill, attention is required for

some stages of processing, and once acquired the skill may be performed without those stages requiring attention. These changes do not
apply exclusively to motor skills, of course, and the interactions
between attention and the performance of cognitive skills also concerns
the following section of this discussion.

2. ATTENTION, CONSCIOUSNESS AND INFORMATION PROCESSING

2.1. Attention as a control process

The term *control process* refers to those processes that are not permanent
features of memory, but are instead transient phenomena under the
control of the subject; their appearance depends upon such factors as
instructional set, the experimental task, and the past history of the
subject (Atkinson and Shiffrin, 1968, p. 106).

Given that humans have a number of operations or stages of processing
which can be performed upon information which is presented or is
retrieved from memory, we must also take account of the choice of
which operations are applied under different circumstances. The
"control process" referred to by Atkinson and Shiffrin, being under the
volitional control of the individual, is what others have referred to as
attention. The selection of information from iconic memory (e.g.
Mewhort *et al.*, 1969), the selective rehearsal of some members of the
memory set in preference to others (e.g. Rundus, 1971), the selective
"forgetting" of some items previously encoded (e.g. Woodward and
Bjork, 1971), the selective search of one category of remembered items
(e.g. Naus *et al.*, 1972) and the selective enrichment of alternative
associations by imagery (e.g. Bower *et al.*, 1969), are all examples of
volitional control, or attention to selected components from the total set
available.

By way of illustrating the role of attention in the information processing system, the discussion will first proceed via a few experiments
concerning the strategical manipulation of memory systems, the
systems in which Atkinson and Shiffrin's (1968) control processes
operate.

Perhaps the most obvious effect of attention in any memory experiment is that of rehearsal: if the subject rehearses the words presented
to him, he is, in general, more likely to remember them than if he
diverts his attention elsewhere. Rehearsal is a manifestation of attention
and has been held to have a variety of functions all aimed towards
facilitating recall. Rehearsal is of importance only to a single channel

processor (such as the speech production system) in that it selects one item at a time and selectively prevents loss of that item at the risk of other items. The onset of the decay process is postponed by rehearsal, and the repetition of an item by the subject may increase the trace strength of the item, or it may provide more attributes to aid retrieval, but repetitive rehearsal itself has only short-lived advantages. Attention to an item which is to be remembered will only keep the item in episodic rather than semantic memory (Tulving, 1972), unless an additional process gives the item a deeper level of coding (Craik and Lockhart, 1972). Episodic memory is said to be a representation of our cognitive autobiography, the diary of information which has been processed, and which is organized temporally. Semantic memory is said to accumulate via the operation of episodic memory, and is an organized repository of the rules, concepts and relationships between words and other symbols. Accordingly "semantic memory does not register perceptible properties of inputs, but rather cognitive referents of input signals" (Tulving, 1972, p. 386). Any entry or use of semantic memory must be directed through episodic memory, and so repetitive rehearsal may leave no mark on the semantic system but will produce the corresponding number of entries in episodic memory. To gain access to semantic memory, the associations between the item and others already in store must be attended, and this form of elaboration will lead to what Craik and Lockhart (1972) refer to as a deeper level of processing.

As an illustration of the significance of the depth of processing consider an experiment reported by Weist and Crawford (1973), who instructed their subjects to use one of two rehearsal strategies. Some subjects were instructed to rehearse the items in the same order as that in which they were presented, and others were allowed to organize their rehearsal of the words, which for both sets of subjects were semantically related. The lists of words were thirty-six items in length, with six words in each of six categories, but the words were not organized into categories during the presentation. Other groups of subjects were presented with lists of unrelated words. The presentation of disorganized lists of related words did facilitate recall in this experiment, but only for subjects who were free to rehearse the words in their own style. Subjects who rehearsed sequentially, and who did not appear to develop the associations between words in the categorized list performed no worse on the list of unrelated words. Rehearsal provides the opportunity for a deeper level of processing, but does not ensure it. The style of rehearsal is important here, and will depend upon the expectations of the subject. If the subject is misled into believing that an item will be required for no longer than a few seconds, a repetitive rehearsal strategy may well be adopted, and used effectively over that time scale. When tested after a few minutes in a final test of all that he has been presented with during the course of an experimental session, then repetitive rehearsal may be of no advantage whatever, and Meunier *et al.* (1972) found that subjects prevented from rehearsing during storage were as successful as subjects who had rehearsed repetitively, when tested unexpectedly for final recall at the end of the session. Subjects who did rehearse did not develop the spread of elaboration coding necessary for sustained storage. Attention to the item in isolation does not ensure that the item will be available for recall as few retrieval cues will be established. The more associations there are elaborated, the more possible routes of retrieval there will be available.

An indication of the variety of strategies of retrieval which are available has been provided by a series of experiments reported by Mary Naus (Naus *et al.*, 1972; Naus, 1974). These studies have extended the Sternberg (1966) memory search paradigm to situations which are a closer approximation of working memory than those previously investigated. Sternberg presented a list of homogeneous items (e.g. digits), followed by a probe to which the subjects responded "yes" or "no" according to whether or not the memory set had included the probe. By presenting various numbers of items in the memory set, and comparing response times to positive and negative probes, Sternberg was able to infer that the search of the memory set was both serial (rather than in parallel for each item in the set) and exhaustive (rather than self-terminating on location of a positive probe in the set). Naus *et al.* (1972) presented their subjects with memory sets containing two types of items (animals' names and girls' names) to investigate the entry strategy. Would subjects presented with an animal name as the probe go directly to the appropriate set of items, or would they plough straight in, checking item by item regardless of the category? If the experiment reflected non-laboratory behaviour then presumably a *directed entry* strategy would be applied, with the subject first matching the probe category with the subset category. When asked a geographical question of the form "What is the capital city of Iran?" a subset of possibilities arises within the total set of "capital cities" or the set of "Middle Eastern cities" (whichever location search is used), in one case excluding non-Middle Eastern cities and in the other case excluding non-capital cities. The best strategy of answering the question may be to exclude unreasonable possibilities before proceeding with a serial search of the reasonable-sounding possibilities ("Amman, Beirut, Tashkent, Teheran, Jerusalem . . ."). Such searches and strategies are appropriate only where the solution is not immediately available, of course, but is known to be stored somewhere. Directed entry searches have the advantage of excluding all non-category items from consideration, and the disadvantage of requiring the subject to categorize the probe and match that category with a category already in storage. The alternative strategy is one of *random entry* and involves the selection on a random basis of the category to be searched first. Naus *et al.* (1972) found that their subjects preferred the random entry strategy when presented with only two categories in the memory set, presumably because of the savings made by the non-necessity of the category match made before the search. Some subjects, it should be noted, preferred, on at least some trials, to use the direct entry strategy and thus incur time penalties before entry and gain by not searching the inappropriate strategy. When subjects are cued in advance which of the categories is to be probed then selective, direct entry strategies are also employed (Darley *et al.*, 1972), even when the entire memory set is required for later use. Presumably, as the number of categories in the memory set is increased, the likelihood of a direct entry search will also increase, but even with as many as four categories in the set, Naus (1974) found a preference for the random entry strategy. The use of serial and exhaustive ·searching continued to be a feature of the retrieval strategy in these experiments, but these features too may be used strategically. If the memory set is particularly large, for example, it may be more economical to be prepared to terminate the search on successful location of the positive probe in the set, but this may require more search time per item. If the memory set is particularly overlearnt the search may be conducted by matching these items in parallel. Discussions concerning the controversial serial and exhaustive nature of the search have been provided by Baddeley (1976), Murdock (1971), Sternberg (1975) and Theios (1973).

These experiments illustrate some of the manipulations of cognitive structure which can be apparent in simple laboratory situations. The choice between a direct entry and a random entry search is influenced by the demands of the task, but it remains as a choice made by the individual subject. Naus (1974) was able to train her subjects to use direct entry rather than random entry, and observed the corresponding increase in entry time resulting from the additional matching process. There are structural features of memory which influence performance in tasks such as these, but the manipulation of information within these structural limitations is at least partly under the volitional control of the individual, with the information being attended to gaining access to the more powerful processes.

The modes of retrieval mentioned above, volitional and involuntary, are representative of many cognitive skills in their relationship with the attention process. Ask a regional geographer or an Arab "What is the capital of Iran?" and the instant reply "Teheran" will be accompanied by a questioning look, as if he were adding "What's the problem? Isn't it obvious?" Certain facts do not have to be searched for by any of the strategies outlined in the preceding discussion. As soon as we specify the question the answer is retrieved immediately, and without our having to attend to a set of likely possibilities. Retrieval in these instances appears to be *automatized*, and by this we mean that the process is an involuntary reflex which does not require guidance from consciousness, only an input from that source. The required word is presented to consciousness without our being aware of any of the search processes which are involved. Supporting these somewhat intuitive statements is not quite so straightforward, however, and this controversy is a subissue of the perceptual-selection/response-selection discussion of the role of the attention process. Attention might be viewed as being necessary to admit sensory data to the cognitive processing systems, or for organizing responses to the processed data. Similarly, attention might or might not be necessary for the retrieval of information from memory; if it is not necessary then support is given to response selection theories of attention, on the basis that many pieces of information may be retrieved at one time, and selection would then be necessary for their organization (*see* Keele, 1972). As is evident with the case of retrieval, the solution to the problem is that attention is sometimes required, and it depends upon the information involved and the current state of the memory system as to whether or not the individual will have to attend to the retrieval programme. Once this statement has been generalized to the many other stages of processing for which attention might be necessary, then the complexity of the total system can be appreciated, and attempts to find a single location of selectivity put into perspective. The following discussion examines the empirical search for the locus of selectivity within this framework.

2.2. Attention and selective processing

Broadbent (1958) accounted for the apparent absence of semantic processing of unattended speech messages by postulating that attention was necessary for the word analysis of a message, and that only one message could be processed at a time. Selection of the message to be analysed was said to be made on the basis of the physical characteristics of the available messages (e.g. spatial location, loudness, pitch of the speaker's voice), and all unwanted messages were said to be filtered away before analysis of their meaning. Attention is thereby necessary for word analysis, and without attention a message cannot be understood, remembered or responded to. This particular theory of attention was rejected very soon after it was formulated, on the basis of experiments showing occasional effects of the meanings of unattended words which were important to the listener (Moray, 1959) or highly probable in the context of the attended message (Treisman, 1960). These two experiments were indications that attention was not located at a single site in the information processing chain, but at the time they were interpreted as giving support to the notions that attention aided either perception (Treisman, 1960) or response organization (Deutsch and Deutsch, 1963).

Progress in the two decades since the formulation of Broadbent's model has been hampered by both conceptual and methodological problems. The methodological problems associated with the investigation of attention concern the use of the shadowing procedure (which biases selectivity, masks the stimuli, and consumes processing capacity which might otherwise be used for stimulus analysis) and the subject's knowledge that he might be tested for reception of an "unattended" message. These problems have been discussed in some detail elsewhere (Davis and Smith, 1972; Underwood, 1976a, b; Underwood and Moray, 1971). The conceptual problems here, as with the investigation of any cognitive process, are profuse, but centred around the feature that whereas attention is the manifestation of strategical control it has been discussed as a structural and invariant feature of a processing system away from the influence of the individual. Even at a basic level, the alternative strategies of focusing closely upon an attended message and dividing attention more between competing messages will produce qualitative differences in the processing completed by the invariant stages (Moray and O'Brien, 1967; Ostry et al., 1976; Treisman, 1969; Underwood, 1976b). One of the implications of this view of attention having a number of modes is that sometimes certain classes of information will be admitted to certain stages of processing whereas at other times the same information will not be processed at that level. This possibility in itself is sufficient to produce apparently contradictory results when different experimental paradigms are used. A second serious flaw with the traditional theories of attention has been discussed by Erdelyi (1974). Unless we have invariant sequences of processing without selectivity then attention must be apparent at many locations, and not simply as a gate to perception *or* response. Attention may be used for selecting information which is to be perceived *and* for selecting that which is to be responded to, as well as selecting for any number of intermediate or subordinate processes. The notion of a single site of attention may have arisen initially from the unity view of consciousness: only that information which gains admittance to consciousness is thereby processed. Attention might then be seen as the process by which information is made available for the scrutiny of the conscious processes. This view is clearly unacceptable, for there are any number of stages of processing which do not require monitoring by consciousness. We are not aware of the activity of the feature detectors at work while we are listening or looking, only of the transformed outputs from these stages. When our knowledgeable subject immediately replies to a question about his speciality he answers without being aware of the stages of retrieval, only the answer. Given an unusual display of data points, or a difficult retrieval problem, then we may direct our awareness to the setting up of perceptual hypotheses or to the search of possible locations of the required information. Consciousness is not a passive stage of processing. Not only may it reflect the selection of the particular processes which may be applied to information (attention to the output), but it also reflects the selection of the information which is to be made available to these processes (attention to the input). Attention may be directed to the perceptual input, or to the response effectors at different times. The problem is not one of whether attention is necessary for perception or response, but of *when* attention is necessary for perception and *when* it is necessary for response, as well as when it affects other stages.

A further problem is also evident (Kahneman, 1973; Neisser, 1967; Treisman, 1969) in the description of what is admissible as a "response". In one sense only observable outputs by the organism should be considered as being responses, but if we are prepared to be less behaviouristic then entry into memory, or indeed any stage of processing, is a response to an available input. The distinction between input and output becomes tenuous when we consider that the output from one stage of processing forms the input to the next stage, and attempting to decide then whether attention is required singularly for input or output is an unsound approach. When a number of inputs are available, then it may even be described as a selective response, and the selection may follow the redirection of attention to the choice. It is possible to extend this argument regressively until the primary act of perceiving a stimulus is regarded as a selective response to that stimulus, and at this point the differences between perceptual-selection and response-selection theories of attention completely disappear. Both classes of theories are then in the position of arguing that attention is sometimes necessary for the selection of stimuli which are to gain perceptual analysis. Don Norman's (1969) late-selection model in his book *Memory and Attention* is not as flexible as this analysis suggests, however, and by his model all signals contact their representations in memory (i.e. perception and access to memory are both pre-attentive), but only the most "pertinent" signal gains access to "further analysis". Although Norman (1968) argues that "sound might be decoded into morphemes or words, but the

temporal integration of these basic units into more meaningful structures is not performed in the absence of selection" he does go on to say
that "subjects should retain in primary storage material which has been
presented to them, even if not attended at the time of presentation"
(Norman, 1968, p. 528). These statements clarify one issue, and are
supported, and confuse another issue, and are not supported. Words
which are attended gain full analysis of their meaning and may be
integrated with each other, associations derived, and contribute to the
identification of the deep structure of their enveloping sentence. Words
which are not attended are said to be analysed as isolated symbols,
which are meaningful in themselves, but which do not contribute to a
schema of what their sentence is intended to convey. It is this position
which the present discussion will support. Norman's view that unattended words gain entry to what James (1890) called primary
memory merely confuses the issue, and is not supported here. Primary
memory is said to reflect that which is in consciousness, that which the
individual is aware of and is contributing to his perception of the
psychological present, whereas it is clearly the case that unattended
messages do not enter the awareness of the individual even though their
isolated meanings are analysed and may affect other ongoing processes.
A straightforward demonstration that unattended words do not gain
entry to any fixed-capacity primary memory system has been provided
by Davis and Smith (1972).

Norman's views of the representation of unattended words in one
memory store or another are based upon a misapprehension that is
necessary to postulate more than one memory system. The varieties of
evidence said to support a dichotomy are being eroded convincingly
(Craik and Lockhart, 1972; Kay, 1968; Melton, 1963, Murdock, 1974;
Tulving, 1970, Wickelgren, 1973, 1975) in favour of a unitary-trace
model with a number of strategies of attribute-encoding and retrieval
available. There is clearly a dichotomy between the stored information
of which we are aware at any one time, and the enormous amount of
stored information of which we are not aware. This is the Jamesian distinction between primary and secondary memory, but this introspective
distinction does not compel a view of distinct systems. Rather, information "in primary memory" may simply be that information being
acted upon by volitional processes. Consciousness then is an attribute
of volitional processing. When an item of information "in secondary
memory" is actively used, it is not transferred to primary memory, but
the process of search and retrieval which allows us to become aware of
the item simply adds the attribute of current activation. A limited
number of items may be maintained at the level of activation required
for their entry to awareness, possibly as a result of sequential inspection

and spontaneous decay, and this limit represents the apparent capacity of the primary memory store.

It should be noted that the present view of consciousness as a unitary system is contentious, however, and Neisser (1976) argues that "introspection does *not* necessarily show that one is aware of only a single thing at a time" and that "people report the singleness of consciousness largely because the philosophical assumptions of our culture require it" (p. 104). Neisser similarly dispenses with notions of limited capacity, stages of processing, "mechanisms of attention", selective filters and passive, fixed mechanisms. His views of automatized activity are somewhat ambiguous, however, for at one point he argues that "I do not mean to deny the existence of automatic mechanisms altogether", but prefers to interpret the results of experiments demonstrating simultaneous processing as a result of "the intermittent exercise of casually acquired skills [rather than] the operation of automatic mechanisms" (p. 94). The relationship between the acquisition of a skill and the onset of preattentive automatized performance of that skill is not clear from Neisser's discussion, for it seems that automatization of the components of a task is a necessary condition for skilled performance. This is not to suggest that initiation of the activity itself becomes a passive, automatized activity, and indeed Neisser's emphasis upon the active mind applying skilled strategies of information pickup and processing is in complete accord with each of the discussions contained in this volume.

The current model of cognitive organization holds that under certain conditions word recognition is an automatized activity, and that whereas attention may be directed to the analysis of individual words or to their component features, attention is necessary, and thus more often engaged in, the processes dependent upon word recognition. These processes include the elaboration of attributes, the assimilation of the recognized words into the schema of the constituent sentence, and the derivation of the relationship between the current sentence and others. Attention is not necessarily essential for the recognition of individual words, but it is necessary for the comprehension of language. Words which are structurally associated may, when presented together, be related in that temporal context, but words which are unassociated require manipulation by attention before they may become associated. The following section examines the evidence for this model, develops the discussion of attention and capacity, and outlines some of the effects of attentional strategies.

2.3. The recognition and manipulation of words

Early investigations of the visual recognition of words indicated that the stimulus factors of exposure duration, size, clarity and illumination could all influence the probability of a word being identified. These might be described as examples of data-limited processes, after Norman and Bobrow (1975), in that the determinants of processing are with the visual display. In contrast are the resource limits of attention, and the question here concerns the extent to which a diversion of attention away from the stimulus impoverishes its recognition. We are not concerned with the manifestation of attention in the manipulation of the sense organs, and it is assumed that an eye fixation to one point in visual space may or may not be associated with attention to the object or other display at that point. Fixation upon a point does not imply attention to that point, of course, for attention may be directed inwards to our thoughts, or outwards towards another, non-fixated point in space (Littman and Becklen, 1976), but only within a few degrees of fixation will a word be sufficiently distinct for us to consider that it may be processed as efficiently as it would if fixated. Such qualifiers are fortunately not necessary for the case of spoken presentations, and the interpretation of dichotic listening experiments is accordingly more straightforward.

Doubt as to the validity of Broadbent's filter model of attention was first spread by the appearance of effects of unattended spoken words in dichotic listening experiments. Moray (1959) reported that listeners occasionally responded to unattended instructions when they were prefixed by the listeners' own names, and Treisman (1960) noticed that an unattended word was occasionally recognized and repeated when preceded by contextually congruous attended words and accompanied by a simultaneous dichotic attended word which was incongruous with the preceding attended words. As an example of this effect Treisman gives the following example, where the listener was instructed to attend to and shadow the spoken words presented on the top line here, but instead repeated those words in capitals:

"... I SAW THE GIRL   song was   WISHING ..."
"... me that bird   JUMPING   in the street ..."

After the word "girl" in the attended message the two dichotic messages had been transposed, with a previously rejected message then coming from the location of the previously attended message. As noted above, it is not viable to instruct experimental subjects to ignore a message and respond to it, although a number of studies employ just these demands. Most of the useful evidence relating to the attention process has been derived from studies investigating the effects of unattended messages upon other processes. This evidence shows a reliable effect of individual words although there is no evidence of the assimilation of unattended words into meaningful structures. "Reliable" in this sense is intended to mean an effect observable in a number of situations. A number of specific effects of unattended words have proved to be difficult to replicate, and this is interpreted here as a reflection of the capriciousness of attentional strategies and their influence by experimental demands, and this is not inconsistent with the interpretation drawn by Neisser (1976) who ascribes these differences as being a result of differences in the levels of skill demonstrated by subjects in different experiments. The acquisition of skill in this context might be interpreted as meaning the development of adaptive strategies of handling the incoming information and organizing the responses, and certainly involves the process of automatization. If we can process certain classes of information without passing it through a limited capacity system then we have freed that system for other more general processing. And so it is with words. The skilled reader and the skilled listener do not have to process individual words except in conditions of difficult reception.

Effects which demonstrate the two points of pre-attentive processing of words, and the difficulty of replicating the experiments demonstrating such processing, are provided by the initial experiments of Lewis (1970) and Corteen and Wood (1972). In Lewis' study, subjects shadowed one message from a dichotic presentation, and their shadowing latencies were recorded for a number of the words to which they responded. When the simultaneous unattended word was a synonym of the word being shadowed then the shadowing latencies were increased in comparison with latencies when the unattended word was not semantically related to the shadowed word. The meaning of an unattended word had influenced the processing of a temporally adjacent attended word. Antonyms, in contrast, tended to speed up the shadowing response, and although this is another demonstration of the effect of the meaning of unattended information, it is not clear why there should be a difference in the effects of synonyms and antonyms. Bryden (1972) has provided an extension of this result, finding that presentation of an unattended antonym *prior to* the related shadowed word increases the amount of facilitation in proportion to the proximity of the shadowed word. Synonyms also showed a slight facilitation effect in this experiment, however, and so the interpretation of Lewis' synonym–antonym differences becomes pleonastic. Of some interest is the attempted replication by Treisman *et al.* (1974), who found evidence of *interference* with the shadowing response when simultaneous synonyms were presented. This experiment regrettably did not test for the effects of antonyms. The effect appeared only for those synonyms presented in the early positions of the dichotic lists (the third unattended item), and no significant difference was observed between synonyms and unrelated words when presented later in the lists (as the seventh unattended item). Indeed, by eliminating the longest shadowing latency from the data provided by each subject for responses to the early list positions, the difference between synonyms and unrelated words disappears altogether. Treisman *et al.* (1974) interpreted their result as possibly being due to serial processing of the two related words at a time when capacity was not fully occupied by one message, thus allowing some semantic analysis of the other message. The effect appears only when attention might be argued to be divided between the two messages to some extent. We shall return to this point in the discussion of attentional strategies. A further point is worth making about this experiment. When the synonym was presented in list position 7, with no reliable effect upon shadowing, there was a tendency for the effect to be one of facilitation. So, although this is a non-significant result, the mean shadowing latencies indicate that early synonyms (565 ms) interfere in comparison with unrelated words (530 ms), but that later synonyms (617 ms) facilitate shadowing, in comparison with unrelated words (633 ms). This may also be a reflection of the different attentional strategies used as the list progresses, but the caution of interpreting this statistically unreliable result should be emphasized.

Corteen and Wood (1972) first had their subjects associate certain words with the presentation of an electric shock until the galvanic skin response was elicited by the words in the absence of the shock. These words were then presented as part of the unattended message while subjects shadowed in a dichotic listening task. Not only did the shock-associated words (city names) produce more skin conductivity changes than previously heard words (other nouns) which had not been associated with the electric shocks, but semantic associates (other city names) also elicited GSR deflections more often than new nouns also introduced into the experiment for the first time. This result indicates that unattended words are recognized as previously having significance, and that they are recognized categorically. The new city names were processed to the level of category membership. Although some variations of this technique have successfully shown effects of shock-associated words which are not attended (Corteen and Dunn, 1974; Moray, 1969; von Wright *et al.*, 1975), there have also been reports of a failure to replicate the effect (*see* Wardlaw and Kroll, 1976). We shall ascribe the difficulty of replication to differences in the strategies used by subjects in slightly different experimental situations, rather than accepting the possibility that the effects are in some way not real, on the basis of the generality of the effects of unattended words in a variety of situations. Slight modifications in experimental technique may bias the subjects to use attentional strategies which prevent certain effects from appearing. The conclusion that attentional strategies may affect the automatic processing of words is not necessarily self-contradictory, for automatic processing may be dependent upon a general awareness of words, together with a priming of the lexicon, or upon a suitable division of attention between all messages. Attention may be divided between two messages without any of the secondary message exceeding the threshold for awareness. The message which we are aware of may be allocated the bulk of the strategically available capacity, but that is not to say that no capacity will be available for other messages. The allocation of residual capacity may not be open to independent strategic manipulation, however, and may be dependent upon the central strategy of processing.

Demonstrations of the effects of the semantic content of unattended messages are abundant in experiments investigating vision and hearing. Smith and Groen (1974) reported a study of recognition memory for the attended halves of dichotic lists in which attended and unattended words were sometimes related semantically. Similarity between the messages interfered with the correct rejection of a probe when the probe had been presented as part of the unattended message. Effects of unattended words printed between the attended lines of text affected the answers given to comprehension questions (Willows and MacKinnon, 1973), and distracting words have retarded the time required to name pictures in experiments where the word is printed over the picture and freely available for inspection (Rosinski et al., 1975), and where the word is tachistoscopically presented in the periphery of vision (Underwood, 1976b, 1977a). The lexical meaning of a word may be affected by unattended information, but the effect may be local to words. Bradshaw (1974) found that the interpretation of homographs such as PALM can be biased by the simultaneous presentation of a disambiguating word (HAND or TREE) in the periphery, thus extending MacKay's (1973) demonstration that the lexical ambiguity of a sentence may be clarified by unattended words in a dichotic listening task. Deep structure ambiguity as in the sentence "They knew that flying planes could be dangerous" was not resolved by unattended words however, and this indicates that the meaningful relations between words are only derived by attending to them. We may comprehend easily the words of a complex sentence, but to comprehend the sentence we may need to set up and be aware of a number of hypotheses. To put this another way, we must attend not to the words but to their elusive and often intangible relations.

The pre-attentive recognition of words in the periphery of vision has certain adaptive functions whilst reading, and the recognition of such words can be shown to affect the pattern of eye movements prior to the positions of those words in the text. Rayner (1975) and Kennedy (Chapter 6) have shown that words ahead of fixation affect the duration of fixation and the number of fixations according to their semantic relationship with the words being attended to. Peripheral words may be actively directing the strategy of fixation and information acquisition, or these strategies may be affected passively by the recognition of advance information related to that being processed. It would be good to think that advance information could be accepted and used with intention, and indeed Willows (1974) found that good readers showed signs of using such information where poor readers were able to ignore it, but the issue is not clear, and peripheral words may be processed incidentally and without purpose.

The importance of attention for comprehension may be demonstrated in a variety of situations. When I am reading a novel or a textbook at the same time as having some problem to mull over I often find myself reading each of the words, and even whole phrases and short sentences, without attending to the underlying meaning of the text. In consequence when my eyes arrive at the bottom of the page I discover that I have not the slightest idea of the schematic meaning represented by each of the words I have recently read. That I have read the words and not understood the meaning is demonstrated by the familiarity with which I greet each of the words and phrases upon re-reading the page. Without attending to the schematic meaning of the text we can still analyse individual words and phrases, but we will then comprehend little of the whole. Attention to individual words does not necessarily preclude comprehension of the whole, but it does not guarantee comprehension either. My superficial reading of novels and textbooks may be a reflection of the study reported by Mandler and Worden (1973), in which readers processed words and described them as being nouns or verbs but performed poorly on a subsequent recognition task. These words were not encoding by any strategy of elaboration organization, for the readers had no reason to expect the subsequent memory test, but the experiment serves to demonstrate that local understanding does ensure permanent storage. In the terms of the Craik and Lockhart (1972) model of the unitary-memory trace we would argue that the failure of recognition is a result of an inappropriate level of processing during input. If we need to store information permanently, then it must be well associated with information already well encoded and in the permanent memory store. Craik and Tulving (1975) provide evidence that as the encoding processing progresses from structural ("Is the word in capital letters?") to phonemic ("Does the word rhyme with WEIGHT?") to categorial ("Is the word a type of fish?") to semantic ("Would the word fit the sentence "He met a . . . . . in the street"?"), so the probability of recognition increases in an unexpected recognition test. This effect may be due in part to the amount of time engaged by the initial processing, for the response latencies to the questions requiring a deep level of processing were proportionately longer than those to questions about the physical attributors of the word. The time spent on the initial processing is not the primary determinant of the success of recognition, however, for in one of Craik and Tulving's experiments a difficult non-semantic task was associated with long decision times and poor recall, whereas an easy semantic task produced faster decisions and better recall.

When we do not attend to the relationships between words, recall is impoverished, and ambiguities may remain unresolved. Hence, in the dichotic listening experiments reported by Treisman and Geffen (1967) and Glucksberg and Cowen (1970) subjects who were attempting to detect target digits embedded in spoken prose messages were unable to distinguish between the digits "two" and "four" and their homophones "to", "too", "fore" and "for" when these words were presented in the unattended message. The homophones could be disambiguated only by their contextual relationship with the sentence in which they were presented. That these words should be detected falsely is an indication that this relationship had not been appreciated. Attention may not be necessary for the recognition of individual words, but it is essential for the analysis of the relationships between words, a process necessary for the resolution of lexical ambiguity. The appreciation of context is clearly demonstrated in the experiment reported by Tulving and Gold (1963) in which the tachistoscopic recognition of individual words (e.g. "performer") was increasingly facilitated by increasing amounts of appropriate context (e.g. "The actress received praise for being an outstanding . . .") presented immediately prior to the words to be recognized. This effect is restricted to situations in which the context is attended to, however, and the presentation of increasing amounts of unattended context does not provide increasing amounts of facilitation. Underwood (1977b) had listeners shadow short messages, of between five and eleven words, which were complete sentences, or the final few words of sentences with the early words replaced. The dependent measure was the shadowing latency to the final word of the message. In reflection of the Tulving and Gold result, the latency was decreased as the number of semantically and syntactically related words increased, i.e. context facilitated word recognition and output. In other experimental conditions the context was presented as the unattended message, whilst the subjects shadowed lists of unassociated words terminating with the critical context-associated word. Increasing the amount of unattended context did not continue to decrease the shadowing latency, but the presentation of *some* context did facilitate processing. A few words of context speeded the response over a list composed entirely of unrelated words, but the presentation of more context failed to improve the facilitation. The initial facilitatory effect of a few unattended and associated words may be ascribed to the effect of spreading excitation within the lexicon (Collins and Loftus, 1975; Meyer and Schvaneveldt, 1971), and the failure to observe an increasing effect of increasing context may be a consequence of the failure to attend to the deep structure of the developing sentence. Meyer and Schvaneveldt (1971) demonstrated the effect of a semantic relationship between two words even when the words are to be processed individually and sequentially, and in a task which does not *require* the associates of either word to be accessed. This may be an effect of excitation spreading spontaneously from one lexical representation to its associates, and may be responsible in part for the many effects reported which show an influence of a semantically related word which is incidental to the main task of processing a target word (e.g. Bradshaw, 1974; Jacobson, 1973; Lewis, 1970; MacKay, 1973; Treisman, 1960; Underwood, 1976b). Spreading excitation from a word to its associates would then be observable whether the influential word is attended to or not. It is a pre-attentive and structural feature of the lexicon, and its effects are apparent in Underwood's (1977b) experiment as a result of the pre-attentive recognition of the unattended context spreading to the associates of the contextual content words, and these associates will include the final attended word. The spreading of this activity will serve to reduce the recognition thresholds of all the associates of the context words, and so the final attended word will be processed more efficiently than when no such context is available. The failure to observe an increased effect with increased unattended context may result from the necessity to attend to the contextual relations available, or from the rapid dissipation of spreading excitation over time (*see* Collins and Loftus, 1975). Excitation from early contextual words may have dissipated by the time of presentation of the target words which they had previously and momentarily affected.

2.4. Strategies and recognition

Not all unattended words affect behaviour, and the extent of their effect will depend upon an interaction between the semantic relationship of the attended and unattended words, and the attentional strategy in operation. With attention closely focused upon the primary message, only words which are related in meaning to the attended words will show any effect, although the admission of any word to the recognition device for analysis of meaning must imply that all words have access to this stage of process. There is the recurrent danger here in concluding that only one category of words may be analysed, and that analysis tells us about the category of those words. This is similar to the problem faced by theorists of the perceptual defence effect—do we perceive in order not to perceive?—and a restricted set of words, defined by their related meanings, cannot be assumed to have preferential access to the recognition device where those very meanings would be analysed. Preferential access can only follow an effect upon the recognition process itself, and in the case of attention studies the effective agent may be the processing of the attended message. As the individual processes an attended word, comprehending it and preparing the response which is based upon it, so spreading excitation will reduce the recognition thresholds of all of the associates of that word. A restricted set of words defined by their related meanings has then been formed. They are the associates of the attended word. When one of these associates is presented in the unattended message, sufficient stimulus information will be available to raise the level of activation further, and so differentiate the unattended words from other associates of the attended word. The activation of two words in the lexicon may be sufficient to require a process of discrimination to be applied before the required word can be processed further, and finally responded to. Bilexical activation may facilitate or inhibit the ongoing task, of course, depending upon the demands of that task. If the subject is attempting to determine the category membership of a target word, the presentation of an additional instance of that category may reduce the decision time necessary before the response can be made. The processes outlined in this view of word recognition are compatible with the available evidence concerning the effects of synonyms and disambiguating words from a number of auditory and visual tasks discussed above. The model is based heavily upon the assumptions of lexical access suggested in Morton's (1969) "logogen" model of the factors affecting word recognition.

When attention to the primary message is less focused, then a different pattern of results will emerge. In their attempted replication of the Lewis–Bryden effect, the experiment reported by Treisman et al. (1974) found an influence of unattended synonyms only when these were presented at the beginning of a trial, when attention might be more divided between the two messages. When observer's divided their attention between two equally likely signal sources in Underwood's (1976b) picture-naming experiments, both related and unrelated words which were presented as unattended "distractors" slowed down the naming of the picture. Unrelated words had the greater effect in this experiment, whereas they had no effect upon the naming latencies in the focused attention experiment. With the divided attention strategy subjects accepted more stimulus information from the unwanted source than when focusing, and this information was evidently sufficient to provide discriminative activation of the lexical representations of these unrelated words in the absence of priming from attended related words. Once activated beyond a threshold level of discrimination from spontaneously active representations (noise), the influence upon processing may resemble the influence of related words. These events in no way depend upon intentional manipulation of the words in consciousness—they do not need a "primary memory" representation (James, 1890; Waugh and Norman, 1965)—but for *any* unattended words to be pre-attentively recognized, the subject may have to adopt a strategy of receptiveness to words: a general language-processing strategy. Treisman and Fearnley (1969) give a good grounding for this qualification in a Stroop experiment. Irrelevant colour words only caused interference with the processing of colours when colour-naming was a necessary part of the task. A language-processing strategy is clearly not necessary for the pre-attentive recognition of all words. The low thresholds of certain important words may be exceeded without attention to language at all, as in the case of sleeping subjects who give autonomic responses to their own spoken names (Oswald *et al.*, 1960).

The focusing of attention upon one message acts to attenuate the processing of unattended messages, as suggested by Treisman (1960), in that less evidence is available to activate the appropriate lexical representations and so priming has a relatively smaller influence. When unrelated "distractors" do affect the processing of the attended stimulus the observers are generally aware of the identity of the word. Underwood (1977a) asked subjects to name a picture as the primary task with focused attention, but to subsequently report the word whenever it became available to them. For unreported words, those which were related to the picture had the greater effect, in line with the earlier investigation of focused attention (Underwood, 1976b). This result supports the notion of two independent thresholds of word recognition suggested here and elsewhere (Dixon, 1971; Underwood, 1976a), by which all unattended words produce lexical activation, but discriminative activation (recognition threshold) is achieved only for words receiving a certain accumulation of contextual and/or stimulus information. The amount of information available from any source, which is necessary to exceed this threshold, will depend upon such factors as subjective frequency of occurrence. Morton (1969) provides a full discussion of these factors and their influence upon recognition. Words may enter awareness following the presentation of sufficient stimulus and contextual information (this is what Norman and Bobrow, 1975, refer to as a data-limited process) to overcome the attenuation affecting an unattended message, or following the presentation of less stimulus and contextual information which can be attended to (a resource-limited process). A greatly degraded message may be synthesized if attention is available to construct the necessary tests, but will not be recognized if attention is diverted elsewhere. The awareness threshold is dependent upon the attentional strategy in use, and may be set to prevent awareness of a clear message, or to gain awareness of a brief or degraded message.

These discussions have provided a model of how attention affects the immediate processing of information—how attention can degrade the processing of an unwanted message, and how that message is processed in the pre-conscious lexicon with consequences for other processes. The following discussions concern the use of information which is admitted to the awareness of the individual.

3. CONSCIOUSNESS AND THE SERIAL ORDERING OF BEHAVIOUR

3.1. Awareness and choice

For microbes and machines the world must be a very simple place. Information is received, and is responded to: behaviourists' paradise! Not so for men, for theirs is a world not restricted to the present. We are aware of events long past and can anticipate events long into the future. To an already complex three-dimensional world is added the dimension of time. (Other dimensions may exist, but as we can be aware only of the information available from our sense organs, we can have no idea of the amount of unavailable information in any number of dimensions in the world beyond our sense organs. This, one of the more popular themes taken up by Science Fiction writers, will not be taken up here in a chapter ostensibly concerned with Science Fact.) The task of men is to use their experience to select their goals and their paths to those goals, and our task here is to describe how the multitude of previous experiences can be organized into a coherent pattern given the continuous and unitary stream of consciousness. We have a multi-dimensional world available to us, from which we selectively encode our experiences to record not just events, but inferences about those events. Our representation of that world is encoded serially, and our responses are organized and produced serially. We are not concerned, in this section, with those responses which do not require control and monitoring by any volitional process—the overlearnt and automatized activities which do not demand continuous awareness. Mandler (1975) has suggested that consciousness is necessary in man for:

1. The choice and selection of action systems (cf. TOTE systems),
2. The modification of long-range plans,
3. The retrieval of information from permanent memory,
4. The coding of comments derived from presented information, and
5. The solution of occasional problems arising from activities which have become automatized.

For all of these reasons microbes and machines do not require consciousness: they are simple S–R organisms. Complex, programmable machines are being developed which can synthesize, extrapolate and choose between alternatives, and if man is viewed as a "complex programmable machine" then other analogies may also follow. When machines are developed which can perform man's activities then they might display characteristics which we recognize as being those of consciousness. Such machines might also display an awareness of themselves, for conscious organisms are not only aware of the world and are able to select their own experiences, but they are also aware of their ability to make these selections and are aware of their identity as agents in the world. We can be aware of the ticking of a clock, and we can be aware of our awareness of the clock. Consciousness became necessary as organisms evolved in order to be able to choose between courses of action, to modify long-range plans, to retrieve the increasing amounts of information being stored in permanent memory etc.

Selection and choice are fundamental concepts in the function of consciousness, and are present in the prologue to Arnold Toynbee's dissertation *Mankind and Mother Earth*:

Certainly Man is both a spectator and a censor. These roles are corollaries of his faculty of consciousness and of his consequent unavoidable power and need to make ethical choices and ethical judgements (Toynbee, 1976, p. 14)

and the importance of consciousness in these events is stated clearly earlier in the prologue:

In the relations of non-conscious species with each other, neither co-operation nor competition is an act of deliberate choice; but the choice is deliberate in human beings, and in us it is bound up with the human sense of the difference and antithesis between right and wrong and between good and evil (Toynbee, 1976, p. 3)

Choices between stimuli in a display may be made by automatic devices, and by non-conscious species, for only the stimuli with an appropriate representation will be detected. Other stimuli will not be recognized, and so the required stimuli may be said to be selected from the display. If the set of stimuli consist of the contents of memory or if the choice is to be made on the basis of actions appropriate to goals which are to be achieved well into the future, then the selected stimulus or selected response will be taken from well recognized alternatives. When we know the alternatives then judgement is required rather than stimulus selection, and as Toynbee points out so logically, this is a function of conscious organisms alone. Machines which can play games involving the achievement of long-range goals (such as chess) must certainly evaluate the relationship between alternative actions and the difference between the present position and the desired position. However, the better machines become at performing these evaluations then the more they will resemble conscious beings.

3.2. The response characteristics of consciousness

Consciousness aids the consideration of the paths to our goals, but the problem of why consciousness should appear to have a unitary identity remains unclear. Neisser (1976) considers that we give the impression of being aware of only one thing at a time because of a cultural response bias, and he may be right. The view here is that we are aware of what we are capable of responding to by volition. If we are able to attend to a number of response patterns executed through a number of effectors then we will be aware of all of those response patterns. Consciousness reflects our capacity of response, and its unitary nature may stem from the association of thought and language. This is not an acceptance of a variety of the Whorfian hypothesis, but if language is prepared by thought then our awareness of thought must be as serial as our production of language. The serial order of consciousness is thus a preparation of the response. As information is transformed by conscious manipulation so it becomes available as a potential response in various forms. We can respond to any number of characteristics of a word (physical, phonemic, categorical . . .) according to the transformations applied to that word. As each transformation is completed the result is available as a volitional response which may be submitted to further covert processing or produced overtly. To produce a volitional response the information must be present in consciousness, and it must be present in the form required by the response mechanisms. The response may thus be rehearsed in consciousness, and this gives rise to the notion of primary memory as a response buffer (*see* Atkinson and Shiffrin, 1968; Crowder and Morton, 1969). Consciousness serves not only to select information from the world and from our memories of the world, but also to provide anticipations of some local effects of the set of potential responses. The advent of such a response-rehearsal device also means that responses can be delayed for short periods whilst the information is kept available. If consciousness must be a unitary experience then the rehearsal of responses must be serially organized, and this serial organization is well reflected in our behaviour. This serial organization, according to Lashley (1951) is produced by a "central scanning mechanism" (identified here as consciousness). Bryden (1967) argued that this mechanism must be influenced by the sensory input, the mental set operating and by learned associations, to determine the serial response sequence. The "mental set" might be otherwise described as the strategy of information processing in this description, and Lashley's notion of a scanning mechanism, which selects the information required for the response as a reflection of the response, is a solution to the serial order problem in which the force of strategies is appreciated.

3.3. Consciousness, attention and time

The representation of our personal world of the operations we perform upon the information gained from that world, and of our responses, gives us the quality of awareness of those events. It also gives us an awareness that we are processing information, and that we have processed information. The appreciation of this change over time gives rise to an awareness of time. Our records of what has passed through consciousness are said to be stored serially in episodic memory (Tulving, 1972), and so our record of the passage and storage of information gives us a temporal order upon which we can base estimates of the passage of time. This relationship between the amount of information processed, the perception of the duration of processing, and of the span of awareness as reflected by the span of attention has been discussed in part by Ornstein (1969), although the picture is far from complete. On different occasions focused attention may result in a perception of a long duration or a short duration. In a recall experiment the more difficult tasks resulted in longer estimates of the duration allowed for performance (Underwood, 1975), but waiting for a pot to boil also produces long estimates of the duration of the event. Ornstein's demonstrations that duration estimates are directly related to the complexity of information produced during the interval are perhaps a measure of the amount of attention paid to the tasks. The focusing of attention upon the information being processed is just as reliable an indication of the passage of personal time. In tasks with little information content, time appears to pass slowly, possibly due to the focusing of attention upon the passage of clock time. This is particularly noticeable in situations when we are waiting for events to occur—for a person to meet an appointment, or for a pot to boil. In such situations the event is time-dependent and so we are very much aware of time. Our perception of time may be based on the information processed during the interval, but the variety of information attended during the interval is also a potent factor. The relationship between the perception of time and the attention paid to the information being processed is also indicated by the "time-gap" experience (Reed, 1972). Certain highly automatized activities which may engage a number of action systems simultaneously and over long periods of time may operate for several minutes without attention being directed to the input or the output during that interval. When this occurs the experience is one of having "lost" time. We may have no record of processing the information necessary to get to that particular point in space and time, and so no episodic record upon which to infer the passage of time. During an automobile drive over a regularly taken route, the journey taken to work each morning for instance, we may automatize not only our procedures for operating the car, but also the major structural features of the route. We may have appreciated the redundancy of the route and the driving characteristics necessary to handle that route to an extent where the behaviour of other road-users is the only non-redundant feature of the journey. Under such circumstances automatization can lead to regular "time-gaps" in which we may arrive at a certain point on the journey with no recollection of the immediately preceding sections of road, or of the procedures we used to handle them. In consequence we may feel that we have a gap in our experience of time. Reed ascribes this phenomenon to a failure to attend to the environmental stimuli which are affecting our behaviour, but implies that rather than attention being directed elsewhere the operator is aware of very little: he is inattentive to anything. A time-gap resulting from inattentiveness *per se* may be feasible, but it certainly is not adaptive for the organism, and it seems more likely that automatization does not take over so that we can switch off consciousness but so that attention may be directed to other processes. These processes involve the retrieval of information from memory, and would include the updating of information relevant to long-range goals. In order that we can organize our long-term behaviour in advance without allowing this organization to occupy our complete set of action systems, we need to automatize, and perform the organization during automatization. The automatization of the performance of skills is necessary for us to employ attention in the hierarchical ordering of skills into subskills and then into sub-subskills, and so on. If we must attend to accelerator–clutch coordination every time we change gear then we will never attend to the steering at that time and will certainly miss any conversation offered during a gear shift. There are a number of problems which arise when automatization is completed, however, and these concern the processing of essential information arriving in "messages" which are not gaining attention. If the automobile driver is attending to the day's work whilst driving to the office, then how can he handle a novel and dangerous traffic situation as it arises? The re-direction of attention may be called whenever information arises which cannot be handled by the automatic processes, and this is what Mandler (1975) describes as the trouble-shooting function of consciousness, but there is a problem here of describing a system which calls for help whenever it is overloaded. Given that we can demonstrate that the recognition of words does not demand attention, then perhaps we can argue that the recognition of a class of events ("dangerous situations") may likewise be automatized. This would have an adaptive function for inattentive and sleeping organisms alike.

A more practical problem concerns the automatization of activities which, when automatized, lead to information processing errors. When we cannot remember where we left an umbrella, or leave for the office without picking up a letter to be posted, it seems possible that automatization is to blame. Putting down an umbrella or leaving for the office are tasks which we can perform whilst engaged in conversation or emerged in thought, and so we need not attend to them. In consequence events associated with these unattended tasks (remembering where the umbrella was, or remembering to pick up the letter before leaving) are forgotten. These signs of absent-mindedness are no more than an indication of automatization and of attention being directed elsewhere. A related error is apparent when we attempt to transfer our automatized skills to slightly different situations. After becoming very familiar with the five-gear characteristics of my own car I have some difficulty in transferring to a standard four-gear vehicle in that I often find myself attempting to shift into fifth gear. The habit of making that gear shift is evidently so strong as to appear in inappropriate situations, when we should not attempt to rely upon automatized behaviour.

In serial order of consciousness, a preparation of the serial order of behaviour gives us the impression of the passage of time. We cannot experience time directly, but we base our estimates upon the information processing demands of the task in hand. The strategical manipulation of our processes handling these tasks is thus the cognitive feature responsible for our anomalies of time perception.

4. SUMMARY

If we are to describe the factors which affect the variability of behaviour then we must take account of volitional choice. We choose between features of the environment to gain more information about features of interest, and we choose between alternate courses of action to satisfy our needs and to approach our goals. Attention is sometimes used for the analysis of aspects of the environment, but this process can be automatized. It is essential for the extraction of the meaningful relationships between aspects of the environment, because this process requires the integration of some features with other features stored in memory. The features used will be optional, and whereas in most cases the interpretation will make sense if only one combination is fitted together, these options can lead to the appreciation of deep structure ambiguity in such sentences as: "I was going to take the plane to Chicago, but it was too heavy". The words of this sentence may be processed pre-attentively, but the meaning is processed consciously, and the alternate relationships made available for selection. The selection of the appropriate interpretation will in most cases be apparent by the context of the passage in which the sentence appears. If the immediately preceding sentence had concerned a last-minute business trip one interpretation would be appropriate, but if the passage had described a child's baggage allowance another interpretation might have been obvious. Each sentence we produce can be made to sound ambiguous given a different context, and the assimilation of context and stimulus is a skill which requires attention and conscious processing.

The entry of information into consciousness, often mediated by the direction of attention, has consequences for the organization of our responses to the word, even though the relationship is not causal. The conscious manipulation is necessary for the evaluation of the choice of responses, and the linear patterns of potential responses are available to us first as a pattern of events in consciousness. Consciousness is thus as serial and unitary as the responses which we are producing volitionally. Responses which are automatized and which do not need the control which can be exerted by consciousness can be produced in parallel with other automatized and volitional responses. Multiple task performances are thus instances of multiple automatization, and do nothing to challenge the view of consciousness as a limited-capacity process.

ACKNOWLEDGEMENTS

I should like to thank Neville Moray and Joel Singer for their extensive comments upon the discussions presented here.

REFERENCES

Atkinson, R. C. and Shiffrin, R. M. (1968). Human memory: A proposed system and its control processes. *In* "The Psychology of Learning and Motivation" (K. W. Spence and J. T. Spence, eds), Vol. 2. Academic Press, London and New York.

Baddeley, A. D. (1976). "The Psychology of Memory". Harper and Row, New York.

Bower, G. H., Lesgold, A. and Tieman, D. (1969). Grouping operations in free recall. *Journal of Verbal Learning and Verbal Behavior* **8**, 481–493.

Bradshaw, J. L. (1974). Peripherally presented and unreported words may bias the perceived meaning of a centrally fixed homograph. *Journal of Experimental Psychology* **103**, 1200–1202.

Broadbent, D. E. (1958). "Perception and Communication". Pergamon, Oxford.

Bryden, M. P. (1967). A model for the sequential organization of behaviour. *Canadian Journal of Psychology* **21**, 37–56.

Bryden, M. P. (1972). Perceptual strategies, attention and memory in dichotic listening. Unpublished report No. 43, University of Waterloo.

Collins, A. M. and Loftus, E. F. (1975). A spreading-activation theory of semantic memory. *Psychological Review*, **82**, 407–428.

Corteen, R. S. and Dunn, D. (1974). Shock-associated words in a non-attended message: A test for momentary awareness. *Journal of Experimental Psychology* **102**, 1134–1144.

Corteen, R. S. and Wood, B. (1972). Automatic responses to shock-associated words in an unattended channel. *Journal of Experimental Psychology* **94**, 308–313.

Craik, F. I. M. and Lockhart, R. S. (1972). Levels of processing: A framework for memory research. *Journal of Verbal Learning and Verbal Behavior* **11**, 671–684.

Craik, F. I. M. and Tulving, E. (1975). Depth of processing and the retention of words in episodic memory. *Journal of Experimental Psychology: General* **104**, 268–294.

Crowder, R. G. and Morton, J. (1969). Precategorical acoustic storage (PAS). *Perception and Psychophysics* **5**, 365–373.

Darley, C. F., Klatzky, R. L. and Atkinson, R. C. (1972). Effects of memory load on reaction time. *Journal of Experimental Psychology* **96**, 232–234.

Davis, J. C. and Smith, M. C. (1972). Memory for unattended input. *Journal of Experimental Psychology* **96**, 380–388.

Deutsch, J. A. and Deutsch, D. (1963). Attention: Some theoretical considerations. *Psychological Review* **70**, 80–90.

Dixon, N. F. (1971) "Subliminal Perception: The Nature of a Controversy". McGraw-Hill, London.

Erdelyi, M. H. (1974). A new look at the new look: Perceptual defense and vigilance. *Psychological Review* **81**, 1–25.

Glucksberg, S. and Cowen, G. N. (1970). Memory for nonattended auditory material. *Cognitive Psychology* **1**, 149–156.

Jacobson, J. Z. (1973). Effects of association upon masking and reading latency. *Canadian Journal of Psychology* **27**, 58–69.

James, W. (1890). "The Principles of Psychology". Holt, New York.

Joynson, R. B. (1972). The return of mind. *Bulletin of the British Psychological Society* **25**, 293–302.

Kahneman, D. (1973). "Attention and Effort". Prentice-Hall, Englewood Cliffs, New Jersey.

Kay, H. (1968). Learning and aging. *In* "Theory and Methods of Research on Aging" (K. W. Schrie, ed.). West Virginia University Press, Morgantown.

Keele, S. W. (1972). Attention demands of memory retrieval. *Journal of Experimental Psychology* **93**, 245–248.

Lashley, K. S. (1951). The problem of serial order in behaviour. *In* "Cerebral Mechanisms in Behaviour: The Hixon Symposium" (L. A. Jeffries, ed.). Wiley, New York.

Lewis, J. L. (1970). Semantic processing of unattended messages using dichotic listening. *Journal of Experimental Psychology* **85**, 225–228.

Littman, D. and Becklen, R. (1976). Selective looking with minimal eye-movements. *Perception and Psychophysics* **20**, 77–79.

MacKay, D. G. (1973). Aspects of the theory of comprehension, memory and attention. *Quarterly Journal of Experimental Psychology* **25**, 22–40.

Mandler, G. (1975). "Mind and Emotion". Wiley, New York.

Mandler, G. and Worden, P. E. (1973). Semantic processing without permanent storage. *Journal of Experimental Psychology* **100**, 277–283.

Melton, A. W. (1963). Implications of short-term memory for a general theory of memory. *Journal of Verbal Learning and Verbal Behavior* **2**, 1–12.

Meunier, G. F., Ritz, D. and Meunier, J. A. (1972). Rehearsal of individual items in short-term memory. *Journal of Experimental Psychology* **95**, 465–467.

Mewhort, D. J. K., Merikle, P. M. and Bryden, M. P. (1969). On the transfer from iconic to short-term memory. *Journal of Experimental Psychology* **81**, 89–94.

Meyer, D. E. and Schvaneveldt, R. W. (1971). Facilitation in recognizing pairs of words: evidence of a dependence between retrieval operations. *Journal of Experimental Psychology* **90**, 227–234.

Moray, N. (1959). Attention in dichotic listening: Affective cues and the influence of instructions. *Quarterly Journal of Experimental Psychology* **11** 56–60.

Moray, N. (1969). "Attention: Selective Processes in Vision and Hearing". Hutchinson, London.

Moray, N. and O'Brien, T. (1967). Signal-detection theory applied to selective listening. *Journal of the Acoustic Society of America* **42**, 765–772.

Morton, J. (1969). Interaction of information in word recognition. *Psychological Review* **76**, 165–178.

Murdock, B. B. (1971). A parallel-processing model for scanning. *Perception and Psychophysics* **10**, 289–291.

Murdock, B. B. (1974). "Human Memory: Theory and Data". Erlbaum, Potomac, Maryland.

Naus, M. J. (1974). Memory search of categorised lists: A consideration of alternative self-terminating search strategies. *Journal of Experimental Psychology* **102**, 992–1000.

Naus, M. J., Glucksberg, S. and Ornstein, P. A. (1972). Taxonomic word categories and memory search. *Cognitive Psychology* **3**, 643–654.

Neisser, U. (1967). "Cognitive Psychology". Appleton-Century-Crofts, New York.

Neisser, U. (1976). "Cognition and Reality". Freeman, San Francisco.

Norman, D. A. (1968). Toward a theory of memory and attention. *Psychological Review* **75**, 522–536.

Norman, D. A. (1969). "Memory and Attention". Wiley, New York.

Norman, D. A. and Bobrow, D. G. (1975). On data-limited and resource-limited processes. *Cognitive Psychology* **7**, 44–64.

Ornstein, R. E. (1969). "On the Experience of Time". Penguin, Harmondsworth.

Ostry, D., Moray, N. and Marks, G. (1976). Attention, practice and semantic targets. *Journal of Experimental Psychology: Human Perception and Performance* **2**, 326–336.

Oswald, I., Taylor, A. and Treisman, M. (1960). Discriminative responses to stimulation during sleep. *Brain* **83**, 440–453.

Rayner, K. (1975). The perceptual span and peripheral cues in reading. *Cognitive Psychology* **7**, 65–81.

Reed, G. F. (1972). "The Psychology of Anomalous Experience". Hutchinson, London.

Rosinski, R. R., Golinkoff, R. M. and Kukish, K. S. (1975). Automatic semantic processing in a picture-word interference task. *Child Development* **46**, 247–253.

Rundus, D. (1971). Analysis of rehearsal processes in free recall. *Journal of Experimental Psychology* **89**, 63–77.

Smith, M. C. and Groen, M. (1974). Evidence for semantic analysis of unattended verbal items. *Journal of Experimental Psychology* **102**, 595–603.

Sternberg, S. (1966). High-speed scanning in human memory. *Science* **153**, 652–654.

Sternberg, S. (1975). Memory scanning: New findings and current controversies. *Quarterly Journal of Experimental Psychology* **27**, 1–32.

Theios, J. (1973). Reaction time measurements in the study of memory process: Theory and data. *In* "The Psychology of Learning and Motivation" (G. H. Bower, ed.), Vol. 7. Academic Press, London and New York.

Toynbee, A. J. (1976). "Mankind and Mother Earth". Oxford University Press, Oxford.

Treisman, A. M. (1960). Contextual cues in selective listening. *Quarterly Journal of Experimental Psychology* **12**, 242–248.

Treisman, A. M. (1969). Strategies and models of selective attention. *Psychological Review* **76**, 282–299.

Treisman, A. M. and Fearnley, S. (1969). The Stroop test: Selective attention to colours and words. *Nature* **222**, 437–439.

Treisman, A. M. and Geffen, G. (1967). Selective attention: Perception or response? *Quarterly Journal of Experimental Psychology* **19**, 1–17.

Treisman, A. M., Squire, R. and Green, J. (1974). Semantic processing in dichotic listening: A replication. *Memory and Cognition* **2**, 641–646.

Tulving, E. (1970). Short- and long-term memory: Different retrieval mechanisms. *In* "The Biology of Memory" (K. H. Pribram and D. E. Broadbent, eds). Academic Press, London and New York.

Tulving, E. (1972). Episodic and semantic memory. *In* "Organization of Memory" (E. Tulving and W. Donaldson, eds). Academic Press, London and New York.

Tulving, E. and Gold, C. (1963). Stimulus information and contextual information as determinants of tachistoscopic recognition of words. *Journal of Experimental Psychology* **66**, 319–327.

Underwood, G. (1975). Attention and the perception of duration during encoding and retrieval. *Perception* **4**, 291–296.

Underwood, G. (1976a). "Attention and Memory". Pergamon, Oxford.

Underwood, G. (1976b). Semantic interference from unattended printed words. *British Journal of Psychology* **67**, 327–338.

Underwood, G. (1977a). Attention, awareness, and hemispheric differences in word recognition. *Neuropsychologia* **15**, 61–67.

Underwood, G. (1977b). Contextual facilitation from attended and unattended messages. *Journal of Verbal Learning and Verbal Behavior* **16**, 99–106.

Underwood, G. and Moray, N. (1971). Shadowing and monitoring for selective attention. *Quarterly Journal of Experimental Psychology* **23**, 283–295.

Wardlaw, K. A. and Kroll, N. E. A. (1976). Autonomic responses to shock-associated words in a non-attended message: A failure to replicate. *Journal of Experimental Psychology: Human Perception and Performance* **2**, 357–360.

Waugh, R. C. and Norman, D. A. (1965). Primary memory. *Psychological Review* **72**, 89–104.

Weist, R. M. and Crawford, C. (1973). Sequential *vs.* organized rehearsal. *Journal of Experimental Psychology* **101**, 237–241.

Wickelgren, W. A. (1973). The long and the short of memory. *Psychological Bulletin* **80**, 425–438.

Wickelgren, W. A. (1975). More on the long and the short of memory. *In* "Short-Term Memory" (D. Deutsch and J. A. Deutsch, eds). Academic Press, London and New York.

Willows, D. M. (1974). Reading between the lines: Selective attention in good and poor readers. *Child Development* **45**, 408–415.

Willows, D. M. and MacKinnon, G. E. (1973). Selective reading: Attention to the "unattended" lines. *Canadian Journal of Psychology* **37**, 292–304.

Woodward, A. E. and Bjork, R. A. (1971). Forgetting and remembering in free recall: Intentional and unintentional. *Journal of Experimental Psychology* **89**, 109–116.

von Wright, J. M., Anderson, K. and Stenman, U. (1975). Generalization of conditioned GSRs in dichotic listening. *In* "Attention and Performance V" (P. M. A. Rabbitt and S. Dornic, eds). Academic Press, London and New York.

Eight

Strategies in the Control of Movement

C. I. Howarth

University of Nottingham

1. INTRODUCTION

In this introduction the basic arguments to be presented will be stated in a rather dogmatic fashion. The detailed justification for individual statements will be found in the later sections.

The complex articulation of the body and the physical separation of the different spatial senses create difficulties in the control of body movement. The relationships between visual, kinaesthetic, vestibular and auditory information about orientation, and between each of these and the motor system, appear to be too complex to be completely known. For this reason skill in any particular type of movement is relatively specific to that movement. Three clearly identifiable strategies are used to minimize these difficulties. These are:

1. The continuous "recalibration" of the spatial senses relative to each other and to the motor system,
2. The combination of information from more than one spatial sense with weighting according to its reliability, and
3. The continuous monitoring and correction of movements.

These strategies lead to phenomena which are usually explained in other ways. Autokinesis, adaptation to prism spectacles, ventriloquism, the intermittent control of movement, and the relationship between speed and error of controlled movement can all be understood as the consequences of strategic adaptations to the difficulties we experience in knowing, predicting and controlling the position of the body.

All of the spatial senses provide essentially angular information. The eyes register visual separations; kinaesthesis the angles of the limbs. In both cases distance must be deduced from a combination of angular information. Hearing also provides angular information about the direction of sounds, and the vestibular organs about the angle of the head relative to gravity, or about the angle through which the head has been rotated. Difficulties arise when we try to relate the angular information from different senses. The angles are measured from different positions on the body and from positions whose relationship to each other may not be constant. This leads to some well known phenomena.

Autokinesis can be demonstrated in all intersensory judgements of location and reflects the uncertainty of these relationships in a poor stimulus environment. Autokinesis is abolished by anything which assists the calibration of one spatial sense against another. Similarly, when the relationship between two senses is distorted, as for example by the wearing of prism spectacles, the new relationship can be learned quite rapidly, given adequate feedback, but this learning is surprisingly specific to the situation in which the learning takes place and its effects may be rather transient. The function of many training and "warm up" strategies is to facilitate this kind of learning. Autokinesis itself may be a search strategy, seeking for a meaningful relationship between different kinds of sensory information. The susceptibility of autokinesis to suggestion is consistent with this view.

A second set of phenomena are concerned with the combination of information from different senses. The stabilization of autokinesis by additional spatial information can be interpreted in this way. When information is available from more than one sense, it seems to be weighted according to its reliability. Ventriloquism is an example of this. Many habitual movements seem to be designed to increase the efficiency with which information from different senses is combined. Head movements produce movement parallax and so improve visual judgements of depth. They can also be used to provide more than one "fix" on a sound source.

The complexity and unreliability of spatial information makes it impossible to plan and initiate movements with complete accuracy. Hence they must be continually monitored and corrected. These corrections are necessarily intermittent, since they can only be initiated when an error is detected, and themselves introduce a lag into the system. The subject's strategic response to this situation determines the relationship between speed and error in the execution of these movements. In the past these relationships have usually been explained in terms of some variant of information theory, but these explanations are easily shown to be inadequate. In target-aiming tasks, unskilled people show comparatively little variation in speed as they approach the target, while practised subjects decelerate sharply towards the end of the movement, so that final corrections to the movement can be made as near to the target as possible. The function relating speed and error varies, but is always identical with the one which relates time and distance from the target for a particular person, whether skilled or unskilled. When speed is constant, as in some continuous control tasks, speed and error are linearly related. When speed has to be adjusted, as when the skilled car driver adjusts his speed to the effective width of the road, a simple theory enables the ideal degree of adjustment to be calculated. Unskilled drivers do not usually achieve the necessary degree of adjustment.

Body movements are not only a matter of making and monitoring simple movements. They are planned and purposive, integrated with other movements and adapted to the situation in which they are made. Visual search is perhaps the most efficient of all skilled movement. Our understanding of the structure of the visual world is such that we are nearly always looking in the right place at the right time, and are usually unaware of the startling deficiencies of vision which only allow us to see clearly objects which fall within a two-degree cone centred on the direction in which we are looking.

Neisser (1976), Gauld and Shotter (1977) and others have claimed that human behaviour is best understood in terms of human purposes, rather than mechanisms. They argue that with a suitable degree of skill, behaviour can transcend mechanism. In this paper some strategies are described which make this possible. But these strategies can only be understood as adaptations to the mechanical limitations of the body, and any discussion of them without reference to mechanism would be meaningless.

2. THE SPATIAL SENSES

The position of the body in space, and the position of the parts of the body relative to each other, can be sensed in many ways. Vision gives the most detailed and accurate information, but is itself dependent on information about the direction in which the eyes are pointing, derived either from kinaesthetic receptors in the eye muscles and the neck, or from monitoring the neural messages to the eye muscles. Kinaesthesis can include information from joint receptors as well as from the Golgi tendon organs and the muscle spindles, and together with the monitoring of motoneuron activity, can indicate the relative disposition of our limbs, head and trunk. Receptors present in the skin indicate the position of external objects relative to the limbs. Gravity receptors, in the utricle and saccule of the inner ear, indicate the orientation of the head relative to gravity or to the vector of the forces produced by gravity and acceleration. Touch and kinaesthesis are also sensitive to gravitational forces. The semicircular canals respond to rotation of the head in all three planes of space. Hearing is sensitive to the direction of sound, most sensitively in the horizontal plane, but with some sensitivity to up and down displacement of complex sounds. In addition to all this sensory information, changes in the position of the body can be predicted on the basis of the activity of those parts of the central nervous system which control the muscles.

This multiplicity of sensory information is not all equally reliable. In measuring the accuracy of spatial information, it is important to distinguish between "intrasensory" localization, in which the relative position of two objects perceived by the same sense organ is judged, and "intersensory" localization, in which the position of an object perceived in one sense organ is judged in relation to the position of an object perceived by another sense organ. In general, "intrasensory" localization is very much more accurate than "intersensory" localization for reasons which will be discussed in detail in the next section. Here it is sufficient to say that the accuracy of intrasensory localization is very much dependent on the two objects being perceived simultaneously. If the two objects appear successively, accuracy falls off very rapidly when the time interval between them is increased (Kinchla and Smyzor, 1967; Holding, 1968). With an interval of only a few seconds, the accuracy of "intrasensory" localization is no better than that for "intersensory" localization (Fisher, 1962b).

The most accurate "intrasensory" localization occurs in vision. Vernier acuity and movement acuity displays are sensitive to differences of as little as 10″ of arc. On the finger tips, touch is sensitive to differences of about 1 mm, which at arm's length is about 3′ of arc. Under optimum conditions we can detect a difference of about 1° of arc in the position of two sources of sound.

We have no good information about the "intrasensory" sensitivity of kinaesthesis because no one has yet found a way of doing intra-sensory kinaesthetic judgements simultaneously. Experiments have been done in which a subject is asked to place a limb twice, in rapid succession, into the same position. Cohen (1958) reported that this could be done with an accuracy of about 2°, while Merton (1961) who asked the subject to make a much smaller movement between the two positionings of the arm, obtained an accuracy of about 6′ of arc. In both cases the time delay between successive positionings of the arm prevented this from being a true measure of intrasensory localization. Similarly, Breslaw (1978) has recently shown that, even in the presence of a fixation point, the eyes cannot be repositioned with an accuracy better than 1° of arc. Cleghorn and Darcus (1952) claim that at $0 \cdot 2°$ s^{-1} a passive movement of about 1° could be detected by the elbow joint. Goldscheider (1899) obtained similar figures for most of the joints of the body, with surprisingly, a greater sensitivity of the larger joints, such as the hip and shoulder, than of the smaller joints such as the finger joints. However, it is difficult to know whether the subjects were responding to movement of the joints as such, or to the forces which were required to produce the movement.

There is a similar difficulty in estimating the sensitivity of the semi-circular canals. The smallest amount of head rotation which can be detected depends on the velocity and acceleration of rotation even more than on its extent. Moreover, it is very difficult to rotate the whole body smoothly so that the detection of rotation may be based more on body senses than on the semicircular canals. Fortunately, rotation induces a particular type of eye movement called nystagmus which is entirely dependent on the stimulation of the semicircular canals. This allows us to be certain that they are capable of responding to rotations at least as slow as $1 \cdot 0°$ s^{-1}. Unfortunately, for nystagmus to develop, the rotation must continue for some time, so that this method cannot be used to determine the minimum perceptible rotation.

M. A. Babaei and I have recently determined subjects' ability to estimate or repeat rotations of about 180°. They can do this with standard deviations of between 7° and 70° (*see* Tables II and III) depending on conditions, but there is inevitably a time delay of about 3 s between the conclusions of the two movements. It is likely that the subject's monitoring of his own muscular activity is at least as important in this task as the sensations derived from the semicircular canals.

The effect of time delays in intrasensory localization may be related to autokinesis. Autokinesis usually means the apparent movement of a small spot of light in a dark room, but a faint sound source may also appear to move in a very similar way (Bernadin and Gruber, 1957). It was first reported by von Humbolt in 1799 as a problem for astronomers and extensively studied since then. Most early work concentrated on the effect of additional visual stimuli, which in quite modest amounts destroy the illusion, and on its relationship to eye movements. Most early workers found no relationship to eye movements, and in particular that there was no correlation between the small spontaneous eye movements of the subject and the distance and direction in which he "saw" the spot move. However, Matin and MacKinnon (1964) showed that under conditions which reduce eye movements, auto-kinesis is also reduced, while Carr (1910) and Gregory and Zangwill (1963) have shown that unidirectional autokinesis can be induced as an after-effect of strong aversion of the eyes.

Similar after-effects can be induced in kinaesthesis. A common party trick is to exert strong pressure against someone's arm, so that when the pressure is removed and for some time afterwards, the arm if relaxed, tends to move in a direction opposite to that in which the pressure was applied. This tendency can be resisted, but is never-theless compulsive. Hick (1953) has studied the phenomenon quanti-tatively under the name of the "after contraction", but more attention has been given to after-effects of posture, without any strong muscle tension. For example, Selling (1930) and Nachmias (1953) asked subjects, with their eyes closed, to hold out both hands horizontally in front of them, then to raise one arm 45° above the horizontal for a brief period, and then to return it to the horizontal. Both workers found that, in the absence of a visual check on the position of the arms, the arm which had been moved was held several degrees above the hori-zontal, while being judged by the subject to be both horizontal and level with the other arm. Jackson (1954) demonstrated "postural persistence" for postures other than those which are held against gravity, and has shown that significant effects can be obtained after as little as 5-s exposure.

In the next section, it will be argued that autokinesis is properly seen as a phenomenon of intersensory localization. The only alter-native to this is the view (e.g. Roelofs, 1959) that we have some sort of absolute sense of our own position and orientation in space, and that all the spatial senses relate the direction of objects in space to this. Helmholtz (1962) called visual space "cyclopean" because visual direction is judged as it would be if we had only one eye in the middle of the forehead. Roelofs called this the "egocentre", and Fisher (1962b) did some tests of this idea, suggested by me and summarized in Howard and Templeton (1966).

Fisher asked his subjects to judge the relative directions of sounds, lights and objects which could be touched. The judgements were made at varying distances from the body. If all these judgements were referred to a single "egocentre" then all the judgements should be consistent. If, however, visual, auditory and kinaesthetic judgements of direction were referred to a different centre, then tell-tale inconsistencies should show up in the subject's reports. None did. However, this is not conclusive evidence for the "egocentre", since instructions such as "Point at this seen object", "Point at this heard object", or "Is this seen object, which is close to you, in the same direction as that heard object which is some distance away?" are all ambiguous. It is easy to show how variably this ambiguity can be resolved.

I have recently done a pointing experiment, but varying the instructions given to the subject. The subject was positioned 1·8 m away from the experimenter, and told to obey one of the following instructions immediately after closing both his eyes:

1. Place the index finger of your outstretched hand on a line between your nose and the experimenter's right eye.

2. Place the index finger of your outstretched hand on a line between your dominant eye and the experimenter's right eye.

3. Place the index finger of your outstretched right hand on a line between your right shoulder joint and the experimenter's right eye.

4. Place the index finger of your outstretched right hand on a line between your left shoulder joint and the experimenter's right eye.

Since the subject is pointing at the experimenter's right eye in all four conditions, the experimenter, with his left eye closed, can easily judge the variability with which the task is performed and the average position of the "egocentre" implied by the judgement. Variability within and between subjects is approximately the same in all four conditions (*see* Table I).

It seems as if there is no single "egocentre" but that the centre of personal space, as defined by pointing, may be the dominant eye, a point between the eyes, or the shoulder joint of the pointing arm or some compromise between these. When the ambiguity of the instruction is removed, each of these definitions of "pointing" serves equally well. It is a little more surprising to find that instruction 4 gave the subjects little more difficulty than the others, although it implies a centre of personal space which is never a spontaneous interpretation of the ambiguous instruction "Point at this object". There is some suggestion

TABLE I. Defined origin of pointing. All errors are measured in centimetres on a scale across the subject's shoulders. The experimenter was 1·8 m away from the subject so that the pointing finger was approximately half-way between the subject and the experimenter; 1 cm corresponds to approximately 0·5°. Negative constant errors imply that the egocentre is to the left of the defined origin of pointing. Subject PB was left-handed, the other subjects right-handed.

Each subject pointed twenty times under a given instruction and the mean error and standard deviation were calculated. Each subject then repeated all four conditions a second time in reverse order. Note that there are several significant differences between the constant errors from the first to the second set of trials. This is characteristic of all such experiments and is related to autokinesis.

Subject		Shoulder of pointing hand		Dominant eye		Nose		Opposite shoulder	
		1st series	2nd series	1st series	2nd series	1st series	2nd series	1st series	2nd series
CIH	c.e.	− 0·4	− 0·35	− 2·0	− 2·15	+ 0·06	− 0·35	− 6·8	− 1·85
	s.d.	1·66	2·31	2·65	1·71	1·71	1·01	2·56	2·04
FB	c.e.	+ 7·90	− 4·1	+ 1·2	− 4·7	− 3·05	+ 0·25	+5·3	+ 7·62
	s.d.	1·89	2·41	2·54	1·45	1·83	2·17	3·34	0·9
PB	c.e.	− 12·55	+ 0·95	− 3·25	+ 3·75	− 0·50	− 0·45	+ 4·1	+ 5·2
	s.d.	2·54	2·33	1·97	2·12	1·02	3·41	2·32	2·38
Mean s.d.		2·19		2·07		1·85		2·26	

in the data that the nose is the easiest egocentre to use, but the differences, with only three subjects, are not significant.

From these experiments we must conclude that subjective space does not have the structure of simple polar coordinates measured from a single centre. Instead the information provided by the multiplicity of spatial senses is used in different ways for different purposes. The literature on adaptations to distorted space shows that these adaptations can also be surprisingly specific (*see* Section 4). It will now be argued that these specificities are inevitable given the complex articulation of the human body.

3. INTERSENSORY LOCALIZATION

The pointing experiment, referred to in the last section, is just one of many possible experiments on intersensory localization, i.e. the comparison or combining of spatial information from more than one sense organ. In the pointing experiment, the object was localized visually, then the eyes were closed and the pointing was controlled kinaesthetically. If the eyes are kept open, then pointing is controlled visually and the localization would be intrasensory, not intersensory. By placing a horizontal screen between the arm and the eyes, intersensory pointing can be done with the eyes open. This is, for example, the technique used by Held and others in their studies of adaptation to the wearing of prism spectacles which will be described later.

Intersensory localization is much less accurate than intrasensory localization. The different dispositions of the various senses in the body make knowledge of the relationship between them depend on kinaesthetic and muscular information about the orientation of the limbs, trunk and head, and about the direction in which the eyes are pointing. It is unfortunate that we do not know anything directly about the accuracy of this kind of kinaesthetic information. The situation is made more difficult by the complex articulation of the body, so that, for example, mapping of visual information onto kinaesthetic information from the hand, will be different for each of the possible orientations of eye, neck, trunk, shoulder, elbow, wrist and fingers. The permutations are so complex, that it is something of a surprise that intersensory localization is possible. Exactly the same difficulties are faced when planning and executing the simplest of movements.

The simplest systematic studies of intersensory localization experiments are those done by Fisher (1960a, b, 1961, 1962a, b) based on some of my own theoretical ideas (described in some detail by Howard and Templeton, 1966). Fisher asked his subjects to judge the relative position of two stimuli at arm's length in a horizontal plane level with the subject's head. The experiments were done in a dark, quiet room. This prevented the development of a visual or an auditory framework which would have allowed *absolute* judgements of the position of the visual or auditory stimuli.

To prevent the development of a kinaesthetic framework, five identical fixed scales were used for each modality. These scales were displaced from each other by five 1° steps. The stimuli to be judged were presented in pairs, but on each trial the scale to be used was chosen at random from each of the five available scales. This elaborate procedure was necessary because an attempt to break down the kinaesthetic framework by rotating the subject slightly between each trial was a failure. The subject was always very well aware of the angle through which he had been rotated, and hence of the direction in which he was facing. Because of that he was able to make absolute judgements of the direction of a touched point. Since rotating the subject did not work, the experiment, in effect, rotated the whole experimental world about the subject. This did succeed in preventing the development of a kinaesthetic framework.

The three stimuli used were a point source of light (V), a point source of sound (A), and a tangible point which the subject touched with the forefinger of his preferred hand (K). The stimuli were presented in pairs, VK, VA and KA, and the subject was asked simply to report which of the two was to the left of the other. Using a staircase method (or up-down method as it is sometimes called), the mean and variance of these three judgements were determined. The following were the main findings:

1. The constant errors were consistent over short periods of time, so that, for example, if the stimuli were in the same place, but on average K was judged to the right of A, and V was judged to the right of K, then, also on average, V would be judged to the right of A. Indeed the consistency was such that, within the accuracy of the method, the three constant errors summed to zero, provided they were obtained within an overlapping time period. To show this, it was necessary to interleave trials of the three possible intersensory judgements.

2. Over reasonably long periods of time, the constant errors were not in fact constant (cf. similar phenomenon in Table I). They showed a continuous slow drift, reminiscent of the autokinetic effect. It is tempting to equate these drifts in intersensory localization with autokinesis, since, for example, the movement of the light in visual autokinesis can only have meaning in relation to a kinaesthetically appreciated body position. However, in autokinesis the subject reports movement where none exists. In Fisher's experiments the subjects were judging stimuli to be in the same place when they had in fact been moved as much as 20° apart. Other authors have found that people can be quite unaware of differences in direction of as much as 30° between a visual stimulus and an auditory stimulus (Witkin et al., 1952; Jackson, 1953).

3. Each of the three intersensory localizations had a characteristic variance with VK least and KA greatest. This suggests that the variance contributed by the three modalities increases in the order VKA. This is consistent with intrasensory measures of accuracy of localization in each of the three senses.

If we assume that each sense contributed independently and without interaction to the intersensory variance, we can write three equations:

$$\left.\begin{array}{l} \sigma_{VK}^2 = \sigma_V^2 + \sigma_K^2 \\ \sigma_{VA}^2 = \sigma_V^2 + \sigma_A^2 \\ \sigma_{KA}^2 = \sigma_K^2 + \sigma_A^2 \end{array}\right\} \qquad 3.1$$

where σ_{VK}^2, σ_{VA}^2 and σ_{KA}^2 are all empirically determined and σ_V^2,

$\sigma_K{}^2$ anc $\sigma_A{}^2$ are three unknowns. When these equations are solved using the experimentally determined values for $\sigma_{VK}{}^2$, $\sigma_{VA}{}^2$ and $\sigma_{KA}{}^2$, it was found that:

σ_V was a little less than 1°,
σ_K was a little greater than 1°,
σ_A was approximately 3°.

That these values are meaningful is indicated by the very similar values obtained from comparable intrasensory localization experiments by Fisher and by other workers. These comparable intrasensory experiments must avoid the special mechanisms which make Vernier acuity and movement acuity so good. Fisher found that the simplest way to do this was to introduce a small time delay between the two stimuli. This seems to have a much greater effect on intrasensory localization than on intersensory localization. Although these constant and variable errors have been labelled V, K and A, they must all three be largely a measure of kinaesthetic and muscular information about the position of the eyes in the head, the position of the head on the shoulders and the orientation of the arms relative to the shoulders. Howard and Templeton (1966) undervalue the consistency Fisher observed in these variances. He encountered considerable methodological problems, but was not totally defeated by them. Recently Auerbach and Sperling (1974) have found a similar consistency in constant and variable errors, thus confirming points 2 and 3 above.

These experiments suggest two important conclusions about intersensory localization. The first is that they have a relatively simple and coherent structure, as shown by the consistency of the constant and variable errors. The second is that they are unstable, as shown by the autokinetic instability of all three intersensory judgements. The simple structure of these judgements would lead one to expect them to be stable. The observed instability may be due to the complexity of the interrelationship between the three senses when the body is moved into different positions, and when the stimuli are presented at different distances. Because of these complexities we probably deal with each new situation as it comes, and quickly learn how to cope with it. Autokinesis occurs when there is too little information available for learning to take place, and may be interpreted as a search strategy, trying varying hypotheses about the relationships between the parts of the body and the outside world, until sufficient information is available to make it possible to settle on one. Regarding autokinesis as a search strategy is consistent with its susceptibility to suggestion and to environmental influences.

4. THE "RECALIBRATION" OF SPATIAL SENSES

It is a relatively simple matter to "learn" a new relationship between two spatial senses. For example, Heyes and Gazely (1975) have shown that when a hard-of-hearing person is fitted with two hearing aids, he can usually recover his ability to judge the direction of a sound. Initially however, his auditory "space" is narrower than his kinaesthetic, motor or visual space. A. D. Heyes (personal communication) has shown that a minimum of experience is necessary to recalibrate and expand the auditory space. Merely to shake a matchbox at arm's length and at various positions round the head is enough. In everyday life, when moving actively in a rich auditory, visual and tactile environment, we have many opportunities to learn or relearn the relationships between information from the different spatial senses. In this way we cope with the problems created by our complexly articulated bodies and the relative unreliability of our spatial senses, to the extent that we are usually unaware of those problems.

In everyday life, and in Heyes' experiments, the subject has the opportunity to compare information from many sources about the location of an object. The matchbox, held at arm's length is heard, seen and felt simultaneously. The position of the hand holding it is appreciated both kinaesthetically and from a knowledge of the muscle movements previously made to put it there. The position of the box in the hand is felt through the skin. Which of these additional sources of information is most important for the recalibration of the auditory localization is not clear. However, many experiments have been done which seem to indicate:

1. That the calibration can be very specific to the situation in which it occurs, and
2. That recalibration seems to occur more easily when active movement is involved.

Harris (1963) and Hamilton (1964) showed that, in an experiment in which the subject wore prism spectacles to distort the relationship between visual direction and information derived from other senses, learning to point correctly with one hand produced no transfer of the adaptation to the other hand. Harris also found that after wearing prism spectacles for some time, pointing behaviour showed some adaptation while auditory localization did not. Helmholtz, a hundred years earlier (new translated edition 1962), claimed that adaptation to a prism in front of one eye did not transfer to the other eye. However, in other experiments contradictory results have been obtained. Helmholtz himself obtained transfer from one hand to another, while Bossom and Hamilton (1963) found transfer from one eye to another in a monkey. It seems likely that the precise conditions of the experiment and the instructions given to the subject could eventually explain these contradictions. Hamilton, for example, found that there was some transfer of adaptation from one hand to the other if the subject was allowed to move his head and body during the training period. Harris did most of his experiments by asking his subjects to judge when a light or a sound was "straight ahead". This is an ambiguous instruction in the same way that the instruction to point at an object beyond arm's length is ambiguous.

Hardt *et al.* (1971) found that even when adaptation of the felt position of the arm had occurred after wearing prisms, no adaptation was shown when the subject was asked to return his arm to a remembered position, i.e. one taken up by the arm before adaptation took place. They argue that this demonstrates adaptation to be sensorimotor and specific to the particular sensorimotor system involved. However, Howard (1971) suggests that their results could be equally well explained by a change in the felt position of the neck or eye. Wilkinson (1971) has shown that, in some cases at least, the adaptations in different systems sum in a linear fashion. If this were a general phenomenon, it would reduce the specificity of adaptation, although, given the complexity of the systems involved, there would still be considerable scope for specificity of adaptation. No one has yet investigated the effect of a change in body posture on adaptation, or on the transfer of adaptation from one body system to a completely different one.

Hay and Pick (1966) have shown that the time course of adaptation may be different in different systems. For example, they found that subjects wearing prism spectacles showed a steady adaptation of eye–hand coordination up to 44 h experience, but ear–hand coordination showed a maximum effect after 12 h and subsequently decreased. Welch and Rhoades (1969) obtained similar effects by manipulating the type of feedback the subject was given, while Warren and Platt (1975) showed that individual differences in adaptation were related to individual differences in other types of perceptual ability.

Held (1961, 1963) has argued that adaptation can only occur in relation to reafferent information, that is, sensory stimulation produced by active body movement. He cites as evidence for this the lack of adaptation produced by passive experience, particularly the experience of passive body movement (Held and Hein, 1958; Held and Freedman, 1963). However, Howard and Templeton (1966) argue that since all Held's tests for adaptation involved active movement, his results could equally well be explained as another example of the specificity of adaptation. Templeton *et al.* (1966) indeed showed that a passively arranged position of the arm could be correctly judged in relation to a prism distortion after as few as sixteen trials, provided proper know- ledge of results was given. They also found some transfer to active pointing. In their experiment the transfer was only one-third of that shown for passive judgements, but they thought that longer training might have produced greater transfer. They explain Held's total failure to find transfer from passive to active pointing to be due to the poor knowledge of results he provided in the passive condition. Pick and Hay (1965) have also demonstrated passive adaptation.

More extreme distortion, such as the inversion and reversals of visual space produced by wearing lens spectacles (Stratton, 1896; Snyder and Pronko, 1952) or by looking at the world entirely through a mirror (Kohler, 1962), has also been studied. Adaptation to these distortions is much slower than to simple prism induced displacements. However, if the spectacles are worn continuously over a period of weeks, considerable adaptation occurs, so that eventually activities such as walking, skiing, climbing, cycling and driving can be carried out reasonably skilfully. However, each task has to be learned piecemeal, and there is almost no transfer from one complex task to another.

Kohler describes the strategies used by his subjects to overcome their difficulties. Well practised movements, such as writing, could be performed best if visual feedback was, to some extent, ignored. Some subjects were able to use vision to adjust the position of the writing on the paper, but they had to rely on kinaesthetic-motor automatism to produce the detailed shape of the letters. Another strategy was the conscious reversal of each intended movement. Similar strategies are occasionally described in relation to prism displacements. Surprisingly, no one seems to have commented on the compulsive active movements, apparently seeking the information necessary for reorientation, although these are the most obvious features of the behaviour of anyone wearing distorting spectacles for the first time. They wander around, gently and timidly it is true, but nevertheless seeking and experiencing as much conflict as they can with safety.

Let me now return to the question of active *vs.* passive adaptation. There is no doubt that passive adaptation can occur. What is un- certain is the extent of it, the conditions under which it can be demon- strated and the reasons why, under most conditions, it appears less effective than active adaptation. Held's original view, that adaptation only occurs in response to reafferent, i.e. self produced movement, can still be rescued if we assume that totally passive experience is very difficult and that the effect of passive instructions is merely to reduce but not totally to eliminate the active control of the position of the limbs. Unfortunately, the opposite, but equally strong view that adaptation can occur equally well for passive as for active experience, cannot be ruled out either. The relative ineffectiveness of passive adaptation would then be explained by differences between the training and test situations. For example, Pick and Hay (1965) showed greater transfer from active training to passive testing, than from passive training to active testing. This may be because, following active training, it is even more difficult to remain entirely passive during the subsequent passive testing, whereas, if the subject is relatively successful in remaining passive during training, he may not learn much that is useful during subsequent active testing.

This latter explanation depends on the assumption that spatial learning is highly specific to the situation in which it occurs. M. A. Babaie and I have recently demonstrated the specificity of spatial learning in an experiment on body rotation. The subjects were blind-folded and rotated through 180° on a turntable. The rotation was done actively by the subject shuffling round until told to stop or passively as a result of the experimenter rotating the turntable. The subject was then asked to turn through 180° back to the starting point, again either actively or passively. In the latter case the subject instructed the experimenter when to stop the rotation. Thus active learning (or instruction) could be followed by active or passive testing and passive learning could also be followed by active or passive testing. Two other variables were also used, the initial rotation could be to the left or right and the testing rotation could be to left or the right, the testing rotation being either in the same direction or in the opposite direction.

Each subject did each of the eight conditions once, in random but balanced order. None of the constant errors individually were significant (*see* Table II) and indeed there was no reason to expect that they would be; but for passive rotation followed by active testing there was a tendency to over-rotate when continuing in the same direction, but to under-rotate when turning in the opposite direction, while for active training followed by passive testing this pattern was reversed. Similarly, active testing following active instruction produced all positive errors while passive instruction followed by passive learning led to all negative errors.

The variable errors showed a statistically significant and more understandable pattern. In general, the variability was twice as great for active learning followed by passive testing than for active learning followed by active testing. Similarly passive learning followed by active testing was twice as variable as passive learning followed by passive testing. Thus the movement is repeated more accurately when it was performed in the same mode (active or passive) as the original learning. Rather to our surprise there was no difference in variable errors between continued and reversed movements. We had expected continuation to be more accurate than reversal because of the greater similarity of the two movements.

However, the degree of adaptation in prism adaptation experiments is not simply a function of the similarity between the training and testing situation. Howard *et al.* (1974) have recently shown, to their surprise, that the judged position of a stationary limb is more affected by prism adaptation than the judged position of a moving limb. They attribute this to the greater information available about the position of a moving limb. They argue that the discrepant information from vision has less effect the more reliable the kinaesthetic information. If the argument is correct it should also apply to other situations in which information from different senses is being compared and combined (see Section 5 for a fuller discussion of this).

TABLE II. Transfer from active to passive performance and vice versa. Passive testing is twice as variable after active learning as after passive learning, while active testing is twice as variable after passive learning as after active learning.

Data from twenty-four subjects, each of whom did each of the eight conditions once only in random order, are presented. None of the constant errors are significant but seven of the eight standard deviation ratios are significant at better than 0·05, while the eighth (AP ÷ PP continuing to the right) is significant at the 0·1 level. It is also noticeable that active testing gives, on the average, slightly more accurate results but this is probably due to the difficulty subjects have in telling the experimenter when to stop the rotation in the passive testing condition. For that reason the only valid comparisons are between those conditions which use the same testing procedure.

		PA	AA	Ratios s.d.	f	AP	PP	Ratios s.d.	f
Constant Errors									
Continue	R	12·0	8·64			− 17·0	− 1·82		
	L	3·68	6·18			− 3·95	− 4·45		
Reverse	R	− 1·0	6·59			16·68	− 10·27		
	L	− 3·73	1·59			11·73	− 17·27		
Standard Deviations									
Continue	R	40·26	21·21	1·90	3·61	43·38	31·86	1·36	1·85
	L	33·43	15·17	2·20	4·84	63·29	27·61	2·29	5·24
Reverse	R	39·61	22·9	1·73	2·99	66·6	42·89	1·55	2·40
	L	33·04	15·62	2·12	4·49	58·69	25·54	2·30	5·29

When preparing to perform a skilled task such as playing cricket, tennis or throwing the discus, athletes "warm up". One function of this is to get the blood flowing to the muscles, so that they are ready to deliver their maximum power. It may also serve to "recalibrate" the relevant senses and the relevant motor activity which may have lost their fine tuning as a result of autokinesis, or have been set to another calibration for a different kind of activity. It is characteristic of "warm up" activities that they closely resemble the activity for which they are in preparation and that they are usually identical with it. The necessity for this follows from the specificity of spatial learning. When practising, athletes often say they are "getting the feel of things again", or that "things are beginning to click into place". These phrases are consistent with the present interpretation. Vision is immensely important in resolving sensory conflict. It is not very useful in the experiments of Fisher, Held and others because of the artificial situations. But in most everyday situations we not only see objects in space, we also see our own bodies, and the other spatial senses can be recalibrated instantly with reference to vision. Many habitual patterns of movement can be seen as strategies designed to make the best use of vision for this purpose. For example, in ball games, the novice is told to keep his eye on the ball. Experts do not always follow this advice. They look around the field of play to preserve their sense of where they are in it, and where their opponent is. They may even look briefly at their own body or their racquet or bat. The purpose of this may be to preserve the calibration of the different spatial senses. Vision is not only dominant because it is such a rich source of information about the outside world, but also because it provides a spatial framework against which all the other spatial senses can be calibrated (cf. Pick, 1974).

5. COMBINING SPATIAL INFORMATION FROM DIFFERENT SENSES

Information from different senses is not only used to recalibrate the senses relative to each other. Information from different senses may also be combined to provide the best possible estimate of the position of objects in space. Studies of the "ventriloquism" effect (e.g. Jackson, 1953) have shown that vision dominates hearing to the extent that the voice appears to come from the dummy's mouth. But these experiments do not rule out the possibility that the apparent position of the dummy's mouth may be affected by the presence of the voice.

Fisher (1962b) investigated this possibility, again testing some of my own theoretical predictions. Howard and Templeton (1966) have described and discussed these experiments also. Fisher used the apparatus which has already been described, presenting, in the dark, quiet room, various combinations of a visual stimulus (V), an auditory stimulus (A) and a kinaesthetically appreciated stimulus (K). In the first of these experiments on the ventriloquism effect he presented all three stimuli simultaneously, but informed the subject that two of them were in the same place, and that his task, as before, was to say whether the third stimulus was to the left or the right of the pair. In fact the paired stimuli had always one of three possible relationships to each other, either they were as described, in the same place, or one was 10° to the left of the other, or it was 10° to the right of it. These three conditions were used in three temporally interleaved, but quite independent, series of trials according to the "up-down" or staircase rule. In this way, comparable mean and variance estimates were obtained from all three conditions, and for all three possible stimulus pairs.

Fisher found that the variances were the same in all conditions, and were no less when the paired stimuli were in the same place than when they were in different places. This shows that on each trial the judged position of the paired stimuli was based on an average of the positions of each one and that discrepant positions are no more difficult to average than coincident positions.

Secondly, he found that vision dominated audition in the sense that paired auditory and visual stimuli were always judged to be very close to the position of the visual stimulus. So by judging the position of the paired stimulus with respect to a third sense, Fisher demonstrated not only that the voice and the dummy's mouth are judged to be in the same place, but that their location is indeed the visual location of the dummy's mouth. He also found that kinaesthesis dominated audition, but when kinaesthetic and visual stimuli were paired, their apparent position was almost midway between the two. The order of dominance corresponds to the order of the accuracy of spatial information from the three senses calculated by Fisher from equation 3.1.

Pick *et al.* (1969) have demonstrated similar effects even when the subject is aware that two stimuli are discrepant. They asked their subjects to point, with the right hand, at either the *seen* position of a finger of their left hand or the *felt* position of the finger, when wearing prism spectacles. They showed that the seen position was deviated towards the felt position, and the felt position deviated towards the seen position. The seen and felt positions never coincided, but the felt position was more affected than the seen position. Similar experiments with a hand-held clicker and a pseudophone demonstrated the dominance of kinaesthesis over audition. The dominance of vision over audition was demonstrated by asking the subject to point at either the heard or seen position of a clicker when wearing prisms (or equally effectively when wearing a pseudophone).

These experiments can be compared with those of Howard *et al.* (1974) since all three show the importance of the accuracy of spatial information. Fisher showed that the weighting of information is proportional to its accuracy. Pick *et al.* (1969) showed the greater instantaneous stability of accurate information while Howard *et al.* (1974) showed its greater stability over time in a spatial learning stituation.

Choe *et al.* (1975) have shown that the ventriloquism effect only operates for simultaneous stimuli. A time difference of as little as 0·7 s totally destroys the illusion.

Fisher attempted to manipulate the accuracy of spatial information, and hence the weighting it was given in the ventriloquism situation. He did this by adding extra visual or auditory stimuli. Unfortunately, these created a stable framework in which subjects were able to make absolute judgements of the target stimulus relative to the additional stimuli. He did apparently change the dominance hierarchy, but this was almost certainly an artefact. The experiment needs to be repeated using different positions for the additional stimuli on each trial.

More recently, Babaei and I (Babaei and Howarth, 1978) have studied the summation of information about rotation, derived from the semicircular canals and from active movement of the body. This was partly inspired by a desire to understand the behavioural consequence of the after-effects of rotation. A blindfolded subject standing upright was rotated through 180° in a horizontal plane, and then asked to judge the angle of rotation and to report the duration of the illusory after-effect of rotation in the opposite direction. Three conditions of rotation were used; an active self-determined movement in response to the instruction "Rotate 180° to the right (or left)"; an active, experimenter-determined condition in which he was instructed "Rotate until told to stop"; and a passive experimenter-determined condition in which the experimenter rotated him through 180° on a turntable. Each subject experienced only one of the conditions, and did it twice only, once to the left and once to the right. In the active self-determined condition, the actual angle of rotation was measured. In the other two the subject was asked to judge the angle of rotation by drawing on a piece of paper the direction in which he was originally facing. Since these two measures are very different, comparisons between them must be treated cautiously.

Table III shows the result of the experiment. The pattern of constant errors is not very clear but the variable errors suggest that active movement is more accurately perceived than passive movement. This may be because at least two different sources of information are available whereas only one is present in the passive rotation. It may also be the case that active body movement gives better information than the

TABLE III. Errors of estimation and after-effects of rotation. In relation to errors, the differences between the first condition and the other two, although almost all significant, are almost certainly due to the difference in the way the errors are measured. The comparison between conditions 2 and 3 do, however, reflect a real difference in the appreciation of active and passive movement. The pattern of constant errors is not consistent but the pattern of variable errors shows that active movement is significantly more accurately judged than passive movement ($p < 0.01$, $p < 0.05$ for right and left rotation, respectively). The significant difference in variances between left and right judgements in condition 2 is puzzling.

In relation to the after-effects, the picture is much clearer. There is virtually no after-effect following any kind of active movement. The times recorded are merely reaction times. However, for passive movement the after-effect is about 1·5 s which is significantly different from both active conditions. $N = 24$.

		Errors (deg)		After-effect (s)	
		R	L	R	L
1. Active self-determined	$\bar{x}$	4·4	− 2·5	0·30	0·19
	s.d.	17·6	7·4	0·71	0·37
2. Active experiment determined	$\bar{x}$	21·6	8·7	0·14	0·27
	s.d.	28·1	46·7	0·35	0·65
3. Passive experiment determined	$\bar{x}$	31·3	− 8·8	1·50	1·44
	s.d.	67·0	69·6	1·41	1·80

semicircular canals. This could only be decided by an heroic experiment in which the information from the semicircular canals was blocked.

However, the most interesting effect is on the perceived duration of the after-effect. The duration of the effect is, on average, six or seven times longer after passive movement than after either kind of active movement. The most likely explanation of this is that when additional information is available, less weight is given to information, including illusory information, from the semicircular canals. In this respect, this experiment resembles Fisher's experiment on dominance in the "ventriloquism" situation. The clear result obtained here suggests that the effect of the additional stimuli in Fisher's experiment may not have been entirely an artefact.

As well as averaging information, the spatial senses can be used in combination to provide new information which would not otherwise be available. The putting together of information from shoulder, elbow and wrist to indicate the position of the hand, is one example of this. So too is all the complexity of stereoscopic vision. Sometimes movement strategies increase the efficiency of this kind of combination. It is characteristic of people listening to a faint sound which they wish to localize, to tilt their head slightly. With the head upright, hearing localizes a sound somewhere on a vertical plane running through the centre of the head. When the head is tilted the plane of localization is tilted, and the intersection of the two planes gives the precise direction of the sound.

6. THE ACCURACY OF THE MOTOR ELEMENT IN A MOVEMENT

So far we have been concentrating on the adequacy of the sensory information on which movements can be planned and executed. But the movements themselves probably contribute their own characteristic errors. It is difficult to estimate neuromotor error independently of the error of the sensory information on which it is based, but it seems more than likely that the complex articulation of the body creates difficulties in the execution of movement which are similar to the difficulties it presents to the spatial senses. It is possible to go from A to B by an infinity of different routes and indeed, when learning a new skill, performance is both varied and inaccurate. Performance improves with practice and this is, at least partially, the result of learning the most economical and efficient series of movements to get us from A to B. Having settled on the best sequence, practice increases the accuracy of the movement.

One indication of the accuracy of the motor element in a movement might come from the comparison of slow and fast movements, in the presence of an excess of accurate sensory information. One could argue that the accuracy of slow movements would depend on the accuracy of the sensory information about the position of the limb in space, while the accuracy of a fast movement would depend on both the accuracy with which the target is located and the accuracy with which the motor element is executed. For this reason fast movements are sometimes called ballistic movements, by analogy with the uncontrollable trajectory of a cannon ball once it has left the cannon's mouth.

Unfortunately, provided there is no visual monitoring of the movement, the accuracy of movement is independent of speed (Beggs et al., 1972a). In their experiments the movement was a highly practised pointing movement so that the motor component might be contributing a negligible amount to the total error. Alternatively, since the target for the movement was visual, kinaesthetic monitoring of the movement may have been inhibited, even for slow movements. However, even when the target is kinaesthetically appreciated, fast movements are no less accurate than slow movements.

Another way of estimating the accuracy of the motor element might be to ask people to repeat the same movement without a target. Again, the difference between fast and slow movements could indicate the error contributed to the movement by the muscles, but the result is likely to be contaminated by autokinetic effects.

Although we have no good estimates of the error due to the neuro-muscular element of a movement, it is unlikely to be negligible, particularly in novel tasks. Some muscular movements are innately programmed, but most have to be learned. The visual monitoring of motor activity has been demonstrated in four-month-old babies (McDonnell, 1975) and vision provides a good form of feedback for the correction of motor programmes.

Beggs *et al.* (1972b) have shown that the accuracy of ballistic move-ments varies greatly among different tasks. They also found no correla-tion between the accuracy with which their subjects performed three different tasks, rolling a ball at a target, touching a target with the hand, and walking along beams of wood of different widths. The last two are not strictly ballistic movements but the theory to be described in the next section allows a measure of ballistic accuracy to be deter-mined for a small section of the movement. This lack of correlation between the subject's performance on the three tasks, is consistent with the idea that spatial skills are specific to the situation in which they are learned, although it does not differentiate between the sensory and the neuromuscular elements of the skill.

7. THE INTERMITTENT CONTROL OF MOVEMENT

The inaccuracies resulting from the combination of fallible spatial information and fallible planning and execution of movement, make the monitoring and correction of movement unavoidable. Ballistic movements occur in well practised situations in which the terminal accuracy of the movement is not critical, as in rapid piano playing. Under all other circumstances movement is controlled by what von Holst called "reafferent stimulation", that is, stimulation produced as a result of the subject's own movements.

The relationship between the speed and accuracy of movement has usually been explained in terms of information theory, which relates the accuracy of information to the duration of the message which contains it (e.g. Fitts, 1954; Welford, 1968). Information theory cannot explain the observation of Beggs *et al.* (1972a) that in the absence of visual feedback, movement accuracy is independent of speed. Beggs (1971) has shown that the logarithmic function, predicted by information theory, only holds when error is measured in the direction of move-ment. When error is measured at right angles to the direction of movement the relationship between speed and error is a power function (Howarth *et al.*, 1971), and moreover, the exponent of the function changes with practice (Beggs and Howarth, 1972). Recently a simple and empirically justifiable explanation of all these phenomena has been given by myself and Alan Beggs (Howarth *et al.*, 1971; Beggs and Howarth, 1970, 1972). This new theory is a quantitative development of Craik's (1947) description of the intermittent control of movement. The most important features of the theory are the way it relates errors to movement patterns and its descriptions of strategic adaptations which occur with practice. The continuous monitoring and intermittent correction of movement can be regarded as yet another way in which we deal with the difficulty of perceiving and controlling the movements of our complexly articulated bodies. Our theory makes this strategy explicit and deals with it quantitatively.

Information theories require a logarithmic relationship between the speed and accuracy of movement aimed at a target. Klapp (1975) has shown that, for reasonably long movements, all of the relationships between speed and accuracy are due to changes in the speed of movement rather than in the reaction time before the movement is initiated. The new theory relates speed and accuracy by a function which is entirely determined by the movement strategy the subject uses in approaching a target. If the target is approached with a constant speed, the relationship should be linear. If the subject slows down near the target, then deceleration can be described by a power function relating time and distance. This same function should also describe the relationship between speed and accuracy. This is because an initially fast movement, which decelerates near to the target, allows corrections to be applied closer to the target and therefore more effectively. The identity of the function describing the trajectory of the hand as it approaches a target and the function relating speed and accuracy is one of the strongest pieces of evidence for the theory.

Figure 1 illustrates this in more quantitative detail. It is observed that the trajectory of the hand as it approaches the target can be described by a power function:

$$d = kt^n \qquad\qquad 7.1$$

where k and n are arbitrary constants. The distance of the hand from the target is d and t is the time remaining before impact (note that t is the reverse of ordinary time, as when counting down 5, 4, 3, 2, 1, 0). If the total time for a movement is T, then 7.1 can be rewritten as:

$$d = k\left(\frac{t}{T}\right)^n \qquad\qquad 7.2$$

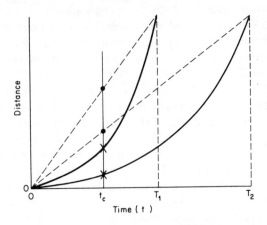

FIG. 1. The trajectories for movements towards a target with movement times T_1 and T_2 and with linear trajectories (dotted lines) or power function trajectories (solid lines). Time t is measured as time remaining before the target is hit and the distance is simply the distance from the target at time t. If t_c is the corrective reaction time, d_c, the distance from the target at which the last correction is made, can be read off from the distance axis. Knowing d_c, the error on target can be calculated by equation 7.4.

It is found empirically that when T varies, for a given distance of movement, k and n are relatively unaffected, so that equation 7.2 is a powerful descriptive equation. If we now assume that there is a corrective reaction time t_c, such that, even if an error is noticed when the movement is t_c away from the target, there will not be time to correct it, we can, as a first approximation, calculate that the last corrective movement will be made when the hand is at least a distance of d_c away from the target where d_c is calculated from equation 7.2. as follows:

$$d_c = k \left(\frac{t_c}{T} \right)^n \qquad\qquad 7.3$$

If we further assume that each correction is made with an accuracy described by a standard deviation of an angular measure (σ_θ), we can calculate σ_ϵ (also a standard deviation), the accuracy with which the target is hit.

$$\sigma_\epsilon = d_c \sigma_\theta \qquad\qquad 7.4$$

Putting 7.3 and 7.4 together we get:

$$\sigma_\epsilon = k \left(\frac{t_c}{T} \right)^n \sigma_\theta \qquad\qquad 7.5$$

Howarth *et al.* (1971) found that the results of a target-aiming experiment, in which the subject's movement was paced by a metronome, fitted this equation very well, but that an even better fit could be obtained by assuming that σ_e^2 was the sum of a variance derived from equation 7.5 and a variance due to tremor. This addition to the theory is obviously necessary since equation 7.5 implies that infinitely slow movements will be infinitely accurate.

Beggs and Howarth (1972) have demonstrated that the chief effect of prolonged practice in the task is to increase the value of n. The effect of this is to reduce d_c, the distance from the target at which the last correction is made. By equation 7.4 this reduced the error on target.

In most experiments by Beggs, Howarth and their co-workers, the error is measured at right angles to the direction of movement. If it is measured, in whole or in part, in the direction of movement, the task ceases to be one of simple aiming, since the critical element in the task is to stop in the right place. However, subjects deal with this more complex situation in much the same way as the simpler one. They approach the general area of the target as quickly as possible and then make corrections in the vicinity of the target (Annett *et al.*, 1955). It is difficult to apply equation 7.5 completely rationally to this situation, which is the one used by Fitts (1954), but despite this, equation 7.5 describes the results of these experiments surprisingly well, particularly if we ignore the constant errors and consider only variable errors (Beggs, 1971).

Another difference between Fitts' experimental situation and that used by us, is that Fitts varied the size of the target and allowed the subject to choose his own pace. The reason why Fitts obtained a logarithmic function seems to be because, under these conditions the value of n in equation 7.2 is not independent of speed. Particularly at slow speeds, subjects adopt approach strategies which give high values of n. Another way of putting this is to say that practice has a greater effect on n in Fitts' situation, particularly at slow speeds. This assertion has not yet been experimentally tested, but it is of course a relatively easy experiment to do.

The smallest value of n so far obtained occurs in continuous control rather than target-aiming tasks. When speed is constant n necessarily takes a value of 1, and we predict a linear relationship between, for example, speed and the width of a road when driving a car (Rachevski, 1959), the width of a track traced by a pencil (Drury, 1971), or the width of a beam on which the subject is walking (Beggs *et al.*, 1972b). This simplest form of the theory was in fact first proposed by Rachevski for car driving and, independently, by Drury. Beggs *et al.* (1972b) were also unaware of the work of either Rachevski or Drury, so that the intermittent control theory account of the relationship between speed and error for continuous movement has been independently developed on at least three occasions. The most general form of it, which can be equally well applied to intermittent target-aiming tasks, was first proposed by Howarth *et al.* (1971).

Strangely enough, no one has yet extended the theory to account for strategic adjustments of speed in car driving and other continuous control tasks. This is an extremely important feature of such tasks and the skilled driver is one who can, among other things, adjust his speed according to the demands of the situation.

When equation 7.5 is adapted to the case of continuous movement we get:

$$m\sigma_\theta St_c = W \qquad\qquad 7.6$$

where S is the speed of movement, W is the width of the road, t_c and σ_θ are as previously defined, and m is a constant determining the acceptable probability of hitting the side of the road.

The rationale of equation 7.6 is the assumption that a car aiming straight down the road will do so with an accuracy σ_θ; that the acceptable error is defined by the constant m; that the error will be detected and corrected only after an appreciable corrective reaction time t_c; and that the speed will be adjusted so that $m\sigma_\theta St_c \leqslant W$, thus keeping the probability of hitting the kerb down to an acceptable level. It follows from equation 7.6 that, when the width of the road varies, the speed should vary proportionately. However, when a road narrows the speed should be adjusted in anticipation so that, for example, when moving at speed S_1 along a road of width W_1 and the road narrows to width

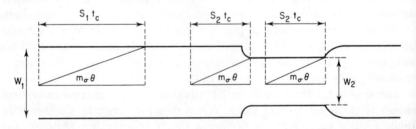

FIG. 2. This diagram shows:
    1. The basic relationship between $m\sigma_\theta$ (the acceptable error of aiming), S_1 the speed, and t_c the corrective reaction time for a road of constant width W_1,
    2. The distance S_2t_c at which the speed must be adjusted prior to a narrowing of the road, and
    3. That the speed can begin to be increased at the same distance S_2t_c before the end of the constriction in the road.

W_2, then the new speed S_2 (where $S_2 = S_1 \times W_2/W_1$) should be achieved when the car is a distance $S_2 t_c$ from the narrowing of the road, otherwise the risk of running off the road will be increased. Similarly, when the road widens again the driver can begin to speed up, before the road widens again at a distance $S_2 t_c$ from the end of the constriction. Figure 2 illustrates some of these relationships.

8. PLANNED MOVEMENTS, EYE MOVEMENTS AND VISUAL SEARCH

Babaei and Howarth (1978) have recently done an experiment which shows an unexpected simplicity in the planning of movements. They found that the accuracy with which a movement is made is unaffected by the simultaneous planning of further movement. They presented their subjects with pieces of paper on which there were five dots in the form of a pentagon. They were asked to place a pencil on one of the dots, to close their eyes and then, in one condition to move the pencil with deliberate speed to touch in turn each of the remaining four dots. In the other condition they were merely required to move to the nearest dot. At least in this simple situation, planning ahead does not interfere with current movement.

The planning of movements is essential to the strategic control of movement. It has already been argued that many strategies can be best understood as ways of overcoming the deficiencies of our spatial senses. "Warming up" strategies and the rapid deceleration of the hand near the target are probably best understood in these terms. Other strategies reflect our understanding of the structure of the perceptual world. Visual search while driving a car or reading are good examples of these.

The eye can only see clearly with a 2° cone which represents the part of the visual field which falls on the fovea. We are normally quite unaware of this because our eye movements are so skilful that we are nearly always looking directly at the thing we need to see at the moment we need to see it. So, in driving car, if we fail to see the pedestrian who steps suddenly on to a zebra crossing, or the turn indicator of the car in front, or a stop sign, we are considered to be morally at fault, driving without due care and attention. It is no use telling the judge that we can only see clearly on a 2° cone which happened to be directed elsewhere at the crucial moment. We are all so skilful at looking in the right place at the right time that an appeal based on a lapse of skill is not acceptable. We are expected to know where to look and when to look, and this requires very skilful prediction based on good road sense.

Road sense is largely an understanding of what is likely to happen in different situations.

Similarly, rapid readers make so few fixations per page that they could not possibly see all the words on it. The skilled reader probably makes use of his knowledge of the structure of English to direct his eyes to those parts of the text which contain the most information. The rest can be guessed.

Unfortunately, we do not have any quantitative theory of the way the structure of a situation determines the eye movements. This is because we have no appropriate ways of describing the structure of a visual scene. The most successful treatments of visual search are concerned with search in unstructured situations. For example, Howarth and Bloomfield (1969) have shown that search times in an unstructured field can be predicted very successfully from:

1. A measurement of the angular distance from the fovea at which the target can be perceived with a duration of exposure (250–300 ms) which matches the average fixation time during normal eye movements, and

2. The assumption that the eye makes a random scan of the search field at the rate of 3–4 fixations s^{-1}.

Eye movement studies show that fixations are not at random, but neither are they particularly regular or systematic. This has led many people to believe that visual search could be improved by training people to search regularly. This expectation has always been disappointed (*see*, for example, Gottsdanker, 1960) since training in regular search either has no effect or actually makes the searcher less efficient.

The reason for this is easy to understand in terms of Howarth and Bloomfield's theory. The distance from the fovea at which an object can be seen depends on its contrast with the background, whether in terms of brightness, or in terms of size or shape differences between the target and non-target objects also in the search field. If the object is easy to see, it can be seen within a large area around the fixation point of the eye. If it is difficult to see, the area within which it is visible is small. Random placing of these areas of visibility on the search area results in the search area being covered more quickly by the large areas of visibility, although some fixations will be wasted because they cover again areas which have already been covered. If we know in advance how easy the target is to see, so that we can calculate the area of visibility, then search time should be reduced by regular search, with each fixation separated by approximately the diameter of each area of visibility. However, if the difficulty of the target is not known, no regular search strategy is appropriate and the random strategy is most efficient.

An important part of Howarth and Bloomfield's theory is the linear relationship between such measures of contrast and the distance from the fixation point at which an object can be seen. This enabled them to develop a simple equation relating stimulus measures to search time. These equations work very well in randomly structured search fields. They are quite inappropriate in structured search situations in which random search is not the most efficient strategy.

Yarbus (1967), Mackworth and Morandi (1967) and others have shown that visual search is systematic, in that the eye concentrates on the most interesting and informative parts of a scene. It is unfortunate that this aspect of planned movement still awaits adequate theoretical treatment. It is likely that some systematic eye movements have the function of building up our knowledge of our position in space, so helping to overcome the difficulties our spatial senses have in dealing with our complexly articulated bodies. No studies of this function of eye movements have yet been made.

Gross body movements must also be planned ahead. Untrained, unfamiliar movements are conservative and slow, leaving adequate opportunities to recover from mistakes. With practice, the margin of error can be reduced, movement can be speeded up and long sequences of related movements put together. These changes are consistent with the improved accuracy of spatial information specific to a well practised situation.

REFERENCES

Annett, J., Goldby, C. and Kay, H. (1958). The measurement of elements in an assembly task—the information output of the human motor system. *Quarterly Journal of Experimental Psychology* **10**, 1–11.

Auerbach, C. and Sperling, P. (1974). A common auditory-visual space: Evidence for its reality. *Perception and Psychophysics* **16**, 129–135.

Babaei, M. A. and Howarth, C. I. (1978). The influence of forward planning on the accuracy of movement (in preparation).

Beggs, W. D. A. (1971). Movement control. Ph.D. thesis, University of Nottingham.

Beggs, W. D. A. and Howarth, C. I. (1970). Movement control in a repetitive motor task. *Nature* **225**, 752–753.

Beggs, W. D. A. and Howarth, C. I. (1972). The movement of the hand towards a target. *Quarterly Journal of Experimental Psychology* **24**, 448–453.

Beggs, W. D. A., Baker, J. A., Dove, S. R., Fairclough, I. and Howarth, C. I. (1972a). The accuracy of non-visual aiming. *Quarterly Journal of Experimental Psychology* **24**, 515–523.

Beggs, W. D. A., Sakstein, R. and Howarth, C. I. (1972b). The generality of a theory of intermittent control of accurate movements. *Ergonomics* **17**, 757–768.

Bernadin, A. C. and Gruber, H. E. (1957). An auditory autokinetic effect *American Journal of Psychology* **70**, 133–134.

Bossom, J. and Hamilton, C. R. (1963). Interocular transfer of prism-altered co-ordinations in split-brain monkeys. *Journal of Comparative Physiology and Psychology* **56**, 769–774.

Breslaw, P. I. (1978) The accuracy of repeated eye movements (in preparation).

Carr, H. A. (1910). The autokinetic sensation. *Psychological Review* **17**, 42–75.

Choe, C. S., Welch, R. B., Gilford, R. M. and Juola, J. E. (1975). The ventriloquist effect: visual dominance or response bias. *Perception and Psychophysics* **18**, 55–60.

Cleghorn, T. E. and Darcus, H. D. (1952). The sensibility to passive movement of the human elbow joint. *Quarterly Journal of Experimental Psychology* **4**, 66–77.

Cohen, L. A. (1958). Analysis of position sense in the human shoulder. *Journal of Neurophysiology* **21**, 550–562.

Craik, K. J. W. (1947). Theory of the human operator in control systems 1. The operator as an engineering system. *British Journal of Psychology* **38**, 56–61.

Drury, C. G. (1971). Movements with lateral constraints. *Ergonomics* **14**, 293–343.

Fisher, M. H. (1960a). Intersensory localization in three modalities. *Bulletin of the British Psychological Society* **41**, 24–25A.

Fisher, G. H. (1960b). Intersensory elements of phenomenal space. *Proceedings of the 16th International Congress on Psychology* 840.

Fisher, G. H. (1961). Autokinesis in the spatial senses. *Bulletin of the British Psychological Society* **44**, 16–17A.

Fisher, G. H. (1962a). Resolution of spatial conflict. *Bulletin of the British Psychological Society* **46**, 3A.

Fisher, G. H. (1962b). Intersensory localization. Ph.D. Thesis, University of Hull.

Fitts, P. M. (1954). The information capacity of the human motor system in controlling the amplitude of movement. *Journal of Experimental Psychology* **47**, 301–391.

Gauld A. O. and Shotter, J. D. (1977). "Human Action and its Psychological Investigation". Routledge and Kegan Paul, London.

Goldscheider, A. (1889). Untersuchungen Uber den Muskelsinn. *Archives of Anatomy and Physiology*, Leipzig, 369–502. Quotes by Howard and Templeton (1966).

Gottsdanker, R. (1960). The relation between the nature of the search situation and the effectiveness of alternative strategies of search. *In* "Visual Search Techniques", NAS-NRC Pub. 712, 181–186.

Gregory, R. L. and Zangwill, O. L. (1963). The origin of the autokinetic effect. *Quarterly Journal of Experimental Psychology* 15, 252–261.

Hamilton, C. R. (1964). Intermanual transfer of adaptation to prisms. *American Journal of Psychology* 77, 457–462.

Hardt, M. E., Held, R. and Steinback, M. J. (1971). Adaptation to displaced vision: a change in the central control of sensorimotor co-ordination. *Journal of Experimental Psychology*, 89, 229–239.

Harris, C. S. (1963). Adaptation to displaced vision: Visual, motor or proprioceptive change? *Science* 140, 812–813.

Hay, J. C. and Pick, H. L. (1966). Visual and proprioceptive adaptation to optical displacement of the visual stimulus. *Journal of Experimental Psychology* 71, 150–158.

Heyes, A. D. and Gazely, D. J. (1975). The effect of training on the accuracy of auditory localization using binaural hearing aid systems. *British Journal of Audiology* 9, 61–70.

Held, R. (1961). Exposure history as a factor in maintaining stability of perception and co-ordination. *Journal of Nervous and Mental Disorders* 132, 26–32.

Held, R. (1963). Movement produced stimulation is important in prism-induced after-effects: a reply to Hochberg. *Perceptual and Motor Skills* 16, 764.

Held, R. and Freedman, S. J. (1963). Plasticity in human sensorimotor control. *Science* 142, 455–462.

Held, R. and Hein, A. (1958). Adaptation of disarranged hand-eye coordination contingent upon re-afferent stimulation. *Perceptual and Motor Skills* 8, 87–90.

Helmholtz, H. von. (1962). "Treatise on Physiological Optics". Dover, New York.

Hick, W. E. (1953). Some features of the after-contraction phenomenon. *Quarterly Journal of Experimental Psychology* 5, 166–170.

Holding, D. H. (1968). Accuracy of delayed aiming responses. *Psychonomic Science* 17, 125–126.

Howard, I. P. (1971). Perceptual learning and adaptation in "Cognitive Psychology". *British Medical Bulletin* 27, 248–252.

Howard, I. P. and Templeton, W. B. (1966). "Human Spatial Orientation". John Wiley and Sons, London.

Howard, I. P., Anstis, T. and Lucia, H. C. (1974). The relative lability of mobile and stationary components in a visual-motor adaptation task. *Quarterly Journal of Experimental Psychology* 26, 293–300.

Howarth, C. I. and Bloomfield, J. R. (1969). A rational equation for predicting search times in simple inspection tasks. *Psychonomic Science* 17, 225–226.

Howarth, C. I., Beggs, W. D. A. and Bowden, J. M. (1971). The relationship between speed and accuracy of movement aimed at a target. *Acta Psychologica* 35, 207–218.

Jackson, C. V. (1953). Visual factors in auditory localization. *Quarterly Journal of Experimental Psychology* 5, 52–65.

Jackson, C. V. (1954). The influence of previous movement and posture on subsequent posture. *Quarterly Journal of Experimental Psychology* **6**, 72–78.

Kinchla, R. A. and Smyzor, F. (1967). A diffusion model of perceptual memory. *Perceptual and Psychophysics* **2**, 219–229.

Klapp, S. T. (1975). Feedback *vs.* motor programming in the control of aimed movements. *Journal of Experimental Psychology: Human Perception and Performance* **104** (1), 147–153.

Kohler, I. (1962). Experiments with goggles. *Scientific American* **206**, 62–86.

Mackworth, N. H. and Morandi, A. J. (1967). The gaze selects information details within pictures. *Perception and Psychophysics* **2**, 547–552.

Matin, L. and MacKinnon, G. E. (1964). Autokinetic movement: selective manipulation of directional components by image stabilization. *Science* **143**, 147–148.

McDonnell, P. (1975). The development of visually guided reaching. *Perception and Psychophysics* **18**, 181–185.

Merton, P. A. (1961). The accuracy of directing the eyes and the hand in the dark. *Journal of Physiology* **156**, 555–577.

Nachmias, J. (1953). Figural after-effects in kinaesthetic space. *American Journal of Psychology* **66**, 609–612.

Neisser, U. (1976). "Cognition and Reality". Freeman, San Francisco.

Pick, H. L. (1974). Visual coding of non-visual spatial information. *In* "Perception: Essays in Honour of J. J. Gibson" (R. B. MacLeod and H. L. Pick, eds), Cornell University Press, Ithaca, N.Y.

Pick, H. L. and Hay, J. C. (1965). A passive test of the Held reafferance hypothesis. *Perceptual and Motor Skills* **20**, 1070.

Pick, H. L., Warren, D. H. and Hay, J. C. (1969). Sensory conflict in judgement of spatial direction. *Perception and Psychophysics* **6**, 203–205.

Rachevski, N. (1959). Mathematical biophysics of automobile driving. *Bulletin of Mathematical Biophysics* **21**, 375–385.

Roelofs, C. O. (1959). Considerations on the visual egocentre. *Acta Psychologica* **16**, 226–234.

Selling, L. A. (1930). An experimental investigation of the phenomenon of postural persistence. *Archives of Psychology* **118**.

Snyder, R. W. and Pronko, N. H. (1952). "Vision with Spatial Inversion". McCormick-Armstrong, Wichita, Kansas.

Stratton, G. M. (1896). Some preliminary experiments in vision without inversion of the retinal image. *Psychological Review* **3**, 611–617; (1897) **4**, 182–187, 341–360, 363–481.

Templeton, W. B., Howard, I. P. and Lowman, A. E. (1966). Passively generated adaptation to prismatic distortion. *Perceptual and Motor Skills* **22**, 140–142.

Warren, D. H. and Platt, B. B. (1975). Understanding prism adaptation: an individual difference approach. *Perception and Psychophysics* **17**, 337–345.

Welch, R. B. and Rhoades, R. W. (1969). The manipulation of informational feedback and its effects on prism adaptation. *Canadian Journal of Psychology* **23**, 415–425.

Welford, A. T. (1968). "Fundamentals of Skill". Methuen, London.
Wilkinson, D. A. (1971). The visual-motor control loop: A linear system?
Journal of Experimental Psychology **89**, 250–257.
Witkin, H. A., Wapner, S. and Leventhal, T. (1952). Sound localization
with conflicting visual and auditory cues. *Journal of Experimental Psychology*
43, 58–67.
Yarbus, A. L. (1967). "Eye movements in Vision". Translated from Russian
by B. Haigh. Plenum, New York.

Nine

The Strategic Control of Information Processing

Neville Moray
University of Stirling

For our purposes understanding why is usually more important than understanding where (Baron *et al*, 1970).

1. INTRODUCTION

The quotation heading this chapter is in contrast with most modern work on information processing. From the classical work of Broadbent (1958) onwards, the most influential models of attention, skill and information processing have concentrated on the question of "Where" in the sense of Baron *et al.* (1970). Where does selection take place? Where is the channel limited? Where is memory accessed? The aim has been to discover, in flow-chart terminology, what black boxes need to be postulated and what their order and interrelationship must be to account for the known phenomena of these fields of human behaviour. What is the canonical form of the flow-chart, and what functions are computed by the various boxes? Models of attention have postulated switches, attenuators, filters, pattern analysers, and so on. Models of skill have postulated limited capacity channels, parallel and serial recoding, feedback loops, and comparators. Frequently a decision that a particular component exists has been made on the basis of remarkably inadequate evidence considering that the claim amounts to an existence proof, and often the results have been inconclusive as in the problem of whether selective attention behaves as an all-or-none switch or as an attenuator. But whatever the success or failure of particular models and theories, they have tried to answer the question, "With what components is the head stuffed?"

The study of strategies of behaviour is not primarily, if at all concerned with that question. Rather does it speak to the question, "How is the hardware of the brain used by its owner, whatever the hardware may be?" In the language of the theory of signal detection (TSD), strategies would be more concerned with the criteria for decisions, the placing of decision cut-offs, and the interpretation of biases and pay-offs than with the structure of the neural circuits (whether conceptual or physiological) which deliver the evidence to the decision axis, except in so far as the properties of those circuits impose certain constraints on the nature of rational and optimal behaviour.

A *rapprochment* between the two approaches is clearly needed if a full understanding of an adaptive and purposeful system such as a human is to be achieved. The main theme of this chapter is to emphasize the less common approach so as to show to what extent we are now ready for such a *rapprochment*.

"Strategy" implies the goal-directed, purposeful use of resources. The agent desires to bring about some end, and takes steps which seem most likely to achieve that end given the resources available to him. Strategy consists of the subtle striving of a rather rational agent in a fairly orderly universe. If the agent were not at least in part rational he could not determine goals and ways of achieving them; and if the universe were totally unstructured there would be no point in planning. The existence and use of strategies implies in the agent a knowledge of the structure of the universe and consequent expectancies about events distant in time and space, especially with respect to future time. The strategist is the complement of the S–R organism: he is not concerned with what has just occurred in the past, but responds to what will occur in the future.

It is probably this last point which accounts for the relatively small amount of work which has been done on the nature of strategies in skill, attention and control. Strategy will tend to be idiosyncratic, since the precision of the observer's knowledge of the world and his ability to predict will vary widely between individuals, unless very time-consuming and expensive steps are taken to ensure that different operators have equivalent models. In most psychological work the emphasis is on general laws which it is hoped will hold despite individual differences, and steps are taken to minimize the opportunity for individual rational strategies to develop. Therefore stimuli are randomized, probabilities are equalized, pay-off matrices have value unity, and everything is balanced so that the situation has no structure encouraging a sensible strategy, whether conscious or unconscious.

On the other hand, there is abundant discussion of such topics in engineering literature, for engineers and engineering psychologists have become increasingly concerned in recent years with modelling human skills in the context of designing man–machine systems. With the growth of automatic control systems, many human skills have been taken over by machine, and a proper understanding of skill, both human and inanimate, has become central to problems of design. It is something of a paradox that as automatic systems become more and more sophisticated it becomes more and more important to understand human information processing capabilities. On the one hand the ways in which humans behave can provide valuable insights into adaptive system design, and on the other a failure will always arise sooner or later which will require the human, usually acting as monitor, to regain control of a system whose behaviour may be almost, if not quite, beyond his capabilities to control. As automatic control systems have developed they have evolved from the early simple servo-controls in which error was controlled by negative feedback, and have become adaptive and predictive. They can respond to the future and adopt strategies of behaviour, as can humans. Providing that the universe is at least locally predictable in time and space the apparent limitations of systems made from relatively slow components such as neurons can be overcome, and both man and machine can escape the tyranny of reaction time as they become skilled.

Let us start by a somewhat unfashionable assertion. Despite the known difficulties of applying Information Theory as a model for the human operator, the latter does behave on many occasions as if he were a limited capacity channel (Shannon and Weaver, 1949; Attneave 1959; Garner, 1962; Leonard, 1959; Mowbray and Rhoades, 1959; Davis *et al.*, 1961). Although by extensive practice, high stimulus response compatibility, or a combination of both we can produce what look like cases of infinite rates of information transmission or parallel processing, in the everyday world man usually behaves as if he were severely limited. For many practical tasks such as driving a car, flying an aeroplane, or even talking to people in a crowded room, we will obtain a reasonable approximation to performance if we assume that information theory is true. This may be because much of human skill is visually guided, and therefore detailed pattern information is acquired only close to the point of fixation. Consequently the observer must scan the world with his fovea, taking sequential samples of information at discrete intervals of time. (This is not of course to deny that certain kinds of information, especially to do with the rate of movement of objects, can be picked up in the visual periphery. But even then one must turn one's head to sample the world behind one.)

Many possible scanning sequences may be imagined. It might be that the eye jumps to parts of the visual array where sudden changes occur, drawn by the occurrence of change, as in the orientation reflex or the fixation reflex. On the other hand, the eye might scan the array in a series of sequential sweeps like a TV raster. If such modes exist, and are "given" in the sense that they are neurally wired permanently and genetically, they are uninteresting for our purpose. They may be strategies adopted by natural selection, but they are not strategies based on a predictive statistical model of the world, acquired by the observer in his own lifetime and adapted to his own needs. The orientation reflex calls up a response: the viewer is acted upon not acting. The response is independent of the changing properties of the environment. But if the next fixation is decided by a rational operation on the outcome of the previous ones, then we may be looking at a strategy.

Similarly one may look at a behaviour in the time domain. If a stream of information arrives over a single channel it will not, in the real world, be statistically homogeneous. Some moments contain information that is adaptively more important than that of other moments, just as some spatial regions do. "Adaptively important" information allows one to predict where or when other important information may occur, or what responses are likely to be needed in the near future.

To identify such moments and regions is valuable because to do so allows the limited capacity of the organism's information processing systems to be deployed optimally in the light of past experience. The world represents itself in the nervous system as a model which predicts the world's future properties, and the model is then used to govern behaviour—a strategy develops.

As an example, let us consider the model (*see* Fig. 1) proposed by McGruer and Krendel for skill acquisition, as described by Young (Young, 1969; McGruer *et al.*, 1968).

Consider a tracking task. A spot of light is displayed on an oscilloscope screen. The light moves sometimes slowly, sometimes rapidly. The task of the operator is to hold it still at a defined position on the screen. As far as the operator knows its movements are random. Let us assume

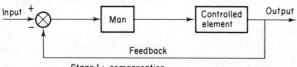

Stage 1 : compensation

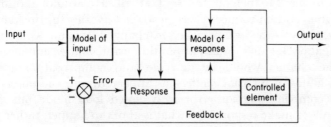

Stage 2 : development of open loop response

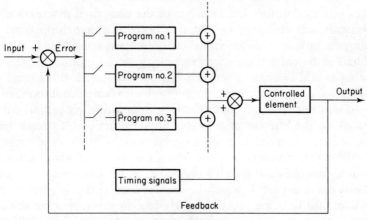

Stage 3 : precognitive open loop

FIG. 1.

that the motion has in fact two components and is a linear combination of a function of time $s(t)$ which is deterministic, and noise $n(t)$. The noise is white, Gaussian and band-limited. The combination of the two functions provides the observed display, $y(t)$, according to the equation

$$y(t) = s(t) + n(t).$$

For the purposes of exposition we assume that $s(t)$ is a pure sine wave, whose frequency w_s is constant over a duration d s, where $30 < d <$

600. At the end of a period d, the frequency of the sine wave changes at random to one of three values $w_s = w_1$, w_2, or w_3. The operator controls the movements of the spot of light by means of a joystick, and its movements or the force he applies to it act on the spot to offset its movements. The task is what is known as "compensatory" tracking.

If $s(t)$ were uncontaminated by $n(t)$ and $w_s < 1\cdot0$, the task would be extremely easy. Indeed after a short period of practice the operator would no longer lag behind the spot at all. He would abolish his reaction time and introduce phase lead, *anticipating* the movements of the spot. Only at the instants when w_s changed its value would there be a momentary lag or substantial position error, and within a second or two the change would be detected and compensation applied (Young, 1969). An internal model has appeared, and the observer is no longer compensating for error in a closed loop mode but going "open loop", to make responses to what is about to happen rather than to what has just happened. He has become a generator. Pew *et al.* (1967) have shown that humans can track in this way for periods of several seconds or more with considerable accuracy.

This is a straightforward example of the adoption, or creation, of a strategy. It will obviously be effective providing that the properties of the target, in this case the value of w_s, remain constant. If a second task had to be carried out, for example, a visual monitoring task, the tracking would appear to proceed "in parallel" with the second task, the operator only occasionally sampling the tracking input to make sure that w_s had not changed, but otherwise generating his output without reference to the current state of the input function. As described by McGruer and Krendel, the operator has constructed a set of programs, or models of the properties of the input, the statistical distribution over time of the moments at which a change in w_s is likely, and of the effects of particular movements which he makes; and he is using them intelligently to gain time for other tasks. He has, in short, become skilled.

Problems arise at the moments when w_s changes. Indeed the one problem about being skilled and basing performance on strategies and models is that they imply a commitment to a stable world. If sudden and hitherto unexperienced changes occur, or if the distribution of times at which the known changes can occur changes suddenly without the operator being aware of it, then maladaptive behaviour can occur and go unnoticed until the next time that the operator feels it necessary to check on the state of the forcing function. The more skilled he is, the longer the interval prior to that will be. This suggests a paradox of considerable practical importance. Consider, for example, an air traffic controller who watches a radar display. He knows the flight characteristics of the aircraft appearing on the screen, and has experience of the effects of the usual patterns of turbulence and weather conditions. Hence, when he has noted the position, speed, and course of a particular plane he may not examine the plot again until such a time as his internal model suggests that considerable uncertainty has arisen due to the cumulative effects of random disturbances. The better he knows the aircraft, and the more experienced he is, the longer will be the interval before he needs to check on his prediction. If an aircraft appears whose characteristics are unknown or unusual, he does not have a good model for it, and so will sample its position more frequently, both to check on its movements and to build up at least a temporary model. It follows that the more experienced an observer is, the less likely he is quickly to notice the occurrence of an abnormal flight pattern in a well known aircraft flying a scheduled route. Although no research seems to exist on the topic, the above scenario (which is here suggested only speculatively and to show the bad side of the adoption of strategies by skilled operators) seems to bear a marked resemblance to the situation surrounding certain midair collisions and near misses, such as the Yugoslavian crash in 1976.

Returning to more general considerations of skill, and in particular to·the account of the development of open loop generative behaviour from closed loop, error correcting, reaction time bound behaviour, we see that this development corresponds to the construction of internal models and their adoption, consciously or unconsciously, as adaptive strategies of behaviour. When we later consider recent models of man as a controller, we will see that there is clear evidence that he is a dynamic modeller of the statistics of the environment, constantly updating his representation of the world and using it to derive predictions and drive behaviour.

Young (1969) has provided a particularly clear picture of man as an adaptive controller (*see* Fig. 2). He emphasizes the great richness of the dynamic factors which must be taken into account in acquiring a control skill. "Plant adaptation" is outside the operator's control, and can best be thought of as wear and tear on mechanical systems, "running in", and other factors which influence the physical elements being controlled. The two blocks in the lower part of the diagram represent McGruer and Krendel's "programs" in their Stage 3 operator, and are the embodiments of strategies in our sense. These blocks represent weighting and cost functions, and knowledge of the effects of responses ("The road ahead is icy and so I must reduce rate of change of velocity and torque applied to the steering wheel", "It is now more important to detect targets than to avoid false alarms and so I will lower my response criterion"). The first block is the most interesting, being the means by which the internal model of source dynamics is constructed.

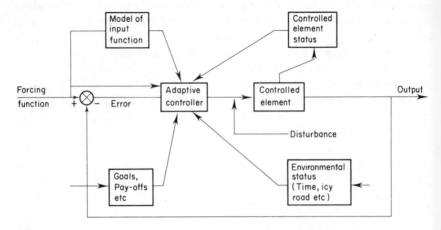

FIG. 2.

This block is where the past history of the input is used to build a statistical model from which its future can be predicted and dynamic program developed. This allows future behaviour to be prepared and initiated before it is needed, thus reducing the decision load as the future unfolds. As Kelley (1968) has pointed out, information from displays in general (temperature gauges, speedometers, pressure gauges, fuel gauges etc.) is required *not* to tell the observer what the condition of a system is at present, but what action may be needed in the future; how things *will be* if no action is taken.

Let us now take a closer look at less predictable inputs. In developing the above discussion we assumed that the process being controlled was a sinusoidal function of time, $s(t)$. We now assume return to the more general case of the signal being contaminated by noise, and the observer trying to control the function $y(t) = s(t) + n(t)$. It is realistic to make the assumption that real-life control problems involve compensating for Gaussian noise disturbances because any real system is likely to be subject to many small independent disturbances acting simultaneously, and their joint effect may, by the central limit theorem, be regarded as equivalent to Gaussian noise. What behavioural strategies are then appropriate, assuming that the signal to noise ratio is rather small? What should, or could the observer know about the process $y(t)$ which would allow a rational strategy to be adopted?

In the first place, the observer could, as a result of practice or prior knowledge, know the mean and standard deviation of the input when no control is exercised. He could also have an implicit or explicit knowledge of its bandwidth, since noise in the real world is bandlimited.

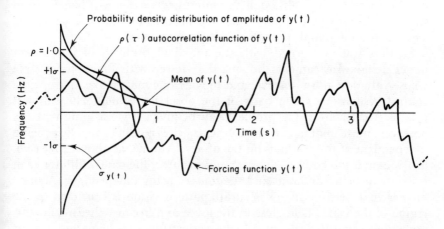

Fig. 3.

Given a reasonable estimate of those parameters, he will be able to make quite accurate predictions of the future history of the function $y(t)$, even though it is, in the main, random. We proceed to show how this can be so. Consider Fig. 3. Three things are shown, the function $y(t)$ of time, its amplitude distribution with mean $\mu = 0$ and standard deviation $\sigma = 1\cdot0$, and the autocorrelation function $\rho(\tau)$ of $y(t)$. The function is bandlimited to $w = 1\cdot0$ Hz, and consequently its autocorrelation function is non-zero to about $t = 2/w = 2\cdot0$ s. The autocorrelation function is a measure of the predictability of future values of $y(t)$ from an observed value at t_0. Therefore if the observer embodies implicitly or explicitly the amplitude distribution and the autocorrelation function, he has a model of the temporal statistical parameters of the process, and can predict, probabilistically, future values of $y(t)$ from the value observed at t_0. The ability to foretell the future course of the function ceases when $\rho(\tau) = 0$, which is at approximately twice the inverse of the bandwidth, or in this case about 2 s ahead.

If the observer is asked to make a response appropriate to the value of $y(t)$ at a time further into the future than $2(1/w)$, the best he can do is to assume that it will be at its mean value, which is the most likely value. But between t_0 and $t_{2/w}$ he can do much better *without making any further observations of* $y(t)$ providing that he has an internal model of the process, even though the process $y(t)$ is random.

These sort of considerations have led to a series of models for visual attention and tracking behaviour derived from an initial proposal by Senders *et al.* (1964) for a normative model of the human observer viewed as an information seeker. There is no time here to do more than outline these models, although the interested reader will benefit from studying the sequence of papers in their historical relation. Two will be treated in some detail, the others merely mentioned.

Senders was concerned with the practical problem of instrument panel design. Instruments present the viewer with functions of time whose values he must observe, and to which he must make appropriate control responses on the basis of the observed values. The simplest possible treatment of the problem can be given if we assume that the observer must monitor m instruments, the reading on each being independent of the readings on the others. Assume, as above, that each instrument is forced by a Gaussian noise source, the bandwidth for each instrument being different and the sources being independent. Assume further that because man's accurate pattern vision is restricted to the region of the visual field close to the fovea and because the instruments are widely separated, he must fixate an instrument if he wishes to read it accurately. The task is to detect "abnormal" readings, defined as a pointer position greater than some specified scale value. What is the best strategy for the observer as he moves his gaze over the array of instruments?

According to classical information theory the answer is given by Nyquist's Sampling Theorem. We assume that the observer in carrying out the task is trying to transmit all the information in the display generated by the functions $m_i(t)$, $m_j(t) \ldots m_q(t)$. It is both necessary and sufficient for him to sample an instrument m_i at a rate $2w_i$ s^{-1} where w_i is the bandwidth of the forcing function on instrument i. Samples taken at intervals shorter than $1/2w_i$ are redundant, and samples taken at longer intervals result in a loss of information. Whether or not the observer can achieve the necessary sampling rates depends on the dynamics of the oculomotor system, on the control mechanisms which are prone to "psychological refractory period" effects, and to the degree of accuracy with which each observation is required, since the information per observation is given by $\log_2 (1 + A/a)$ bits per observation, where A is the root mean square (r.m.s.) amplitude of the function and a is the r.m.s. "permitted error" (or degree of precision required). The greater the required accuracy, the longer each observation will take.

Senders *et al.* (1964) found remarkably good agreement between the predictions from information theory and the empirical data they obtained in several experiments in the laboratory and in simulators, and the model can be summarized in Fig. 4.

The most important idea from our point of view is that the observations made by the observers serve both to initiate responses and also to construct a model or set of models of the observed processes, and it is

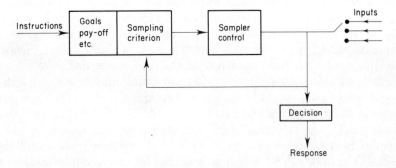

FIG. 4.

the latter, weighted by externally or internally imposed goals and cost functions that determine the observing strategy. Note that the model is dynamic, and is dependent on either practice or specific instructions for its construction.

2. INTERNAL MODELS

Despite the success of his predictions Senders has himself criticized the model on a number of grounds, and it is known from his own work that there are many situations where its predictions do not hold when fairly minor changes are made in the experimental situation. However while its details may be incorrect the central idea of the internal model remains valuable.

Some of the failures stem from the simplifying assumptions that were made. The values of instruments in the real world are frequently, if not usually, correlated. Thus altitude, pitch and airspeed tend to covary, and in industrial process control, several instruments may represent a causal sequence of operations in an industrial process. Furthermore, the result of making an observation that an instrument is in an abnormal or "danger" region will usually be that the controller tries to restore the process to its permitted values, rather than merely reporting that it is abnormal, so that in practice the future time course of $y(t)$ is not independent of the operator's observations. Such considerations led to the development of more sophisticated models such as those of Smallwood (1967) (relating to a Markovian analysis of instrument readings) and Carbonell (1966) (in which the effect of control on observing strategies was treated). The most general theory which can be seen as a descendent of Senders' original proposals is the Supervisor Theory due to Sheridan (1970).

The Supervisor is a close relative also to the various expressions of the idea that skills are controlled by hierarchies of commands (Kelley, 1968). (Kelley's book is the best currently available introduction to the kinds of ideas being discussed here for those without an engineering background.) The Supervisor is a mechanism whose task is to control the flow of information, information processing and action through a device whose purpose is to monitor and control a source of information. In more familiar psychological terms it could be regarded as the source of control for the setting of the Filter in Broadbent's model, or of the thresholds and analyser biases in Treisman's model (Broadbent, 1958, 1971; Treisman, 1969), although Sheridan himself does not relate it to these. The Supervisor has a representation of the world and a knowledge of the pay-off structure of the world with which it decides what operations should be performed so as to optimize the adaptive control exercised by the information processing device of which it is the supervisor. The criterion of success is not the minimization of error as in the classical servo-loop model discussed earlier, but the maximization of profit for the device.

Sheridan presented the Supervisor in the context of a single channel perceptual-motor task. The simplest case would be a single axis, zero order, compensatory manual tracking task, in which the observer tries to hold steady a spot of light within a small limit using a joystick or force stick to compensate for its movements while it is subjected to a bandlimited Gaussian disturbance.

Sheridan notes that one may set two limits on possible control and observation strategies, concentrating on the nature of the observations taken. Assume that either through practice or through being told the operator knows the mean and standard deviation of the forcing function, $y(t)$. One very weak strategy would be simply to assume that the best estimate of the value of $y(t)$ would be the mean, and to set the control stick on the mean, and thereafter take neither observation nor action. This would result in zero time being spent on taking observations, and an r.m.s. error score equal to the standard deviation of the function $y(t)$. No processing load would be placed on the observer, whose information capacity could be used for other tasks. Another very strong strategy would be to observe $y(t)$ continuously, so that there was never any observation error other than that due to the limited sensory acuity of the observer. The accuracy of control would be limited only by the accuracy of motor commands in the operator's nervous system. This strategy represents too much time spent in observing, since we saw earlier from the sampling theorem that it would be sufficient to sample $y(t)$ at no more than twice its bandwidth, and hence some time that could be available for other tasks would be lost.

We have therefore two limiting strategies, never to observe and always to observe, one being too lax and the other too strict. There must therefore be an optimal observation interval, and Sheridan's theory of the Supervisor aims to define that interval.

We have seen earlier that the autocorrelation function of a band-limited function of time shows it to be locally predictable, in a probabilistic sense. Following an observation, however, the observed value $y(t_0)$ becomes a less and less good predictor of the value of $y(t)$ at times $t > t_0$. If we wait long enough the weak strategy becomes the only strategy, and we must assume that the best estimate of the position of the function is merely the mean (*see* Fig. 5).

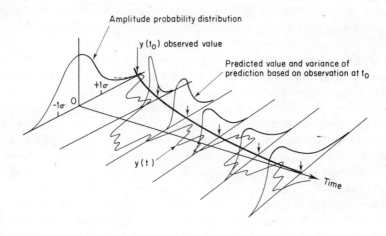

FIG. 5.

Suppose that there is a cost c associated with making an observation. If observations are made at intervals Δt the average cost per observation is $c/\Delta t$, and the longer we wait for an observation the less its average cost.

There are therefore two functions associated with the passage of time in addition to the process $y(t)$. One is the declining value of the last observation made, and the other is the decreasing average cost of an observation. If we represent value as positive and cost as negative, we can represent the two processes as in Fig. 6, and the difference between them will be non-monotonic for a large range of cost and value functions. The interval t_{vmax} at which this difference is a maximum represents the required optimal sampling interval, and to sample at that time is the required rational strategy.

If the operator is given some extra constraints, for example that the process $y(t)$ must not be allowed to exceed a certain value, then the

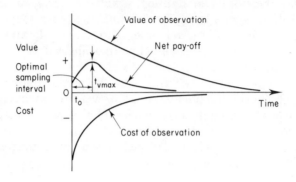

FIG. 6.

sampling interval Δt will not in general be constant, since if $y(t)$ is observed and found to be near the critical limit, it is more likely to exceed that value shortly afterwards than to be above it some time later, due to the tendency of the autocorrelation function to die away to zero and the long-term best estimate of $y(t)$ being its mean. Constraints of this kind act as weighting constants on the computation of Δt_{max}, and Δt is a function or ensemble of values rather than a constant. Thus the net cost is a complicated function of task demands, and any experiment on "switching time" or "sampling rate" which assumes a fixed interval is doomed to failure.

"Costs" are associated with making an observation. But what are these costs? Sheridan presents his models in terms of cash costs: the Supervisor has control of a money tap which is opened by finding the appropriate strategy. This may be true for some tasks, or may be an approximation in the sense that many outcomes can be mapped onto a cash value axis by human operators. But there is a more general, and for our purposes more interesting, interpretation of observation cost, which was developed by Senders (1964).

3. THE COST OF ATTENTION

If we assume as a working approximation that the human operator is a single channel then the cost associated with an observation on one channel is the probability of missing an event in a channel which is not currently being observed. For the purpose of exposition let us consider four instruments at the cardinal points of the compass with our observer situated in the middle of the array. Unless he moves his gaze sufficiently to lose sight of one instrument he cannot accurately read another. As an observer he is certainly a single channel. (Whether or to what extent he is truly a single channel observer when all the instruments are within his fixed visual field, or when the sources are auditory is an open question. The particular example is used for the sake of clarity. There are in fact a number of other situations in which the single channel approximation is plausible.) Now if the probability of occurrence of a critical value y_c on the four instruments is P_n, P_e, P_s and P_w respectively, then the cost of observing y_n is the union of the probabilities of target events on the other three channels. In terms of Sheridan's control paradigm the cost of observing $y_n(t)$ is the probability that while the observation is made the value of $y(t)$, another function to be controlled, will become so uncertain with the passage of time that the uncertainty becomes intolerable. (Note that the amount of uncertainty which can be tolerated will be a function of the task demands and the Supervisor's value system.)

T. Sheridan (personal communication) has found that human observers behave suboptimally in terms of his model. This is not entirely surprising, since to behave optimally requires an exact knowledge of the statistics of the process $y(t)$, and also an exact knowledge of the pay-off structure of the task, each of which is difficult to ensure. But the general idea of the Supervisor is extremely attractive. Viewed as part of Young's Adaptive Manual Controller it once more emphasizes the central role one might expect of adaptive learning and active prediction in optimal information processing by rational operators (Kelley, 1968).

It is important to emphasize that the observer, controller or supervisor may not be consciously aware of the details of the model he is using, of its parameters, or even of the overall strategy; but he is considered to embody these things, and his strategy observed as behaviour will reflect them. Only sometimes will he be able to estimate quantitatively their values to a reasonable accuracy. It should also be noted that this approach assumes that the parameters of the models he uses will constantly be varying. Steady-state performance is regarded as unusual and in some sense abnormal, in so far as it means that the operator is not for the moment regarding the world as a dynamic system, which is its inherent nature. Normally the adaptive controller must constantly change the parameters of his internal model in response to the dynamic characteristics of the environment. This is emphasized by the remarkable success of optimal adaptive control theory using the Kalman–Bucy filter as a model for the human operator (Baron *et al.*, 1970; Veldhuyzen and Stassen, 1976; Curry and Gai, 1976; Rouse, 1977).

4. ADAPTIVE OPTIMAL CONTROL THEORY

As an example of adaptive optimal control, consider the work of Stassen
and Veldhuyzen on the control of the steering of large ships. The records
of the adaptive automatic control system and of the human operator are
virtually indistinguishable for long periods in real time, measured not
merely as an average, but on a moment to moment basis. Some of
their results are shown in Fig. 7, from which the success of the automatic controller will be apparent.

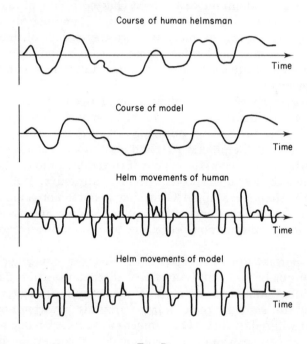

Fig. 7.

Conceptually it is not clear whether one should regard Stassen's
model as an "explanation" of the human operator's performance, or
merely as a description of it. As with classical information theory,
optimal control theory is normative, and provides a standard against
which to measure human performance. If all one can say is that the
adaptive control system is a successful controller, at least one can add
that the human operator behaves as if he were an optimal adaptive
controller.

The difference between the "classic" control theory (servo-control theory) account of skill and the adaptive optimal controller lies in the nature of the control loop. The most common account of perceptual-motor skill proposes that the observer makes use of the observed error signal to adjust his output until error is minimal. That is, he behaves only as a Stage 1 system in the series proposed by McGruer (*see above*). The problem for such a system is that it is inherently limited by transmission delays in the forward and feedback paths. There are a number of problems associated with negative feedback systems which are generally overlooked when they are used as models of skill—for example, their inherent instability when the loop delays are long and/or the amplification round the loop is high. But more importantly, it is known that the human operator can abolish reaction time delays and can introduce phase lead when tracking repetitive patterns or when tracking "precognitively". Such predictive behaviour implies zero or negative reaction time (more appropriately called "transmission delay" or "transport lag" in continuous tasks). This is true whether the behaviour is only locally predictive (as is possible with bandlimited Gaussian noise) or independent of input (as in the case of repetitive functions where the operator goes open loop). Such behaviour implies that the controller possesses and is using a model of the process to be controlled, and a model of the forcing function, in the sense of knowing the parameters of its statistical structure and being able to use them. The classical servo-loop theory cannot handle this problem.

An adaptive optimal control system, however, can. It both constructs and uses a model of the controlled process, and updates the model continuously in the light of the changing error. It can be regarded as a system which takes a sample of the error, estimates its parameters, passes the estimates to the model, and uses the model to plan control behaviour which is optimal in some well defined sense (usually in practice the minimizing of the root mean square error). It predicts the future, initiates the response, and then repeats the cycle on the basis of a new error estimate. In short, the system constantly evaluates parameters and uses them to estimate the future and initiate responses appropriately. The result is a highly dynamic controller which can respond to a wide variety of changes in the input and plant characteristics. Humans also have such abilities which are in marked contrast to the prediction of most psychological models which can account at best for steady-state performance with constant experimental parameters in the relatively impoverished environment of the well controlled laboratory experiment. The continuous learning which occurs both in the optimal adaptive controller and in the human accounts for their both being so effective in the real world, and also why it has been so difficult to transfer experimental results to the real world. For our purposes it is sufficient to note that the impressive agreement between man and model in Stassen and Veldhuyzen's data stems from the fact that each system incorporates a *predictive model* which, as we saw earlier, is a prerequisite for, indeed the embodiment of, strategy. This is why they are so much better models for skill than most current "psychological" models.

5. PROCESSING CAPACITY

Let us return to the main theme of the allocation of processing capacity, bearing in mind the ideas which have led us down this long and complex path. We had suggested that such allocation is carried out in the light of known pay-offs and probabilities, and such factors can be included as weighting functions in an optimal control model. Thus the allocation of capacity, or the direction of attention, can itself be regarded as a control skill, the skill of controlling the flow of information optimally through an organism whose information processing rate is in some sense finite. The concept fits the facts very well, whether or not we assume that the human is a discrete sampler or operates continuously in time and whether or not he is in a strict sense always single channel. (Mathematically either discrete sampling or continuous processing can be readily incorporated into optimal control models.)

If the ideas are so powerful one might expect similar behaviour to be discovered throughout the attention field, not merely in visual attention and tracking. It will be recalled that we proposed that strategies can be expected to show themselves in changes in criterion settings in TSD analyses, while they would only indirectly affect sensitivity. However, in the massive literature on selective listening, systematic changes in response bias have been conspicuous by their absence. A close inspection of the details of the experiments shows that this can be attributed to the experimental designs. Most experiments have been designed so as to make the use of strategies inappropriate. Usually experiments have either asked listeners to report one message and ignore another, or have made the occurrence of targets equiprobable on the two messages, and their occurrence statistically independent. The occurrence of targets has been at random moments, and under such circumstances there is no strategy which can usefully be employed by observers, since there are no constraints similar to the statistical constraints among the sources in Senders' dials or the bandwidths of the courses in tracking experiments. Moreover it has been customary to analyse experiments by averages based on long runs, or even to average data across observers before calculating statistics, both of which would tend to conceal short-term strategic fluctuations in performance.

Recently, however, new methods of analysis have appeared which, taken with appropriate experimental designs, should reveal strategies—and they have appeared. Moray *et al.* (1976) and Ostry *et al.* (1976) observed strategies, including the development of optimal settings of β during prolonged practice, as the observers acquired knowledge of the message structure even in the absence of any formal instruction or feedback from the experimenters. Using a range of signals from pure tone intensity increments to the identification of nouns of a specified category in strings of nouns of many classes they observed very large and systematic changes in response criteria. They purposely used messages in which the occurrences of targets were not statistically independent, but where the detection of a target in one message could convey information about the likelihood of the occurrence of a target simultaneously in the opposite channel. Thus the occurrence of a target in one message was 0·1 but the occurrence of a target in the second message given the occurrence of a target in the first was 0·5. Measuring the response criterion dependent on what happened at each moment in the opposite channel rather than averaging over whole runs, they found that when an observer thought that there was no target in one channel his β was approximately 10·0 for the other channel, while given a hit or false alarm in one channel his β for the opposite channel was about 1·5, where the optimal values from TSD are respectively 9·0 and 1·0. The authors concluded that the observers were using internal models of the statistical properties of the sources to control their decision strategy by choosing appropriate response biases, and that they were able to change the latter at least two to four times per second. Where the statistical structure of the task made the use of strategies appropriate, people used strategies.

6. SPEED–ACCURACY TRADE-OFF

Many aspects of attention and skill can thus be seen as the use of internal models to control sampling behaviour, response generation and decision-making. At a more general level still the whole concept of the speed–accuracy trade-off can be seen in this light. The human operator chooses what he believes to be an appropriate strategy when faced with rather indefinite task demands such as "Go as fast as you can but don't make too many errors". Annett pointed out that one might, for example, conceive of the psychological refractory period as due to the operator's interpretation of the rules of the game which he was being asked to play by the experimenter. Green and Luce (1973), among others, have documented the relation between RT and d' which is linear over a wide range, longer RTs producing higher d' values; and there is a similar relation between RT and β. A pilot experiment in our laboratory required a two choice RT to be made as fast as possible without insisting on a low error rate, and resulted in the relationships shown in Fig. 8.

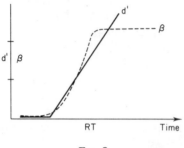

Fig. 8.

There could be two reasons for the relationship between RT and d'. If the information processing system integrates energy, then a high d' means a large signal, due to a rapid integration of energy leading to an early passing of the decision threshold. On the other hand one can envisage the observer deciding to be very accurate and so delaying his response until the strength of the events set in train by the arrival of the stimulus reached some high value. In the latter case one might say that a decision to produce a reaction time distribution within a certain range could determine the value of d', so that in some sense the value of the RT determines the value of d' rather than the other way round. On the other hand there is no such ambiguity about the response criterion—the RT function. In fact it is so clear that the experiment hardly needs to be done, resembling rather one of the "ideal experiments" indulged in by theoretical physicists. If I want the fastest possible RT, I must be satisfied with very poor evidence when I make my decision to respond: anything which looks even remotely like a signal must be enough for me to initiate the response. Many false alarms or anticipations will occur but the RTs will be fast. If accuracy is demanded I must set a high criterion and wait for abundant evidence to accumulate, so that few false alarms and anticipations will occur, but the RTs will be slow. Changes in experimental conditions which result in an inverse relation between speed and accuracy will almost always reflect a change in the strategy adopted by the observer. This is due to his seeing that the rules of the game have been changed, whether by explicit instructions from the experimenter or as a result of something about the task demands as he sees and interprets them.

7. INTERNAL MODELS AND STRATEGY IN CONTROL

Finally, let us return to some pure control models and look at tasks where the observer has a variety of models at his disposal and chooses them appropriately to the demands of the situation.

Although it is known that its application is limited, the quasi-linear control theory model of the human operator proposed by McGruer and Krendel (1957) works rather well within its limits. The original formulation has been progressively refined and predicts moment to moment performance by a human operator who is well practised, in a steady state, where the situation does not allow prediction (which cannot be handled by classical linear theory), and where the dynamics of the equipment being controlled do not vary. The detailed time history of compensatory tracking and the overall spectral characteristics of the human operator's responses are quite well explained (Fig. 9); sufficiently well, certainly, for the model to be used as a design tool to predict the handling characteristics of aircraft. McGruer and Krendel have recently applied the model to an analysis of pilot behaviour, and it is from that work that the following findings are taken.

The role of a human operator in controlling a complex system such as an aircraft in flight, can be regarded as providing compensation for

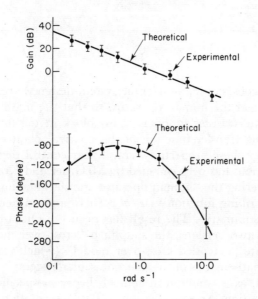

FIG. 9.

the properties of the thing controlled when it is subjected to disturbance by the environment. Any vehicle is more or less stable depending
on its physical characteristics and the properties of the disturbances to
which it is subjected. Where the vehicle has several degrees of freedom,
as is the case of an aircraft which can roll, pitch or yaw, and can change
velocity or acceleration on each axis, the physical laws governing its
motion may be quite different in respect of changes on the different
axes. The physics of the situation and the structure of the control
system may require extremely complex behaviour from the human
operators.

The man–machine system taken as a whole can be approximated by
a linear combination of the physical properties of the object and the
properties of the human operator, such as his bandwidth, transmission
delays (RT) etc. The overall flow diagram then becomes one such as is
shown in Fig. 10.

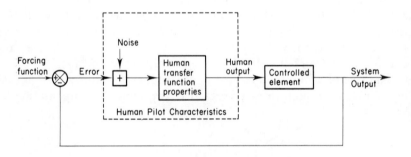

Fig. 10

For the purposes of man–machine system design we require to know
the properties of the human operator, so that the mathematical combination of the transfer function of his block in the diagram can be
made with the transfer function of the physical plant characteristics.
The search for these properties, using linear control theory in steady-
state applications has been pursued by McGruer and Krendel with the
aim of discovering the "human operator transfer function" or "human
operator describing function" (see also Sheridan and Ferrell, 1974, for
an excellent summary). The result has been the Quasi-linear Control
Model, in its two versions, the simplified "cross-over model" and the
more elaborate "extended cross-over model" (which explicitly incorporates the mathematics of the neuromuscular system).

The model, as is common in control theory, is specified in Laplace
transform notation. An introduction to Laplace notation can be found
in Toates (1976), Milsum (1966), or in the first few pages of McGruer

and Krendel (1974). Table I below shows the Laplace transforms of several functions and operations. The use of Laplace transforms greatly simplifies the mathematics involved much as logarithms allow long division to be performed by subtracting two numbers. Thus if a signal passes through a black box in such a way that the output of the box is the time integral of the input we label the box in Laplace notation, $1/s$. An input itself can be described by its Laplace transform. For example, a step function has the Laplace transform $1/s$. The output of the box when forced with an input is obtained by multiplying the two transforms to obtain the output in Laplace transform notation, and then consulting a set of tables to find the inverse transform and get the answer in the original domain (in as much as we use a table of anti-logarithms to find the answer to our division problem). So if we force

TABLE I.

		Laplace Transform
Input Function		
Impulse		1
Step		$\dfrac{1}{s}$
Ramp		$\dfrac{1}{s^2}$
Operator		
Integration		$\dfrac{1}{s}$
Differentiation		s
Gain (amplification)		K (constant)
Pure delay		$e^{-\tau s}$
Lag		$\dfrac{1}{1+ts}$
Lead		$1+ts$

an integrator with a step function, we find that the output is, in Laplace notation,

$$1/s \cdot 1/s = 1/s^2.$$

Consulting a table of transforms (such as that given in Table I) we can see that the output is a ramp, which corresponds to the fact that a non-zero d.c. voltage applied to an integrator results at its output in a linearly increasing voltage as a function of time. A black box which is merely an amplifier of constant gain has a Laplace transform which is a constant, K, the gain factor. A pure time delay (such as we might use to model the reaction time delay) has a transform in Laplace notation of $e^{-\tau s}$ where τ is the time constant of the exponent, and so on. To find the result of a series of operations performed in series we merely multiply the several transformed variables together and then, after appropriate algebraic manipulations, use tables to transform back into the time domain. By using different forcing functions, such as impulses, steps, ramps and sinusoids it is possible to discover the characteristic "describing function" of a particular black box, and hence the overall mathematical operations performed on its input to produce its output.

As a result of this kind of analysis, McGruer and Krendel suggest the following black box analysis of the human operator, in which we have omitted the details of the neuromuscular system for simplicity (Fig. 11). The elements in which we are presently interested are those labelled "Integral", "Rate", "Proportional" and "Acceleration". These are all operations which are at the disposal of the human operator, as experiments have shown. But he does not always use them all. Rather, the experienced controller chooses an appropriate control law according to task demands.

When the controlled element characteristics are a pure gain, with Laplace transform K_p, the human operator transfer function is that of an integrator, gain and delay ($K_h e^{-\tau s}/s$). When the controlled element has a transfer function of an integrator with gain, K_p/s, the human operator's transfer function tends towards $K_h e^{-\tau s}$, that is, a gain and delay. When the controlled element is K_p/s^2, the human approximates to $K_h s e^{-\tau s}$. When the controlled element is $K_p/s(s + a)$ the human tends to $K_h(s + a)e^{-\tau s}$, and so on. Without being concerned here with the exact interpretation of the various transfer functions in the time domain, we can construct a table of these relations such as Table II, which shows a striking regularity.

This is of course only a partial and simplified account of man as a controller. But it is clear that the human operator is choosing his own

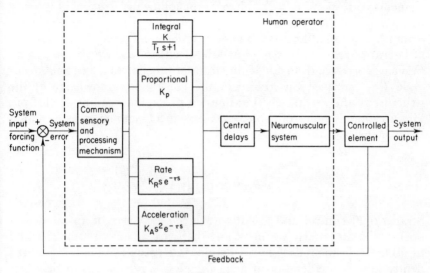

Fig. 11.

TABLE II. Choice of transfer function by the human operator as a function of the characteristics of the controlled element.

Machine	Man	Man–machine combination
K_p .	$K_h e^{-\tau s}/s$	$= K_m e^{-\tau s}/s$
K_p/s .	$K_h e^{-\tau s}$	$= K_m e^{-\tau s}/s$
K_p/s^2 .	$K_h s e^{-\tau s}$	$= K_m e^{-\tau s}/s$
$K_p/s(s+a)$.	$K_h(s + a)e^{-\tau s}$	$= K_m e^{-\tau s}/s$

In this table, K_p, K_h and K_m are the gain constants for the controlled element, the human and the man–machine system combination, and $K_m = K_p \cdot K_h$. The value of τ varies according to the particular combination in such a way as to compensate for changes in the time characteristics of the controlled element, such as phase lags produced by integration, and has a limited lower value equal to the reaction time.

control law from the battery available in a remarkably elegant way so as to produce a combined man–machine system transfer function which approximates a gain, a delay and integration. In other words, human operators like working with inputs which are rates of change of information and will compensate for machine properties in order to be able to do so. More complex transfer functions also appear, using more complex combinations of the functions available in the human operator, as the situations demand. [In the "real world" the machine elements correspond to such things as the following. Control of velocity in an automobile has a transfer function K_p. Directional (heading, azimuth) control at low speeds has a transfer function K_p/s. The control of lateral position on the road at low speeds in fog, where there is no preview, corresponds to a machine transfer function of K_p/s^2, and so on.]

So we again see the ability of the controller's knowledge of the structure of the world, whether implicit or explicit, calling forth from him a rational choice of control strategy, nicely chosen so as to match the exigencies of the situation.

8. CONCLUSION

Strategies of control and attention are the responses of an intelligent operator in an orderly world. While there are advantages for research in using experimental designs where events occur randomly, independently and unpredictably in a meaningless way, the world does not have those properties, nor have the nervous systems of the world's occupants evolved to function as though it did. Rather, information processing proceeds on the assumption of law, albeit stochastic; on the assumption that God is an artificer, not a random number generator or an experimental psychologist. It is not then surprising that when we turn our eyes from the structure of information processing systems to their use that we do not find reaction time delays and stimulus–response pairings. Rather we find adaptive performance of great elegance and rationality, perfected and fitted for its purpose to a remarkable degree, and oriented towards what concerns all organisms —the future.

We find, in short, strategies.

REFERENCES

Attneave, F. (1959). "Applications of Information Theory to Psychology". Holt, Rinehart and Winston, New York.

Baron, S., Kleinman, D. and Levison, W. (1970). An optimal control model of human response. *Automatica* **6**, 357–369.

Broadbent, D. (1958). "Perception and Communication". Pergamon, Oxford.

Broadbent, D. (1971). "Decision and Stress". Academic Press, London and New York.

Carbonell, J. (1966). A queuing model for many-instrument visual sampling. *IEEE Trans. Human Factors in Electronics.* HFE-7, 157–164.

Curry, R. and Gai, E. (1976). Detection of random process failures by human monitors. *In* "Monitoring Behavior and Supervisory Control" (G. Johannsen and T. Sheridan, eds). Plenum Press, New York.

Davis, R., Moray, N. and Treisman, A. (1961). Imitative responses and the rate of gain of information. *Quarterly Journal of Experimental Psychology* **13**, 78–90.

Garner, W. (1962). "Uncertainty and Structure as Psychological Concepts" Wiley, New York.

Green, D. M. and Luce, R. D. (1973). Speed–accuracy trade-off in auditory detection. *In* "Attention and Performance IV". (S. Kornblum, ed.). Academic Press, London and New York.

Kelley, C. (1968). "Manual and Automatic Control". Wiley, New York.

Leonard, J. (1959). Tactual choice reactions: I. *Quarterly Journal of Experimental Psychology* **11**, 76–83.

McGruer, D. and Krendel, E. (1957). Dynamic response of human operators. WADC Technical Report, 56–524.

McGruer, D. and Krendel, E. (1974). Mathematical models of human pilot behaviour. Agardograph No. 188, NATO.

McGruer, D., Hoffman, L., Jex, H., Moore, G., Phatak, A., Weir, D. and Wolkovitch, J. (1968). New approaches to human-pilot/vehicle dynamic analysis. AFFDL-TR-67-150, Wright Patterson.

Milsum, J. (1966). "Biological Control Systems Analysis". McGraw-Hill, New York.

Moray, N., Fitter, M., Ostry, D., Favreau, D. and Nagy, V. (1976). Attention to pure tones. *Quarterly Journal of Experimental Psychology* **28**, 271–285.

Mowbray, G. H. and Rhoades, M. V. (1959). On the reduction of choice reaction times with practice. *Quarterly Journal of Experimental Psychology* **11**, 16–23.

Ostry, D., Moray, N. and Marks, G. (1976). Attention, Practice, and Semantic Targets. *Journal of Experimental Psychology: Human Perception and Performance* **2**, 326–336.

Pew, R., Duffendack, J. and Fensch, L. (1967). Sine wave tracking revisited. *IEEE Trans. Human Factors in Electronics*, HFE–8, 130–134.

Rouse, W., ed. (1977). "Human Factors". Special edition on applications of control theory to psychology. Vol. 19, nos. 4 and 5.

Senders, J. (1964). The human operator as a monitor and controller of multidegree of freedom systems. *IEEE Trans. Human Factors in Electronics*, HFE-5, 2–6.

Senders, J., Elkind, J., Grignetti, M. and Smallwood, R. (1964). An Investigation of the visual sampling behaviour of human observers. NASA, CR-434.

Shannon, C. and Weaver, W. (1949). "Mathematical Theory of Communication." University of Illinois Press, Illinois.

Sheridan, T. (1970). On how often the supervisor should sample. *IEEE Trans. Syst. Sci. and Cybernetics*, SSC-6, 140–145.

Sheridan, T. and Ferrell, R. (1974). "Man–Machine Systems". M.I.T. Press, Cambridge, Massachusetts.

Smallwood, R. (1967). Internal Models and the Human Instrument Monitor. *IEEE Trans. Human Factors in Electronics*, HFE- 8, 181–187.

Toates, F. (1976). "Application of Control Theory in Biology and Experimental Psychology". Hutchinson, London.

Treisman, A. (1969). Strategies and models of attention. *Psychological Review* **76**, 282–299.

Veldhuyzen, W. and Stassen, H. (1976). The internal model—what does it mean in human control? *In* "Monitoring Behaviour and Supervisory Control" (G. Johannsen and T. Sheridan, eds). Plenum Press, New York.

Young, L. (1969). On adaptive manual control. *Ergonomics* **12**, 635–675.

Ten

Problem Solving—The Nature and Development of Strategies

University of Nottingham

1. INTRODUCTION

One of the areas within which psychologists have played an active role in public policy making concerns the factors which supposedly underlie effective problem solving, particularly that sort of thinking which guarantees success in school learning situations and in tests of academic potential. In the United States and Great Britain several substantial attempts have been made to have direct, predictable influence on the linguistic and cognitive abilities of children who are considered socially and economically disadvantaged. Broadly speaking, these interventions were inspired and explained at least in part on the basis of certain views about relationships between language and thought. Although no proper scientific conclusion has been reached about the role of language in the development of thinking, psychologists and others, perhaps rightly, have acted as though it had, accepting as a provisional

329

truth the view that specific forms of language use have a direct and causal influence on the development of certain types of thinking. Indeed, such is the state of our knowledge about role of interaction in development that these attempts at intervention represent one of the best potential methods for trying to prove the hypothesis. It is also the case, however, that no explicit analysis has been offered within these interventions about processes which supposedly go on in thinking and problem solving. Consequently, no detailed mapping has been made of social, linguistic processes on to the cognitive activities which guarantee success in directive thinking.

This chapter explores certain hypotheses about the possible relationships between cultural and intellectual variables, starting out with a brief consideration of some of the processes which go on in adult problem-solving and, later, asking what we know about the ontogenesis of these processes. Central to this endeavour is the concept of strategy. At one level, the definition of this term is relatively straightforward, something along the lines of a "programmatic assembly of operations aimed at a common goal". But there is more to it than this. In employing the term at all, one is tacitly introducing a concept of choice or optionality into thinking and a suggestion that the "rules" which govern such activities are, at one level, "man-made". It stands opposed to the view that intellectual operations are somehow a natural or universal product of experience or of the automatic operation of the nervous system. This is not to argue, of course, that at some level experience does not have necessary intellectual consequences or that there may not be innate biological laws governing nervous functioning. Rather, it implies that intellectual activity is eminently adaptable to the local environment. The real heart of the argument is that the "rules" of thought are not fixed by very basic common experience as say a Piagetian theory might hold, but that they take much of their form and procedures from rather specialized experience. The general point of view explored below is, in fact, that intelligent, directed thinking involves a process akin to an inner dialogue. It has a topic-comment structure within which the mental activity is itself the basis for reflection, analysis and evaluation and a potential basis for new rules or strategies of thought. Furthermore, the form, clarity and extent of this dialogue together with the zest with which it is undertaken are the product of experience, particularly social experience. We know that correlations exist between social and intellectual factors and the point of view explored here is that the concept of strategy is a useful intervening construct for the analysis and explanation of this relationship.

2. ADULT PROBLEM SOLVING

The solution to a problem, like skinning a cat, can be achieved in more than one way. Different people with the same problem, even one person with a problem on separate occasions, may perform quite differently in achieving a solution. And these differences cannot all be accounted for in terms of familiarity with particular operations or with differential speed and accuracy of formally similar performances. Techniques and strategies differ qualitatively and in quite important respects. Consider the problem below, for example. This can be solved by at least three methods. You are asked simply to look at it and deduce the answer:
Who is taller, John or Ian, if . .

John is taller than Paul
Dave is taller than Paul
Tom is taller than Dave
Ian is taller than Tom
Dave is taller than John

First, you might solve the problem by constructing a "list" or "ladder" in your head. As you read each successive item, you attempt to combine it with what you already have in store constructing a "spatial para-logic" (De Soto *et al.* 1965), "image" (Huttenlocher, 1968) or "representation" (Wason and Johnson-Laird, 1972) in which "tall" items come at the top of the list and less tall ones at the bottom. Periodically you may check to see if the list which you are holding in memory connects the two names in the question. If it does, you may "read off" the solution. If not, you try to add more items or you may have to back-track, deleting items, perhaps, to fashion new potential solution paths. The majority of subjects given such problems start out this way (Wood, 1969a, b). However, when they are given protracted experience with the problems, more than half of them report a different technique. Here, they take the first name in the question and search down the left-hand side of statements looking for its occurrence. If they find one, they see if this connects it to the second name in the question, for if it does the problem has been solved. If not, they search for occurrences of this new item (remembering where they had picked up the last statement) to see if this links to the second name in the question. This search continues until the problem is solved or a dead-end is reached. Entry in a dead-end demands some backtracking, essentially discarding the last focus of search to look for new occurrences of the one immediately before it.

This too continues until a solution is reached or all dead-ends have been explored. In the latter eventuality, search begins afresh with the second name in the question. This *must* lead to solution if the initial search was exhaustive and accurate for all the problems given are soluble. Eventually, subjects come to recognize this "higher order" constraint too and having exhausted an initial search *immediately* announce solution— "If A is not taller, B must be". This effectively reduces their mean search times by some 25%. Some subjects go even further than this with the realization that an initial *scan* of the left-hand side of the statements can, on some problems, reveal if one or other of the names could *not* be the taller. As one subject put it, "If one's not taller than somebody, he cannot be taller than the other". Similarly, a search of the right-hand side can reveal, on some problems, whether one could not be *less* tall than the other.

It is relatively simple to construct computer programs to simulate these different strategies (Wood, 1969a, b). These can be constructed to keep count of the number of hypothetical operations (like "examine next item", "add item to list", "delete item") which they execute in solving a given problem. Over a range of problems, these counts provide theoretical rankings of relative difficulty, and such rankings, compared with empirically derived solution time measures, yield significant correlations between predicted and obtained levels of difficulty.

Where a subject mentions more than one strategy, there is *always* a privilege of occurrence—"list" before "search" and "search" before "scan". The implication is that the later strategies are somehow more efficient and economic than earlier ones, an expectation that has been confirmed in another study (Quinton and Fellows, 1975) in which groups of subjects were trained to use the different techniques with the expected results. Those using what we have called the "list" technique fared worse than those using the "search" approach. Possible reasons for such changes in performance with experience are not hard to find. In the first place, subjects using the first method often complained that they kept "losing hold" of the information. Since the problems used contained up to eight statements and possessed a quite complicated structure, some subjects were stretched to their limits actually remembering information currently in store. And in addition to doing this, they might have to add, delete or substitute items and occasionally must search through their mental list looking for two names, paying due regard to their order or occurrence. The search approach, on the other hand, seldom takes the subject beyond a depth of search involving more than four items, demanding that he remember what he is currently searching for and the location of past relevant items. Here, one suspects, recognition can be employed in place of recall, since he only needs look back up the list after a failure of search to "see" where he found the last focus of search.

A major implication of the proposed shift in strategy is, then, that the deployment of capacity is different. The subject supposedly moves from a reliance on "symbol" memory to a more positionally governed technique where merely to *read through* statements in a rule-governed sequence is to solve the problem.

This analysis implies a prediction which can and has been tested. If the subject really does as the simulations suggest, then, having just solved a problem in the initial stages of his trial, he or she should have a list of items in store. However, if that same problem were to be handled later, he should have no such list, merely knowledge of the solution and, perhaps, decaying information which would enable him to recognize items-in-location. Suppose then he is asked immediately after solution to answer a new and unexpected question, one whose answer relies on information just employed to solve an initial problem. If he still has a list in store (the information has been removed, of course) he should be able to answer the question. If he has not, then he should not be able to answer it. So, subjects should show a diminishing capacity to answer probe questions as they gain experience with the problems. This is exactly what happens (Wood *et al.*, 1974).

This diminution in probe-answering ability is only found with visual presentation, however (Wood and Wood, 1976). If problems are read out to subjects they never report a shift from the list strategy to the search one. And we would not expect them to be able to do so, for the search and scan techniques identified rely on *positional* coding made possible by the continuous problem display. It thus seems that with some problems at least, auditory presentation impedes the development of new strategies *but* in so doing, it leaves the subject with a memory for material which enables him to answer fresh and unexpected questions even after protracted experience. So, auditory presentation, though more laborious, facilitates greater generalization. Visual presentation, on the other hand, engenders strategies which are more economical and less "content" oriented, ones that make less demands on working memory but which eventually lessen generality. In view of some recent proposals about the importance of visual artefacts like the printed word in the ontogenesis of intellectual skills (Olson and Bruner, 1974; Olson, 1975), we will return to a more general consideration of this and related results later in the chapter.

To underline the main initial point, then, it seems that a given type of problem may encourage the development of more than one technique or solution strategy. More recent work by H. Simon and others indicates that this conclusion holds for a variety of other problems too, including non-verbal problems like the Tower of Hanoi (Simon, 1975) and "teasers" like the Cannibal and Missionary problem (Simon and Reed, 1976) or the formally similar Hobbits and Orcs one (Thomas, 1974). These findings raise some methodological problems for the investigation of "models" of thinking and these are perhaps worth mentioning briefly before a consideration of more interesting theoretical implications.

It is often the case in attempted analyses of directed thinking that theorists only consider single-factor explanations. Take the vigorous investigations of the three-term series problem, for example (e.g. Hunter, 1957; De Soto *et al.*, 1965; Huttenlocher, 1968; Clark, 1969). It has been argued by De Soto and his colleagues that people solve these problems using a "spatial paralogic" in which "end" items (e.g. the longest and shortest in "A is longer than B, C is shorter than B") first have to be "anchored" leaving the third term to the middle. In a development of another "image" theory, Huttenlocher has provided a theoretical explanation for this "end anchoring" effect in terms of proposed relationships between linguistic structure and mental activity. She argues that the grammatical subject in each statement is pre-disposed to be mentally handled first. Difficulty of comprehension and inference is thus determined by the immediacy with which grammatical form permits location of elements in imaginary space.

Where the structure of the sentence permits immediate placement then the problem will be relatively easy. For example, consider Problem 1 below:

Problem 1: Which is longest if A is longer than B and C is shorter than B?

First, according to Huttenlocher, A and B are located in the image, A being placed above B. Then, once A and B are located, the problem is to place C relative to them. Since C is the subject of the second statement this can be done without any transformation of the premises. In Problem 2, however, some transformation is required.

Problem 2: Which is longest if A is longer than B and B is longer than C?

Here, once A and B are located, the second statement needs reorganization. B is the subject of that statement but its position has already been established relative to A. So the statement must be transformed to "C is shorter than B" so that C, now the subject of the sentence, can be located. Thus, Problem 2 is counter-intuitively more difficult than

Problem 1 because it involves an extra step in the achievement of comprehension and inference. Interestingly enough, children attempting to follow instructions with real objects (e.g. "Put the red block on the green block and the blue block under the green block") show similar relative levels of difficulty in handling formally similar structures (Huttenlocher and Strauss, 1968). This, according to Huttenlocher, demonstrates a continuity between physical and mental activity.

In another theory, Clark and his colleagues have dismissed the "image" altogether as an explanatory concept arguing that the relative difficulty of comprehension and inference can be explained on purely linguistic grounds. He claims, essentially, that the processes which go on in verbal problem solving and normal language use are the same. He adapted and developed ideas from Chomsky's (1965) transformational linguistics to argue that it is factors like the nature of the underlying "base strings" which determine a problem's difficulty. In Problem 1, for example, the statements give the strings: "A is long, B is long" and "C is short, B is short". A is marked unambiguously "long" and C "short". In Problem 2, however, the strings given are "A is long, B is long" and "B is long, C is long". Here B is double-marked "long", implying, against the state of the world or "deep structure" represented in the problem, that it is longest. Thus, Problem 2 generates extra sources of difficulty.

In a series of experiments following on this controversy Clark's linguistic theory has emerged as a better predictor of the relative difficulty of various problems than Huttenlocher's image theory. This seems to justify Clark's rejection both of the image as an explanatory principle and the concept of strategy too. Clark points out that his model unites problem solving with a general theory of linguistics where transformational rules operate automatically below the level of consciousness to guarantee solution to problems. Subjects' reports about their strategies should thus be treated as epiphenomena, not as direct insights into the fundamental basis of their activity. If the solution to problems *is* ensured by natural rules embedded in the nervous system, then to be sure we must reject the notion of strategy in our explanations of such intellectual activity. For the concept of strategy tacitly assumes an element of conscious choice in how a problem is handled, a choice between different approaches to a problem where such differences are non-trivial. If people are driven by unconscious linguistic rules then it is reasonable to dispense with the concept altogether, at least in relation to verbal problems. However, this conclusion is premature. In the first place, not everyone can solve such simple inferential problems even though they have "full" linguistic competence, as we shall see in the next section. And there is a deeper issue too. What would happen if

Huttenlocher acted as Clark's subject? She could, of course, follow the dictates of her own theory thus violating the predictions of Clark's model. If this is so, what is the status of Clark's theory or indeed of Huttenlocher's performance? The question is neither a flippant nor a trivial one. Huttenlocher's experiences have led her to develop a valid system for solving these problems, one based perhaps in uncommon sense, for she may be wrong in assuming that the majority of her subjects utilize their own experience in such a way. Clark's model is conceivably more general than Huttenlocher's because it is based in more common areas of experience in everyday tasks and problems which most of us share. However, both approaches I would argue are strategic in that they involve a potentially optional application of different areas of knowledge to the problem at hand. People who are not American undergraduates or the products of Western technological society do not make such strategic applications. We may draw on many different types of experience to solve a problem, including immediate past experience with such problems, as we saw above. The central question then becomes not whether one rule system exists in human performance to the exclusion of another. What we must ask is how and why different areas of experience may be drawn on in particular contexts to provide the "metaphors", "analogues", "frames" or strategies for solving problems.

It is interesting in this connection that Huttenlocher should report that subjects in her experiments were ashamed of their strategy: "They regarded their own spatial imagery as an intellectual crutch, unseemly for the solution of formal reasoning problems". If they were following the dictates of some obligatory rules why should they feel so inelegant? They are reflecting on the nature of their own mental activity, and for some reason which is obscure, finding it wanting, even though it guarantees solution to the problems. Unfortunately we are given no information which would enable us to decide whether subjects did ever get better or feel more satisfied as they gained experience. But the expression of dissatisfaction itself I would argue indicates a push towards more economical, situation-specific strategies. What is it, then, that subjects do as they not only solve problems but also seek for and, at least on some occasions, discover hypotheses about potentially more acceptable ways of solving such problems in future? This is the question which we take up in the next section.

3. THE BASES OF STRATEGY CHANGE

Consider the following problem: What relationship is a woman to her mother's brother's daughter? Several factors seem to determine the difficulty of such problems. For example, the initial transition from "mother" to "brother" involves two distinguishing features, namely *sex* and *co-lineality*. The second also involves two features, in this case *sex* and *descendancy*. In all, then, four distinguishing features mark the statement of the problem. This renders it more difficult than, say "What relationship is a woman to her mother's sister's daughter" which, though it yields the same solution term, only involves a total of two distinctive feature transitions. Generally speaking, the number of such transitions relates systematically to problem difficulty, though there is probably more than one psychological mechanism underlying the effect (Wood and Shotter, 1973). There *are* different mechanisms because, here too, subjects employ more than one strategy to solve the problems. In one experiment for example, eight out of twenty-four subjects first mentioned using their own families as a basis for achieving solution. They "pictured" their *own* mother's brother's daughter, achieving solution by recognizing *who* was being referred to in the problem. This "personal" strategy was, of course, severly limited by individual experience. Take a problem which gives, say, great-niece as a solution and most subjects using such an approach are likely to flounder—their family simply does not extend that far. Most subjects (about 70%) came to employ an image or representational approach in which *descendancy* was represented in an imaginary vertical dimension and *co-lineality* long a horizontal one. *Sex* was handled separately when the subject came to disambiguate the final solution term (e.g. choose between "nephew" and "niece" by looking at the sex of the last term).

These problems proved much easier than the series problems already discussed and, perhaps for this reason, comparatively few subjects (5) developed beyond a representational approach—though here too many protested that their technique was inelegant. However, about 20% did report another strategy. One subject said, for example, "When you say the words, I translate them so that 'father's father' is 'up-up' and I know that 'up-up' must be a 'great-something'." Another subject said "Up-across-down *means* cousin". Here, then, subjects seem to have been *reflecting on the structures inherent in their own past mental activities*, using hindsight to discover a new approach. Their new "coding" of the problem was not given "directly" in any statement of the problem or in its lay-out. Rather, it was generated from characteristics of the mental activity used to solve the problems initially, for the ups and downs which formed the basis of new coding were *descriptions* of such past mental events.

With the series problems, too, certain characteristics of the later strategies may well have been developed through such a process of reflective abstraction. It is possible to simulate a transition from the search to the scan technique by generating a new set of processes which keep track of the fate of past problem solving episodes (Wood, 1969b). Such a system "discovers", for example, that on every past encounter with the problems, having shown that "A is not taller than B" it always transpires that "B is taller than A". So, any activity following an initial, fruitless search for A is redundant and may be "pruned" away. This generates a major characteristic of the scan technique. Other lessons gained from the same simple procedures permit the search or scan strategist to change his behaviour for reading the problems. It picks up any biases in problem presentation which load the occurrence of information at particular locations in the lists of statements. In short, if relevant items have been found to occur most frequently at the bottom of lists of statements it comes to read these first. More recent studies of eye movements in problem solving (Willmot, 1975) confirm that subjects do in fact change their reading behaviour to reflect such structural constraints in the problems.

Here, then, we have a truly classical explanation for changes in behaviour with experience. Patterns emerge in the subject's activity because he responds systematically to elements of the problem. These systematic "molecular" responses produce *sequences* of moves which may be picked up by the subject if he reflects on his past experiences. The basic idea that the creation of higher-order behaviour derives from a hierarchical assembly of lower-order ones in this way is, of course, a familiar one. Miller and his colleagues (Miller *et al.*, 1960) conceived of behaviour in terms of "Plans" seeing these as hierarchical assemblies of constituent "TOTE" units while Bruner *et al.* (1959) observed that "Much of what we classify as learning, recognition and problem solving consists of being able to identify recurrent regularities".

Results from the experiments employing series problems are generally consistent with this "skills" paradigm. Male subjects, who shifted more frequently than female subjects from the list to the search technique, also solved problems faster and with fewer errors, and those subjects who started out with faster solution times were also most likely to finish faster and the most likely to report an early strategy shift (Wood and Wood, 1976). One can hypothesize, therefore, that subjects who began with relatively clear, skilled, spatialized constructions most readily appreciated the higher-order patterns and regularities within these and, as in all skill development (e.g. Bryan and Harter, 1897), were then able to utilize these sooner in the service of a new approach.

The argument is, then, that the development of new strategies for problem solving often involves a process of reflective abstraction in which previous problem solving behaviour becomes itself data in an attempt to discover patterns and regularities. These patterns, on occasion at least, rely on the description of mental acitivities which are essentially "paralogical" in nature. From a psychological standpoint, this suggests that we cannot predict the form of skilled problem solving behaviour from a "formal" examination of the problem alone. We must know something about the subjects' initial strategic responses if we are to anticipate the later form of their behaviour.

But the concept of reflective abstraction alone cannot adequately characterize the development of complex problem solving behaviour. Clearly, what a subject recalls of his past problem solving will depend, in part at least, upon how he conceptualized and planned that behaviour in the first place. Subjects sometimes think ahead, beyond the level of a single move, organizing their actions in sets of pre-meditated operations. For example, Greeno (1974), discussing Newel and Simon's General Problem Solver, argues that this achieves its ends by a brute use of memory, organizing all its activities at the level of single moves and continually keeping track of the fate of each of them. Yet subjects in his experiment, which faced them with the Hobbits and Orcs problem, often planned several moves ahead. Such pre-planning of their behaviour or foresight is at the very least likely to *bias* the course of any hindsight and recall. Only by doing justice to the subjects' own conceptions or hypotheses about his own activities are we likely to gain insights into the processes which he eventually employs to describe, evaluate and change his own strategies.

Another line of evidence which questions the reflective abstraction view and raises the question of foresight comes from a study of "geographic" problems like those given below.

Where would a man be, relative to his starting place, if he took:

one step east
one step north
one step east
one step south
one step east.

Here too, subjects report more than one solution strategy (Wood and Wood, 1976). Twenty-two out of twenty-four subjects reported a representational approach in which they attempted to construct a "map" or "grid" incorporating each successive step. Another technique (again, only with *visual* presentation) was akin to the positional, search technique found with the series problems and it involved "search and delete" operations. One subject explained the approach particularly clearly: "There's no sense in taking a step 'north' if I'm going to have to step 'south' again. I look at norths and souths and cancel them out and I remember if any are left. Then I do the same with easts and wests. What I'm left with is the answer." Another subject went further: "Norths and souths stick out further than easts and wests." And that, of course, makes cancelling out easier. Here too the subject is searching systematically, mentally "blanking out" those complementary pairs of statements which can be deleted. On the first five of sixty problems, eight out of twelve female subjects reported a change to this approach. By that time, none of the twelve men had done so, although nearly all of them did by the time they had solved fifteen problems. So, women changed strategy significantly earlier than men even though, as with the series problems, initial reports suggested *spatial* strategies in which men supposedly excel. And, on the very first problem, eleven of the female subjects complained about the problems and expressed doubts about their ability to solve them. None of the men did so. Here, then, women seem to be developing a new technique *before* protracted experience and any possible benefits of hindsight. The result of this was a significant interaction between "sex" and "experience". Men started relatively faster but finished relatively slower.

Parenthetically, it is perhaps worth noting the implication of this result for discussions about sex differences in intellectual ability and about the relationships between hemispheric dominance and intellectual performance. Evidence favouring the view that men on average are superior to women on tests of spatial ability is overwhelming (e.g. Hutt, 1972). However, *task* classification which underlies any predictions about likely sex differences is another matter. While there may well be functional connections between cerebral hemispheres and intellectual performance, without an effective task taxonomy we cannot expect to predict how well each sex will do in a particular situation. And "face" inspection of tasks is a poor basis for classification without a knowledge of the strategies that subjects are likely to bring to bear in their attempts to solve them.

In conclusion then, it seems that we can understand *some* aspects of strategy change in terms of relatively straightforward processes of hindsight and reflective abstraction. There are occasions where subjects achieve a level of experience and skill with a problem solving technique which enables them to anticipate regular patterns and contingencies in their mental activity. They are then able to exploit these in various ways, by *recoding* the problem space, perhaps, or by pruning away whole sequences of operations which, in the given context, always yield predictable outcomes. But there are other factors involved too. Subjects may bypass extended experience with a "primitive" method to develop a new one. Thus, they presumably entertain more than one hypothesis about the task, each of which may be developed into a strategy. Another crucial question concerns the subject's own conception of his behaviour. We know that they may plan their problem solving beyond the level of a single move and, consequently, any attempt to characterize processes of self-description and evaluation must gain access to this level of organization. All this moves our attention away from a formal description of the task itself to a consideration of the knowledge and experience of the would-be problem solver.

An effective characterization of mental activity in problem solving must look, then, beyond the mere application of operations to representations of the problem. In the language of linguistics, problem solving involves a "topic-comment" structure in which the thinker not only applies operations to transform the problem space but also attempts to construct a model of his own activity as he does so. The studies of strategy development represent one attempt to externalize these processes. But there are relevant studies elsewhere, in the field of Developmental Psychology, where the debate about the connections between cultural and cognitive variables has generated a series of studies designed to investigate the "socialization of cognitive modes" in development. They are concerned in part with the identification of the factors acting in development which shape the flexibility and "generativity" of thinking, and viewed from this perspective they complement the problem solving studies just outlined.

4. CULTURE AND THOUGHT

Members of Western culture, in general, and subjects in psychology experiments, in particular, tend to be habitual problem solvers. Such is the uncertainty of their lives that they must continually meet and master unfamiliar situations. In our working lives, many of us must adapt to new knowledge, techniques and tools, develop new routines and change old habits. In our social and interpersonal lives, we are continually meeting new people, encountering strangers who have lived through experiences which we did not share, but with whom we must communicate and cooperate. Much of our interaction, commerce and coordination with others is governed by tacit definitions of office and role; by special knowledge and expertise rather than by familiarity, common experience and personally negotiated contracts. In such situations, our dealings with others can seldom be governed entirely by shared habits and values; rather we must often appeal to the force of rational argument and to abstract laws. In our handling of the world we must be prepared to adapt and transfer experience from one domain to another, to develop and use general purpose tools and operations fitted to a range of task situations. In other, less technological societies such uncertainties are relatively rare. The skills needed for survival in an environment that changes only by season and the vicissitudes of nature remain relatively stable. Interpersonal contact in a geographically constrained group is grounded in continuous contact and shared experiences and is basically predictable.

A number of cross-cultural studies have suggested that these idealized differences in cultural design go hand-in-hand with differences in intellectual capacities and problem solving ability. In their studies of the Kpelle in central Liberia, for example, Cole and his colleagues gave a range of tasks and problems to various individuals to reveal quite substantial differences between Kpelle and Western thinking (Cole *et al.*, 1974). One class of problems, for example, were syllogisms of the following general kind:

Experimenter: Flumo and Yakpalo always drink cane juice (rum) together. Flumo is drinking cane juice. Is Yakpalo drinking cane juice?

Subject: The day that Flumo was drinking the cane juice Yakpalo was not there on that day.

Experimenter: What is the reason?

Subject: The reason is that Yakpalo went to his farm on that day and Flumo remained in town on that day (pp. 187–188 in Cole *et al.*, 1974).

Replies were seldom compelling. Rather, they reflected a comparison of what was said with reality and personal knowledge. The reply may have been *plausible* but not logically necessary. Cole and his colleagues used several different variants of such problems trying to employ terms and characters which would be familiar to the Kpelle in an attempt to overcome any misunderstandings which they might have about nature of the task being set, but to no avail. The Kpelle it seems, in company with other non-literate, unschooled peoples did not appreciate that force of logical necessity in the statements which, to Western minds, seems so natural. Such deductions or inferences, it seems, do not arise spontaneously out of linguistic experiences or internalized actions; rather they seem to be dependent on certain specific forms of cultural experience. They are essentially strategic in nature.

There have been at least two hypotheses about the processes underlying such differences. Greenfield and Bruner (1969) have argued that the mediating factor is the form of instruction characteristically employed in a culture. In traditional or non-technological societies the child learns the skills he will need to survive by a process more akin to induction than instruction. There are no schools, no one person specializes in the instruction of the young and learning is not seen as a distinct process at all. The child is simply expected to find his own place in society, naturally acquiring those skills and the knowledge that he will eventually need to play a full part in it. He learns in context, often by observing and being helped by those who are slightly more advanced and skilled than he is. Such help is seldom verbal in nature and is closely tied to the immediate practical content. His actions and operations are thus not linguistically encapsulated, not coded into language beyond the pragmatic demands of face-to-face communication. In a schooled culture on the other hand, much of what is learnt is out of context and direction and feedback are often social in origin. There is a push towards the representation of absent events and the mental manipulation of these. There is a splitting-off of word and referent increasing the psychological distance between language and the events or objects to which it refers. Thinking and learning become distinct processes to be described, analysed and evaluated. In parallel with Luria's (1961) hypothesis about the "second signal" properties of language, Bruner and Greenfield see in this growing emphasis on language and linguistic feedback the generation of new levels of mental activity. Linguistic symbols can be decontextualized, once "liberated" from practical contexts they can be easily juxtaposed and transferred to produce creative combinations of elements of experience in a manner not possible before. The strategic use of knowledge is thus tied to patterns of instruction and learning. It is simply not sufficient that an individual possesses the operations which are logically necessary to solve a problem. For "knowing how" resides also in the manner of its acquisition. The capacity to transfer experience from one domain to another depends on the way in which experience is conceived which, in turn, resides in processes of communication and instruction. For Bruner, then, the nature of knowledge itself is fundamentally changed by the advent of schools and those processes which the presence of schools entails.

Schooling, of course, is contaminated with other variables, rendering any causal explanation hazardous. Generally speaking, the advent of schools within a society accompanies a shift from ascribed to achieved roles, indicating a fundamental change in economic and political structure. It also goes hand-in-hand with literacy and other depersonalized media for the transmission of information. Olson (1975) has recently argued that it is literacy, in fact, which underlies the hypothetical, stage-like shifts in thinking across societies.

The unschooled, illiterate Kpelle (and pre-literate children) fail to respond logically to questions, according to Olson, because they lack a capacity to *represent* hypothetical situations *and* the competence needed to subject these to logically disciplined interrogation. Logical operations arise from literacy, because the printed word permits the individual to transcend the temporal and spatial limitations inherent in speech and common-sense knowledge. The literate thinker is able to check back over previous thoughts and to relate experiences removed in time when inconsistencies and illogicalities in his thinking are apparent. With literacy comes a new perspective on experience which comes to be treated in a *hypothetical* spirit, answerable not to reality, actuality and plausibility but to internal coherence and logical consistency. It is difficult to see, however, how literacy could lead to a sense of logical compulsion without an existing competence for making such judgements. How does the individual come to realize that different states of affairs could not coexist logically if he did not possess already a sense of logical coherence, one based on "common sense" knowledge? Whilst it is possible, say, to see necessity arising out of the fabric of sensory motor experiences, a formalization of the constraints which have been found to govern activity in the world, it is difficult to see how it could arise out of marks on paper, if these did not, in turn, excite such a more primitive, everyday basis for logical necessity. A weaker interpretation of Olson's position is that the presence of literacy helps articulate and formalize logic on a new and more abstract plane. If so, what we are discussing is not the development of logical necessity *per se*, but its expression at a more abstract level.

Both Olson and Bruner see a causal relationship, then, between forms of language use and general aspects of strategic thinking. The manner in which language is used to code experience underlies the capacity to generalize, to transfer knowledge from one domain to another and to solve problems, particularly where these demand the construction and disciplined interrogation of hypothetical representations. The thinker must be capable of taking on a particular attitude towards his own experience and knowledge if he is to free operations from one context for use in another and he must have been enjoined to conceptualize, describe and evaluate his own experience in a particular way during development if he is to be capable of this. Whether the primary influence supplying the push towards the establishment of the skills and operations underlying decontextualized thinking is schooling or exposure to the printed word we cannot say. What empirical evidence there is about the relationships between gross cultural variables like schooling, literacy and problem solving abilities is equivocal (e.g. Dasen, 1972). However, there does seem to be some measure of agreement that substantial differences do exist in the intellectual abilities of peoples in technological and non-technological societies (Dasen, 1972; Goodnow, 1969; Serpell, 1976). Goodnow's generalization still seems to hold up in the light of more recent studies. She argues that the major difference in the intellectual abilities of traditional and techno-logical societies reside in the capacity to mentally manipulate events:

> as we move away from a technological society there is not any overall lag or retardation . . . tasks not handled well outside the traditional (Western technological) group . . . seem to be predominantly tasks where the child has to transform an event in his head, has to shift or shuffle things around by some kind of visualising or imaging rather than by carrying out an overt series of changes (Goodnow, 1969, p. 249).

Elsewhere (Howarth and Wood 1977), we have argued that this generalization also fits the intellectual profile of congenitally deaf people, indicating that dislocations in normal patterns of communica-tion disrupt the development of such intellectual abilities. Again the argument is that the capacity to create abstract representations and to solve problems which demand other than a pragmatic, realistic and personal attitude towards the information given reside in patterns of social interaction and instruction.

5. INSTRUCTION AND PROBLEM SOLVING

The evidence demanded by a proper scientific attitude to this general thesis about the relationship between language and problem solving simply does not exist. Ideally, it should be shown that specific use of written language or particular styles of verbal instruction have pre-dictable effects on problem solving performance. It should clarify the variables underlying such effects and identify the problem solving processes which are being differentially effected. The cross-cultural research has not and arguably cannot provide such evidence. However, there is another line of research which has pursued very similar hypo-theses about the relationships between language and thought and this does go some way towards the provision of such evidence. A good deal of this work has been inspired by Bernstein's theory about the relation-ships between social class and language codes.

He has argued (Bernstein, 1961, 1960) that two distinct language "codes" can be identified in spoken English. One, the *elaborated code*, is essentially context free. So, anyone listening to the elaborated code speaker but not sharing his perceived or recalled experiences will none-theless be able to understand him. For elaborated code language approximates to written language in that, for example, it displays a preference for first references to objects by name rather than by gesture or pronoun. In elaborated speech, syntax bears a good deal of the burden for specifying semantic relations. The speaker does not assume that his listener is privy to information which will enable him to judge who is acting with what on whom, for example. The idealized *restricted code* user, on the other hand, does act in accordance with such assumptions. He uses fewer explicit labels and often fails to employ syntactic devices for specifying or disambiguating semantic relations. Bernstein's thesis is highly controversial, particularly in its suggestion that differences in language codes correlate with and help perpetuate social class differences (e.g. Labov, 1970). Elaborated code language is supposedly characteristic of the middle classes and embodies solutions to the problems of management, planning and control. Restricted code language is essentially working class, more pragmatic, task specific and adapted for face-to-face usage. Thus it is seen to be less adequate as a tool for the control and regulation of behaviour at a distance in time and space.

Bernstein's analysis leads us to examine the relationships between linguistic function and problem-solving competence. The explicitness of linguistic descriptions and instructions affect what is learned and remembered and the ease with which experiences in one situation can be related to that in others. Where the same explicit references are used in different contexts, for example, the problem of extracting common, recurrent features in experience, of establishing certain types of continuity and discontinuity, will be facilitated (and, of course, constrained). Where reference is more pragmatic and situation-specific the problem of appreciating patterns and regularities will be made more difficult. It can also be argued that the likelihood of a child's actions being placed in a wide temporal framework establishing a sense of continuity and planning is intimately dependent upon how language is deployed in relation to him. The strategic use of knowledge, a capacity to transfer knowledge from one context to another, fitting it to the demands of a new situation, is thus also tied to aspects of language use.

The thesis is, then, that the scope and generativity of thinking are determined by processes of socialization and in particular by the way in which language is used to coordinate and control behaviour. If Bernstein's thesis holds then it should follow that the processes of foresight, hindsight and reflective abstraction which we have placed at the heart of strategic development are rooted in patterns of social interaction and social control. But does it hold? A series of experiments performed in the 1960s gave encouraging support to Bernstein's central hypothesis. In one, for example, Hess and Shipman (1965, 1968) observed mothers and their children in an investigation of the relationships between maternal language and various aspects of the child's intellectual abilities. They found, as Bernstein had led them to expect, correlations between the two. Broadly speaking mothers displayed three different styles or strategies for instructing, controlling and helping their child. Some, for example, displayed a high proportion of elaborated code language and usually, when trying to instruct the child, they used invitations rather than orders to try and get him to do something. They tended to be highly task-oriented, continuaiiy reminding the child of the overall goal and relating his current task efforts to this in an explicit task analysis. They tended to underline the intrinsic rewards arising out of successful task completion, adopting a decentred or non-personal perspective. Other mothers, however, tended to emphasize rewards which were extrinsic to the task itself (e.g. doing something because it would please mummy or the experimenter). They adopted restricted code language, ordering rather than inviting. In short, different mothers placed their child's behaviour in totally different perspectives or plans, plans varying in specificity and generality, in the depth of forward-planning and the degree of decontextualization that they tacitly offered the child.

These differences in maternal teaching strategies correlated with several aspects of the child's problem solving style. For example, when asked to *sort* objects, the children of mothers who emphasized intrinsic reward factors tended to offer a formal, explicit category system. Those whose mothers had emphasized extrinsic personal reasons for doing things tended, on the other hand, to use more idiosyncratic and informal criteria, *classifying*, for example, according to whether they possessed an object of the same type or not. There are also low but significant correlations between the child's performance on intelligence tests and the incidence of elaborated code language.

Other studies have produced strikingly similar results to those of Hess and Shipman (e.g. Bee *et al.*, 1969; Haavind and Hartmann, 1977). Unfortunately, there are many problems in the interpretation and evaluation of these studies. In the first place it is difficult to estimate how representative the rather artificial laboratory observations are of anything enduring in the parent/child relationship. Are they merely tapping the adults' attitudes or expectations about what the experimenter is seeking, or really revealing behavioural predelictions for helping and controlling the child? And there are other methodological and conceptual problems which caution against too ready an acceptance of the evidence apparently favouring the Bernstein thesis. Behaviour of mother and child is interdependent and the use of correlational techniques as a basis for statements about causation is unsound. Behaviour of both mother and child might be expressions of underlying genetic factors, effective instruction and effective learning being bound by heritability. Or it may be that the child who is good at problem solving helps shape a mother who seems to teach well. There are problems too in estimating the scope of those factors which supposedly influence problem solving performance. Early work seemed to suggest that the differences revealed between subgroups of the culture were qualitative and all-or-none. In fact, the use of language by the two groups is somewhat context specific and there are occasions when both utilize elaborated code language (Labov, 1970). Nonetheless as Cole and Bruner (1975) have pointed out, it still seems to be the case that social class differences in use of language do extend over those situations which are most likely to shape the child's reactions to a formal school situation and other public domains, where his future is being decided. They would still argue that the capacity for setting up and solving problems, making creative and productive use of personal experience in the service of arbitrary problematic situations, relates to differences in forms of language use. However, it seems to be the case that the influence of language on problem solving may be much more task specific than was originally supposed.

This conclusion also accommodates the results of other empirical studies (e.g. Jones, 1972) which have failed to discover correlations between measures of children's linguistic ability and their capacity to solve some types of problems, namely those used by Piaget to diagnose concrete operational thinking. It seems, in fact, that cultural and social class differences exert little influence over a range of problems which essentially demand that the thinker construct *practical* models of reality and run this mentally to produce predictions and expectations about the outcome of events. However, where the problem is more abstract and calls for a hypothetical attitude to information and the use of logic to govern "non-sensical" events, then cultural and social factors do seem to play a central part. Furthermore, as we saw in the first section of this chapter, there is often more than one strategy for solving a problem. The relationship between problem solving performance and social-linguistic factors is more likely, perhaps, to operate at the level of strategy rather than that of sheer competence. In other words, by leaving out the possibility of strategic differences in problem solving, studies of the relationships between language and thought may have masked the very links they were supposedly investigating.

More recent studies of the relationships between social interaction and problem solving have overcome some of the methodological difficulties which characterized the earlier work, though they have not convincingly overcome the conceptual difficulty contingent on the use of correlational methods. Haavind and Hartmann (1977) using a Norwegian sample, performed another study in the Hess and Shipman tradition but with a number of methodological changes. Most important of these was the separation of mother and child in their observations, thus overcoming at least some of the problems of inter-dependency of behaviour. They observed the mother teaching a stranger child while her own was being taught by an experimenter. They used factor analytic techniques to reveal three teaching strategies used by mothers. These corresponded roughly to those identified by Hess and Shipman. They also found three factors in their descriptions of the children's use of the experimenter and quite striking correlations across mother/child behaviour. For example, where a mother charac-teristically approached the task of helping the child by a rational, pragmatic and a forward-looking technique, one which emphasized reasons, her child was also likely to display a similar pattern in his own interrogation and exploitation of the teacher. Rather than waiting passively to be told what to do or acting on impulse, as children taught by less effective strategies tended to do, he was more likely to operate analytically, to look and ask for reasons, giving evidence of thinking ahead.

The major implication, like that from Hess and Shipman's study and a good deal of intervening work, is that different adults place children's activities in the context of plans varying in scope and analytical specificity. Some enjoin the child to see his current efforts in an extended framework, relating it *forward* to future goals and operations and reflecting *back* to the child in rational terms what he has done and how he has performed as seen from the vantage point of someone more task-effective than himself. Other adults place the child's actions in a more limited programme, operating very much on the basis of the here-and-now and talking, not from an abstract analysis of the task, but from their own immediate perceptions of task requirements. These planning and controlling activities are supposedly internalized by the child thus tending to perpetuate the cognitive style of his "teachers". The work of Haavind and Hartmann suggests that the teaching style of the mother is a trait in that the strategy she uses generalizes to other children whom she has never met before. And her child's responses to her also generalize, helping to dictate further what he will learn from his instructional contacts with others.

In spite of improvements in methodology, however, neither this nor other contemporary studies can claim to have overcome the basic conceptual difficulties which such research faces. The fundamental problem is how to analyse the behaviour of two interacting systems, given that each can have both long- and short-term effects on the actions and interactions of the other. This analysis needs to be translated both into statistical techniques and suitable empirical methods of investigation. Today, so far as the present writer knows, no such analysis exists. There is, however, at least one way of steering around this conceptual wrangle. If we cannot properly analyse causation from observations of "spontaneous" interaction, what we can do is to try and idealize those aspects of the interaction which are supposedly having the differential effects, express these as formally stated teaching strategies and then see if we can administer these with the predicted results to matched subjects. There have been at least two attempts to follow this general strategy, one working with face-to-face teaching of pre-schoolers (Wood and Middleton, 1975; Wood et al., 1976; Wood et al., 1978) and the other in the classroom (Wright and Nuthall, 1970; Nuthall and Church, 1973). Such studies, of course, do not tell us how the initial correlations came about nor could they establish the original direction of causation. What they do do, however, is demonstrate whether the patterns of instruction per se are affecting the dependent measures.

In the study of face-to-face teaching with pre-schoolers Wood et al. (1976) looked at the techniques used by mothers to teach their own child how to solve a complex construction problem. The most important aspect of effective instruction, according to this study, was not simply a particular style or code of language use, but the sensitivity of the instructor to the child's ever-changing level of task mastery, which involved them in both verbal and non-verbal instruction. As in earlier studies, the mothers who were really effective in teaching their child how to solve the problem displayed a good, tacit task analysis; a knowledge of how to break the task down into useful subgoals for the child. Such mothers systematically varied the specificity of their verbal and non-verbal help tending to decrease control (i.e. setting more "remote" subgoals) after the child successfully followed an instruction and becoming more controlling immediately he failed to do so. So, although the ultimate outcome might have been a capacity on the child's part to understand the task in analytic, formal terms, he arrived at that knowledge by a process of negotiation from shared, overt activities, through specific verbal suggestions to the comprehension of very general prompts and instructions.

There were various ways in which mothers biased this contingent strategy. Some relied on a higher incidence of verbal help; some tried demonstration almost exclusively, and so on. These various patterns were idealized and expressed as four teaching strategies. When a trained teacher used these to instruct matched groups of children, the results were as predicted. Patterns of instruction per se were instrumental in determining rate of task mastery.

The New Zealand studies by Nuthall and his colleagues are much more extensive and representative of real educational activities. They observed teachers giving classes in various subjects—natural history and electromagnetism, for example, using an elaborate coding system to describe their behaviour. When they compared these descriptions with the child's memory for material given in the lesson they found several correlations. One, for example, was a positive relationship between the teacher's use of "closed" questions (which essentially left the children with only one degree of freedom when answering) and the children's retention of relevant material. The use of *open* questions, which involved subquestions in their answer, was negatively correlated. However, in another study, they found that the most effective teaching strategy seemed to vary according to the objective being pursued by the teacher. Where the teacher was trying to present the children with material to prompt them to think about it and consider its implications rather than to remember it, then the frequency of open questions went up and that of closed questions down, and the children's use of logical argument (as indicated by the frequency with which they used logical connectives) was, this time, positively correlated with frequency of open questions. When teachers were specifically asked to adopt one objective rather than the other, they varied their behaviour appropriately, and with it that of their children. When scripts of such lessons were used to teach other, independent groups of children, they too displayed the predicted relative capacities to remember and reason. Again, style of instruction, as identified, was central to the learning process. What the children learned and how far they were overtly pre-disposed to reason about the material hinged on strategy of presentation.

The work of Nuthall suggests that we might do well to question the wisdom of single-factor explanations as an adequate explanatory basis for the effects of instruction of cognitive growth. Different activities, it seems, are best fostered by quite different strategies of teaching. Possibly, it means that intellectual activities like remembering and reasoning do not have a common ontogenesis.

6. INTERVENTION AND ITS EFFECTS

The great weakness of such studies, of course, is that they have only established, as yet, short-term and relatively specific effects. However, there have been other attempts, on a much larger scale, to engineer more fundamental and long-lasting effects. Working from ideas like Bernstein's various intervention programmes have taken place with the aim of modifying, extending and improving the intellectual and linguistic abilities of "deprived" children.

In a recent endeavour along these lines, Tough (1977) has itemized various linguistic functions which, she claims, are differently distributed across the speech of children from different social classes. For example, over 70% of verbal exchanges from lower-class children were distributed over just three functions—"self-maintaining", "monitoring their own actions" and "identifying present objects or events". In other words, they seemed pre-occupied with the "personal" and the here and now, paying little apparent attention to the past, future or to other people's perspective. Advantaged children, on the other hand, distributed their utterances over a wider range of her functions, being particularly more active in "predictive" activities and in monitoring and anticipating the future consequences of their intended actions. They also displayed a much higher incidence of logical reasoning and made more detailed analyses of the objects and events around them. Tough's goal is to work with primary school teachers in order to develop their strategies for interacting with children, "pushing" the disadvantaged child, through verbal interchanges, to explore those functions which he supposedly lacks.

It is too early to say whether Tough's approach will have any real effects on the intellectual abilities of children. However, numerous past studies (*see* Tizard, 1975; Woodhead, 1977) have all produced relatively consistent results. Basically, while they usually have managed to have the desired effects on measures of intellectual and linguistic abilities during the period of intervention, shortly after active intervention had ceased the effects were washed out. It *is* possible, then, to have predetermined effects on children's measured abilities, but it is clear that the problem of engineering lasting changes has been far from solved. Either the abilities involved are too complex to be handled through short-term intervention or we simply do not know how to pass on psychological knowledge to those who continue to have responsibility for children after the psychologist leaves the scene. In any event, it is clear that one mental "shot in the arm" is not good enough to counteract the supposed differences in the children's backgrounds. If it *is* the form of control and dialogue which underlies effective problem solving and thinking, then it is a dialogue which must continue extensively through the period of the child's intellectual development.

7. SUMMARY

The numerous studies which started in the early 1960s and are continuing in the 1970s, looking at the relationships between the child's capacities to solve certain types of problem and the way in which his behaviour is monitored and assisted by those around him during development, have produced quite strikingly similar and consistent results. Although the correlation-cause issue has not been resolved, what evidence we have, though inconclusive as it stands, suggests that when we simulate those strategies which both theoretically and empirically go together with effective learning we can use them with predictable results. In other words, it does seem to be patterns of instruction *per se* which underlie the effective transmission of knowledge about how to solve problems. Whilst attempts to change the intellectual capacities of "underprivileged" children have not produced lasting changes they have, generally speaking, obtained the expected effects in the short term. And it may well be that the failure of intervention studies results from our poor techniques for "giving psychology away" than it does from a lack of knowledge about the factors which influence intellectual development. In sum, then, while the thesis with which I opened this chapter concerning the two levels or types of mental activity in problem solving has not been proved beyond proper doubt, it has held up reasonably well against numerous lines of investigation.

The concept of "strategy" serves as a useful construct mediating the relationships between cultural and educational factors on the one hand and mature, directed thinking on the other. The effective problem solver has a range of potential experiences upon which to draw as he attempts to solve his problem. And his behaviour is open-ended, in the sense that the act of problem solving or attempted problem solving itself furnishes fresh data from which he can invent new codings or representations of the problem space and new, perhaps task-specific operations, for manipulating these. A fresh juxtaposition of old experiences and the accumulation of new ones potentially creates new distinctions in the problem space, and highlights new features. Many of the operations manufactured in this way and codings achieved will be dispensed with once the task at hand is over. But where such new discoveries lead to the solution of common, important problems or to the invention of new ones they will obviously be exploited. Words may be invented to label both those features which have gained new significance and the tools or operations which have been designed to operate on these. A new technology will be created. But this type of constant growth and exploitation through problem solving is a cultural phenomenon. The "scientific", hypothetico-deductive thinking which it demands, the ability to create representations of, as yet, imaginary states of the world and the capacity to subject these to disciplined logical interrogation rest in certain cultural factors. They are not "natural" achievements in that they do not grow out of "ordinary" sensory-motor experience in the physical world. The proposition which has been explored here is that they are, in fact, the outgrowth of relatively specific aspects of socialization and language use.

Perhaps when we have achieved a richer and more convincing characterization of the intellectual processes which underlie intelligent problem solving, we will be able to go back to a study of development with a more articulate set of questions. If we ever do, what we discover will not only increase our knowledge of the processes of growth, but will also put into our hands the knowledge we need to become better and fairer educators.

ACKNOWLEDGEMENTS

The work on adult problem solving referred to in the chapter was financed by grants from the Science Research Council. The studies of face-to-face teaching strategies with pre-school children was financed by Grant No. HR 2520/2 from the Social Science Research Council. The chapter is a modified version of the Spearman Medal Lecture given to the British Psychological Society at York in April 1976, with the title "Nurturing Nature".

REFERENCES

Bee, H. L., Van Egeren, L. F., Streissguith, A. P., Nyman, B. A. and Leckie, M. S. (1969). Social class differences in maternal teaching strategies and speech patterns. *Developmental Psychology* **1**, 726–734.

Bernstein, B. (1960). Language and social class. *British Journal of Sociology* **2**, 217–276.

Bernstein, B. (1961). Social class and linguistic development: A theory of social learning. *In* "Economy, Education and Society" (A. H. Halsey, J. Floud and C. Anderson, eds). Free Press of Glencoe.

Bruner, J. S., Wallach, M. A. and Galanter, E. H. (1959). The identification of recurrent regularity. *American Journal of Psychology* **72**, 200–209.

Bryan, W. L. and Harter, N. (1897). Studies of the telegraphic language: the acquisition of a hierarchy of habits. *Psychological Review* **6**, 545–575.

Chomsky, N. (1965). "Aspects of the Theory of Syntax". M.I.T. Press, Cambridge, Massachusetts.

Clark, H. H. (1969). The influence of language in solving three term series problems. *Journal of Experimental Psychology* **82**, 205–215.

Cole, M. and Bruner, J. S. (1975). Cultural differences and inferences about psychological processes. *American Psychologist* **26**, 10, 867–876.

Cole, M., Gay, J. A., Glick, J. A. and Sharp, D. W. (1974). "The Cultural Context of Learning". Methuen, London.

Dasen, P. R. (1972). Cross-cultural Piagetian research: a summary. *Journal of Cross-Cultural Psychology* **3**, 23–40.

De Soto, C. B., London, M. and Nandel, S. (1965). Social reasoning and spatial paralogic. *Journal of Personality and Social Psychology* **2**, 513–521.

Goodnow, J. (1969). Cultural variations in cognitive Skills. *In* "Cross-Cultural Studies" (H. Price-Williams, ed). Penguin, Harmondsworth.

Greenfield, P. M. and Bruner, J. S. (1969). Culture and cognitive growth. Reprinted in "Beyond the Information Given" (J. Anglin, ed.). Norton, New York.

Greeno, J. G. (1974). Hobbits and Orcs: acquisition of a sequential concept. *Cognitive Psychology* **6**, 270–292.

Haavind, H. and Hartmann, H. (1977). Mothers as teachers and their children as learners. Paper to the XXI'st Congress of Psychology, Paris, June, 1976.

Hess, R. D. and Shipman, V. C. (1965). Early experience and socialization of cognitive modes in children. *Child Development* **36**, 869–886.

Hess, R. D. and Shipman, V. C. (1968). Maternal influences upon early learning: the cognitive environments of urban pre-school children. *In* "Early Education" (R. D. Hess and R. M. Bear, eds). Aldine, Chicago.

Howarth, C. I. and Wood, D. J., (1977). Research into the intellectual abilities of deaf children. *Teacher of the Deaf* **1**, 5–12.

Hunter, I. M. L. (1957). The solving of three term series problems. *British Journal of Psychology* **48**, 286–298.

Hutt, C. (1972). "Males and Females". Penguin Books, Harmondsworth.

Huttenlocher, J. (1968). Constructing spatial images: a strategy in reasoning. *Psychological Review* **75**, (6), 550–560.

Huttenlocher, J. and Strauss, S. (1968). Comprehension: relations between perceived actor and logical subject. *Journal of Verbal Learning and Verbal Behavior* **7**, 527–530.

Jones, P. A. (1972). Formal operational reasoning and the use of tentative statements. *Cognitive Psychology* **3**, 467–471.

Labov, W. (1970). The logical non-standard English. *In* "Language and Poverty" (F. Williams, ed.). Markham, Chicago.

Luria, A. R. (1961). "The Role of Speech in the Regulation of Normal and Abnormal Behaviour". Pergamon Press, London.

Miller, G. A., Galanter, E. and Pribram, K. H. (1960). "Plans and the Structure of Behaviour". Holt, New York.

Nuthall, G. and Church, J. (1973). Experimental studies of teaching behaviour. *In* "Towards a Science of Teaching" (G. Chanan, ed.). NFER, Slough.

Olson, D. R., (1975). The languages of experience: on natural language and formal education. *Bulletin of the British Psychological Society* **28**, 363–373.

Olson, D. R. and Bruner, J. S. (1974). Learning through experience and learning through media. *In* "Media and Symbols: The Forms of Expression, Communication and Education" (D. Olson, ed.). University of Chicago Press, Chicago.

Quinton, G. and Fellows, B. J. (1975). Perceptual strategies in the solving of three-term series problems. *British Journal of Psychology* **66**, 1, 69–78.

Serpell, R. (1976). "Culture's Influence on Behaviour". Methuen Essential Psychology, London.

Simon, H. A. (1975). The functional equivalence of problem solving skills. *Cognitive Psychology* **7**, 268–288.

Simon, H. A. and Reed, S. K. (1976). Modelling strategy shifts in problem solving task. *Cognitive Psychology* **8**, 86–97.

Thomas, J. C. (1974). An analysis of behaviour in the hobbits–orcs problem. *Cognitive Psychology* **6**, 265–269.

Tizard, B. (1975). "Early Childhood Education". Education Research Board of the Social Science Research Council.

Tough, J. (1977). "The Development of Meaning". Unwin, London.

Wason, P. C. and Johnson-Laird, P. N. (1972). "Psychology of Reasoning". Batsford, London.

Willmot, C. (1975). Eye movements in problem solving. Dissertation, Dept. of Psychology, University of Nottingham.

Wood, D. J. (1969a). Approach to the study of reasoning. *Nature* **223**, 101–102.

Wood, D. J. (1969b). The nature and development of problem solving strategies. Ph.D. Thesis, University of Nottingham.

Wood, D. J. and Middleton, D. J. (1975). A study of assisted problem solving. *British Journal of Psychology* **66**, 2, 181–191.

Wood, D. J. and Shotter, J. D. (1973). A preliminary study of distinctive features in problem solving. *Quarterly Journal of Experimental Psychology* **25**, 504–510.

Wood, D. J. and Wood, H. A. (1976). A study of sex differences in reasoning. Paper read to the *British Psychological Society*, April, Nottingham.

Wood, D. J., Shotter, J. S. and Godden, D. (1974). An investigation of the relationships between problem solving strategies, representation and memory. *Quarterly Journal of Experimental Psychology* **26**, 252–257.

Wood, D. J., Bruner, J. S. and Ross, G. (1976). The role of tutoring in problem solving. *Journal of Child Psychology and Psychiatry* **17**, (2), 89–100.

Wood, D. J., Wood, H. A. and Middleton, D. J. (1978). An experimental evaluation of four face-to-face teaching strategies (in press).

Woodhead, M. (1977). "Intervening in Disadvantage". NFER, Slough.

Wright, C. J. and Nuthall, G. (1970). The relationships between teacher behaviour and pupil achievement in three elementary science lessons. *American Educational Research Journal* **7**, 477–491.

Eleven

Strategies and the Structure of a Cognitive Skill

Richard M. Young
University of Edinburgh

1. PRELIMINARIES

1.1. Introduction: strategies in cognitive skill

The notion of *strategy* is intimately bound up with the fact that many tasks can be carried out in several different ways. Although it may still be linguistically correct to refer to "the strategy" used to perform a task that can be done in only one way, the idea of strategy is of interest to psychologists mainly in cases where there is some degree of choice, so that what method will be adopted on a particular occasion is not always known beforehand. One approach to dealing with such cases

357

is to classify the different methods, and to suppose that everyone has at his command a number of different strategies from which he chooses according to the occasion. Regarded in this way, each strategy is seen as a self-contained module of problem-solving ability, pertaining to a particular task or part of a task. The analogy between such strategies and the *subroutines* used by computer programmers to organize large programs has been widespread for a while now, both in cognitive psychology (e.g. Miller *et al.*, 1960) and in the study of motor skills (e.g. Connolly, 1971).

From this starting point, it is but a small step to a position where one treats these strategies as part of the actual structure of a person's ability, or in other words regards his problem-solving skill as being organized into a collection of subroutines. Even so, this step is logically unwarranted, and the position it leads to is misleading or even factually wrong. To take the step is to adopt the view, widely held though rarely explicitly stated, that strategies are psychologically real.

One purpose of the present chapter is to argue against this view of cognitive skill. The argument centres round an experimental and theoretical analysis of a particular cognitive skill, that of *length seriation* (Young, 1976). The task studied was one where 4- to 6-year-old children are presented with a heap of wooden blocks of different lengths and asked to arrange them in a straight line in order of size. Seriation was originally introduced into the literature by Piaget, two of whose books report studies dealing with the task (Piaget, 1952; Inhelder and Piaget, 1964). For Piaget, the ability to seriate is of great importance for the child and underlies many of the other operations of concrete thinking. For instance, seriation and classification together provide the twin supports on which the child's (or the adult's) conception of number is based. For an investigation into the nature of cognitive skill, a developmental setting can be particularly fruitful since it provides an opportunity to observe the skill while it is still emerging and growing. Using either *cross-sectional* data from different groups of children of different ages, or *longitudinal* data from a single group of children at different times, it is comparatively easy to examine the skill at various points during its acquisition.

Our use of the term "cognitive skill" is intended as a deliberate reference to two traditions in cognitive psychology which provide the historical context for the work reported below. One tradition stems from the work of Bartlett. In his book *Thinking* (1958), he puts forward a view of cognition as a form of mental skill analogous to the more familiar notion of physical skill, and points out similarities between the two. The other tradition is the work of Piaget, which proposes a different view of the relationship between bodily movement and mental activity (*see*, e.g. Piaget and Inhelder, 1969). For Piaget, cognition is seen as an extension (rather than an analogy) of physical skill, thought being based on and developing out of a child's own sensory-motor activities. In studying a task such as seriation which on the one hand involves a considerable component of physical manipulation in addition to pure cerebration, and on the other is best studied in young children nearing their concrete-operational level of development, we are dealing with a topic to which both kinds of analysis can apply.

The general lay-out of this chapter is as follows. The rest of Section 1 is spent introducing a notation known as a *production system* (PS). Section 2 summarizes an experimental study in which PSs are used to analyse children's problem-solving behaviour and to describe the structure and acquisition of their seriation ability. The results of this study serve in Section 3 as the basis for some general observations on the nature of cognitive skill. In particular, the ability of PSs to exhibit different patterns of behaviour in different circumstances leads us to question the role of "strategies" in the organization of cognitive skill, and to propose an alternative view in which it is seen as a heterogeneous but adaptive collection of independent rules.

1.2. Production systems and protocol analysis

The starting point of the work described below is a recent theory of human problem solving developed by Newell and Simon (1972) which provides the basis for a new approach to the modelling of cognition. This approach typically involves the close analysis of an extended protocol of human problem-solving behaviour, followed by the construction of an information-processing model to reproduce the protocol as faithfully as is practicable.

A central technique in Newell and Simon's theory is the use of *production systems* to capture the regularities in a subject's behaviour. A production system (PS) is a set of rules expressing what the subject does under what conditions. Each rule is a condition–action statement of the form $C \Rightarrow A$, and means simply that in the circumstances specified by C the subject performs action(s) A. As a simple example, Newell and Simon give the following PS to describe the behaviour of a thermostat intended to keep the temperature of a room between 70° and 72°:

Th1: Temperature $< 70°$ and Furnace $=$ off $\Rightarrow$ Turn-on [Furnace]
Th2: Temperature $> 72°$ and Furnace $=$ on $\Rightarrow$ Turn-off [Furnace]

The action on the right-hand side of Th1 applies whenever the condition on its left is satisfied, and similarly for Th2.

A production system for a given task is an information processing model of the subject's cognitive processes, expressed in a form explicit enough to be programmed on a computer which can then be used to simulate the subject's behaviour. The use of such models in psychology is typically associated with the use of data from individual subjects rather than groups, and with a concern for the details of the subject's performance instead of just a summary measure like a pass/fail score or the time to completion. Unlike a *functional* approach, which tends to ask questions about the effects of various controllable factors on certain gross measures of the subject's performance—such as, does altering the size differences between the seriation blocks affect the time to solution?—the information processing approach prefers to ask questions directly about *how* the child is carrying out the task, seeking an answer in terms of the psychological processes and representations that underlie his behaviour. These concerns dictate the need to work with the detailed blow-by-blow record, or *protocol*, of the subject's behaviour, in the way pioneered by Newell and Simon.

The first work to make use of PSs was concerned with the analysis of verbal protocols gathered from adults tackling symbolic problems in crypt-arithmetic, formal logic and chess (Newell and Simon, 1972). More recently, this line of work has led to attempts to model the control of short-term memory (Newell, 1973a), the interface to the perceptual system (Newell, 1972a; Klahr, 1973) and the coding of visual information (Baylor, 1971; Moran, 1973). The research discussed below is concerned with a different application of PSs: their use in describing the course of cognitive development (Young, 1976). Cognitive development is among the potentially most fruitful topics to which the new information processing techniques are applicable (e.g. Farnham-Diggory, 1972). In part, this is because information processing psychologists have begun to recognize the significance of Piaget's developmental analysis of "genetic epistemology" (Piaget and Inhelder, 1969; Elkind and Flavell, 1969). But Piaget's formulations tend to remain at a rarified level of abstraction and, as has often been noted, it is hard to bring them into close contact with actual behaviour. This is especially frustrating from an information processing point of view, since Piaget seems so nearly to be talking in process terms. He deals with "representations", his "schemata" can be identified at least tentatively as fragments of program, and many of his observations seem to demand a processing explanation. Providing such an explanation consists of more than a mere "working out of the details" of Piaget's theories. It involves the challenging task of designing information processing models of cognitive development, based on Piaget's notions (modified where necessary), which serve both to explicate those notions in concrete terms and to square them with observed facts of human development.

This work on cognitive development extends the Newell and Simon analysis by dealing with the non-verbal protocols of children performing a manipulative task, rather than with the verbal protocols of adults working on symbolic mental puzzles. In this respect, it resembles Olson's (1970) analysis of children's attempts to copy a diagonal pattern, but of course is concerned with a much finer level of detail and adopts a quite different theoretical approach. Other groups using the PS technique to model cognitive development include Klahr and Wallace, and Baylor and his colleagues at the University of Montreal. Klahr and Wallace have been primarily concerned with the study of class inclusion (Klahr and Wallace, 1972) and with quantification processes—their origins, and their role in the development of conservation (Klahr and Wallace, 1976). Baylor has been examining seriation in a way complementary to the study reported here (Baylor and Gascon, 1974), and in particular has investigated the causes of the 2–4-year lag (known as *horizontal décalage*) between the ages at which children master length seriation and the seriation of weight (Piaget, 1952; Baylor and Lemoyne, 1975).

1.3. An example

An example of a PS used to analyse a seriation protocol may help to clarify some of the points made above. This example will deal explicitly with just a single seriation by one subject, although the analysis is in fact supported by consistent evidence from a number of trials with this same subject (Young, 1976).

Consider a seriation of six blocks carried out by a 5-year-old boy, Del. Figure 1 shows the lay-out of the blocks from Del's point of view. The blocks lying on the table drawn in solid lines show the initial configuration, and are labelled from A, the smallest block, to F, the largest; the box-like structure depicts the final seriated line, with all the blocks standing upright; and the dashed outline represents a block in a temporary intermediate position. Figure 2 presents a summary of Del's behaviour on the task, divided into *episodes* each concerned with the placing of one block.

It is not hard to summarize Del's seriation technique. As far as the choice of blocks is concerned, he starts with the biggest block in Episode 1 but thereafter simply takes successive blocks as they come to hand, regardless of their size. (The one exception is in Episode 5, where he picks block A instead of the nearer block D.) Each new block is added to the right-hand end of the line, and is accepted there provided

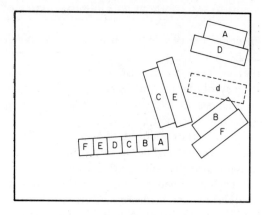

Fɪɢ. 1. Lay-out of Del's seriation.

that it preserves the ordering of the line (Episodes 2, 4 and 5). Other-
wise the new block is switched with its neighbour and then re-evaluated
(Episodes 3, 6), this switching being repeated as often as necessary
(Episode 6).

Before we look at the PS to model this performance, we must deal
briefly with a couple of technical points. First, we assume that behaviour
—that is, a production rule—is evoked always in the context of some
active *goal*. These goals are organized into a stack, so that whenever a
new goal is set up the old one is saved by being "pushed down" on the
stack. And conversely, when the active goal is satisfied it is "popped
off" the stack and the previous goal is reinstated.

Secondly, the matter of conflicts. Running a PS basically consists of
repeatedly finding the rule whose left-hand conditions are satisfied and
then executing the actions on its right. But it can sometimes happen that
two or more rules have their conditions satisfied at the same time, and
the question then arises as to which of them to evoke. It is necessary in
such cases to have some way of resolving the conflict. The convention
adopted here is to give priority to the rule whose conditions are the
most restrictive. The usual situation is that the conditions of one rule,
R1, are included in those of another, R2; in which case R2 is given
precedence when both apply. We will meet several examples of this in
just a moment. (Notice that other conventions are possible. For example
Baylor and Gascon (1974) follow Newell and Simon (1972) in *ordering*
their rules by priority, and then always choosing the highest-priority
rule whose conditions are satisfied.)

Figure 3 gives a PS to model Del's behaviour. The notation used is
fairly informal, and most of the rules should be self-explanatory. Rules

Episode	Summary	Line
1. Add F	Scan Pool Reach towards E Get F, put at left	
2. Add C	Get C, put next to F Examine	F C
3. Add E	Get E, put next to C Examine	F C E
	Switch C, E Examine	F E C
4. Add B	Get B, put next to C Examine	F E C B
5. Add A	Move D to d Get A, put next to B Examine	F E C B A
6. Add D	Get D, put next to A Examine	F E C B A D
	Switch A, D Examine	F E C B D A
	Switch B, D Examine	F E C D B A
	Switch C, D Examine	F E D C B A
	Straighten B, A	F E D C B A

FIG. 2. Summary of Del's seriation.

T1 through T2 are concerned with the cyclic behaviour of getting blocks from the pool and adding them to the line. P1 through PG3 govern the actual placing of the blocks, and finally rules B1 to B3 deal with the very first block. Rather than going through the whole PS and explaining the function of the rules one by one, let us watch what happens during a typical episode.

Suppose we plunge into the seriation at the beginning of Episode 3, when blocks F and C have already been placed. The top goal is SERIATE, and the only rule applicable is T1, so it fires off with the result that the active goal now becomes ADD.ONE. Now rule S1 is evoked, and Del reaches out and gets hold of the nearest block, E. At this point, rule S1 still has its condition satisfied, but so also does T2, which being more specific than S1 is therefore the next rule to fire:

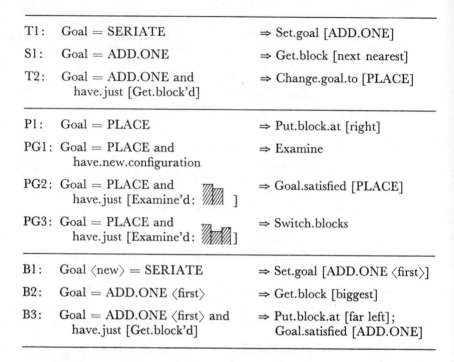

T1:	Goal = SERIATE	⇒ Set.goal [ADD.ONE]
S1:	Goal = ADD.ONE	⇒ Get.block [next nearest]
T2:	Goal = ADD.ONE and have.just [Get.block'd]	⇒ Change.goal.to [PLACE]
P1:	Goal = PLACE	⇒ Put.block.at [right]
PG1:	Goal = PLACE and have.new.configuration	⇒ Examine
PG2:	Goal = PLACE and have.just [Examine'd: ▨]	⇒ Goal.satisfied [PLACE]
PG3:	Goal = PLACE and have.just [Examine'd: ▨]	⇒ Switch.blocks
B1:	Goal ⟨new⟩ = SERIATE	⇒ Set.goal [ADD.ONE ⟨first⟩]
B2:	Goal = ADD.ONE ⟨first⟩	⇒ Get.block [biggest]
B3:	Goal = ADD.ONE ⟨first⟩ and have.just [Get.block'd]	⇒ Put.block.at [far left]; Goal.satisfied [ADD.ONE]

Fig. 3. Production system for Del's seriation.

the active goal now becomes PLACE. Rule P1 is evoked, and Del moves block E to the end of the line. This results in a "new configuration", so rule PG1 fires (taking precedence over the less specific P1) and Del examines the shape of the line in the vicinity of the block just added. The outcome satisfies the condition for rule PG3, so he switches blocks E and C. That switch yields another "new configuration", so PG1 fires and Del examines the line again. This time rule PG2 is evoked, so the goal of PLACE is satisfied and it is popped off the stack, returning Del to the context of the top goal of SERIATE. And so on. In Episode 6, rules PG1 and PG3 fire in alternation no less than three times.

Rules B1 to B3 deal with the treatment of the very first block, and are included to reflect the fact that Del (and other children) handle the first block in a distinctive way. Rules B1 and B2, which are evoked instead of T1 and S1, respectively, during the first episode, lead to the initial choice of the largest block, while B3 indicates that once found, that block is put over on the left of the table without the attention and checking that accompany the later placements.

2. EXPERIMENTAL ANALYSIS OF SERIATION

2.1. The experimental study

There are evidently close connections between the notion of strategy and Piaget's well-known idea of *stages* in cognitive development, since each stage is typically associated with, or even defined by, one or more characteristic strategies. As with the other concrete-operational skills, Piaget divides the development of seriation into three main stages. A child at *Stage I* is unable to construct an ordered line. At first he simply aligns the blocks in an arbitrary order. Later he may construct two or more short series which he cannot combine, or else a single series omitting some of the blocks. *Stage II* is the level of "empirical seriation". A child at this stage succeeds in building an ordered series, but does so by what Piaget calls "trial and error", that is, by repeated rearrangement of the blocks in the line being built (as we have just seen Del doing). "Operational" seriation makes its appearance in *Stage III*. A Stage III child seriates by choosing the blocks in order of size, and constructing the series step by step from the smallest block, say, to the largest. It is at this stage too that he is first able to insert further, intermediate blocks into an existing series.

It should be noted that the only seriation strategy accepted by Piaget as being "operational" is the one used in defining Stage III. This is a point we will return to later, in Section 3.2.

One can of course quarrel with Piaget's distinctions or attempt to refine them (Flavell, 1971; Pinard and Laurendeau, 1969), but in either case Piaget's classification provides a valuable starting point for characterizing a child's seriation ability. The classification is, though, concerned primarily with providing information about what one might call the outer aspects of seriation, such as what strategies get used and in what order they appear. The classification is less appropriate for answering questions about the inner aspects of seriation, questions for example concerning what the methods used in successive stages have in common, or how the transition from one stage to another takes place. Indeed, the division into discrete stages encourages one to regard the strategies as simply being *different*, and like Piaget, to talk of the transition from one stage to the next as involving a "restructuring" of the child's ability. But doing this raises more questions than it answers. The aim of the study reported here was to look at these inner matters more closely. The goal was to analyse the internal structure of the various methods of seriation, and to use these analyses to understand more deeply the relationship between successive stages.

2.1.1. Experimental methodology

The experiments consisted of giving 4- to 6-year-old children a series of seriation and seriation-like tasks, and observing their problem-solving behaviour. Subjects were run individually, in sessions lasting between 10 and 20 min. The whole of each session was recorded on videotape, allowing the experimenter to review it later as often as he needed. The recorded behaviour was later transcribed, then analysed and subjected to a detailed protocol analysis, as described above.

A special feature of the research is its concern for empirical validation. Whereas most other PS analyses have been content to take a protocol (or a set of protocols) from a subject and proceed from there to the PS analysis, this study used a kind of *adaptive experimentation* involving a much closer coupling between theory and data. The research attempted to provide empirical support for a proposed analysis of a child's seriation ability by examining his behaviour on a variety of problems related to the original task. For example, in addition to performing straightforward seriation, a child might be asked to seriate a set of blocks from which one of the middle-sized ones is missing, or to build the seriated line out of sight behind a screen. In attempting to analyse the data from a session, the experimenter would usually find himself without sufficient information to actually write a PS. So the child would return a few days later for a second experimental session, to face a series of problems devised expressly to resolve the points still at issue. This observation–analysis cycle could be repeated as often as necessary, though in practice most of the children ran in either two or three sessions.

2.1.2. Preliminary task analysis

Before we actually look at some sample protocols, it will prove helpful if we introduce a modest amount of terminology. In all cases of seriation to be considered, the initial heap of blocks, called the *pool*, is geographically distinct from the series being constructed, called the *line*, and the child performs the task by moving blocks one at a time between them. As was noted in the case of Del's seriation, the children's behaviour consists of a sequence of *episodes* each initiated by the selection of a block and terminated by its addition to the line (or sometimes its return to the pool). The course of behaviour within an episode is determined by three aspects of a child's skill: selection, evaluation and placement. Exploring the nature and details of these aspects is the purpose of the analysis about to be described, but we define here some of the terms associated with them:

Selection: the choice of which block to work with next. As was seen in Del's protocol, the choice is often based not on considerations of a block's size, but simply its location in the pool. In such a case, the block chosen is not necessarily physically the closest to the line, but simply the one that comes first to hand. This is referred to as *proximate* selection, or selection by *proximity*.

Evaluation: the decision whether or not to accept a block as a suitable addition to the line. If not, the block may be returned to the pool: this is called *rejection*. Blocks which are compared to their neighbours and judged to be too big or too small will be referred to as *oversize* or *undersize* respectively.

Placement: whereabouts in the growing line a block should be put. Sometimes a block may be put in one position, judged to be wrong, and then moved to another position: this is *correction*. *Insertion* is a special form of placement in which a block is positioned between two others.

The following sections, 2.2 to 2.4, consist of protocol analyses typical of those in the original study. They are given here to provide examples of the kind of evidence on which the discussion of Section 3 is based. But one cannot pretend that they make easy going, and on a first reading they can—and probably should—be omitted.

2.2. Alf's protocols: methods of empirical seriation

From the example of Del's seriation discussed earlier (summarized in Fig. 2), it is easy to classify him as being at the level of Piaget's Stage II, so-called trial-and-error seriation. We saw that once he had chosen and placed the biggest block, his selection thereafter was based on proximity and that in adding each block to the line he could start at one end and switch it with its neighbour as often as was necessary to bring it to the right position. But this is only one of several different possible ways of performing the task. In the rest of Section 2 we will be examining and analysing a sample of further seriation protocols that illustrate other ways of tackling the problem, not all of them necessarily successful. As well as providing some idea of the variety of seriation techniques to be met with in practice, these protocols also serve to illustrate how the technique of adaptive experimentation described was used to explore the structure of the children's ability. These protocols are all taken from the report of the original study (Young, 1976), to which the reader is referred for further details. We begin with some seriations by 5-year-old Alf.

During his first experimental session, Alf was given a number of problems involving the seriation of eight wooden blocks, A to H (A being the smallest and H the largest). Like Del, Alf would clearly be classified as being at Piaget's Stage II level of seriation. But his method differs from Del's in a number of interesting ways.

First, in the matter of selection, whereas Del merely takes whichever block comes first to hand, Alf makes a deliberate effort to choose a block of about the right size, which means in practice a block not too different to the last one he placed. Although he is definitely not following the operational method of always picking the largest block in the pool—in one protocol, for example, four out of ten selections from the pool were of blocks other than the biggest—neither is he choosing them at random. The block he picks is almost always a plausible candidate for the next position in the line. In the PSs this selection technique will be referred to as the operation of Get [suitable] (*see* rule S2 in Fig. 6). Alf also shows consistent evidence of a quite different kind of selection technique, in which he chooses any block which he happens to have "in mind" (*see* rule S3). A block is considered to be "in mind" if it has recently been attended to for any reason, for example, if it has been considered as a candidate for selection but eventually passed over, or if it has actually been tried but rejected. It should be noted that the plausibility of this technique is *psychological* rather than *logical*. It is easy to imagine why when Alf needs a block he goes back to one that he has been dealing with recently. What is less clear is that such a block is necessarily a good candidate for selection, though it is possible to visualize circumstances in which this would be the case. Anyway, this selection will be referred to as the operation of Get [in mind].

Secondly, in the matter of evaluation, whereas Del would accept any block provided it was smaller than its neighbour, Alf is more fussy about what he is prepared to regard as a correct addition to the line. For him, not only must the new block be smaller than its neighbour, it must also be not too much smaller. In his first three protocols, Alf consistently accepts a block as correct only if it is either one or two step sizes smaller than its neighbour.

Thirdly, Alf again differs from Del in the matter of correction. Whereas Del switches an oversize block with its neighbour until it is correctly positioned, Alf simply rejects a wrong block, i.e. moves it back to the pool. Because of this, if he happens to omit a block early on in the course of a seriation, it will simply be omitted from the line and left over at the end. It then has to be inserted into its correct position in a later episode that follows, and is distinct from, the main seriation itself. When doing this final insertion—or when simply asked to insert an extra block into a completed line—Alf makes use of a switching technique similar to Del's, but he never does this during the original seriation.

2.2.1. *Insertion and Screen tasks*

In addition to the standard seriation problem, Alf was given a number of variants of the task to probe into the different facets of his ability. His behaviour on the variants serves to confirm the description of his seriation skill just outlined. After his first seriation he was handed a further intermediate-sized block and asked to "Put this where it belongs". He readily did so, using a version of Del's switching technique. Next Alf was presented with the Screen task, in which the line being built is kept covered by a screen so that the subject is unable to see the blocks he has already placed. Alf's method of seriation depends crucially upon his getting visual feedback from the line he is building, so that when this is denied him the PS model of his skill (*see* Fig. 6) predicts that he will simply add blocks to the line one at a time, thereby constructing an unordered line. This is just what he did. He began well enough, placing first block H and then G next to it. But thereafter, as the line was kept hidden and the experimenter insisted that Alf not be allowed to peek behind the screen, he was unable to continue the seriation. He ceased all attempts to select blocks according to their size, merely placing them behind the screen in the order they came to hand. The result was the line D F A E B C G H.

2.2.2. *One Extra and One Missing tasks*

The next two problems are intended to diagnose Alf's seriation skill more finely, and to identify the information on which he bases his problem solving decisions. They are presented to him as straightforward replications of the original seriation task, but in fact one of them, the One Extra task, has two identical blocks D1 and D2 instead of the single block D, while in the other, the One Missing task, block D has been surreptitiously removed. In both cases, the principal contrast is with what would have happened if Alf had been using the operational method and choosing blocks from the pool in order of size. In the case of One Extra, the operational method would lead us to expect nothing out of the ordinary, since after blocks H, G, F and E had been placed, first one of the D blocks and then the other would be chosen as the largest remaining. (The only other possibility might be if Alf were to notice the identity of the two blocks *in the pool*, in which case he might be surprised.) In the event, what actually happens is quite different. One of the critical blocks, D1, gets selected early on, rejected, then reselected and placed after H, G and F. D2 is then selected, and it is only when the two D blocks are standing side by side *at the line* that Alf notices their similarity and reacts to it. After a certain amount of playing around with them he puts D2 aside, completes the seriation without it, and then finally reinserts it next to D1.

In the case of the One Missing task, the two methods differ even more sharply in their predictions. For the operational method, there should be nothing whatever amiss. For if block D is absent, the rest should simply be chosen and placed in the order H, G, F, E, C, B and A, since each one is in turn the largest block in the pool.

Alf's protocol is summarized in Figs 4 and 5. This seriation differs from his earlier ones in showing more evidence for a careful choice of block, and none at all for selection by proximity. This improvement is matched by a sharpening of the evaluation, so that Alf accepts only blocks one unit smaller than their neighbour. Blocks two units smaller are now rejected (Episodes 4 and 7). The behaviour of interest occurs in Episodes 7, 8 and 9, at the point in the seriation where block D would be placed if it were present. The missing block causes a noticeable disruption of Alf's ongoing behaviour. In Episode 7 Alf chooses C quite deliberately, puts it in the line and examines it. Since it is two units smaller than E he rejects it, following the pattern established earlier in the protocol with block E (Episodes 2 and 4). Block B is tried (Episode 8), somewhat reluctantly, and of course decisively rejected ("No, no, no, no!"). At this point Alf seems to understand the situation and what to do about it. He turns and grins at the experimenter, then replaces C and quickly concludes the seriation. The disruption of Alf's problem solving behaviour by his discovery of the missing block bears out our earlier conclusion based on his performance in the standard seriation situation and the Screen task. Although the pool plays a part in his selection of the blocks, the crucial information for the success of his seriation technique comes from the growing line.

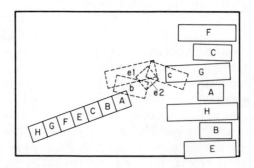

FIG. 4. Lay-out of Alf, seriate One Missing.

2.2.3. Production system for the One Missing protocol
Figure 6 shows a PS summarizing our analysis of Alf's seriation skill. It is broadly similar to the PS given for Del's seriation (Fig. 3). The differences reflect the new mechanisms we have discussed:

Episode	Summary	Line and Comments
1. Add H	Get H, put at left	
2. Try E	Get E, put next to H Examine Reject, to e1	Hand before eye "No!" On way to G
3. Add G	Scan pool Get G, put next to H Examine: accept	H G
4. Try E	Get E, put next to G Examine Reject, to e2	H G E On way to F
5. Add F	Scan pool Get F, put next to G Examine: accept	H G F
6. Add E	Hand hovers over B, then A Get E, put next to F Examine: accept	H G F E "Yup"
7. Try C	Grasp A, release Get C, put next to E Examine Reject, to c	H G F E C "Nope" Near where came from
8. Try B	Scan pool Get B, put next to D Examine Reject, to b	H G F E B "No, no, no, no" On way to C
9. Add C	Look at *Exp.* Grasp C, put next to E Examine (?)	H G F E C
10. Add B	Scan A, then B Get B, put next to C Examine: accept	H G F E C B "Yup"
11. Add A	Get A, put next to B Examine: accept Examine line, especially near FEC	H G F E C B A "Yup"

Fig. 5. Summary of Alf, seriate One Missing.

1. Alf's selection is now predominantly of plausible blocks, as specified by rule S2.

2. Alf selects any block that he has "in mind", if there is one (rule S3). The "⟨new⟩" on the goal condition is needed to prevent a rejected block from being immediately reselected.

3. The evaluation rule PG2 has been sharpened to accept only blocks one unit smaller than their neighbour.

4. Unacceptable blocks are rejected back to the pool, by rule P2.

T1:	Goal = SERIATE	⇒ Set.goal [ADD.ONE]
S2:	Goal = ADD.ONE	⇒ Get.block [suitable]
S3:	Goal ⟨new⟩ = ADD.ONE and have.block.in.mind	⇒ Get.block [in.mind]
T2:	Goal = ADD.ONE and have.just [Get.block'd]	⇒ Change.goal.to [PLACE]
P1:	Goal = PLACE	⇒ Put.block.at [right]
P2:	Goal = PLACE and have.just [Examine'd ⟨wrong⟩]	⇒ Reject.block; Change.goal.to [ADD.ONE]
PG1:	Goal = PLACE and ⟨have new configuration⟩	⇒ Examine
PG2':	Goal = PLACE and have.just [Examine'd: ▨]	⇒ Goal.satisfied [PLACE]
B1:	Goal ⟨new⟩ = SERIATE	⇒ Set.goal [ADD.ONE ⟨first⟩]
B2:	Goal = ADD.ONE ⟨first⟩	⇒ Get.block [biggest]
B3:	Goal = ADD.ONE ⟨first⟩ and have.just [Get.block'd]	⇒ Put.block.at [far left]; Goal.satisfied [ADD.ONE]

Fig. 6. Production system for Alf, seriate One Missing.

How well does this PS fit Alf's protocol? Of course this modest PS is intended to account for only those aspects of Alf's behaviour directly concerned with the performance of the seriation and seriation-like tasks, so it makes no claim to explain precisely what happens when Alf finally realizes in Episode 9 that a block has been left out. It would predict that *something* will go wrong after he has placed block **E**, but exactly what form the trouble will take and how Alf will cope with it are questions beyond its scope. So we should not expect it to predict Alf's decision to try block B after block C in Episode 8, nor in Episode 9 his decision to accept C after all. Apart from that incident, the only misfit occurs in Episode 2 where the PS fails to predict the choice of block E, which could be a residue of Alf's earlier tendency to choose blocks by proximity. Otherwise the scanning of the pool and the overt hesitations and indecisions all indicate that Alf is mostly carrying out a careful selection, as specified by rule S2. The choices that differ from this pattern are themselves predicted by the PS: the first block, H, has its own selection rule B2; the reselections of E in Episodes 4 and 6 both occur after E was previously rejected and can therefore be supposed to be in mind; and almost certainly C is similarly in mind in Episode 9. The evaluation and placement rules fit the protocol without error.

2.3. Beth's protocols: seriation by placement

We turn now to another subject, Beth, who at $6\frac{1}{2}$ years is the oldest child run in the study. (Indeed, at one point she informs the experimenter: "You can't fool me—I'm in first grade!") Her general ability and style of seriation is close to that of Del and Alf, though her technique differs from theirs in depending more on the use of a variety of tactics for positioning the blocks within the line. We therefore discuss first the matter of her placement rules.

2.3.1. Beth's placement rules
Figures 7 and 8 summarize Beth's seriation of six blocks differing in length by only half as much as the blocks in the previous protocols. Perhaps the most immediately striking feature of this protocol is the irregular order in which the blocks are chosen, but we defer discussion of that for the moment and turn our attention instead to the technique Beth uses for putting the blocks into the line. Notice that although the smaller blocks are added, as usual, to the growing end of the line, Beth is willing to try a big block first at the *larger* end of the line (Episodes 5 and 6). This is also what she does with block H in Episode 2 of the subsequent seriation, which will be discussed in a moment (Fig. 11). This regularity in her behaviour can be captured as a new production rule, rule P4 of Fig. 9. The other new feature is that once Beth has decided that a block does not belong at either end of the line, she sets about putting it wherever it should go. This behaviour can be captured in a PS for the Place operation, as shown in Fig. 9. Rules P1 and P4

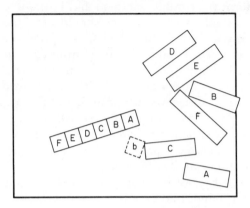

Fig. 7. Lay-out of Beth, seriate six blocks.

are responsible for the initial placement at one or other end of the line, as just discussed, and rules PG1 and PG2 have been seen often enough before. The new feature is that whereas in Del's case rule PG3 detected a reversal pattern and led to the specific remedy of switching the end two blocks, Beth has a more general form of this rule, in which the block's inappropriateness leads to the modified operation of putting it *wherever* it belongs. This goal is achieved by insertion, as specified by rule PW, the details of which will not be spelled out.

This analysis helps to explain in retrospect one of the puzzling aspects of Alf's seriations. Note that in Beth's case it is the existence of rule PG3' that accounts for her willingness to insert blocks during the course of the seriation. In Alf's case, recall that he was *able* to insert blocks into the line, but did not do so unless he was either explicitly asked to or else found himself with a block left over at the end of a seriation (Section 2.2). Presumably this means that he possesses a rule like PW, but fails to evoke it because he has no rule corresponding to Beth's PG3' to set up the appropriate goal.

This tentative analysis of Beth's placement technique yields a testable prediction. Since her acceptance rule PG2 implies that she is content, like Del, to accept an undersize block, it follows that her seriation should remain unaffected if one of the middle-sized blocks is missing. Recall that this is just the opposite prediction as was made for Alf, whose acceptance rule demands a block exactly one unit smaller than its neighbour, so that the absence of one of the blocks seriously disrupts his performance (Fig. 5). The relevant evidence comes from Beth's performance on the One Missing task, summarized in Figs 10 and 11. Her seriation can be summarized as follows. Like the other

Episode	Summary	Line and Comments
1. Add F	Scan pool Get F Put at left	Only a brief glance at F
2. Add B	Get B Put next to F Examine	F B
3. Add C	Get C Put next to B Examine Switch B, C	"I keep on getting mixed up" F B C → F C B
4. Add A	Get A Put next to B Examine	F C B A
5. Add E	Get E Put at left of F Examine Move aside A, B, C Put E at right of F	E F C B A F E C B A
6. Add D	Get D Put near left of F Examine Put next to E Close up C, B, A	D F E C B A F E D C B A F E D C B A

FIG. 8. Summary of Beth, seriate six blocks.

children, Beth knows enough to start the seriation with the biggest—or at least, a big—block. Otherwise her selection is hard to characterize. She seems to put effort into choosing blocks deliberately, unlike Del for example, who simply takes the first block that comes to hand. And, like Alf, although the block she picks is not always actually correct, nor is it ever wildly inappropriate. Like Del, she accepts a block in the line provided it is smaller than its neighbour, and on the one occasion where the new block is oversize she simply switches the end two blocks. The important point is that on the two occasions when she adds to the line a block *two* units smaller than its neighbour (E next to G in Episode 3, C next to E in Episode 5), in neither case does she show signs of detecting anything amiss, and so the prediction is borne out.

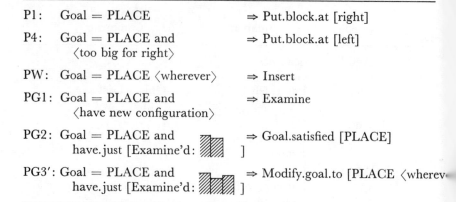

FIG. 9. Partial production system for Beth's placement.

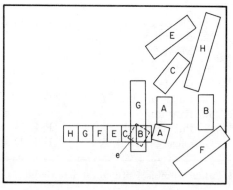

FIG. 10. Lay-out of Beth, seriate One Missing.

Further evidence to the same point comes from her performance on an insertion task (Fig. 12) in which she is asked to add block F′, intermediate in size between blocks F and G. Her behaviour leaves little doubt about her preference for, and hence *a fortiori* her ability to detect, an equal-increment line. For even when she has inserted F′ correctly, she is sufficiently unhappy about the line's appearance that she tries switching F′ with G to see if that improves matters. Further, when asked if it is right, she pulls F′ out and considers inserting it elsewhere. But finally she removes it altogether, remarking that "It shouldn't be here", i.e. that it really doesn't belong in the line at all.

Thus her acceptance of undersize blocks is not to be taken as indicating an ignorance that they *are* too small. The reader may already have

Episode	Summary	Line and Comments
1. Add G	Get G Put at left	Keep looking at H while placing G
2. Add H	Get H Put at left of G Examine	"This is the biggest" H G
3. Add E	Grasp C Get E Put next to G Examine	H G E
4. Add F	Get F Move to near E Switch E, F Examine	Smile at *Exp.* H G F E
5. Add C	Grasp A, release Get C Put next to E Examine	H G F E C
6. Add B	Get B Put next to C Examine	H G F E C B
7. Add A	Get A Put next to B Examine Pat the blocks in turn: H, G, F, E, C, C, B, A	H G F E C B A Not break rhythm at C

FIG. 11. Summary of Beth, seriate One Missing.

drawn a similar conclusion from the protocol summarized in Fig. 11. In Episode 7, when the line is complete, Beth runs her hand down the "stairs", rhythmically patting each block once, except for block C which she pats twice. What likely explanation is there for this, other than that one of the pats is meant for the missing block D?

2.3.2. Beth's selection rules

To close this discussion of Beth's seriation we return briefly to the matter of her selection. It will be recalled that in the seriation of Fig. 8, after the first one she seems to make little effort to choose blocks appropriately, taking them in the order F, B, C, A, E, D. In comparison with

Summary	Comments
Move aside A, B, C, D, E, F	
Move aside H, G	
Put F' in gap	H G F' F . . . .
Examine	
	"Yup!"
	"No!"
Rotate F', G	H F' G F . . . .
Examine	
	"No!"
Switch G, F'	H G F' F . . . .
Straighten F, E, D, C, B, A	

	Exp.: "Can you find one that's wrong?"
Grasp F'	

	Exp.: "Where should it be?"
Withdraw F'	H G F E . . . .
Consider putting F' in another place.	
Say "Shouldn't be here" and leave it out of the line.	

Fig. 12. Summary of Beth, Inset F'.

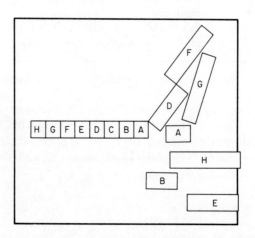

Fig. 13. Lay-out Beth, Tellme.

Experimenter	Subject
1. "Which one shall I start with?"	
	Tap H
"That one?" Points to H	
2. "Which one shall I place next?"	
	Tap G
"Okay"	
3. "Which one next?"	
	Tap F
4. "And then?"	
	Tap D twice, while looking at *Exp.*; then say "That one", tapping E
"This one? How d'you know it's that one?"	
	"Because . . ."
"Because what?"	
	"Same size as this one" Indicate F, E
"It's what?"	
	"It looks like the same as this." Back and forth between E, F
"Okay"	
5. "Now which one?"	
	Point to D
6.	Point to C
7.	Point to B
8.	Point to A
"That's very good"	

FIG. 14. Summary of Beth, Tellme.

the blocks used in the seriation of Fig. 11, the reduced discriminability of the smaller-increment blocks may partly explain her poorer selection, but even with the easier blocks she still makes two avoidable mistakes: choosing G instead of H in Episode 1, and E instead of F in Episode 3.

What, then, are the rules governing Beth's selection? From the lay-out of the blocks on the table (Fig. 7), it can be seen that the order of choice is not haphazard. The blocks seem to come in pairs, B following F, A following C, and D following E, so that after the initial block F, each block is either adjacent to the one just placed or else is the closest one to hand. It would be hard to make these notions precise enough to actually predict her choices, but the nature of the pattern is revealing and suggests that Beth tends to grasp a block her attention is drawn to without bothering to scan the whole pool to find a better one.

One possibility that comes to mind is that Beth makes errors in selection because she is simply unable to do any better. But it is easy to show experimentally that this is not so. Figures 13 and 14 show a seriation in which the blocks are actually placed by the experimenter instead of the subject, but the subject still has to choose which one should be used.

By experimentally divorcing the selection of the blocks from their subsequent placing, this forces the subject to pick blocks in the right order if the final line is to be correct. Figure 14 shows that Beth is in fact able to choose the blocks in order of decreasing size. (One incident of possible interest occurs in Episode 4 when Beth first chooses block D—near to blocks F and G just placed—but then changes her mind to E, away on the other side of the pool. From this, and the brief dialogue which follows, the reader is left to draw his own conclusions.)

So if Beth's poor selection is not due to an inability to choose the blocks in the right order, what then? It must be that she doesn't pick the blocks in order because she *has no need to*; she has access to other ways of seriating the line. She is able, as we have seen, to put any block in its correct position in the line, so it follows that she can seriate a set of blocks correctly no matter in what order she deals with them. There is a parallel here with what we have found when examining her evalua-tion rules, where she was happily accepting undersize blocks even though she knew there was a block missing. The point is that Beth has mastered the task sufficiently for her skill to possess a kind of redun-dancy: she has alternative ways of using the information available in order to produce a correct seriation. In the case of the evaluation rules, she can afford to accept an undersize block temporarily because she will still be able to place the missing block correctly when (or if!) it turns up later. In the case of the selection rules, even though she can choose the blocks in order when she needs to, she can afford to pick blocks lazily because she can cope with them in any order. This aspect of her behaviour is crucial for understanding the nature of seriation skill, and we will return to it in the later discussion (Section 3.2).

2.4. Inability to seriate: rejection without correction

Among our subjects, even children unable to seriate can nonetheless recognize a correct solution, that is, they can distinguish between seriated and non-seriated lines. This ability suggests a possible method of attempting seriation in which the discrimination serves as the basis for a *test*. A block could be added, and the line checked to see whether it is still in order. If the line passes the test, then the block is accepted; if not, then it is returned to the pool. Figure 15 shows part of a PS to implement this technique; none of the rules is new. The protocols which follow demonstrate what happens when a child chooses blocks from the pool without regard for their size and accepts them at the end of the line unless they are oversize, but otherwise is unable to put them where they belong.

T1:	Goal = SERIATE	⇒ Set.goal [ADD.ONE]
S1:	Goal = ADD.ONE	⇒ Get.block [next nearest]
T2:	Goal = ADD.ONE and have.just [Get.block'd]	⇒ Change.goal.to [PLACE]
P1:	Goal = PLACE	⇒ Put.block.at [right]
P2:	Goal = PLACE and have.just [Examine'd: ⟨wrong⟩]	⇒ Reject.block; Goal.failed [PLACE]
PG1:	Goal = PLACE and ⟨have new configuration⟩	⇒ Examine
PG2:	Goal = PLACE and have.just [Examine'd: ▨] 	⇒ Goal.satisfied [PLACE]

FIG. 15. Partial production system for rejection without correction.

The general form of these protocols, then, is that the child begins by adding successively smaller blocks to the line, but at some point can proceed no further. The problem is that once a small block has been put in the line, all the larger blocks still left will be rejected when tried and so inevitably omitted from the seriation. The result is thus a *partial seriation* in which some of the blocks are built into an ordered line, but the rest are left over and the subject is unable to place them. The line that gets built is guaranteed to be ordered, since any out-of-order block would be removed by the rejection rule, but once a block has been skipped there is no way for it to be added back to the line later. To a certain extent, the first seriation of Alf that we described in Section 2.2 exhibited this feature: because block E was accepted after block G, block F was eventually left over. The difference is that Alf, when prompted, was able to insert the left-over block. The children described here are unable to do so.

2.4.1. Lot's protocols

Lot's attempts to seriate eight blocks illustrate dramatically the limitations of the method. Her first attempt is summarized in Figs 16 and 17. After trying to extend the sequences G B and G B A, she finds herself holding just blocks A and B, and she rotates them to conform to the direction of the line she is trying to build. She then proceeds to put

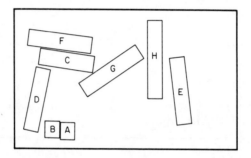

FIG. 16. Lay-out of Lot, first seriation attempt.

	Episode Summary	Line
1.	Try various blocks to extend the sequences G B and G B A	
2.	Have A B, rotate them	B A
3.	Reach for H; get E, put next to A; examine; turn E upside down; examine; reject E	B A E
4.	Put G next to A; reject it	B A G
5.	Put C next to A; reject it	B A C
6.	Put D next to A; reject it	B A D
7.	Put F next to A; reject it	B A F

FIG. 17. Summary of Lot, first seriation attempt.

the remaining blocks (except H) one at a time next to A—and of course rejects them all. At this point the experimenter intervenes by removing blocks A and B and giving her block H: at least with H to start with she has a chance of finding some acceptable blocks (*see* Figs 18 and 19). She grasps G, which is standing upright and nearby, and puts it next to H. Then she reaches for block A and that too is added to the line. But again the effect of accepting A is that she rejects all the other blocks she tries: B, D, C. Rules PG2 and P2 appear to be working inexorably. Block A is accepted by PG2 in Episode 3 despite the enormous size difference, since the line H G A is indeed monotonic; and blocks B, C, D are rejected by P2 since they are indeed larger than A.

2.4.2. *Kap's attempt*

Kap too illustrates the same phenomenon, though this time in less extreme form. In his attempt to seriate six of the blocks (Figs 20 and 21) the order in which he chooses them—F, B, D, E, C, A—indicates

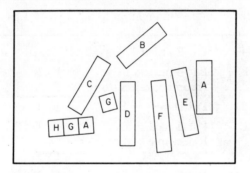

FIG. 18. Lay-out of Lot, second seriation attempt.

Episode Summary	Line
1. Given H	
2. Put G next to H	H G
3. Put A next to G	H G A
4. Put B next to A; reject it	H G A B
5. Reach for F	
Put D next to A; reject it	H G A D
6. Put C next to A; reject it	H G A C
7. Grasp F	

FIG. 19. Summary of Lot, second seriation attempt.

Fig. 20. Lay-out of Kap, seriate six blocks.

Episode	Summary	Line					
1. Add F	Put F at left						
2. Try B	Put B next to F		F	B			
	Examine; reject, to b		F				
3. Add D	Put D next to F		F	D			
4. Try E	Put E next to D		F	D	E		
	Reject to e						
	Say "No"!		F	D			
5. Add C	Put C next to D		F	D	C		
6. Add A	Put A next to C		F	D	C	A	
7. Try E	Put E next to A		F	D	C	A	E
	Reject		F	D	C	A	
8. Try B	Put B next to A		F	D	C	A	B
	next to F	B	F	D	C	A	
	Reject		F	D	C	A	
9. Try E	*Exp.* pulls away						
	E, A, B		F	D	C		
	Put B next to C		F	D	C	B	
	Put A next to B		F	D	C	B	A
	Put E next to F	E	F	D	C	B	A
	next to A		F	D	C	B	A	E

Fig. 21. Summary of Kap, seriate six blocks.

that his selection, like Del's, consists of starting with the biggest block and thereafter choosing by proximity, with the exception of A which is recognized separately. By Episode 6 he has managed to put four of the blocks in order, but since the smallest one is A, neither of the remaining two blocks—B and E—can be placed. In Episode 2, he had avoided the trap that Lot fell into—that of placing a small block early in the protocol, and so being unable to add any of the rest—only by rejecting B when put next to F, presumably because of the large size difference.

2.4.3. Final remark

The purpose of presenting the protocols in this section is two-fold. First, they serve to illustrate the inevitable outcome of a seriation ability like that depicted in Fig. 15. Even if the child begins with the biggest block, if the only means he has available to order the line is to reject oversize blocks, then the series he builds, though ordered, will fail to include all the blocks. It will be short if he is unlucky enough to add a very small block early in the seriation, as did Lot; longer if he is able to avoid those smallest blocks, as could Kap. But there is a second, more subtle, point at issue here. It is the suggestion—on the scanty evidence presented here only a hint, but see Young (1976)—that there is no difference in *form* between the PSs of seriators and non-seriators. The PS of a non-seriator is the same as that of a corresponding seriator except for the absence of one or more critical rules. Indeed the PS analysis discourages one from dichotomizing children into seriators *vs.* non-seriators. Instead of classifying the children's behaviour into "correct solutions" and "errors", as does so much research in experimental and developmental psychology, an information processing approach enables one to understand that there are many different ways of tackling the seriation problem, some of which will be successful (in given circumstances) and others not, but that all are to be understood in terms of the same framework. It was by no means obvious beforehand that this would be the case, for a "stage" analysis of seriation leads one to expect that children who cannot seriate may be doing something quite different from those who can. The analysis here suggests that they are merely, in a certain sense, doing less.

3. RESULTS OF THE STUDY

3.1. Analysis of seriation

The experimental study, based on a number of protocol analyses like those above, yielded three main findings.

3.1.1. Space of seriation skills

First, it is indeed possible to write PSs based on converging empirical evidence that accurately model children's seriation behaviour. The seriation task can be thought of as imposing two conditions for its solution:

1. The blocks are to be built into a straight line; and
2. The line is to be ordered by size.

It so happens that condition (1) was invariably met by the subjects. As is hardly surprising, 4- and 5-year-olds found non-problematic the business of building a set of blocks into a line, and they all succeeded on this aspect of the task. The difference between seriators and non-seriators lay solely in whether or not they could also satisfy requirement (2), the ordering of the blocks. From this fact follows the division of the children's seriation behaviour into a sequence of episodes, as seen throughout the protocols. The need to repeatedly bring new blocks to the line in order to extend it was obvious to all the children, seriators and non-seriators alike; what can be regarded for present purposes as their "real" problem solving takes place within the episodes.

A child's seriation skill can be analysed into three major aspects:

1. Selection: the choice of which block to work with.
2. Evaluation: whether or not to accept a block as a suitable addition to the line.
3. Placement: whereabouts in the growing line a block should go.

The combination of these three components determines the nature and quality of the child's ability: his characteristic techniques, the kinds of problems he can and cannot do, and the typical form of his errors. To some extent these components can be regarded as the dimensions of a *space* of seriation skills in which individual children can be placed. Different regions of the space correspond to the different possible ways of tackling the problem and are associated with the various known seriation (and pre-seriation) phenomena: the building of unordered lines, the construction of subseries or partial seriations, the different methods of successful seriation, and so on. These and the other Piagetian observations each belong to a location in the space.

3.1.2. "Kit" of production rules

Secondly, one can write a set of rules that "spans" this space of seriation skills. The individual rules can be treated as the components of a "kit", from which—merely by an appropriate choice of rules—the experimenter can assemble a range of different PSs that correspond to the different regions of the space, and that therefore also exhibit the various phenomena mentioned above. Figure 22 presents a "kit" of production rules from which it is possible for the experimenter to assemble PSs to implement all the major seriation techniques that have been discussed. It has been divided into four subsets of rules, and we briefly discuss each group in turn.

Episodes

T1: Goal = SERIATE ⇒ Set.Goal [ADD.ONE]

B1: Goal ⟨new⟩ = SERIATE ⇒ Set.Goal [ADD.ONE ⟨first⟩]

S1: Goal = ADD.ONE ⇒ Get.block [next nearest]

T2: Goal = ADD.ONE ⇒ Change.goal.to [PLACE]
     and have.just [Get.block'd]

B3: Goal = ADD.ONE ⟨first⟩ ⇒ Put.block.at [far left];
     and have.just [Get.block'd] Goal.satisfied [ADD. ONE]

P1: Goal = PLACE ⇒ Put.block.at [right]

Selection

S2: Goal = ADD.ONE ⇒ Get.block [suitable]

S3: Goal ⟨new⟩ and ⇒ Get.block [in mind]
     have.block.in.mind

B2: Goal = ADD.ONE ⟨first⟩ ⇒ Get.block [biggest]

Evaluation

PG1: Goal = PLACE and ⇒ Examine
      ⟨have new configuration⟩

PG2: Goal = PLACE and ⇒ Goal.satisfied [PLACE]
      have.just [Examine'd: 🔲]

Placement

P2: Goal = PLACE and ⇒ Reject.block;
     have.just [Examine'd: ⟨wrong⟩] Goal.failed [PLACE]

PW: Goal = PLACE ⟨wherever⟩ ⇒ Insert

P4: Goal = PLACE and ⇒ Put.block.at [left]
     ⟨too big for right⟩

PG3: Goal = PLACE and ⇒ Switch.blocks
      have.just [Examine'd: 🔲]

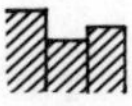

FIG. 22. "Kit" of seriation rules.

As was noted above, all the children asked to seriate manage to take blocks from the pool and add them to the line one at a time. Rules T1 through P1 express this episode structure, and form part of all the seriation (and non-seriation) techniques. The rules should be too familiar by now to require much comment. Suffice it to say that rules T1, S1, T2 and P1 implement the basic cycle of getting blocks and adding them to the line, while B1 and B3 deal with the special treatment accorded to the first block.

Rules S2, S3 and B2 are concerned with selection. The presence of rule S2 in a child's PS indicates that he makes at least some effort to pick appropriate blocks, so that his selection does in fact contribute to his seriation. Rule B2 is responsible for having children start the line with a big block. Notice that both these rules exist in various forms with different degrees of precision, and so contribute to the child's skill in a quantitatively variable way. For example, even among children who have a rule B2, "big" can range in meaning from just "a fairly big block" to a reliable specification of the very biggest.

Rules PG1 and PG2 deal with evaluation. Having PG1, or at least something like it, is a pre-condition for evaluation to occur at all. PG2 is another graded rule. Some versions take the term "monotonic" literally and accept *any* block smaller than its neighbour, while others insist that the block be not too small or even—as in the case of Alf—precisely correct.

The rest of the rules are concerned with placement, in fact all but one of them (P4) with correction. Rule P2 is in some sense the complement of PG2, and represents the most primitive corrective response to a negative evaluation. It gets progressively overshadowed by the more sophisticated techniques, such as the switching of oversize blocks (rule PG3) or their direct insertion at the place they belong (rule PW). Finally P4 expresses a minor placement rule which is helpful but of limited applicability.

This "kit" can be likened to a self-service cafeteria from which a seriation supper is to be composed. So long as the dietary laws of production systems are obeyed—PG1 must be present if there is to be any correction, and P2 must be included whenever PG2 is—then it will be found that the remaining rules are surprisingly independent. When added to the basic cycle, almost any collection of the rules from S2 to P4 yields a PS for seriation (or non-seriation) plausible as what a child might actually be found to have.

3.1.3. Incremental growth

The third finding is that sequences of successive PSs differing solely by the addition of one or more new rules can be shown to display many of the developmental phenomena noted by Piaget. For example, PSs

Group A

T1:	Goal = SERIATE	⇒ Set.goal [ADD.ONE]
B1:	Goal ⟨new⟩ = SERIATE	⇒ Set.goal [ADD.ONE ⟨first⟩]
S1:	Goal = ADD.ONE	⇒ Get.block [next nearest]
T2:	Goal = ADD.ONE and have.just [Get.block'd]	⇒ Change.goal.to [PLACE]
B3:	Goal = ADD.ONE ⟨first⟩ and have.just [Get block'd]	⇒ Put.block.at [far left]; Goal.satisfied [ADD.ONE]
P1:	Goal = PLACE	⇒ Put.block.at [right]

Group B

B2:	Goal = ADD.ONE ⟨first⟩	⇒ Get.block [big]

Group C

PG1:	Goal = PLACE and have.new.configuration	⇒ Examine
P2:	Goal = PLACE and have.just [Examine'd: ⟨too big⟩]	⇒ Reject.block; Goal.failed [PLACE]

Group D

PG3:	Goal = PLACE and have.just [Examine'd: ▨▨] 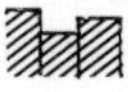	⇒ Switch.blocks

Group E

S2:	Goal = ADD.ONE	⇒ Get.block [similar to last]

FIG. 23. Hypothetical sequence of production systems.

early in the sequence merely arrange the blocks in a line without attempting to order them. Later PSs build partially ordered lines, or lines consisting of two or more subseries, and so on. Figure 23, for example, shows such a sequence representing a hypothetical child who initially can only arrange the blocks in a line, but then gradually acquires the rules that lead him through the observed pre-seriation phenomena, on to simple seriation, and finally more reliable seriation. Some details have been omitted, but roughly, rules T1 through P1 constitute a PS to build the blocks into a line without regard for size (*see* Group A in Fig. 23). Next the child acquires the idea of starting with the biggest—or at least, a big—block; this is represented by the addition of rule B2 (Group B). At this point the child is still constructing an unordered series corresponding to Piaget's Stage I. However, he next begins to satisfy the ordering requirement, at least enough to examine each block after adding it to the line and reject it if it is too big; this is expressed by the addition of rules PG1 and P2 (Group C). At this point he is constructing partial seriations with some of the blocks omitted. Perhaps he next acquires a simple correction technique, that of switching an oversize block with its neighbour, by addition of rule PG3 (Group D). Like Del, he can now seriate successfully provided that the blocks are not too numerous; his performance would be classified by Piaget as Stage II, trial-and-error seriation. Finally, we may suppose that having acquired rule S2 he begins to choose blocks according to their size (Group E). His seriation behaviour then appears to be more or less "operational" depending on the accuracy of his selection. The combination of an at least approximately correct selection rule (S2) with a means for correcting slight errors (PG3) means that he is now able to seriate blocks both harder to discriminate and more numerous than before.

This account of the child's growing ability as a gradual, cumulative acquisition of production rules reveals the continuity underlying the striking (and often discontinuous) changes in his overt performance, and provides a more coherent picture of the development of the skill than does the Piagetian analysis into separate stages. Obviously, this finding is of relevance mainly to an understanding of the *development* of seriation ability, a topic fascinating in its own right but one which we will not pursue here.

3.2. Structure of cognitive skill

Figure 24 shows a typical PS for a child capable of "empirical" seriation, in other words seriation involving the rearrangement of blocks at the line. The rules should all be familiar by now.

It can be seen that this PS portrays the child's seriation skill in a rather unexpected way. The PS appears to be a somewhat untidy conglomeration of bits and pieces, a redundant collection of rules reflecting features of a variety of different seriation techniques. In the context of rules T1, T2, B1 and B3, the rules S2, B2 and P1 supply the core of the "operational" technique of seriating by choosing blocks in the right order, whereas rules B2, P1, PG1, PG2 and PG3 enable the child to seriate "empirically", by taking the blocks as they come and switching any out-of-order ones along the line. Far from embodying a single strategy, the PS provides enough rules to support at least two

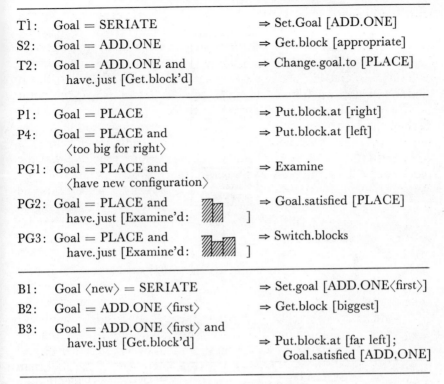

T1:	Goal = SERIATE	⇒ Set.Goal [ADD.ONE]
S2:	Goal = ADD.ONE	⇒ Get.block [appropriate]
T2:	Goal = ADD.ONE and have.just [Get.block'd]	⇒ Change.goal.to [PLACE]

P1:	Goal = PLACE	⇒ Put.block.at [right]
P4:	Goal = PLACE and ⟨too big for right⟩	⇒ Put.block.at [left]
PG1:	Goal = PLACE and ⟨have new configuration⟩	⇒ Examine
PG2:	Goal = PLACE and have.just [Examine'd: ▨]	⇒ Goal.satisfied [PLACE]
PG3:	Goal = PLACE and have.just [Examine'd: ▨▨]	⇒ Switch.blocks

B1:	Goal ⟨new⟩ = SERIATE	⇒ Set.goal [ADD.ONE⟨first⟩]
B2:	Goal = ADD.ONE ⟨first⟩	⇒ Get.block [biggest]
B3:	Goal = ADD.ONE ⟨first⟩ and have.just [Get.block'd]	⇒ Put.block.at [far left]; Goal.satisfied [ADD.ONE]

Fig. 24. "Typical" production system for seriation.

quite different ones. Furthermore, rule P4 does not appear to be part of *any* method of seriation. How are we to make sense of all this?

Figure 26 shows for comparison a PS to realize the operational method given in flow-chart form in Fig. 25. The rules correspond one-for-one to the boxes in the flow-chart, except that there is no essential difference between the two "Select" boxes, so rule T1 takes care of them both. In contrast to Fig. 24 the operational PS seems to have marked advantages in terms of elegance, simplicity, uniformity and parsimony! Why then should we nevertheless prefer a PS like that of Fig. 24 as a model of the child's skill? Of course the main justification is that the protocol analyses have shown it to be a more accurate description of what the child is actually doing, as we have already seen. But it is important to see also that the more heterogeneous PS is more plausible psychologically, and reflects features of human skill not even hinted at by the operational method.

The operational method, in restricting itself to just one source of

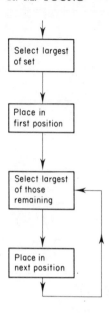

FIG. 25. Operational method of seriation.

T1':	Goal = SERIATE	⇒ Get.block [biggest]
T2':	Goal = SERIATE and have.just [Get.block'd]	⇒ Put.block.at [right]
B3':	Goal ⟨new⟩ = SERIATE and have.just [Get.block'd]	⇒ Put.block.at [far left]

FIG. 26. Production system for the operational method.

information—the relative size of the blocks in the pool—in fact describes a peculiarly imbalanced kind of behaviour poorly matched to the demands of the task. It supposes a subject who goes to all the trouble of making sure of choosing the very biggest block ... but then simply adds it to the line without paying it any further attention. This strategy can be strikingly inefficient, for much of the work needed to find the *biggest* block is often unnecessary. Except when the blocks are unusually easy to discriminate and there are not too many of them, less cognitive processing is required if the subject merely makes a modest effort to pick a *suitable* block, and then puts it at the end of the line, examines it, and corrects it if needed.

Our proposed PS, by contrast, although "unsystematic" in the sense that two consecutive blocks may be added to the line by two quite different processes, manages to mirror the flexibility of the human performance. It shows the child responding to information from a variety of sources—from the size of the block as it lies in the pool, from its appearance next to the other blocks in the line—and moulding his solution to the particular case. In picking up a block he might notice that it was rather big, and so by rule P4 put it directly at the left-hand end, where if it were correct PG2 would have him accept it. With a slightly smaller block he might put it at the growing end (rule P1) and even switch it with another block under the control of PG3 before realizing that it should be tried at the other end. Instances like this abound in the children's protocols.

3.2.1. *Adaptiveness of the skill*

This analysis leads to a view of cognitive skill rather different from that expressed by Piaget and his followers. According to the PS analysis, the "method" "adopted" on a particular occasion depends on the details of the problem. The PS of Fig. 24 shows that the subject tackles the task by whatever appears to make local progress, taking short-cuts when he can by making use of whatever information happens to be available (e.g. rule P4).

This matter of the adaptiveness of a cognitive skill organized as a PS suggests an insight into the nature of adult skill, and is worth exploring a little farther. We suggested above that a subject asked to seriate, say, six easily discriminable blocks may find no difficulty picking them in the right order, whereas faced with a seriation of a larger number of less discriminable blocks, following the operational algorithm can become a painful business indeed. The subject is likely to content himself with selecting merely plausible blocks and performing simple corrections at the line. More generally, it can be seen how in a given task environment there is a psychological effort, or "cost", associated with each "strategy". Under some conditions, such as those just sketched, the cost of making an accurate selection might be relatively high while the correction procedures remain quite cheap. In other circumstances— for example, if the blocks are to be glued together in the line—these costs might be reversed, and we would then expect the advanced seriator to rely on a careful selection. One can see in this way how the subject can exploit the idiosyncracies of the materials to be seriated and adapt his performance to the requirements of the particular task.

In Young (1976) we speculate as to how a set of skills might be organized to exhibit this kind of adaptation without the need to invoke a mysterious process called "adaptiveness" in order to explain how it

$$R4 \quad \left\{ \begin{array}{c} C4 \Rightarrow A4 \\ ----- \\ ----- \end{array} \right\} \qquad \text{etc.}$$

$$R3 \quad \left\{ \begin{array}{c} C3 \Rightarrow A3 \\ ----- \\ ----- \end{array} \right\} \qquad \text{etc.}$$

$$R2 \quad \left\{ \begin{array}{c} C2 \Rightarrow A2 \\ ----- \\ ----- \end{array} \right\} \quad$$ Rules to acquire or derive the necessary information or bring about the necessary physical conditions for rules in R1.

$$R1 \quad \left\{ \begin{array}{c} C1 \Rightarrow A1 \\ ----- \\ ----- \end{array} \right\} \quad$$ Rules that actually carry out the seriation, given the necessary information and physical conditions.

FIG. 27. "Adaptive" production system for seriation.

happens. Figure 27 shows in outline the form of an adaptive PS for seriation. Note that in this, as in the other PSs, the more specific production rules are written nearer the bottom of the figure, so it is best to read this diagram from the bottom upwards. Rules in R1 actually perform some step in the task (such as getting hold of a block), but they can apply only if certain prerequisite information is available and certain necessary physical conditions are met (for example, the block must lie within reach). If these prerequisites do *not* hold, the rules in R2 serve to bring about the state of affairs needed for the rules in R1 to apply, i.e. to derive the necessary information and set up the necessary physical arrangements. But the rules in R2 themselves have pre-conditions for applicability, and the rules in R3 may be needed if these are not already satisfied. R4 may contain rules for satisfying the pre-conditions of R1 directly, but in a more effortful way, and so on. Notice that the rules in successive Rs are evoked only during the course of processes of higher and higher "cost", in other words processes involving increasing amounts of physical and mental activity.

It can be seen that such a PS will adapt to the circumstances of the case it is given. On an easy problem a low-cost strategy will be followed, but in a new situation where the same strategy would involve some high-cost activity a different method will be used which avoids it. An example may help to make this clear. In the case of seriation, R1 may include rules to select the biggest block if it is known, and otherwise simply the nearest one. And R2 may well include a rule that finds the biggest of the blocks provided they are visually accessible and easily discriminable. So in the case of a set of readily distinguishable blocks with the pool in plain view, the seriation will be carried out by choosing blocks in the right order—the "operational method" again! But in another case where the blocks in the pool are kept hidden in little boxes (cf. Baylor *et al.*, 1973), they will be chosen in order of proximity and the seriation will be done by successive comparisons.

Thus the PS adapts to the task without there being any rule or process which "decides" to adapt. "Adaptiveness" is here not a physical or mental *activity*, but simply a feature of the resulting behaviour. The PS is also adaptive in the sense of being able to take advantage of serendipity. If, as a by-product of some activity in a high-cost strategy or as a chance arrangement of the physical environment, information becomes available that permits a low-cost method to be used instead, then it will be.

3.3. The role of production systems

The choice of PSs as the notation used to describe seriation skill should not be regarded as an arbitrary decision. Production systems act as an essential complement to the technique of adaptive experimentation used in this investigation. In order to understand the rationale of this approach, one has to take into account some of the special properties of PSs. One way of viewing PSs is to regard them as a response to a dissatisfaction with current process models in psychology (Newell, 1973b). When we put a child in a situation requiring him to perform a number of different but related tasks, it is the same child who tackles the different tasks. Therefore a satisfactory model of his abilities in that domain will consist of a *single system* capable of handling the whole range. Ordinary computer programs are sadly deficient in this respect. If one writes an arbitrary program to model a child's behaviour on a particular task, then a modified program is needed to model his behaviour on a modified task. We regard this need for reprogramming as unsatisfactory, and PSs give us a way to avoid it.

In other words, we are saying that one of the advantages of PSs of particular relevance here is their generality across situations, i.e. their ability to cope with minor variations of the task. A conventional flow-chart-like model, by imposing a psychologically unwarranted division between processing and control, typically has to be structured anew for each experimental situation. A PS, on the other hand, to serve as an adequate model of a subject has to provide a *single* processing system to handle all the variants. Thus to a far greater extent than is true of conventional processing models, a PS can act as a miniature "artificial subject" whose reactions to different experimental manipulations can be empirically explored.

According to Newell and Simon (1972), "production systems are the most homogeneous form of programming organisation known". One consequence of this homogeneity is that a PS's simple organization as a collection of rules leads to a corresponding structure in the resulting behaviour. Each rule represents a fragment of potential activity that is a meaningful component of the total problem solving process. As a result, individual production rules often possess a kind of local plausibility that makes them intelligible in their own right, independently of the other rules present. In Fig. 24, for example, each of the rules can be seen as reflecting some particular aspect of the seriation task. Rule T1, for instance, acts as a "pacemaker" for driving the cyclic behaviour of repeatedly getting a block from the pool and adding it to the line. It can be seen as a specialized version of a far more general rule which says, in effect: "If you want to do something to each of a collection of objects, do it to one of them"; the rule keeps applying until there are no objects left.

The independence of the production rules is of course what makes it possible to extend a PS incrementally simply by adding new rules (as in Fig. 23), or to combine various sets of rules in different ways to yield working PSs (as in Fig. 22). With a more conventional form of model, the idea of providing such a "kit"—which serves to specify an entire space of seriation processes simply as subsets of its parts—would be unthinkable. In addition, the local meaningfulness of the rules makes it easier to imagine how at least some of them could have originated as specialized forms of more general rules, which it seems plausible the child would have acquired from his extensive experience of manipulating objects during his first few years of life. A deeper grasp of the nature of cognitive skill would enable us to understand how a child tackles the seriation task when he is exposed to it for the first time. Evidently he does not arrive in the experimental situation with a fully specialized PS for seriation ready-formed. Somehow or other he has to deal with the task by assimilating it to his existing skills, and bringing his general abilities to bear on the specific aspects of the new situation (cf. Newell, 1972b). How this happens is a problem for future research.

It is interesting to compare these PSs with the analysis of cognitive skills due to Gagné and his followers (Gagné, 1962, 1968; Gagné and Paradise, 1961; Resnick et al., 1973). The essence of Gagné's technique lies in the subdivision of a given skill into a set of simpler subskills. These in turn can be divided further, so the eventual outcome of the analysis is an *hierarchical structure* for the skill. Thus both Gagné's approach and the PS approach seek to analyse a task into its constituent parts, but the components in the two cases are of different kinds. Gagné *et al.* analyse the task into the actual activities that the child performs. Consequently, something gets left out, for in order to seriate a child must not only "have" the necessary components but must also be able to assemble them correctly. But there are numerous tasks where the difficulty lies precisely in this putting together, the individual components being available to the child long before he can perform the higher-order task itself. (After all, the only *activities* involved in seriation are simple block manipulations and discriminations, all of which the child has mastered long before the age of four.) Gagné tends to overlook this point, since he assumes that if the components of a skill are all present, then verbal instructions alone will suffice to put them together (Gagné and Paradise, 1961; Gagné, 1968). Production systems, on the other hand, analyse the problem solving into components which specify not only what the child does but also *when he does it*. No further "fitting together" is needed: the set of production rules itself forms a working system capable of doing the task.

A final advantage of PSs is their ability to represent the role of the environment in governing the child's behaviour in a way that a more conventional process model cannot. For a PS presents the set of possible actions that the child can take together with the basis on which he decides between them, whereas a flow-chart or algorithm states only the outcome of that decision. In the PS of Fig. 24, for example, it can be seen how rules like PG2 and PG3 isolate the internal and environmental components. Both rules demand that the child must just have performed an Examine, but they respond differentially to the shape of the line. Baylor and Gascon (1974) devote considerable effort to showing how a child's seriation technique uses features of the environment such as the "hole" left in a line of blocks when one of them is removed, and they find that an increased flexibility of response to aspects of the environment is one of the themes characterizing a child's growing skill. Thus PSs are able to indicate explicitly the factors that determine what actions are taken. This is important, since young children are usually given concrete tasks such as seriation which involve a high degree of interaction with the physical world; and also because a pre-operational child relies to a great extent on the environment as an external memory to reduce his cognitive load (Bruner *et al.*, 1966).

4. CONCLUSION

In this chapter we have discussed the nature of a particular cognitive skill, that of length seriation in young children. By using a technique of adaptive experimentation to probe into the structure of the children's ability, it was possible to build information processing models, in the form of production systems (PSs) based on converging empirical evidence, that faithfully reproduced the children's behaviour on seriation and seriation-like tasks. These models yielded a picture of seriation ability different from that painted by Piaget and others, and led us to argue that the notion of discrete strategies is inappropriate for understanding the nature of cognitive skill.

Production systems played a crucial role in the argument. It is the high degree of modularity (or independence) of the individual rules of a PS that makes it possible to write a single, deterministic information processing model of great versatility, which while committed to no one "built-in" method of seriation is nevertheless able to exhibit several different ones as the situation demands.

It is worth giving one further illustration of the difference between an analysis based on strategy, which is a characterization of a subject's overt performance, and one based on an information processing model which specifies the underlying psychological processes that generate that performance. Although it was not mentioned in Section 2, it happens that some children have a selection rule which tells them in effect, to choose the block most similar in appearance to the one last placed (*see* Young, 1976). Now in the context of the standard seriation task, a moment's thought will show that with this rule, provided the child begins with the biggest block (as we have seen most of them do), he will in fact pick the blocks in the "right" order, i.e. in order of decreasing size. In terms of strategy this is the operational method again! An observer would classify the child as being at Piaget's Stage III, even though the child is *not* following a selection rule telling him to choose the largest block in the pool, or anything like it. The important point here of course is that in a given situation, two different seriation procedures can lead to the same observable behaviour. But the two are psychologically different, and with ingenuity can be experimentally distinguished.

The analysis put forward in this chapter suggests that too narrow a pursuit of the goals of elegance, simplicity, uniformity and parsimony can led the investigator astray. Previous studies of seriation by Piaget and others (e.g. Elkind, 1964; Baylor and Gascon, 1974) have tended to stress the regular, algorithmic-like character of operational seriation, and to see it as being in some way optimal. Usually, too, it is implicitly assumed to be the normal "adult" way of solving the problem. But we were led to criticize this method, both for its unhuman-like inflexibility and for its psychologically unwarranted restriction to just a single source of information. According to the PS model, skill is not organized into strategies, but rather consists of a heterogeneous collection of rules, able to support several different strategies and to make use of a variety of information as it becomes available. (Indeed the better developed the skill, the more pronounced this diversity should be, since it is the skilled person rather than the novice who has the wider range of methods for tackling the task.) Which "strategy" actually gets "chosen" on a particular occasion is determined by which of the rules actually get evoked, and that in turn depends on the requirements of the individual task. Thus the technique used is responsive to the actual materials and circumstances of the problem. In a word, cognitive skill is adaptive.

ACKNOWLEDGEMENTS

This chapter was prepared while the author was supported by a grant from the Social Science Research Council. The experimental work reported here was done at Carnegie-Mellon University, as part of a Ph.D. dissertation supervised by Allen Newell. I would like to thank Jim Howe and John Fox for comments on an earlier draft.

REFERENCES

Bartlett, F. C. (1958). "Thinking". Cambridge University Press, Cambridge.

Baylor, G. W. (1971). Program and protocol analysis on a mental imagery task. *Proceedings of the Second International Joint Conference on Artificial Intelligence*, 218–237.

Baylor, G. W. and Gascon, J. (1974). An information processing theory of the development of weight seriation in children. *Cognitive Psychology* **6**, 1–40.

Baylor, G. W. and Lemoyne, G. (1975). Experiments in seriation with children: towards an information processing explanation of the horizontal décalage. *Canadian Journal of Behavioural Science* **7**, 4–29.

Baylor, G. W., Gascon, J., Lemoyne, G. and Pothier, N. (1973). An information processing model of some seriation tasks. *Canadian Psychologist* **14**, 167–196.

Bruner, J. S., Olver, R. R. and Greenfield, P. M. (1966). "Studies in Cognitive Growth". Wiley, New York.

Connolly, K. J. (ed.) (1971). "Mechanisms of Motor Skill Development". Academic Press, London and New York.

Elkind, D. (1964). Discrimination, seriation and numeration of size and dimensional differences in young children: Piaget replication study VI. *Journal of Genetic Psychology* **104**, 275–296.

Elkind, D. and Flavell, J. H. (eds.) (1969). "Studies in Cognitive Development". Oxford University Press, Oxford.

Farnham-Diggory, S. (ed.) (1972). "Information Processing in Children". Academic Press, New York and London.

Flavell, J. H. (1971). Stage related properties of cognitive development. *Cognitive Psychology* **2**, 421–453.

Gagné, R. M. (1962). The acquisition of knowledge. *Psychological Review* **69**, 355–365.

Gagné, R. M. (1968). Learning hierarchies. *Educational Psychologist* **6**, No. 1.

Gagné, R. M. and Paradise, N. E. (1961). Abilities and learning sets in knowledge acquisition. *Psychological Monographs* **75**, Whole No. 518.

Inhelder, B. and Piaget, J. (1964). "The Early Growth of Logic in the Child: Classification and Seriation". Harper and Row, New York.

Klahr, D. (1973). Quantification processes. *In* "Visual Information Processing" (W. G. Chase, ed.). Academic Press, New York and London.

Klahr, D. and Wallace, J. G. (1972). Class inclusion processes. *In* "Information Processing in Children" (S. Farnham-Diggory, ed.). Academic Press, New York and London.

Klahr, D. and Wallace, J. G. (1976). "Cognitive Development: An Information-Processing View". Erlbaum, Hillsdale, N.J.

Miller, G. A., Galanter, E. and Pribram, K. H. (1960). "Plans and the Structure of Behavior". Holt, Rinehart and Winston, New York.

Moran, T. P. (1973). The symbolic nature of visual imagery. *Proceedings of the Third International Joint Conference on Artificial Intelligence*, 472–477.

Newell, A. (1972a). A theoretical exploration of mechanisms for coding the stimulus. *In* "Coding Processes in Human Memory" (A. W. Melton and E. Martin, eds). Winston, Washington, D.C.

Newell, A. (1972b). A note on process-structure distinctions in developmental psychology. *In* "Information Processing in Children" (S. Farnham-Diggory, ed.). Academic Press, New York and London.

Newell, A. (1973a). Production systems: models of control structures. *In* "Visual Information Processing" (W. G. Chase, ed). Academic Press, New York and London.

Newell, A. (1973b). You can't play 20 questions with nature and win: Projective comments on the papers of this symposium. *In* "Visual Information Processing" (W. G. Chase, ed). Academic Press, New York and London.

Newell, A. and Simon, H. A. (1972). "Human Problem Solving". Prentice-Hall, Englewood Cliffs, N.J.

Olson, D. R. (1970). "Cognitive Development: The Child's Acquisition of Diagonality". Academic Press, New York and London.

Piaget, J. (1952). "The Child's Conception of Number." Humanities Press, New York.

Piaget, J. and Inhelder, B. (1969). "The Psychology of the Child". Basic Books, New York.

Pinard, A. and Laurendeau, M. (1969). "Stage" in Piaget's cognitive-developmental theory: Exegesis of a concept. *In* "Studies in Cognitive Development" (D. Elkind and J. H. Flavell, eds). Oxford University Press, Oxford.

Resnick, L. B., Wang, M. C. and Kaplan, J. (1973). Task analysis in curriculum design: a hierarchically sequenced introductory mathematics curriculum. *Journal of Applied Behavior Analysis* **6**, 679–710.

Young, R. M. (1976). "Seriation by Children: An Artificial Intelligence Analysis of a Piagetian Task". Birkhäuser, Basel.

Twelve

Intelligence and General Strategies

Jonathan Baron
University of Pennsylvania

1. THE QUESTION

The question I shall try to answer is whether there are any general strategies underlying intelligent behaviour, behaviour of the short that distinguishes geniuses from retardates, or adults from children.

Before I can try to answer this question, I must explain what I mean by "intelligence", "strategy", "general" and "underlying".

1.1. Intelligence

I hope a better definition of intelligence than we have now will emerge from the kind of effort made here. For now, I shall rely on intuitions. The ultimate goal of the present enterprise is to sharpen and clarify these intuitions in a way that is consistent with empirical fact. In the course of this effort, the intuitions themselves may change, and the initial concept of intelligence may be found to have been made up by putting together parts of other concepts that do a better job of "carving nature at the joints". But these things need not occur; intelligence may turn out to be a perfectly respectable scientific concept.

For a start, we might begin with two general characteristics of people we usually consider intelligent. First, they know a lot. Second, they are able to solve new problems and to deal with new situations they have never before encountered. These two characteristics were surely part of the intuitions of the designers of intelligence tests, as these tests commonly provide direct measures of ability to solve various kinds of problems, and less direct measure of knowledge through sampling various facts to which people are likely to have been exposed. (In fact, the most difficult problem in intelligence testing seems to be that of sampling a body of knowledge to which those taking the test are equally likely to have been exposed.) Stepping back only slightly from these intuitions, we might define intelligence provisionally as the ability to acquire knowledge and to use it in unforeseen situations as well as predictable ones. Later, I shall argue that these two abilities are closely interrelated.

From this simple definition, it is already apparent that there has been very little study of the possible strategies behind many manifestations of intelligence. For example, while there is a great deal of work on the strategies used in acquiring knowledge (e.g. Flavell, 1970; Hagen *et al.*, 1975; Brown, 1975), there is little work on the strategies for using knowledge (however, *see* Ritter *et al.*, 1973; Kobasigawa, 1974). If this chapter serves only to expose gaps of this sort, it will have served well enough.

1.2. Strategies

There are three different kinds of limits on ability to do a task: failure to use the appropriate strategy, inadequate proficiency and limited capacity. Consider, for example, the strategy of rehearsing a list of items when one is instructed to learn the list (Atkinson and Shiffrin, 1968). Young children (Flavell, 1970) and retardates (Brown, 1974) do not use this strategy in situations where older children use it habitually. Failure to use the *strategy* is reflected in such indices as the lack of vocalization during presentation of the items (Flavell, 1970) and different pause patterns when the subject presents the items to himself (Belmont and Butterfield, 1971). When young children are instructed to rehearse, not only does their memory performance improve, but these indirect indices also show them to resemble older children. The instruction has no effect on older children, presumably because the older children are already using the strategy.

Simple instruction does not ordinarily eliminate the difference between younger and older children or retardates and normals, although these differences are reduced. Children may still differ in the *proficiency* with which they use the strategy even if they use it all the time. Such differences in proficiency might be eliminated with extensive practice; however, I know of no studies that address this question.

Group differences that remain even when asymptotic performance is reached must be ascribed to differences in *capacity*. For example, groups may still differ in the rate of rehearsal of the items, or in the rate at which items decay in short-term memory while other items are being rehearsed. Chi (1978), after reviewing the literature on memory span in children, could find no evidence for any differences between ages in the rate of decay. Chi ascribed differences in memory span to factors involving "long-term memory"—possibly factors having to do with the degree of practice at repeating or rehearsing the items used in the tests. However, it is also possible that the remaining differences are due to differences in speed of mental operations, or ability to focus attention or to deploy mental resources. These would be capacity limits rather than proficiency limits. In principle, we can tell which kind of limit is involved by giving practice until the asymptote is reached.

In sum, we may distinguish the kinds of limits on performance in terms of the ways in which they may be overcome and the ways in which we measure them. Ordinarily, failure to use a strategy is overcome only by training that changes behaviour, training such as verbal instruction, modelling or shaping (in the sense used in operant conditioning). Proficiency limits may be overcome only by practice at tasks in which the strategy in question is used. Practice may also help overcome failure to use a strategy, but only if the learner spontaneously discovers, as a result of the practice, that the strategy helps. Capacity limits, by definition, cannot be overcome by psychological manipulations; possibly, they may be affected by drugs or other influences on the brain. We may measure use of the strategy in terms of the probability that it is used in an appropriate situation. Capacities and proficiency may be measured in terms of speed or sensitivity to disruption by concurrent demands on resources.

It is important to point out that these three kinds of limit are not as distinct as they might first appear to be. Limited capacity may affect not only the asymptotic level of skill, but also the ease of acquiring a strategy for the first time. Several accounts of the course of development of children's concepts (e.g. McLaughlin, 1963; Pascual-Leone, 1970) have proposed that the strategies involved in various tasks cannot be acquired because of various kinds of capacity limits such as the size of working memory. Strategies themselves may require minimal levels of certain capacities. Further, proficiency at a strategy may also affect the probability of applying that strategy to a new situation for the first time. Results from studies of both paired-associate learning and discrimination learning (*see* Esposito, 1975) indicate that overlearning facilitates positive transfer of a response (a simple kind of strategy, for our purposes). As yet, we don't know whether the effect of overlearning is mediated by increases in proficiency. It is conceivable that both proficiency and probability of using a strategy are influenced by a single underlying variable, which we might call the strength of a given strategy. At low levels of strength, the probability of using the strategy is affected by changes in strength. At higher levels, the speed may be affected. LaBerge (1975) has presented evidence that the use of resources by a response may continue to decrease even if the speed of the response were to reach asymptote. Thus, only the use of resources may be affected by changes in strength at high levels. For the remainder of this chapter, for simplicity, I shall speak of the strength of a strategy as if strength were a single continuum, reflected in different measures of performance, and influenced by different manipulations in different ranges. I shall also assume that stronger strategies are more likely to transfer to new situations, other things being equal. If this assumption turns out to be wrong, of course, modifications in other suggestions will be required, but these modifications will in every case be peripheral to the main arguments. The advantage of this assumption is that it allows us to speculate about the role of strategies in intelligence by suggesting simply that differences in intelligence are reflected in differences in strengths of the underlying strategies. At low levels of strength, the strategies will not be used at all. Higher levels of intelligence will be distinguished by differences in proficiency, and (perhaps consequently) in tendency to transfer strategies to new situations.

Of course, capacities are also likely to be involved in intelligence, if for no other reason than that they may limit the acquisition and use of strategies. But my concern here is with strategies for three reasons. First, strategies are modifiable by educational manipulations, and it may be useful right now to be able to manipulate intelligence through education in the most direct way. Second, strategies seem to be the more observable manifestation of intelligence. So far, I know of no interesting differences between ages or ability groups that *must* be ascribed to differences in capacities. Yet there are plenty of differences that must be ascribed largely to differences in strategies, such as the differences in memory resulting from differences in rehearsal (described above). Third, capacities influence the manifestations of intelligence in part *through* their influence on the acquisition and use of general strategies. If we knew what these strategies were, we would be in a better position to discover which capacities were most important.

1.3. Generality

General strategies are those that are useful in a wide variety of situations. "Rehearsing" is a strategy that is helpful in memorizing almost any list of items, while "reciting the alphabet" is a strategy that is useful in so few situations that it hardly merits the name "strategy". A strategy that is useful in many situations is one that may become useful as a result of transfer of the strategy from one situation to the other. Thus, the more general a strategy is, the more important it is that the mechanisms by which transfer occurs are working well. (By transfer, here, I mean that using a strategy in one situation can increase the probability of using it in another.)

Beyond this, it is difficult to be more precise about what generality is. In principle, it might be possible to count the number of situations in which a strategy is useful. But many problems arise. For example, it is difficult to say what is to count as one situation. Is memorizing one list of nonsense syllables the same situation as memorizing, for example, a poem, a list of words, another list of nonsense syllables, or the same list on another day or in a different place? A more useful measure of generality might be based on inclusion. One strategy may be said to be more general than another if the first is useful in all situations where the second is, plus others. However, even this definition would have to be dependent upon the opportunities provided by a particular environment. Possibly a different environment could present situations in which the second strategy is useful but not the first.

In spite of these complexities, generality seems to be an intuitively strong idea. And on the basis of this intuitive idea, it also appears that much of the work on strategies has focused on strategies of very limited generality (*see* Baron, 1973, for a review of some of this literature).

Even rehearsal, for example, does not seem to be useful outside of very simple memory tasks presented in psychology laboratories and in few other places; dramatic evidence for the specificity of rehearsal is provided by the finding that "idiot savants", calender calculators who were institutionalized because of overall retardation, perform as well as normals in a digit-span task (Spitz and LaFontaine, 1973).

1.4. Central strategies

I have said that the strategies we are seeking are not only general but also central in the sense that they "underlie" intelligence. This idea is even less clear than the idea of generality, but it may not be meaningless. One way of finding underlying strategies is first to look for the general strategies that are each useful in dealing with a variety of situations in a variety of environments, such as rehearsal. Then we ask what strategies were helpful in acquiring these strategies, and what strategies were helpful in acquiring the helpful strategies, and so on, until we reach some core set of strategies. If we keep coming up with the same core strategies we can be sure either that we are on the right track or that we are biased. Empirical investigation is the best insurance against bias.

If there are such central strategies, we might imagine that they are acquired before the less central ones in the course of development. Such early strategies might define an early "stage" of development. Thus, a child might begin his course of intellectual development by acquiring strategies 1a, 1b and 1c. These might lead to the acquisition of 2a, 2b, 2c, 2d and 2e, which, in turn, might lead to 3a, 3b, 3c, 3d, 3e, 3f and 3g, and so on, until we reach a number of more specific and more advanced strategies. If this is the case, the numbers might correspond to stages in Piaget's sense. Operationally, if we set up a task to pit a higher-numbered strategy against a lower-numbered one, the higher-numbered one will be more likely to be used in older children. But such consistent orderings will be impossible with strategies at the same stage; the particular developmental ordering of the two strategies might change as a function of the individual, the task, or the environment.

However, the central strategies need not be acquired early in development. It is possible that some of the higher-numbered strategies could be learned without the benefit of that learning being facilitated by the lower-numbered strategies. It is also possible that both the central and non-central strategies simply increase in strength with development, in roughly the same way. Even a weak central strategy may facilitate the acquisition of a non-central one. Therefore, while the idea of central strategies is consistent with the idea of stages, one idea does not imply the other.

If we think that the various strategies do form some sort of hierarchy, and that the strategies at the top of the hierarchy are learned first, with the others following in stages, this supposition *seems* to lead to the expectation that the central strategies will reach their full strength early in development, and will play little role in adult intelligence. If this is true, there will be little point in looking for differences among adults in the use of central strategies; instead we should look for the lasting effects, if any, of the weakness of these strategies in childhood, and we should look for differences among children in use of the central strategies. However, this expectation need not be true. Even the central strategies may continue to grow in strength throughout development, or they may level off at different points. If the strengths of the central strategies do differ among adults, we will observe the effects of these differences in the proficiency at applying these strategies in situations where they are habitually used, but, more importantly, in the tendency of these strategies to transfer to new situations. (Recall our earlier assumption that stronger strategies are more likely to transfer.) Thus, even if stages do exist, each stage may continue to increase in strength even while subsequent stages are increasing in strength (presumably at a faster rate), and stages may level off at different strengths in different people. The strength of early stages—and therefore of central strategies—may still influence intelligence in adults. In sum, the existence of stages does not imply that adults are equally good at the central skills.

Another way to think about central strategies is to suppose that they are strategies that are always worth trying before responding to a new situation in which we are required to make a response. At best, such central strategies may help us learn a new general (but not necessarily central) strategy for dealing with a class of situations. Use of a central strategy might also promote transfer of a strategy to the new situation, or learning of a specific strategy for the situation. Presumably, central strategies would *impair* performance only when there was pressure to respond quickly.

I hope these comments have helped to clarify the original question about the existence of general strategies underlying intelligent behaviour. In the rest of this chapter, I shall make an argument for the existence of these strategies, speculate about what they might be, and finally discuss the implications of my general view for future research. The argument for the existence of the central strategies will consist of two parts, an argument for environmental effects on intelligence, and an argument that differences in intelligence, as reflected in specific tasks, can often (if not always) be accounted for by differences in the use of strategies (which is not to say that these differences in use of strategies cannot be accounted for by differences in capacities).

2. EVIDENCE FOR ENVIRONMENTAL EFFECTS

One of the consequences of the possible existence of general strategies is that the acquisition of these strategies ought to be influenced by opportunities in the environment. If we have any hope of using schooling to improve general intelligence by teaching the central strategies directly, it would be nice if we could show that schooling even now affects intelligence.

Some pessimism might arise from studies showing that differences among schools in the same country have only very small effects on differences in basic skills such as reading and arithmetic, once the social class and culture of the students are taken into account (Jencks *et al.*, 1972, p. 91). However, the effects of social class are substantial, and to the extent that school quality is determined by the social class of those who attend it, holding social class constant may mask the effects of school quality (as Jencks acknowledges in a footnote). Further, measuring differences between schools is not the same as measuring differences in schooling: children may get different qualities of schooling within the same school.

When we turn to the effects of school itself, rather than the effects of differences among schools, the effects seem substantial. It is no surprise that basic skills such as reading improve less over summer vacation, or during forced absences from school, than they do when school is in session (Jencks *et al.*, 1972, p. 87) for the schools try to teach just these skills. It is more relevant, however, that schooling seems to have pronounced effects on abilities that are not directly taught in school, such as abilities involved in memorizing (Wagner, 1974), or in solving simple but unfamiliar problems (Cole and Scribner, 1974). Some of this evidence will be examined in more detail below.

In sum, schooling—the aspect of the environment most easily influenced by public policy—can have pronounced effects on intelligence, the acquisition of knowledge and its use in new situations as well as familiar ones. Perhaps an understanding of the basis of these effects can lead to increased effectiveness of schooling in this regard. I now turn to more specific evidence for differences among individuals in general strategies, thus arguing in a different way for the possibility of increasing intelligence through education.

3. INVOLVEMENT OF GENERAL STRATEGIES IN GROUP DIFFERENCES

While there have been practically no attempts to measure the use of central strategies, there have been many attempts to measure the use of strategies of some generality, such as rehearsal. Most of these comparisons involve memory tasks, although some involve tasks requiring selective attention, and others involve linguistic variables. I shall focus on several kinds of comparisons: comparison between older and younger children (or between adults and children) is useful if we make the reasonable assumption that intelligence increases with age. Comparison between normal and retarded children is also of obvious interest, although the deficiencies of retardates may turn out to be along different dimensions than those that distinguish intelligent from less intelligent people in general. I shall also discuss comparisons of highly intelligent adults with less intelligent adults, differences that result from ageing, and comparisons of schooled and unschooled individuals.

In each of these cases, I shall present evidence that many differences in performance between groups can be accounted for by differences in the use of strategies, but few, if any, require explanations in terms of capacity differences. It might be argued that it is impossible to show that performance difference is due to capacity differences. However, I would answer that in principle, at least, it is possible to find some simple, strategy-free task that can measure the purported capacity and then show that groups differ in asymptotic performance of that task. Such a strategy of research has not to my knowledge been used. In spite of the lack of evidence bearing on the question of capacity differences as explanations of performance differences in many tasks, it is none the less surprising how many group differences in performance can be attributed entirely to differences in strategy.

3.1. Differences between older children (or adults) and younger children

Since the literature on age differences constitutes an entire subfield of psychology, I shall focus here only on those cases in which age differences have been analysed with respect to the distinction between strategies and capacities, or in which the age differences in question seem particularly enlightening about general mechanisms of intellectual development. Almost all of the studies in which differences have been analysed concern differences in memory. The major reviews of the literature in this area (Flavell, 1970; Hagen *et al.*, 1975; Brown, 1974,

1975) are in essential agreement that differences in memory abilities can so far be ascribed entirely to differences in strategies (if we include with strategies differences in specific knowledge, such as knowledge of vocabulary). In addition to memory, I shall also discuss age differences in the ability to select relevant information and ignore irrelevant information.

The best example of the development of strategies for memory concerns the development of rehearsal. Flavell *et al.* (1970) asked children to learn the names of an array of pictures for later recall (in order). Children were observed through a one-way mirror; since the names of the pictures were associated with easily observed lip movements, it was possible to observe rehearsal directly. Kindergarteners rehearsed very little during learning, but fourth graders showed considerable rehearsal. Differences in other learning strategies, such as self-testing, were also observed. It was suggested that the failure of young children to use effective learning strategies resulted from their lack of knowledge about the relation between these strategies and performance, a suggestion supported by evidence that young children were poor in predicting the amount of material they could correctly recall. I shall return to this issue later.

Keeney *et al.* (1967) showed first graders an array of pictures, and asked the children to remember (in order) which pictures the experimenter pointed to. On the basis of observation of lip movements, groups of rehearsers and non-rehearsers were selected. These groups differed in performance in the memory task, as we would expect on the assumption that rehearsal helps. Half of the non-rehearsers were then instructed to rehearse, and the task was presented again to all subjects. This time, the non-rehearsers who had been told to rehearse did as well as the rehearsers on the memory task, and better than the other half of the non-rehearsers. The task was given for a third time to all subjects to find out whether the trained group would continue to rehearse. It appeared that only some of the subjects did so. The others reverted back to their old ways, and their performance declined. The failure of such training to transfer to subsequent presentations of the task is a finding that occurs frequently in the literature on strategies; I shall return to this topic later.

If a normal adult is asked to learn a list of items that can be grouped into categories, such as animals, tools and furniture, he will group the items, mentally or physically, as a way of learning them. Moely *et al.* (1969) presented children with a set of pictures drawn from four different categories and asked the children to learn the items for later recall. Kindergarteners did not use the strategy of putting the items together into groups, while fifth graders usually did. This was indicated both by observation of whether the children put related pictures together when the children were learning the pictures and of whether the children grouped pictures from the same category together during recall. Even the kindergarteners, however, could put the pictures into groups when asked to do so. The younger children could also be taught to group the items, and when the children did what they were taught, they remembered more of the items.

Incidental learning procedures, in which the subject does not expect recall to be tested, can be particularly useful in examining the development of learning strategies, since it is often safe to assume that subjects of any age will not use learning strategies unless they expect their memory to be tested. Appel *et al.* (1972), for example, presented pictures to first- and fifth-grade children in two different conditions. In one condition, the children were instructed simply to look at the pictures (under the pretence that looking might help performance in a later task), and in the other, the children were instructed to learn the pictures for subsequent recall. In essence, the first condition was an incidental learning condition, the second an intentional learning condition. For first-grade children, there was no difference in recall performance between these two conditions; only for fifth-grade children did differences between these conditions emerge. Observations of the children also revealed differences in learning strategies. The most effective strategy seemed to be one involving grouping of the items; this was used more by the fifth graders, and was correlated with better performance.

Incidental learning usually involves the use of an "orienting task", a task that takes the place of the learning task and that forces the subject to attend to the items, at least. Sometimes the orienting task may provide a better way of learning the items than the strategies used spontaneously by the subject (although this is often the case because of extra cues that are presented along with the orienting task). M. Brevik and F. I. M. Craik (unpublished), for example, presented a list of words to second-, forth- and sixth-grade children in four different conditions. In one of these conditions, an intentional learning condition, the subjects were simply asked to learn the words. In the other three conditions, the subject performed different orienting tasks with the words: deciding whether the words were presented in upper or lower case, deciding whether each word rhymed with a word presented just before, or deciding whether each word fitted into a sentence presented just before. Memory was tested in two ways. In the recall test, the subjects were asked to recall the words. In the recognition test, the subjects were given a list of words and asked to pick out the words they had seen before.

The different orienting tasks led to different amounts of memory, regardless of age or method of testing; the sentence task was best, the rhyme task next best. In the recall test, older children did better than younger children regardless of the conditions of presentation of the words. However, the effects of age were much greater on the intentional task than on any of the incidental tasks. This suggests that the older children were using learning strategies more, or with greater skill, than the younger children. The data from the recognition test were even more interesting. Here, there were essentially no age differences in performance after incidental learning. There were still differences, however, in performance after intentional learning. These differences in intentional learning probably reflect better use of learning strategies by older children. The fact that recognition performance was unaffected by age, however, suggests that the *capacity* that limits performance here, if any, does not change with age. Differences between ages in the incidental tasks using recall might be due to differences in certain strategies for *retrieving* information that is already in memory. These strategies are presumably useful in a free-recall task, but not in a recognition task. Brown (1975) has found other tasks that show no age differences, again, presumably, because certain retrieval strategies are not helpful.

As yet, we know little about what these retrieval strategies, if they exist, might be. Some attempts have been made to examine the development of retrieval strategies, but the strategies examined seemed to be highly specific ones, useful for retrieval only in the particular task presented—although these strategies might involve more general problem-solving strategies. For example, in one study (Ritter et al., 1973), young children failed to turn over cards that could have reminded them of the contents of boxes, which they were asked to recall. In another (Kobasigawa, 1974), children apparently failed to use pictures that could serve as useful reminders.

All in all, studies of the development of memory yielded much evidence for the view that age differences in memory can be explained in terms of differences in strategies for learning and retrieval. Some studies (Brown, 1975; M. Brevik and F. I. M. Craik, unpublished) suggest that when learning strategies are controlled by using orienting tasks, or made useless, and when retrieval strategies are not helpful, age differences disappear. While the acquisition of strategies for learning and retrieval may be limited by various capacities, there is as yet no convincing evidence that capacities limit performance more directly.

This general conclusion seems to apply to "primary" memory as well as long-term memory. By primary memory, I mean the part of performance in some short-term memory tasks that is limited only by active processes that continue between the time of presentation and recall. It is well known that measures of this ability increase with age and intelligence; in fact, one of the items included on many intelligence tests is a test of the digit span, the number of random digits that can be recalled in order without error after a single presentation. However, there is evidence that at least some of the differences between ages are the result of strategy differences rather than capacity differences (for a fuller statement of this argument, *see* Chi, 1978).

Performance in the digit-span test, or similar tasks, may be decomposed into various strategies and capacities. Most adults do this task by rehearsing the digits as fast as possible as the digits are presented. Thus, memory is limited largely by the amount that can be rehearsed at once. This amount, in turn, is limited by the rate of decay of the memory of each digit, and the speed of rehearsing. For example, if the memory of a single digit decays (during the rehearsal of other digits) to the point where it is lost in 2 s, and if the rate of rehearsal is 4 digits s^{-1}, the digit span will be approximately 8 digits. There is also the problem of simultaneously attending to new digits as they come in while rehearsing old ones. Thus, the less capacity used up by the rehearsal, the better.

Chi (1978) has reviewed a number of studies attempting to measure directly the rate of decay of information in short-term memory (when the subject is attending to other information). The function relating memory to time seems to be unaffected by age in all the studies Chi could find, although most of these studies are questionable for various reasons. On the other hand, we may view the speed of rehearsal as a process limited by reaction time, the time required to repeat quickly a digit that is just about to drop out of one's memory. Children are slower than adults in every reaction-time task examined so far. At least part of this slowness may be due to lack of practice with the specific items involved, that is, in the terms I defined earlier, lack of strength of the strategy of repeating. There is evidence (e.g. Conrad, 1962) that speed of responding in situations like these is influenced by familiarity of the material. Perhaps children would not differ in speed if the material were totally unfamiliar (and totally unrelated to any items that were familiar)—but this is an impossible experiment to do. Another approach is to present the material to be remembered at different rates to adults and children, so as to equate the two groups in terms of the amount of material they can recognize and name in the time taken to present all the material. Chi (1978) has reported that when this is done, age differences disappear.

Further, unfamiliar material seems to require more capacity. LaBerge (1975), for example, has shown that a warning signal providing information about the nature of a stimulus was not helpful when the stimulus was a familiar letter to be named, but such a warning was helpful when the stimulus was a nonsense form to be named with a response only recently learned. Presumably, the helpfulness of the warning signal results from the ability of the subject to mobilize resources to deal with the particular item before it is presented; the warning is not helpful for familiar material because few resources are required. The use of familiar material in primary memory tasks thus frees the subject's resources from rehearsing, so that he may devote more of them to dealing with incoming items and making decisions about which items to rehearse. Almost any material one can imagine is more familiar to adults than to children. In sum, while it may well be that differences in capacity may account in part for age differences in digit span, it is possible to account for these differences now on the basis of familiarity alone, without assuming the existence of such capacity differences. Note that this can be done even under the assumption that all children rehearse in these tasks. The evidence presented above (and below, concerning retardates) indicates that young children or retardates do not even rehearse. This evidence thus strengthens the argument that memory differences may be ascribed to differences in use of, and in skill of using, strategies.

Summarizing the research on the development of memory, there have been several convincing demonstrations that the improvement of memory abilities with age is at least in part the result of the increasing strength of strategies for learning and retrieving, both in primary and secondary memory. There are, to my knowledge, no convincing demonstrations of age difference in such relevant capacities as the rate of decay of memory or the strength of the memory trace that results from the application of a given learning strategy to a given stimulus. This is not to say that no capacities are relevant to memory abilities. However, it is beginning to appear likely that capacities relevant to age differences in memory exert their effects indirectly through the limits they place on the acquisition and use of strategies for learning and retrieving.

To move to a new topic, there is some evidence that strategies for *attending* may change with age in ways that allow us to account for the performance of young children in a large variety of tasks. In particular, it seems that older children are more likely to treat a multidimensional stimulus as a complex of attributes on its respective dimensions, while younger children are more likely to treat the same stimulus as a whole (D. G. Kemler, unpublished). To test such an idea, Smith and Kemler (1977) gave younger and older children groups of three stimuli, on cards, and asked the children to put the two together that went together best. A typical set of stimuli might consist of cards with forms differing in size and brightness. Cards A and B would be identical on the dimension of brightness, but widely discrepant from one another on the dimension of size. The third card, C, would be similar to A in both brightness and size, but identical on neither dimension. Older children tended to put A and B together, while younger children tended to put A and C together. This result, and others like it, indicates that the older children were basing their judgements on the fact that A and B were identical on one dimension, while the younger children were basing their judgements on the overall similarity of A and C. While this perception of overall similarity is—in a sense—determined by the fact that A and C are similar on two dimensions, it appears that the values on the dimensions are not attended to independently of one another. (This developmental change does not occur with all pairs of dimensions. Adults, for example, treat hue and brightness of colour patches the way that children treat brightness and size. Such findings as these have led Garner (1974), to make a distinction between pairs of dimensions that are "integral", as in the A–C response, and those that are "separable", as in the A–B response. From this perspective, most pairs of dimensions appear to move from integrality to separability with age, although some dimensions do not complete the developmental change.)

Other evidence indicates that adults can ignore irrelevant changes in dimensions, but children cannot, in speeded classification tasks. Shepp and Swartz (1976), for example, found that children could sort cards on the basis of colour more quickly when the form containing the colour was held constant, as opposed to another condition in which the form varied unpredictably from card to card. Adults, however, were undisturbed by variations in size. Smith et al. (1975) obtained a similar result.

We can account for this kind of result by making a distinction between two strategies, a "dimension" strategy, which leads to the A–B classification, and a "similarity" strategy, which leads to the A–C classification (Smith and Kemler, 1977). The dimension strategy increases in strength with age, leading to different performance in Smith and Kemler's classification task. As the strength of the dimension strategy increases, its use becomes not only more probable, but also faster and more automatic. Eventually, for some dimensions, it may become faster than the similarity strategy, so that subjects might classify stimuli more quickly on the basis of identity on a single dimension than on the basis of overall similarity (although the speed of both strategies is surely influenced by many specific factors such as the degree of similarity between the two critical stimuli on the relevant dimensions).

This assumption about speed allows us to account for adults' ability to ignore the irrelevant dimension in speeded classification tasks; the similarity strategy here is simply too slow to influence performance, or else the dimension strategy is so automatic that nothing else *can* influence performance. This assumption about increases in speed also allows us to account for another result. Adults who can ignore irrelevant variation on a dimension often seem incapable of using correlated variation to their advantage. For example, if the brighter of two stimuli is always the larger (or always the smaller), someone who attended to both dimensions simultaneously, or to the overall perception that the two stimuli were very different, ought to classify the stimuli faster than he would in a condition in which he must base his response on one dimension, while the other is held constant for all stimuli. For dimensions such as form and colour, this sort of result is found with children but not with adults (Shepp and Swartz, 1976). Adults, according to my strategy explanation, cannot take advantage of the fact that both dimensions are useful, since to do so they would have to switch from a dimension strategy to a similarity strategy, and since the dimensions strategy is so much faster for these stimuli then the switch would not be worth it.

I should point out that there are other explanations of these results besides my explanation in terms of strategies. Capacities may also be involved. Perhaps these developmental changes would occur as a result of maturation of the brain, without any influence of learning. (Cross-cultural studies might shed some light on this possibility, especially if it is found that some cultures do not show age differences.) Or it may turn out that strategies are involved, but that their acquisition is limited entirely by capacities. Perhaps, for example, young children have difficulty judging whether or not two stimuli have identical values on one dimension when the stimuli have discrepant values on another dimension. For the time being, however, I shall assume that strategies do account for these results.

The reason for mentioning the possibility of a dimension strategy that develops, in spite of the lack of conclusive evidence for its status as a strategy, is the potential power of this idea for explaining other changes that occur with age. Many other experimental tasks involve attending to some dimensions while ignoring others, for example the classification tasks of Inhelder and Piaget (1964) and the dimensional discrimination-learning tasks used in so many developmental studies. Beyond these tasks, much of what children have to learn in school involves selective attention to dimensions. I shall have more to say about the possible power of this strategy later on.

To conclude this brief summary of developmental studies of strategies, I should point out that I have dealt only with some of the least obvious cases in which strategies might account for age trends. Many studies of memory and attention have been based on the questionable assumption that capacities could be measured directly. Instead, it now appears that age trends can be accounted for by strengthening of general strategies. It is thus the encroachment of strategy explanations on the territory of capacity that attracts our attention here, as well as the possible generality of these strategies. However, in attending to these surprising recent studies, we should not forget about the massive body of evidence for the involvement of strategies—some of considerable generality—in other developmental changes. In an earlier paper (Baron, 1973), I reviewed some of the evidence for the involvement of strategies in the acquisition of word meanings, logical abilities, moral reasoning and conservation tasks (see also Lawson et al., 1974; Schaeffer et al., 1974; Gelman, 1978; for further discussion of strategies in elementary arithmetic concepts). In a sense, the present discussion begins where that paper left off.

3.2. Differences between retarded and normal children

While there is far less literature on the nature of retardation than on the nature of childhood, the literature that exists tends to be more relevant to the question of strategies and intelligence. Many people who have studied retardates have done so with the ultimate goal in mind of discovering remediable differences, hence differences in strategies, and especially general strategies, between retardates and normals (e.g. Brown, 1974; Fisher and Zeaman, 1973). A number of techniques for assessing differences in strategies have grown out of this research. In general, the findings resulting from the use of these techniques are similar to those comparing children and adults with other techniques. Large differences in use of strategies are apparent, and many of the deficiencies of retardates appear to be remediable in the specific tasks in which the differences are measured. Further, there is no convincing evidence that capacities affect performance directly, although they may account for differences in the strengths of useful strategies.

Again, rehearsal in memory tasks turns out to be a strategy that has been carefully examined. One new technique for studying rehearsal is that of Belmont and Butterfield (1971). Subjects presented themselves with a series of letters for subsequent recall by pressing a button to change the display. Normal subjects almost invariably paused after the fourth letter to rehearse what they had showed themselves so far, but retardates did not. When retardates were taught to rehearse, their pause patterns resembled those of normals, and their recall performance improved, almost to the level of normals.

A second technique for studying differences in rehearsal has been developed by Brown and her coworkers (Brown, 1974). On each trial of a memory experiment, subjects were presented with the latest information about the state of four different variables: animals, vehicles, food and clothing. For example, on a trial, the subject might be shown a picture of a dog, a car, a banana and a shirt. He was then asked to recall the state of one of the four variables; for example, he might be asked what the last animal was. Different variables have different numbers of possible states; there might be two different possible animals but six different vehicles. For normal 9-year-olds performance is independent of the number of states, and of the position in which the probed information was presented during the trial. Retardates, however, recall less when the number of possible states is large and when the critical information was presented early in the trial. If they are trained to rehearse, however, their performance resembles that of normals with respect to the effects of number of states and position in the trial, as well as overall performance. Five months later, eight out of ten trained retardates continued to rehearse in the same task.

Ellis (1970) has presented other evidence for a rehearsal deficit in retardates. Retardates given a task requiring ordered memory for strings of digits showed no effect of the rate of presentation of the digits, while normals performed better with slower presentations.

While differences in rehearsal between retardates and normals are apparent, there is apparently no evidence for differences in forgetting rate when strategies are not involved. Anders (reported in Ellis, 1970) tested retardates and normals in a task in which the subjects counted backwards during a retention interval before trying to recall digits. Memory over the retention interval declined at about the same rate for the two groups over 10 s, although the ultimate level reached was lower in retardates (possibly because of differences in learning strategies). Other investigators (Belmont, 1967; Holden, 1971) have used perceptual memory tasks in which rehearsal would seem to be useless as a strategy, and have found at most only tiny differences between retardates and normals. (Small differences in studies such as these may be due to perceptual deficits accompanying retardation resulting from general biological insults such as birth anoxia.) As yet, there have been no studies of forgetting over a longer period when initial storage is held constant.

Retardates also differ from normals in attention. The most interesting finding in this area is that of Zeaman and House (1963) concerning the role of attention in discrimination learning. In a typical problem, on each trial, subjects are given two stimuli differing in a number of dimensions, such as colour, size and form, and are rewarded for pointing to the one the experimenter defines as correct, which is defined by a certain value (e.g. red) on one of the dimensions. A great deal of evidence (*see* Fisher and Zeaman, 1973) indicates that learning to point to the correct stimulus can be broken down into two processes, learning to attend to the correct dimension, and learning to associate the correct value on that dimension with the response. Before the subject attends to the correct dimension, performance over a series of trials is usually at chance level (50% correct, with two stimuli). Once the correct dimension is discovered, performance rises quickly to 100% correct over a few trials. Zeaman and House (1963) argued that retardates and normals differ only in the process of learning to attend to the correct dimension. This was inferred from the finding that the groups did not differ in the rate of moving from 50% to 100% correct performance once the learning curve started to rise above 50% (which was determined by examining the trials preceding the point at which the learning curve reached 100%).

Several explanations of this attentional deficit may be proposed (and have been proposed), but most of them have to do with strategies rather than capacities. One explanation (Fisher and Zeaman, 1973) holds that the sorts of dimensions used in these tasks are less salient for retardates than normals. If this were the entire source of the deficit, it ought to be possible to find other dimensions that retardates could learn to use more quickly than normals. An explanation in terms of dimensional salience would be the least interesting sort of explanation, since the strategy of attending to colour or form is not a very general one, or one that seems obviously related to intelligence in a number of tasks—although it might be possible to explain salience differences in terms of yet other processes and strategies of greater interest. A second explanation (Fisher and Zeaman, 1973) holds that retardates attend to fewer dimensions on a given trial, possibly only one, and are thus less likely to notice consistent relationships between a value on a given dimension and the correct response. Independent evidence for such a possibility comes from a study in which subjects were presented with a single stimulus and then tested for their ability to recognize the dimensions of that stimulus independently (Fisher and Zeaman, 1973). For example, if the subjects were first shown a red square, they would then be asked to choose between a red triangle and a blue triangle, or between a blue circle and a blue square, on the basis of which was most like the original stimulus. Retardates performed at about a 75% level on these tests, suggesting that they attended only to one dimension and were forced to guess if they were tested on the dimension they had not attended to, but normals performed considerably better. Such a difference between groups is very likely a result of strategy differences, since the retarded subjects were easily capable of remembering two facts about a stimulus (although the modifiability of the strategy was not examined). A third possible explanation (Zeaman and House, 1963) is that retardates are less sensitive to feedback in deciding which dimension to attend to. This might occur for a variety of reasons; for example, retardates might more readily attend to dimensions that have already been ruled out as consistent predictors of reward. (One might think that this problem could arise from differences in memory for hypotheses previously rejected, and thus result from capacity differences rather than strategy differences. However, memory differences themselves may result from strategy differences. Further, Kemler (1978), has found that young children tend to return to ruled-out hypotheses even when the memory problem is made trivially easy by help from the experimenter.) A fourth possible explanation of the differences between retardates and normals is that—following the reasoning of Smith and Kemler (1977) described above—retardates are less likely to attend to dimensions at all. If retardates are more prone to use a similarity strategy rather than a dimension strategy in deciding whether a given stimulus is similar to others that have been associated with reward, they will be correspondingly less likely to notice consistent relationships between attributes and reward. If this is true, differences between retardates and normals should be substantially reduced if the discrimination to be learned is best defined in terms of overall similarity of the stimuli associated with reward rather than in terms of identity on a particular attribute. Differences in the use of a dimension strategy may also serve to explain the finding of Fisher and Zeaman (1973) that retardates appear to remember fewer of the specific dimensions of a stimulus presented once (D. G. Kemler, unpublished).

More generally, it is of some interest that many of the differences between retardates and normals may be traced to possible differences in strategies rather than capacities. Of course, these differences may themselves be the result of differences in capacities. Indeed, in cases of retardation resulting from obvious biological causes, the existence of capacity deficits cannot be disputed. Yet at present there are only a few suggestions about what these capacity differences might be—such as the finding that reaction time is slower for retardates in every task examined. Even when clear capacity differences exist, the question still arises of whether these differences affect intelligent behaviour directly or indirectly through their influence on general strategies.

3.3. Differences between adults of different intelligence levels

In a way, the most obvious test of any proposal about the nature of intelligence is its ability to account for differences among adolescents or adults of the same age. In practice, however, the difficulty of measuring adult intelligence makes this sort of comparison more complicated than it would at first appear to be. Comparisons of adults of different IQ scores, for example, suffer from the possibility that individuals with different scores on the IQ test could actually be identical in real intelligence, whatever that turns out to be. The same applies to other correlates of adult intelligence, such as educational level. In fact all of the various comparisons I have mentioned suffer from the same problem: the groups may differ in other respects than intelligence, and these other differences may account for any observed differences in strategies. Our best insurance against being misled by any particular finding is to make sure that the finding applies to a number of kinds of comparisons, and, perhaps even more importantly, to make sure that the differences we find can in fact account for the different qualities of intelligent and unintelligent behaviour. With these cautions in mind, I shall now discuss a few suggestive results concerning intelligence differences among adults and among adolescents.

One of the most interesting results concerns the development of learning strategies in high-school students from different schools. Rohwer and Bean (1973) gave a paired-associate learning task, using pairs of nouns, to students ranging from the first to the eleventh grades. In the condition of primary interest, subjects were instructed to listen to the pairs and *learn* them. The question of interest here is whether the subjects would use elaborative strategies, such as making up a sentence out of the two words or imagining the two words together in a combined image. To measure elaboration, two other conditions were used, one in which the subjects were instructed simply to *rehearse* the pairs, thus preventing elaboration, and another in which the subjects were instructed to make up a *sentence* out of each pair, thus forcing a kind of elaboration. The sentence condition led to better performance than the rehearse condition by about the same amount for all subjects. The younger children in the sample showed no evidence of spontaneous elaboration, since their scores in the learn condition were identical to their scores in the rehearse condition. Of particular interest is the performance of the high-school students. One group of high-school students was selected from a middle-class school. This group showed no evidence of elaboration. A second group, however, was selected from a school system in which most parents had completed college and in which most families contained a member with a job that could be called "professional". Here, while the younger children still showed no evidence of elaboration, the older high-school students showed considerable evidence of using elaborative strategies in the learn condition. They performed as well in the learn condition as in the sentence condition. Other studies had shown that college students also use elaboration strategies spontaneously in similar tasks. These differences seem to be most easily explained by the idea that college students, and children of college-educated parents, for whatever reason, are more intelligent than other children, and more intelligent people are more likely to use elaborative strategies spontaneously.

A second kind of result concerns the discovery of adults with unusual memory abilities. Hunt and Love (1972), for example, have described a case of a man who has memory abilities far out of the normal range, yet who does not seem to rely on synesthesias or eidetic imagery. His performance appears to be due to a combination of a high (but not extraordinary)mental capacity (as measured by subtests of an intelligence test) and a more extensive use of the kind of learning strategies used by others. While these strategies may not be "central", they are certainly very general, as they can be applied to all the material on which the man was tested. This result makes me hopeful about the possibility of finding people who excel at other general strategies, and about the possibility of teaching such powerful strategies to others.

A third result is of interest not because it shows any clear difference in strategies, as distinguished from capacities, but rather because of the sheer magnitude of group differences found and because of the suggestive nature of the results for our thinking about intelligence. Gleitman and Gleitman (1970; *see also* Geer *et al.*, 1972) measured the ability of adults to paraphrase artificial compound words such as "housebird black". The rules for constructing compounds can be stated clearly, yet these rules are not usually taught in schools, so this measure is uncontaminated by instruction in the task. A group of graduate students in psychology almost always gave correct paraphrases (e.g. a colour named after the colour of housebirds, someone who shines housebirds), a group of part-time secretaries most frequently gave incorrect paraphrases (e.g. a black housebird), and a group of college students was in between. There was almost no overlap between the three groups—none at all between the two extreme groups. I shall return later to the question of how these differences might be explained in terms of differences in general strategies.

A final set of results come from a programme of research being carried out by Hunt and his collaborators (*see* Hunt *et al.*, 1975). These investigators selected a group of college students who scored high on the verbal Scholastic Aptitude Test and another group who scored relatively low, and proceeded to look for differences between these groups in performance on simple tasks, mostly tasks in which reaction time was measured; for example, deciding whether a sentence was true of a picture, or deciding whether a letter was identical to another letter. In general, the results may be summarized by the statement that the high-scoring group was faster than the low scoring group, and that this difference was greater in tasks that would seem to require more effort for good performance. On the face of it, these results would seem to implicate capacity differences between people of different intelligence. I would even admit that this is the most likely interpretation. However, it is also possible that these differences have nothing to do with real intelligence. It might be the case that the verbal Scholastic Aptitude Test measures speed of performance in addition to (other aspects of?) intelligence. Those who finish the test early are more likely to have time to think about the items they had trouble with, and indeed, many students do not even finish the test. Further, there may be many people who are highly intelligent, in the sense of being able to do many novel tasks that many others cannot do at all and able to learn things that others cannot learn, yet very slow in overall speed. The findings of Hunt's group may thus represent a real case in which group differences may have to do with something other than intelligence. Note that in proposing this alternative account I am assuming that intelligence is not necessarily just what the test measures, although I do not deny that intelligent people, other things equal, will perform better on the test.

3.4. Effects of old age

The biological changes that occur with ageing may not prevent people from using general strategies or the knowledge they have acquired from using such strategies in the past, but these changes may make using these strategies difficult enough, at least, so that the normal incentives given experimental subjects are insufficient.

One source of evidence for the decline of learning strategies in the aged comes from a study reported by Craik (1977). Young adults and people over 65 were presented with lists of words under four conditions, one involving intentional learning, and the other three involving incidental learning with different orienting tasks (of the sort used in the study of Brevik and Craik, described above). Memory was tested using free recall and recognition procedures. The inferiority of the older subjects was greater with intentional learning than with any of the incidental procedures, and was greater with recall tests than with recognition tests. The former result suggests that the groups differ in strategies for learning; the latter suggests differences in strategies for retrieval in free recall. The groups were identical in performance under conditions of incidental learning and recognition testing, a result that suggests that the groups do not differ in forgetting, or in the strength of the memory trace (holding the learning strategy constant). As in the case of the memory deficiencies of young children, it appears that the differences in the strengths of strategies can account entirely for the poor memory of the aged. Of course, this finding argues strongly for an influence of capacities on strategies for learning and retrieving, for there is every reason to expect declines in capacity with age, and little reason to expect forgetting (from disuse) of such general strategies as those used for learning and retrieving. (However, it is also possible that the deficiencies of the aged result from poor education rather than age itself.)

Other evidence exists for decreases in the strengths of general strategies in the aged. For example, the aged perform poorly, compared to younger adults, on tests of reasoning of the sort used by Piaget (e.g. Hornblum and Overton, 1976).

3.5. Effects of schooling

A number of studies done in cultures without enforced universal schooling have shown striking deficiencies of natives on tests apparently measuring general strategies. In every case I know of in which the effect of schooling was examined, these deficiencies were found to be absent in those members of the same culture who did have substantial formal schooling.

Cole and Scribner (1974) review a number of such studies. One study done by Sharp and Cole (Cole and Scribner, 1974, p. 106) compared children and young adults with varying amounts of schooling on a classification test. Subjects were asked to classify cards with forms differing in colour, number or shape into two piles so that the cards in each pile were alike in some way, and then to repeat the task, using a different means of sorting. The tendency to classify according to a different dimension was highly correlated with the number of years of schooling, but almost completely uncorrelated with age (with schooling held constant).

Greenfield (Bruner et al., 1966) examined the performance of schooled and unschooled Senegalese children on one of Piaget's conservation tests, and again found that schooling made more of a difference than age.

Finally, Wagner (1974, 1978) studied a number of memory tasks in Mexico and Morocco, using materials familiar to the subjects, such as cards from a Mexican card game (in Mexico). Most strikingly, he found that performance in a serial learning task did not improve with age in unschooled children in both countries, but did improve with age in children who were attending school. In the Moroccan study, Wagner tested both schooled and unschooled children in both cities and rural areas. He found that living in an urban environment had no influence on performance; schooling seemed to have made the difference.

The tasks affected by schooling are among those I have discussed previously with respect to the influence of strategies on performance: sorting, conservation and free recall. The fact that performance on these tasks is affected by schooling supports the claim that performance is limited by acquired strategies, even without explicit instruction in the strategies. This possibility makes me optimistic about the possibility of influencing all of the relevant strategies more efficiently by virtue of knowing what they are.

To conclude this section, I should point out that the evidence I have summarized demonstrates beyond doubt the existence of differences in general strategies between groups differing in intelligence. This is the only point required for my argument so far. Along the way, I have also suggested that differences in capacity affect intelligence primarily through their effects on general strategies, but this suggestion is peripheral to my main argument. The important point is that the use of general strategies is subject to influence by education. If intelligence can be even partly accounted for in terms of the strengths of certain general strategies, we then know how best to use education to increase intelligence. Of course, such a programme would be more successful if we can identify the most central strategies. Rehearsal, for example, seems unlikely to be a central strategy; its value even in rote memory tasks is limited (Craik and Watkins, 1973). I now turn to some speculations about what the more central strategies might be.

4. SPECULATIONS ABOUT CENTRAL STRATEGIES

To my knowledge, there are in the literature only a couple of attempts to deal with the question of central strategies in roughly the way I have posed it (Brown, 1974; Flavell, 1976). Both of these attempts (with Brown in fact drawing on Flavell's work to make her case) have emphasized "metacognitive" strategies, those strategies that monitor and direct other strategies. Flavell seems to have in mind a number of such strategies, including such things as self-testing, which I would classify as general but probably not central. Brown (1974) has suggested that a single metacognitive strategy might be central, the strategy of trying to construct strategies, or, following Miller *et al.* (1960), a plan to make plans (or, for those who want to avoid problems of infinite regress, a *habit* of making plans).

As evidence for her proposal, Brown points to the frequent finding that retardates and children will not use a new strategy spontaneously, e.g. for learning, even after they have used it once successfully (and thus presumably have had an opportunity to perceive its value). Such a failure of use is easily accounted for by the absence of a habit of constructing strategies. When the subject is confronted with a task like the one in which he used the strategy once, he will use it again only if he has developed a habit of using it, which would most likely require several repetitions of the training situation (which seems to work; *see* Brown, 1974; Turnure and Thurlow, 1973), or if he has a plan that involves trying to decide what to do, recalling the previous situation, and repeating the strategy that was successful there. (Note that the distinction between repeating a plan as a result of mere habit and repeating a plan as a result of applying a habit of forming plans assumes that there are two different kinds of learning mechanisms available to humans, the former working automatically and passively, the latter working only as a result of intention and effort.)

There might be other metacognitive strategies worthy of being called "central". For example, strategies for categorizing situations with respect to the kind of strategy required would seem to be necessary in order to learn to use other strategies appropriately. For example, if it is true that different strategies are required for storing and retrieving information (and this may not be as true as it first appears to be), a person must be able to distinguish situations in which these two strategies are appropriate. Or, for a student, it may be important to distinguish situations requiring problem solving from those requiring retrieval. The general problem with the idea that such metacognitive strategies as these are central is that it is hard (at least for me) to think of many cases of unintelligent behaviour that can be accounted for in terms of gross miscategorization of the situation. None the less, it is important for us to be aware that a system for classifying, storing and retrieving information about strategies requires abilities for representation and abstraction beyond what most other species can achieve (*see* Premack, 1976).

Turning now to my own speculations, I began with the rough definition of intelligence as the ability to learn and the ability to use what one has learned in both familiar and novel situations. I then asked whether there are some central strategies for learning and perhaps other central strategies underlying those for using acquired knowledge. There now appear to me to be three such central strategies, which have the advantage of being measurable in simple tasks and definable in terms of simple operations. These may be called relatedness search, stimulus analysis and checking.

4.1. Relatedness search

Relatedness search is the strategy of searching one's memory (not necessarily item by item) for items related to a given stimulus (possibly a mental representation). Asch and Walsh (1978) have shown that intentional application of such a strategy is more effective in bringing about retrieval than is simply attending to the stimulus. Subjects were asked to describe each member of a series of unfamiliar forms. Two of the forms in the series were related. For example, one form could be a part of another, or a rotation. After the series had been presented, subjects were asked whether any form in the series had reminded them of any other form at the time the former was presented, or whether they could think, intentionally, of any pairs of related forms. The latter, intentional condition produced many more reports of the two critical forms than the former, "incidental" condition.

Relatedness search can function as a learning strategy and as a retrieval strategy. As a learning strategy, especially for learning arbitrary associations, relatedness search is a mnemonic device of wide utility. In trying to learn a name, a new word or a fact, it is usually helpful to try to find in our memory things that are related to the new information. This is especially true when the related information found is naturally associated with both members of an otherwise arbitrary association, as in the case of using English cognates to learn the meaning of German words (zeit = time; cognate, tide). Many learning strategies examined in the literature I have discussed may be seen as making use of relatedness search for specific purposes, for example, "elaboration" (Rohwer and Bean, 1973; Turnure and Thurlow, 1973). As a retrieval strategy, when we are given a poor retrieval cue ("the lead actor in *North by Northwest*"), a relatedness search may bring to mind better cues ("Mount Rushmore") that would in turn bring to mind a name or at least an image.

Relatedness search may also be useful in bringing about transfer of learning. When we are not at a loss about what to do in a new situation, such as a difficult problem, it often helps to try to think of a similar or related problem (Polya, 1957). Here, in contrast to the use of relatedness search in learning or retrieval, there are good reasons for some related items in memory to be much more useful than others. For example, if I am faced with a problem involving statistical analysis of an experiment, it is more helpful to think of experiments of the same form than those on the same topic or those done in the same place. If I can think of an experiment of the same form, I can often do the same kind of analysis, thus transferring the solution from one problem to another. Mere use of relatedness search does not ensure that transfer will be appropriate. Prevention of inappropriate transfer, e.g. the wrong kind of data analysis, is the result either of use of *specific* knowledge of what kind of stimulus is likely to yield useful related memories (e.g. a representation of the form of the problem experiment *vs* a representation of the hypothesis), of the impossibility of applying an inappropriate procedure to many problems (e.g. a *t*-test to a 2×2 contingency table), or of other checks on appropriateness. This last method of preventing inappropriate transfer is one of the uses of checking, another one of my proposed central strategies, which I shall discuss later. The point here is that there are ways of preventing inappropriate transfer, and that faced with a choice of giving up on a problem or of searching memory for analogies that may or may not be inappropriate, it can rarely hurt to take the latter course. Those who persist in looking for memories of related situations until they find a memory that helps, may be those who succeed in solving problems where others fail. Relatedness search may thus be an important general strategy for using knowledge to deal with novel situations. [A similar suggestion has been made by Campione and Brown (1977, p. 382).]

The value of relatedness search in solving novel problems is one reason why I think it could be a central strategy. Much learning, including the learning of new strategies, results from solving problems for the first time, in contrast to learning from instruction. Relatedness search can thus facilitate the acquisition of new strategies.

Failure to use relatedness search can also account in principle for failure to transfer a strategy used in one situation to a second, similar situation (e.g. Keeney *et al.*, 1968). Asch (1969) has pointed out that subsequent use of a response (or, by extension, strategy) made to an old situation, repeated later, may depend upon recognition of the relation between the second situation and the first one (the relation of identity). This recognition may be seen as a kind of transfer. Like other transfers, it may be facilitated by relatedness search (Asch and Walsh, 1978). If the children had used the relatedness search strategy to try to think of situations related to the second task they were given, they might have solved the problem of selecting the appropriate strategy to use. This account thus differs slightly from that of Brown (1974) in that she would hold that failure to solve this problem is the result of failure to pose it, while I would argue that failure to solve is the result of failure to use relatedness search in the service of solving it. Of course, both of these failures could occur.

The idea that relatedness search is often essential for both acquiring new strategies (by solving problems) and for transferring strategies already acquired is the clearest way in which I can relate the present speculations to the evidence about other strategy differences between individuals, such as differences in rehearsal. (The other major relation between that evidence and these speculations rests on the idea that whatever capacity differences affect acquisition of other strategies also affect acquisition of the ones I hold to be central.)

Note that the idea of a strategy for transfer departs from traditional views about the determinants of transfer. These views have emphasized the importance of the form of a memory in determining transfer. A rule of mathematics or language would be more likely to transfer if it were represented in a general form. For example, learning the formula for the area of a square as "length times width" would be more likely to promote transfer to rectangles than learning it as "one side squared". Without denying the importance of the form of representation, I would suggest that strategies used at the time of transfer are also important. Neither representation just given for example, would be sufficient to find the area of a diamond or a parallelogram unless the relation between these figures and the original ones are recognized (as they are often not—*see* Wertheimer, 1959), and this recognition may require relatedness search.

This is considerable evidence consistent with the idea that relatedness search is related to intelligence. Most of this evidence uses measures of transfer to show that older or more intelligent subjects are more likely to transfer. I should note that none of the evidence has been gathered with the idea in mind that the tendency to transfer should be related to use of a general strategy, such as relatedness search, and none of the evidence is conclusive with respect to the question of whether the obtained differences in transfer can be ascribed to strategy differences, as opposed to differences in the form or strength of representation of the knowledge that serves as the basis of transfer. There are, however, cases in which such alternative explanations seem implausible.

To begin with, there are many informal observations pointing to failures of children and retardates to use knowledge that they already have. For example, Karmiloff-Smith and Inhelder (1975) studied children's responses to a number of balancing problems, some problems sharing principles with others. The authors noted: "It was as if each block constituted a separate problem for them and . . . as if there was no . . . effort to transfer acquired information intentionally during . . . initial attempts". Similarly, Robinson and Robinson (1970), describing retardates, noted, "Teachers and parents frequently observe that retarded children fail to apply in new context what they already know".

Somewhat more formally, Bullock and Gelman (1977) presented

children aged 2 to 5 years with two displays, one consisting of one object, the other of two, and designated one of these displays as the "winner". The older children spontaneously transferred the implicit relation of "more" or "less" to a pair of displays with three and four objects when asked to pick the winner, but the younger children did not. The failure of the younger children was not a result of failure to notice the relation, since they did transfer the relation when the displays from the original task were covered up (preventing examination) and left in view as a reminder of the original situation. My explanation would be that the original failure to transfer was due to failure to notice the relation between the two pairs of displays, and that this in turn was a result of failure to use a relatedness-search strategy.

A similar finding is that of Parker *et al.* (1971), who taught children of ages from 4 to 8 years to classify objects according to attributes and class membership (e.g. with columns of a matrix defined by colour of toy animals and rows defined by type of animal). Older children improved equally on the dimensions presented during training (compared to a pre-test/post-test control group) and on other dimensions. Younger children improved more on the dimensions presented during training. Possibly, the failure to transfer to new dimensions was the result of failing to apply a relatedness-search strategy at the time the new dimensions were presented. (However, ceiling effects can also account for the results.)

A more convincing finding is that of Rice and DiVesta (1965). They used words as stimuli in a paired-associate learning task, with all age groups learning to the same criterion. Then they examined transfer to lists in which a homophone, a synonym or an antonym of each of the original stimulus words was paired with the response that had been assigned to the corresponding word. Compared to a control condition with new words, unrelated to the original words, third graders showed no transfer at all, but older children showed considerable transfer in all conditions (measured either by first-trial responses or by speed of learning the second list). While the authors, in discussion, emphasize the small differences between the semantic and phonemic transfer tasks, the most dramatic results concern the absence of any transfer at all in the younger children; this finding can explain all of the statistically significant findings the authors present.

A similar finding is that of Bialer (1961). Bialer taught normal and retarded subjects two nonsense names for four visual forms or four colour patches, each name assigned to two items. He then taught them that a candy could be found under one form or colour patch, but not under another. Then, he presented them with the two stimuli not used in the training with the candy, and asked them to pick the one with the candy under it. The stimuli were selected, and the names assigned, so that a different response would be made here depending upon whether the child transferred (or generalized)on the basis of a common name or on the basis of visual similarity. The retardates were much more prone to transfer on the basis of visual similarity, even though they had apparently learned the names to the same criterion. Bialer interprets these results in terms of the idea that retardates are less likely to use acquired names (or other acquired responses) as a way of determining stimulus equivalence. But it is also possible that this result is due to a more general deficit in the use of relatedness search. Generalization on the basis of visual similarity may not require relatedness search, while transfer on the basis of a common name may be more likely as a result of such search.

When a subject learns an arbitrary association between two items, A and B, he may be tested on his memory of the association either in the order he learned it, or in the reverse order, B–A, i.e. he is asked to recall A given B. We may regard this as a type of transfer. Looking at backward association in this way allows us to restate the "principle of associative symmetry" (Asch and Ebenholz, 1962) by saying that transfer is (almost) complete for adult subjects. Baumeister *et al.* (1970) found that normal children, like adults, recalled backward associations almost as well as forward association. However, retarded children showed this symmetry only when the lists presented to test memory consisted of all B terms or all A terms. When mixed lists were used, the performance of retardates on backward associations fell sharply in contrast to performance on forward associations. My interpretation of this result is that normal children were able to maintain a high level of performance on backward associations in mixed lists by using a relatedness-search strategy. Retardates are deficient in this strategy.

Other results (Skanes *et al.*, 1974) relate transfer to intelligence, as measured by Raven's Progressive Matrices, in high-school students. The students were tested on number-series problems of the sort used on IQ tests. Before this test, the students were given training either on the same kind of number-series problem, or else on analogous letter-series problems (mixed in with some number-series problems as well). Students who scored high on the Progressive Matrices were helped just as much by letter-series training as by direct number-series training, but students who scored low were helped much more by the direct training. Again, this failure to transfer from letters to numbers in the low-scoring group may be due to failure to use a relatedness-search strategy.

Earlier, I described this finding of Gleitman and Gleitman (1970) concerning the relation between intelligence and ability to paraphrase compounds such as "housebird black". One factor at work here may be the tendency of intelligent subjects to make an effort to find related compounds in memory (e.g. boot-black), that is, to use the relatedness-search strategy. Of course, the use of such a strategy must be coupled with an appropriate representation of the stimulus in terms of its parts of speech etc. Most likely, specific knowledge about grammar is at work here as well as general strategies, even though subjects had never learned the rules for compounds explicitly (and even though there are so few common compounds as to make the learning of the rules of questionable value).

Baron (1977) has obtained results suggesting that adults can be encouraged to use relatedness search to pronounce nonsense words according to the somewhat complex spelling–sound correspondence rules of English. For example, subjects who had initially pronounced PUCH as "pooch" would switch to pronouncing it by analogy with SUCH or MUCH when told to think of related words. Other evidence suggested that subjects would use this strategy spontaneously when given words such as YAUGH, which was more frequently pronounced by analogy with LAUGH than by correspondences between smaller units of spelling and their corresponding sounds.

Finally, The Rorschach Ink Blot Test (Rapaport et al., 1968) may also serve as a rough measure of relatedness search, as well as of other general strategies. The task is to say what one sees in the ink blot. Without effort, few people see very much besides an ink blot. With a little effort, however, relations between the form of the blot and other forms begin to come to mind. More intelligent people (and adults, as opposed to children) produce better, more integrated responses, larger numbers of responses, and more "movement" responses, which require a more complete perception (Levitt and Truumaa, 1972; Goldfried et al., 1971). Part of the explanation of this difference may be that the more intelligent people are more prone to use relatedness search, which brings to mind a sufficiently large number of possibilities so that the less sensible ones may be weeded out by checking.

In sum, there is a lot of evidence consistent with the idea that use of relatedness search is correlated with intelligence. Introspectively as well, most people will agree that they use something like this strategy fairly frequently when dealing with difficult problems or when learning or trying to recall difficult material. Better evidence than I have presented, however, is still needed.

4.2. Stimulus analysis

Earlier, I discussed the idea (D. G. Kemler, Smith and Kemler, unpublished; 1977) that there is a developmental trend towards classifying stimuli in terms of identity on single dimensions rather than overall similarity. Use of dimensions may be an example of a more general strategy of attending to the features, the parts as well as the attributes, of a stimulus. Parts of stimuli are like attributes in the sense that two stimuli may be classed together on the basis of a common part as well as an identical attribute. The strategy of analysing a stimulus into features, of attending to parts and attributes as stimuli in themselves, can be useful both in learning about a stimulus and in using the stimulus as a retrieval cue. In learning, stimulus analysis increases the opportunity for learning, since each nominal stimulus becomes several effective stimuli as a result. (Elaboration, as a mnemonic technique, may facilitate memory through the same mechanism; a trace consisting of more features of a single whole might be easier to retrieve or less susceptible to interference.) In retrieval, stimulus analysis of a retrieval cue might allow a feature of the stimulus to evoke the memory of an identical feature in the memory to be retrieved.

Likewise, in transfer, identity of features between two stimuli can serve as a basis of transfer. Indeed, this is the traditional view of the main determinant of transfer. I am suggesting that this view must be extended in two ways: first, relatedness search, the active effort to retrieve memories beyond what is spontaneously evoked, will bring about transfer when it would not otherwise occur; secondly, stimulus analysis both at the time of initial storage of a memory and at the time the transfer occurs may increase the probability of attending to a single feature that two stimuli share.

I have already discussed the evidence for the idea that analysis into attributes increase with age. The evidence for increases in other kinds of feature analysis, i.e. parts, is much weaker. One source of suggestive evidence is the literature on "cognitive style". Witkin (1964), for example, has presented evidence that older and more intelligent children are more "analytic". For example, they are more likely to include details in drawings (possibly a motor ability), more able to ignore irrelevant cues (such as a tilted frame) in judging the verticality of a line, and more able to find a hidden or camouflaged figure (possibly a perceptual ability rather than the result of a strategy). While the evidence is consistent with the idea that stimulus analysis, or doing with the features of a stimulus whatever one does with the whole, underlies intelligence, none of this evidence is conclusive.

Parenthetically, I should point out that deficiencies in stimulus analysis may in part account for difficulties in learning letter–phoneme correspondences when learning to read. If a person analyses a printed word into its letters and the spoken response to that word into its sounds, it is easy to imagine that there are learning mechanisms that would form associations between letters and sounds as a consequence of learning associations between printed and spoken words. Baron and Hodge (1978) have in fact shown that adults can apparently learn correspondences between artificial letters and phonemes under such circumstances even when the subjects are unaware of the existence of letter–phoneme correspondences. However, if the parts of either the stimulus or response are not attended to, it seems unlikely that part–part (letter–phoneme) associations would be formed as a consequence of learning whole–whole associations (printed word to spoken word associations). The deficit in children seems to be in attention to the parts of the spoken response. There is a high correlation between performance on tasks that would seem to depend on attention to phonemes and ability to learn to read (Rozin and Gleitman, 1976).

4.3. Checking

Checking is the strategy of withholding the first response that comes to mind, and continuing to use whatever knowledge one has to try to decide on the correct response. Use of such knowledge may reinforce one's original decision, or may lead to other potential responses, which themselves may be reinforced by yet further checking. Checking may be guided by the potential responses that come to mind first; one may look either for knowledge that confirms or that contradicts the original possibility. Checking may be useful in transfer as applied to problem solving, in learning that is meaningful in the sense that it could result from problem solving, and in retrieval.

When we are faced with a problem, a novel situation in which we must make some decision about what to do and in which there is some criterion of success, possible solutions may come to mind either because they are evoked immediately by the problem or because they are suggested by a relatedness-search strategy. Often, these solutions are not the best ones we could produce. Better solutions may be reached by continued search. Evaluation of prospective solutions is the function of checking.

For example, say a child is presented with two rows of objects in one-to-one correspondence, then one row is spread out, and the child is asked whether the rows still have the same number of objects—the classic conservation problem of Piaget. The first strategy to come to mind for producing an answer might be to compare the lengths of the rows; this strategy, of course, would yield the "wrong" answer. Three other strategies might involve counting and comparing the numbers, testing for one-to-one correspondence, and using one's knowledge that number cannot change unless something is added or subtracted. It is of interest that children who err in the problem seem to be capable of each of these strategies under conditions in which other strategies are not evoked (Bryant, 1974; Baron *et al.*, 1975). If all four strategies are used, three of them will agree on the solution. The strategy of comparing lengths will not agree with the others, and will thus not pass the check (assuming that at least one of the three number strategies is attached to the concept of "number" sufficiently strongly so that other length strategies do not win out). It may be because the various number strategies consistently agree that we feel that the solution to this problem could not be otherwise and that we would have to invent a word for "number" if we didn't have one. More importantly, children may err not because they lack specific strategies, but because they lack the general strategy of checking (*see* Baron, 1973; Schaeffer *et al.*, 1974, for similar suggestions).

For another example of the use of checking in problem solving, consider the problem of finding the area of a parallelogram when one knows only how to find the area of a rectangle (Wertheimer, 1959). Two possible solutions might come to mind, multiplying the height by the base, or multiplying two adjacent sides. The first may seem "right" because it can be checked by making the parallelogram into a rectangle, by making (in one's imagination) a cut perpendicular to the base and rearranging the pieces—assuming that the strategy for conservation of area is also available.

Failure to check may account for many other examples of failure to solve simple problems. Still another example is Holt's (1964, p. 10) discussion of a girl producing MINCOPERT as an attempted spelling of MICROSCOPIC, when application of her own knowledge of letter–phoneme correspondence rules could have told her that this was incorrect. While it may be argued that such errors occur as a result of other sources of difficulty, my own observations of highly intelligent people suggest that this is not the case. Such people, when faced with very difficult problems, will not give any answer at all, or will give admittedly tentative answers as a way of eliciting help from others, rather than giving answers that are inconsistent with other things they know.

More generally, checking is almost a necessity when relatedness search is relied upon heavily in problem solving. When I try to solve a problem simply by thinking of related problems I have solved, I will often recall many problems that offer no help at all in solving the problem at hand. There is no guarantee that related problems will always have related solutions, especially in view of the many kinds of relations that can exist, even between appropriately represented problems.

When checking is used to solve a problem, a memory will be stored not only of the problem and solution, but also, most likely, of the checks that were carried out. These memories of checks can serve as a way of enriching the memory of what was stored (as does any sort of elaboration), and also as features on which later transfer can be based. For example, if one has checked one's solution of the parallelogram problem by making the parallelogram into a rectangle, this strategy may aid in finding the area of yet other forms.

Checking may also be used in retrieval. There are often several different associations between a stimulus and response. These may be used to check each other. When trying to think of a word or name, for example, guesses about the response may often be checked by using other associations, including other meanings or images evoked by the guess itself. Or a tentative response may be checked against whatever features are independently remembered, such as the initial and final phonemes or the number of syllables. Checking in retrieval is more useful when feature analysis has occurred at storage, since recall of separate features can serve as ways of checking a tentative response.

Failure to check, when other functions are operating normally, may result in bizarre overproduction of responses, as seen in some forms of schizophrenia. In the Rorschach test, failure to check may lead to a response in which the subject infers the identity of the entire ink blot from the perception of a single part, without checking to see whether the other parts fit in; for example: "It's a face because of the eyes". Such responses in fact occur much more frequently in young children and retardates than in normal adults (Goldfried et al., 1972).

I have already discussed some of the evidence for checking being related to group differences in intelligence: the anecdotal evidence of the sort provided by Holt (1964), and the possibility of explaining such deficits as failure to conserve number when length is changed in terms of failure to check. Other evidence comes from a study done by Kemler (1978) in which children were presented with a standard discrimination-learning problem in which they had to discover the attribute that distinguishes one set of stimuli from another. Kemler found, as had others, that children frequently held hypotheses about the relevant attribute that they had only recently rejected. This fact alone could be the result of poor memory. However, these errors persisted even when the children were given a clear way of keeping track of the hypotheses they had rejected, a way that the children could be shown to understand and use. The most plausible remaining explanation of the behaviour of returning to rejected hypotheses is that the children did not check their new hypotheses against their knowledge of what hypotheses had already been ruled out.

Another source of evidence comes from studies of the Matching Familiar Figures Test (*see* Kagan and Kogan, 1970; Messer, 1976, for a review). In this test, subjects are presented with a standard drawing and (usually) six other drawings, one of which is identical to the standard and the rest of which differ in a small detail. "Reflective" subjects, as opposed to "impulsive" subjects, are those who take longer to make the comparisons, and, as a result make fewer errors. Before pointing to one of the drawings that looks like the standard, they seem more prone to check their answer, either by looking for other possible answers or by looking for differences between the standard and the response they are considering. It has been found, generally, that older and more intelligent children tend to be more reflective. Of course, there are other possible explanations of these correlations. Stimulus analysis might also be helpful in a task of this sort, as might perceptual capacities of a simple sort, or more specific strategies based on the fact that there is usually only one right answer in the set of six (thus making it optimal to proceed looking for differences until differences have been found in all drawings but one).

To the extent that checking is measured by this test, there is evidence that checking is a strategy easily taught, at least in the context of the test itself. Meichenbaum and Goodman (1969) made children more reflective simply by teaching the children to tell themselves to be careful as they were doing the test. A strategy that the subject could represent as "being careful" is one that could be potentially useful in a wide variety of situations. Egeland (1974) found that training on the Matching Familiar Figures Test improved reading comprehension scores several months later. While the success of this experiment is encouraging, we have less idea what was affected by the training than we do in the case of the Meichenbaum and Goodman study.

5. FURTHER SPECULATIONS

So far, I have described three possible central strategies, relatedness search, stimulus analysis and checking, and I have tried to show how each of these strategies might underlie intelligence in the sense I outlined above. In particular, if we begin with a definition of intelligence as the ability to learn, to retrieve what has been learned, and to use one's knowledge for new purposes (described generally as problem solving or transfer to new situations), I have argued that each of these strategies could be useful in all of these manifestations of intelligence. Further, the usefulness of these strategies is, so far as I can tell, almost completely general. The strategies ought to be as helpful in one domain as in another.

Before concluding this section, however, I would like to suggest some further directions for speculation about strategies that might be less general but perhaps even more important in distinguishing superior from merely average intelligence. The strategies I have discussed so far are all ones that can be learned easily by grade-school children. Yet, there is another kind of intelligence that may be better characterized as "intellectual sophistication" of the sort valued by academics. It is easy to think of people who know many things, can remember what they know, and who are even clever and witty in using what they know for new purposes, yet who are also unsophisticated intellectually. Such a person might be the life of the party, and might be an expert on South American birds, yet be totally unable to carry on an intelligent discussion about whether vivisection is immoral.

Two strategies that might be useful in more advanced manifestations of intelligence might be called invention and principle stating. Invention is similar to relatedness search, but is more. Relatedness search can only retrieve a literal memory of what is already known. Invention can embellish a fragment of a memory, continually drawing on other memories, so as to construct a representation of an entirely novel situation. Invention is used not only in all artistic activities (by definition), but also in scientific or philosophical thought. In philosophy, for example, an important technique of exposition or argument is the construction of possible (but often unlikely) situations as examples for testing intuitions of various sorts. We may invent questions as well as situations.

Principle stating is also useful in philosophical or scientific thinking. A common technique is to state a principle, try to check it by thinking of examples and counter-examples, state a new principle to deal with the checks that failed, and so on. Some activities, such as providing definitions, are defined in terms of the goal of arriving at a principle. For example, in defining the word "food", one might first propose the principle, "Food is things that we eat". A check in the form of a search for exceptions might yield an (invented) example of something that we might eat but don't happen to eat, such as lichens. A new principle might be, "Things that we could eat either for taste or nourishment". Further checks might yield further modifications.

Since these speculations are even more speculative than my earlier ones, I shall not try to make any sort of argument for them. The following references, however, might be useful for the reader who wants to think more about these issues: Adelson (1971), Baron (1975), Kohlberg (1971), Peel (1971) and Perry (1970). In lieu of arguments or evidence,

I present Fig. 1—at least for the benefit of those readers who agree with Paivio that one picture is worth at least two words. It may serve to summarize all of the speculations about underlying strategies I have presented.

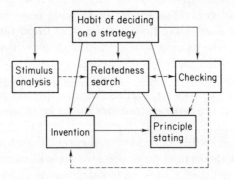

Fig. 1. Interrelations of proposed strategies. Solid lines indicate that a strategy promotes the use of the strategy pointed to. Dashed lines indicate that a strategy makes the strategy pointed to more useful. Strategies at the top are more basic (possibly so basic as to be innate).

At the top of this figure is Brown's (1974) idea of planfulness as a central strategy. If this is a central strategy that differs in strength from person to person, it may be the most central of all, since it would facilitate the acquisition and use of all other strategies. At the next level are the three possible central strategies I have proposed. Of these strategies, relatedness search is especially helpful in promoting the acquisition of the intellectual–sophistication strategies at the next level. Both principle stating and invention would seem to require relatedness search. Principle stating also requires the invention of principles. From the dashed lines in Fig. 1, we can see that the strategies may work together in a number of ways. Stimulus analysis may make relatedness search more effective when the relation between a stimulus and an item in memory is based on identity of parts or attributes. Relatedness search gives checking an additional way of arriving at possible responses, hence an additional way to check a possible response. Similarly, checking evaluates the products of relatedness search, weeding out the inappropriate ones. Finally, checking operates on principles as possible responses. We check principles by trying to recall or invent examples, counter-examples or alternative principles. Thus, sophisticated reasoning can be seen as an extension of checking to more imaginative (or constructive) domains.

6. IMPLICATIONS FOR RESEARCH

I shall conclude with a brief discussion of the implications of my point of view, as presented up to now, for further research on the question of whether there are general strategies underlying intelligence. In a way, the arguments I shall make here are the most important things I have to say. I have been arguing that strengths of general strategies distinguish people of different levels of intelligence, and that such things as central strategies, underlying all intelligent behaviour, may exist. If these arguments are true—regardless of any specific proposals I have made about what the central strategies might be or about the interpretation of particular findings—further investigation of these issues should prove worthwhile both from a theoretical and a practical point of view. From a theoretical point of view, we will come closer to being able to define intelligence in ways less dependent upon particular tools of measurement. From a practical point of view, we shall be in a position to learn what educational techniques are the most useful for increasing intelligence. If we are using these techniques now, we can stop wasting time on others we might be using with the same purpose in mind. If we are using these techniques only haphazardly, we can start using them systematically. Even if widespread adoption of educational practices that increase intelligence does not diminish variations in intelligence, there is little question in my mind that the world would be a better place if everyone were more intelligent. For these reasons, the research I think should be done is too much for a few people to do. I would hope, ideally, that large numbers of the most talented experimental and developmental psychologists would turn their efforts towards the study of central strategies.

The first piece of advice I can offer to those who would turn their efforts in this direction is to worry more about the generality and centrality of the strategies they study than others so far have done. Most research up to now has concerned itself with strategies, such as rehearsal, of limited generality. I am not criticizing this research, for the point needed to be made that individual differences in strategies do exist and do influence performance on simple tasks, and it was easy to make this point with rehearsal as an example. However, it seems to me that the point has now been made, although there may be details here and there that need cleaning up. In this chapter, I have tried to illustrate by example the kinds of considerations that must be raised in evaluating proposals about the generality or centrality of a strategy. Namely, the proposed strategy must be general enough, in principle, to influence the acquisition or use of other strategies or memories.

A consequence of this piece of advice is that we should feel less constrained by experimental procedures that happen to have been well studied. Most of these procedures were invented to try to capture in the laboratory some intuition or experience about what we do somewhere else. While many of these procedures served their initial purpose, few, if any, serve to capture our intuitions about what makes behaviour intelligent. We must now feel free to invent new tasks for this new purpose. In particular, it seems unlikely that we will get very far towards our goal by analysing individual differences in performance on items taken from the intelligence tests that happen to exist, without at least some careful thought about whether we are studying general strategies, the capacities that they draw on, or the specific strategies they produce.

A second piece of advice is apparently less of a problem now than it was, say 50 years ago. In defining general strategies, we must make sure that we define the strategies in terms of procedures that are teachable in their general form. Many old books on "how to think" would describe various qualities of good thinking, such as "clarity", "usefulness" "perception of the essence", "creative insight", and so on. But while these phrases might help a person recognize good thinking when he saw it, they were little help in teaching a person how to do it. The central strategies I have proposed are, I hope, capable of being well defined in this sense. A person who understands the language, and who has the necessary metacognitive abilities, can use an instruction to "think of related situations" as an instruction to change his own behaviour. For one who lacks the linguistic or metacognitive abilities, it ought to be possible in principle to design an instructional programme based on the same principles. The strategy that is taught by such a programme ought to be taught in the same form in which it is used everywhere. That is, the same kind of instruction ought to be effective in all situations in which the strategy is useful. Defining strategies as procedures also leads to better ways of measuring their strength.

A third consideration concerns the testing of any proposals about central strategies. A good way to test such proposals is to show that the strategies have different strengths in groups of people that differ in intelligence. Usually, several such group comparisons are more convincing than one, since it is usually possible that groups that differ in intelligence also differ in other ways that are unrelated to real intelligence, whatever it turns out to be. I have already alluded to some examples of such spurious differences. For example, groups differing in test scores may differ in speed, which may be unrelated to real intelligence. As long as proposals are ultimately checked by several comparisons of this sort, it is not necessary to begin with any particular kind of comparison. For initial tests of a proposal, it might be sufficient to select subjects on the basis of their performance in an experimental task similar to the one used in measuring the strategy in question, although care should be taken to ensure that measures of strategy strength and task performance are not artefactually correlated. For example, in testing for individual differences in relatedness search, using a memory task, performance on the memory task might be used to select subjects, and relatedness search measured by differences in performance between two conditions of presentation of the task.

Fourthly, measures of performance on a single task will rarely, if ever, be sufficient to measure the use of a strategy. Ordinarily, two tasks are required, one in which the strategy in question is helpful, and a second in which the strategy is less helpful but in which most or all other factors are the same as the first task. There is no substitute for this kind of control. Merely picking a wide selection of tasks is not sufficient, for performance on the wide selection might be influenced by other variables than the strategy in question. Inferences about group differences can be further strengthened by using a number of pairs of tasks in this way.

Fifthly, the ultimate test of any proposal about the generality of a strategy is that teaching the strategy in some situations will promote the acquisition of that strategy in other situations. I could find no tests of this sort of generality in the literature I reviewed, for well-defined strategies. Most often, the training is given in a single situation, and use of the strategy is tested in a very similar situation, perhaps after a delay. Training strategies in a general form may require several additions to the usual procedures. First, the training will have to be extensive enough so that transfer will occur at least to closely related tasks. Secondly, consideration will have to be given to the problem of making the strategy transfer to less similar situations. There are two approaches to solving this problem. One is to make sure that the subject has the general strategies for transferring strategies, such as relatedness search, before transfer of the strategy in question is tested. Transfer of the strategy in question to new situations may fail to occur because of individual characteristics that make any transfer unlikely to occur, rather than because the strategy is not itself a generally useful one. The second approach to solving the problem is to teach the strategy in question in a variety of tasks, and then test it in a variety of other tasks. This ought to be possible if the strategy is truly general. We don't know why such a procedure would encourage the transfer of a strategy, but folk wisdom suggests that it would. (We may in practice even need to call the student's attention to the strategy over a period of years, in every situation where it might help; this might be required, for example for teaching the central strategies I have proposed.) In sum, we must be careful to give the generality of a strategy a fair test, by doing whatever we can to encourage its use in situations where it is appropriate other than those in which it was originally taught.

As a final note, I should point out that I have not dealt with the question of how one *tests* whether a strategy is central as opposed to merely general. I leave this as an exercise for the reader.

ACKNOWLEDGEMENTS

I thank Karen Heald, Molly Logan, Don Lyon and Dan Wagner for comments on an earlier draft, many colleagues for discussions of these issues, and the National Science Foundation for financial support.

REFERENCES

Adelson, J. (1971). The political imagination of the adolescent. *Daedalus*, fall, 1971.

Appel, L. F., Cooper, R. G., McCarrell, N., Sims-Knight, Jr., Yussen, S. R. and Flavell, J. H. (1972). The development of the distinction between perceiving and memorizing. *Child Development* **43**, 1365–1381.

Asch, S. E. (1969). A reformulation of the problem of associations. *American Psychologist* **24**, 92–102.

Asch, S. E. and Ebenholtz, S. M. (1962). The principle of associative symmetry. *Proceedings of the American Philosophical Society* **106**, 135–163.

Asch, S. E. and Walsh, W. A. (1978). Gestalt conditions of memory. *Proceedings of the American Philosophical Society* (in press).

Atkinson, R. C. and Shiffrin, R. M. (1968). Human memory: A proposed system and its control processes. *In* "The Psychology of Learning and Motivation" (K. W. Spence and J. T. Spence, eds), vol. 2. Academic Press, New York and London.

Baron, J. (1973). Semantic components and conceptual development. *Cognition* **2**, 189–207.

Baron, J. (1975). Some theories of college instruction. *Higher Education* **4**, 149–172.

Baron, J. (1977). What we might know about orthographic rules. *In* "Attention and Performance VI" (S. Dornic and P. M. A. Rabbitt, eds). Erlbaum, Hillsdale, New Jersey.

Baron, J. and Hodge, J. (1978). Manuscript in press.

Baron, J., Lawson, G. and Siegel, L. S. (1975). Effects of training and set size on children's judgements of number and length. *Developmental Psychology* **11**, 583–588.

Baumeister, A. A., Kellas, G. and Gordon, D. (1970). Backward association in paired-associate learning of retardates and normal children. *Child Development* **41**, 355–364.

Belmont, J. M. (1967). Perceptual short-term memory in children, retardates, and adults. *Journal of Experimental Child Psychology* **5**, 114–122.

Belmont, J. M. and Butterfield, E. C. (1971). Learning strategies as determinants of memory deficiencies. *Congitive Psychology* **2**, 411–420.

Bialer, I. (1961). Primary and secondary stimulus generalization as related to intelligence level. *Journal of Experimental Psychology* **62**, 395–402.

Brown, A. L. (1974). The role of strategic behaviour in retardate memory. *In* "International Review of Research in Mental Retardation" (N. R. Ellis, ed.), vol. 7. Academic Press, New York and London.

Brown, A. L. (1975). The development of memory: knowing, knowing about knowing, and knowing how to know. *In* "Advances in Child Development and Behavior" (H. W. Reese, ed.), vol. 10. Academic Press, New York and London.

Bruner, J. S., Olver, R. and Greenfield, P. M. (1966). "Studies in Cognitive Growth". Wiley, New York.

Bryant, P. (1974). "Perception and Understanding in Young Children: An Experimental Approach". Basic Books, New York.

Bullock, M. and Gelman, R. (1977). Numerical reasoning in young children: The ordering principle. *Child Development* (in press).

Campione, J. C. and Brown, A. L. (1977). Memory and metamemory development in educable retarded children. *In* "Perspectives on the Development of Memory and Cognition" (R. V. Kail, Jr. and J. W. Hagen, eds). Erlbaum, Hillsdale, New Jersey.

Chi, M. T. H. (1978). Knowledge structures and memory development. *In* "Children's Thinking: What Develops?" (R. Siegler, ed.). Erlbaum, Hillsdale, New Jersey.

Cole, M. and Scribner, S. (1974). "Culture and Thought: A Psychological Introduction". Wiley, New York.

Conrad, R. (1962). Practice, familiarity, and reading rate for words and nonsense syllables. *Quarterly Journal of Experimental Psychology* **14**, 71–76.

Craik, F. I. M. (1977). Age differences in human memory. *In* "Handbook of the Psychology of Aging" (J. E. Birren and K. W. Schaie, eds). Van Nostrand, New York.

Craik, F. I. M. and Watkins, M. J. (1973). The role of rehearsal in short-term memory. *Journal of Verbal Learning and Verbal Behavior* **12**, 599–607.

Egeland, J. (1974). Training impulsive children in the use of more efficient scanning techniques. *Child Development* **45**, 165–171.

Ellis, N. R. (1970). Memory processes in retardates and normals. *In* "International Review of Research in Mental Retardation" (N. R. Ellis, ed.), vol. 4. Academic Press, New York and London.

Esposito, N. J. (1975). Review of discrimination shift learning in young children. *Psychological Bulletin* **82**, 432–455.

Estes, W. K. (1970). "Learning Theory and Mental Development". Academic Press, New York and London.

Fisher, M. A. and Zeaman, D. (1973). An attention-retention theory of retardate discrimination learning. *In* "International Review of Research in Mental Retardation" (N. R. Ellis, ed.), vol. 6. Academic Press, New York and London.

Flavell, J. H. (1970). Developmental studies of mediated memory. *In* "Advances in Child Development and Behavior" (H. W. Reese and L. P. Lipsett, eds), vol. 5. Academic Press, New York and London.

Flavell, J. H. (1976). Metacognitive aspects of problem solving. *In* "The Nature of Intelligence" (L. B. Resnick, ed.) Erlbaum, Hillsdale, New Jersey.

Flavell, J. H., Friedrichs, A. G. and Hoyt, J. D. (1970). Developmental changes in memorization processes. *Cognitive Psychology* **1**, 324–340.

Garner, W. R. (1974). "The Processing of Information and Structure". Erlbaum, Hillsdale, New Jersey.

Geer, S. E., Gleitman, H. and Gleitman, L. (1972). Paraphrasing and remembering compound words. *Journal of Verbal Learning and Verbal Behavior* **11**, 348–355.

Gelman, R. (1978). How young children reason about small numbers. *In* "Cognitive Theory" (N. J. Castellan, D. B. Pisoni and G. Potts, eds), vol. II. Erlbaum, Hillsdale, New Jersey.

Gleitman, L. R. and Gleitman, H. (1970). "Phrase, and Paraphrase: Some Innovative Uses of Language". Norton, New York.

Goldfried, M. R., Stricker, G. and Winer, I. B. (1971). "Rorschach Handbook of Clinical and Research Applications". Prentice-Hall, Englewood Cliffs, New Jersey.

Hagen, J. W., Jongeward, R. H., Jr. and Kail, R. V., Jr. (1975). Cognitive perspectives on the development of memory. *In* "Advances in Child Development and Behavior" (H. W. Reese, ed.) vol. 10. Academic Press, New York and London.

Holden, E. A., Jr. (1971). Sequential dot presentation measures of stimulus trace in retardates and normals. *In* "International Review of Research in Mental Retardation" (N. R. Ellis, ed.), vol. 5. Academic Press, New York and London.

Holt, J. (1934). "How Children Fail". Pitman, London.

Hornblum, J. N. and Overton, W. F. (1976). Area and volume conservation among the elderly: Assessment and training. *Developmental Psychology* **12,** 68–74.

Hunt, E. and Love, T. (1972). How good can memory be? *In* "Coding Processes in Human Memory" (A. W. Melton and E. Martin, eds) Winston, Washington, D.C.

Hunt, E., Lunneborg, C. and Lewis, J. (1975). What does it mean to be highly verbal? *Cognitive Psychology* **7**, 194–227.

Inhelder, B. and Piaget, J. (1964). "The Early Growth of Logic in the Child". Norton, New York.

Jencks, C. *et al.* (1972). "Inequality: A reassessment of the effects of family and schooling in America". Basic Books, New York.

Kagan, J. and Kogan, N. (1970). Individuality and cognitive performance. *In* "Carmichael's Manual of Child Psychology" (P. H. Mussen, ed.), 3rd edition, vol. 1. Wiley, New York.

Karmiloff-Smith, A. and Inhelder, B. (1975). If you want to get ahead, get a theory. *Cognition* **3**, 195–212.

Keeney, T. J., Cannizzo, S. R. and Flavell, J. H. (1967). Spontaneous and induced verbal rehearsal in a recall task. *Child Development* **38**, 953–966.

Kemler, D. G. (1978). Patterns of hypothesis testing in children's discrimination learning: a study of the development of problem solving strategies. *Developmental Psychology* (in press).

Kobasigawa, A. (1974). Utilization of retrieval cues by children in recall. *Child Development* **45**, 127–134.

Kohlberg, L. (1971). From is to ought: How to commit the naturalistic fallacy and get away with it in the study of moral development. *In* "Cognitive Development and Epistemology" (T. Mischel, ed.). Academic Press, New York and London.

LaBerge, D. (1975). Acquisition of automatic processing in perceptual and associative learning. *In* "Attention and Performance V" (S. Dornic and P. M. A. Rabbitt, eds). Academic Press, London and New York.

Lawson, G., Baron, J. and Siegel, L. S. (1974). The role of length and number cues in children's quantitative judgments. *Child Development* **45**, 731–736.

Levitt, E. E. and Truumaa, A. (1972). "The Rorschach Technique with Children and Adolescents: Applications and Norms". Grune and Stratton, New York.

McLaughlin, G. H. (1963). Psycho-logic: A possible alternative to Piaget's formulation. *British Journal of Educational Psychology* **33**, 61–67.

Meichenbaum, D. and Goodman, J. (1969). Reflection-impulsivity and verbal control of motor behavior. *Child Development* **40**, 785–797.

Messer, S. B. (1976). Reflection-impulsivity: A review *Psychological Bulletin.* **83**, 1026–1052.

Miller, G. A., Galanter, E. and Pribram, K. H. (1960). "Plans and the Structure of Behavior". Holt, New York.

Moely, B. E., Olson, F. A., Halwes, T. G. and Flavell, J. H. (1969). Production deficiency in young children's clustered recall. *Developmental Psychology* **1**, 26–34.

Parker, R. K., Rieff, M. L. and Sperr, S. J. (1971). Teaching multiple classification to young children. *Child Development* **42**, 1779–1789.

Pascual-Leone, J. (1970). A mathematical model for the transition rule in Piaget's developmental stages. *Acta Psychologica* **32**, 301–345.

Peel, E. A. (1971). "The Nature of Adolescent Judgment". Crosby, Lockwood, Staples, London.

Perry, W. G., Jr. (1970). "Forms of Intellectual and Ethical Development in the College Years: A Scheme". Holt, Rinehart, New York.

Polya, G. (1957). "How to Solve It". Doubleday, Garden City, New York.

Premack, D. (1976). "Intelligence in Ape and Man". Erlbaum, Hillsdale, New Jersey.

Rapaport, D., Gill, M. M. and Schafer, R. (1968). "Diagnostic Psychological Testing". International Universities Press, New York.

Rice, U. M. and DiVesta, F. J. (1965). A developmental study of semantic and phonetic generalizations in paired-associate learning. *Child Development* **36**, 721–730.

Ritter, K., Kaprove, B. H., Fitch, J. P. and Flavell, J. H. (1973). The development of retrieval strategies in young children. *Cognitive Psychology* **5**, 310–321.

Robinson, H. B. and Robinson, N. M. (1970). Mental retardation. *In* "Carmichael's Manual of Child Psychology" (P. H. Mussen, ed.), 3rd edition, vol. 2. Wiley, New York.

Rohwer, W. D., Jr. and Bean, J. P. (1973). Sentence effects and non-pair learning: A developmental interaction during adolescence. *Journal of Experimental Child Psychology* **15**, 521–533.

Rozin, P. and Gleitman, L. R. (1976). The structure and acquisition of reading. II. The reading process and the acquisition of the alphabetic principle. *In* "Toward a Psychology of Reading: The Proceedings of the CUNY Conferences" (A. S. Reber and D. Scarborough eds). Erlbaum, Hillsdale, New Jersey.

Schaeffer, B., Eggleston, V. H. and Scott, J. L. (1974). Number development in young children. *Cognitive Psychology* **6**, 357–379.

Shepp, B. E. and Swartz, K. B. (1976). Selective attention and the processing of integral and nonintegral dimensions: A developmental study. *Journal of Experimental Child Psychology* **22**, 73–85.

Skanes, G. R., Sullivan, A. M., Rowe, E. J. and Shannon, E. (1974). Intelligence and transfer: aptitude by treatment interactions. *Journal of Educational Psychology* **66**, 563–568.

Smith, L. B. and Kemler, D. G. (1977). Developmental trends in free classification: Evidence for a new conceptualization of perceptual development. *Journal of Experimental Child Psychology* **24**, 279–298.

Smith, L. B., Kemler, D. G. and Aronfreed, J. (1975). Developmental trends in voluntary selective attention: Differential effects of source distinctiveness. *Journal of Experimental Child Psychology* **20**, 352–362.

Spitz, H. H. and LaFontaine, L. (1973). The digit span of idiot savants. *American Journal of Mental Deficiency* **77**, 757–759.

Turnure, J. E. and Thurlow, M. L. (1973). Verbal elaboration and the promotion of transfer of training in educable mentally retarded children. *Journal of Experimental Child Psychology* **15**, 137–148.

Wagner, D. A. (1974). The development of short-term and incidental memory: A cross-cultural study. *Child Development* **45**, 389–396.

Wagner, D. A. (1978). Memories of Morocco: the influence of age, schooling and environment on memory. *Cognitive Psychology* **10**, 1–28.

Wertheimer, M. (1959). "Productive Thinking" (enlarged edition). Harper and Row, New York.

Witkin, H. A. (1964). Origins of cognitive style. *In* "Cognition: Theory, Research, Promise" (C. Scheerer, ed.). Harper and Row, New York.

Zeaman, D. and House, B. J. (1963). An attention theory of retardate discrimination learning. *In* "Handbook of Mental Deficiency" (N. R. Ellis, ed.). McGraw Hill, New York.

Subject Index